CRITICAL SURVEY
OF
SHORT FICTION

CRITICAL SURVEY
OF
SHORT FICTION

REVISED EDITION
Woo-Z
Essays

7

Edited by
FRANK N. MAGILL

SALEM PRESS
Pasadena, California   Englewood Cliffs, New Jersey

73909

∞ The paper used in these volumes conforms to the
American National Standard for Permanence of Paper
for Printed Library Materials, Z39.48-1984.

Library of Congress Cataloging-in-Publication Data
Critical survey of short fiction/edited by Frank N.
Magill. — Rev. ed.
      p.   cm.
Includes bibliographical references and index.
1. Short story. 2. Short stories—Dictionaries.
3. Short stories—Bio-bibliography. 4. Novelists—
Biography—Dictionaries.
I. Magill, Frank Northen, 1907-   .
PN3321.C7   1993
809.3'1'03—dc20   92-41950
ISBN 0-89356-843-0 (set)   CIP
ISBN 0-89356-850-3 (volume 7)

Second Printing

PRINTED IN THE UNITED STATES OF AMERICA

LIST OF AUTHORS IN VOLUME 7

CRITICAL SURVEY
OF
SHORT FICTION

VIRGINIA WOOLF

Born: London, England; January 25, 1882
Died: Rodmell, Sussex, England; March 28, 1941

Principal short fiction

Two Stories, 1917 (one by Leonard Woolf); *Kew Gardens*, 1919; *The Mark on the Wall*, 1919; *Monday or Tuesday*, 1921; *A Haunted House and Other Short Stories*, 1943; *Mrs. Dalloway's Party*, 1973; *The Complete Shorter Fiction of Virginia Woolf*, 1985.

Other literary forms

Besides authoring short stories, Virginia Woolf was an acute and detailed diarist (her diary entries occupy five volumes in the authoritative collected edition); a prolific letter writer (six volumes in the authoritative collected edition); a biographer; a perceptive, original, and argumentative essayist and reviewer (her collected essays fill six volumes in the authoritative edition); and a pioneer of the modern novel in her ten works of long prose fiction, which include the acknowledged classics *Mrs. Dalloway* (1925), *To the Lighthouse* (1927), and *The Waves* (1931).

Achievements

A distinguished and distinctive prose stylist, Woolf excelled in fiction, nonfiction, and her own unique hybrid of these genres in her two whimsical books *Orlando: A Biography* (1928) and *Flush: A Biography* (1933), which are variously categorized as fiction, nonfiction, or "other" by critics of her work. In nonfiction, essays such as "The Death of the Moth," "How Should One Read a Book?" and "Shakespeare's Sister" have been widely anthologized, and in their vividness, imagery, and keen analysis of daily life, literature, society, and women's concerns assure Woolf a place in the history of the essay.

In fiction, Woolf's classic novels, sharing much in style and theme with the nonfiction, have overshadowed the short stories. Reacting against the realistic and naturalistic fiction of her time, Woolf often emphasized lyricism, stream of consciousness, and the irresolute slice of life in both her novels and her stories, though she wrote more conventional fiction as well. Whether the conventional "well-made" or the experimental stream-of-consciousness variety, many of her approximately fifty short stories are accomplished works of art. Because of their precise and musical prose style, irony, ingenious spiral form (with narrative refrains), reversal or revelatory structure, and exploration of human nature and social life, they deserve to be better known and to be studied for themselves and not only for what they may reveal about the novels.

Biography

Virginia Woolf was born as Adeline Virginia Stephen and grew up in the literary household of her father, Leslie Stephen, a Victorian and Edwardian literary lion who was visited by many prominent writers of the time. The importance of books in her life is reflected in many of the short stories, such as "Memoirs of a Novelist," "The Evening Party," and "A Haunted House"; her father's extensive personal library provided much of her education, along with some private tutoring (especially in Greek). Despite Katherine Stephen, niece of Leslie Stephen, being the principal of Newnham College at the University of Cambridge (reflected in the story "A Woman's College from Outside"), Virginia was denied a formal college education because of persistent ill health (emotional and physical), as well as her father's male bias in this matter, all of which is echoed with mild irony in "Phyllis and Rosamond" (about two sisters who resemble Virginia and Vanessa Stephen, lacking a college education) and "A Society" (in which the character Poll, lacking a college education, receives her father's inheritance on condition that she read all the books in the London Library).

The early death of Woolf's mother, Julia, in 1895, the repeated sexual molestation by her half brother George Duckworth, her father's transformation of Virginia's sisters Stella and Vanessa into surrogate mothers after Julia's death, and her own attachments to women such as Violet Dickinson and, later, Vita Sackville-West culminated in Virginia's cool and ambivalent sexuality, reflected by the general absence of sexual passion in many of the short stories as well as by what Woolf herself described as the "Sapphism" of "Moments of Being: 'Slater's Pins Have No Points.' "

The more regular element of her adolescence and generally happy life with Leonard Woolf, whom she married in 1912, was the social round of upper-middle-class life, including horticultural outings in London (reflected in "Kew Gardens"), parties, private concerts, and theatergoing (as in "The Evening Party," "The String Quartet," the Mrs. Dalloway party cycle of stories, "Uncle Vanya," and "The Searchlight"), and excursions to the country (as in "In the Orchard"), seashore (as in "Solid Objects" and "The Watering Place"), or foreign resorts (as in "A Dialogue upon Mount Pentelicus" and "The Symbol").

Clustering around Virginia and her sister Vanessa, when they moved to a house in the Bloomsbury district after Leslie Stephen's death in 1904, was a group of talented writers, artists, and intellectuals who came to be known as the Bloomsbury Group and were generally among the avant-garde in arts and letters. (This period is portrayed in "Phyllis and Rosamond.") Many intellectuals from the group continued to associate with Virginia and Leonard Woolf after their marriage, and some, such as T. S. Eliot, had books published by the Hogarth Press, which was set up by the Woolfs in 1917. Indeed, all Virginia Woolf's short stories in book form have been published in England by this press.

In 1919, the Woolfs, for weekend and recreational use, took a country cottage called Monks House, whose reputation for being haunted evoked "A Haunted House" and whose vicinity, Rodmell (as well as Leonard Woolf, by name), is jocularly referred to in "The Widow and the Parrot: A True Story." Because of numerous family deaths as well as, later, the strain and letdown of completing her novels and the anxiety from World Wars I and II (referred to in many of the stories, and responsible in 1940 for the destruction of the Woolfs' London house), Woolf had been and continued to be subject to mental breakdowns. The motifs of liquid's destructiveness and death by drowning in several of the stories ("Solid Objects," "A Woman's College from Outside," "The Widow and the Parrot," "The New Dress," "The Introduction," "A Simple Melody," "The Fascination of the Pool") were actualized when, in early 1941, Woolf, at the onset of another breakdown, drowned herself in the Ouse River, near Rodmell and Monks House.

Analysis

Perhaps related to her mental condition is Virginia Woolf's interest in perception and perspective, as well as their relationship to imagination, in many stories. In two short avant-garde pieces—"Monday or Tuesday" (six paragraphs) and "Blue and Green" (two paragraphs, one for each color)—Woolf attempts to convey the reality of the urban and natural worlds through discrete, apparently disconnected associative impressions. In "Monday or Tuesday," a series of contrasts between up and down, spatially free timelessness (a lazily flying heron) and restrictive timeliness (a clock striking), day and night, inside and outside, present experience and later recollection of it conveys the ordinary cycle of life suggested by the title and helps capture its experiential reality, the concern expressed by the refrain question that closes the second, fourth, and fifth paragraphs: "and truth?" Similar contrasts inform the two paragraphs describing the blue and green aspects of reality and the feelings associated with them in "Blue and Green." These two colors are dominant and symbolic throughout Woolf's short stories. Differing perspectives, which are almost cinematic or painterly, also structure "In the Orchard," as each of the story's three sections, dealing with a woman named Miranda sleeping in an orchard, focuses on, in order, the sleeping Miranda in relation to her physical surroundings, the effect of the physical surroundings on Miranda's dreaming (and thus the interconnection between imagination and external world), and finally a return to the physical environment, with a shift in focus to the orchard's apple trees and birds. The simultaneity and differing angle of the three perspectives are suggested by the narrative refrain that closes each section, a sentence referring to Miranda jumping upright and exclaiming that she will be late for tea.

The ability of the imagination, a key repeated word in Woolf's short stories, to perceive accurately the surrounding world is an issue in many of the stories. In "The Mark on the Wall," a narrator is led into associative musings from speculating about the mark, only to discover, with deflating irony, that the source of the imaginative ramblings is in reality a lowly snail (with the further concluding ironic reversal being an unexpected reference to World War I, whose seriousness undercuts the narrator's previous whimsical free associations). Even more difficult is the imagination's perception of people (who and what individuals really are) in the surrounding world. This is the chief problem of the biographer, a task at which Woolf herself was successful, though not the self-centered and somewhat dishonest novelist's biographer who narrates "Memoirs of a Novelist." In the four stories "An Unwritten Novel," "Moments of Being: 'Slater's Pins Have No Points,'" "The Lady in the Looking Glass: A Reflection," and "The Shooting Party," a major character or the narrator is led through small details into imaginative flights about the life and personality of an individual—only, in the story's concluding reversal, to be proved incorrect or be left very doubtful about the picture or account created. Likewise showing a connection between the literary artist's problem of depicting the truth and the imagination's problem in probing reality is the story "The Three Pictures," in which the first picture, of a sailor's homecoming to a welcoming wife, leads the narrator to imagine further happy events, undercut by the second and third pictures revealing the sailor's death from a fever contracted overseas and the despair of his wife.

The problem of "and truth?" (as phrased in "Monday or Tuesday") can be comically superficial, as in the narrator's wasted sympathetic imaginings in "Sympathy" in response to a newspaper account of Humphrey Hammond's death, only to discover in the story's conclusion that the article referred to the elderly father rather than the son (with ironic undercutting of the genuineness of the narrator's sympathy because of her chagrin about the "deception" and "waste"). In contrast, in "The Fascination of the Pool," the deeply evocative imagery and symbolism of never-ending layers of stories absorbed by a pool over time, and always going inexhaustibly deeper, have a meditative and melancholic solemnity.

Related to imagination and art (which may or may not bridge the gap between human beings), as well as to social criticism and feminist issues (whether roles and identities unite or divide, fulfill or thwart people), is the motif of isolation and alienation in many of the stories. In "Kew Gardens," the first paragraph's twice-repeated detail of the heart-and-tongue shape of the colorful plants symbolizes the potential of love and communication to effect communion, while the colors projected by the flowers from sunlight on various things (mentioned in the first and last paragraphs) symbolize the various couples' imaginations projected on the environs. In the social context of the park, however, the four sets of strollers are isolated from one another, as is the other major "character" described, the snail; each is solipsistically involved in its own affairs. Only in the fourth set, a romantic young couple, do love and communication seem to promise, though not guarantee, the hope of communion.

In "Solid Objects," the first paragraph's emphasis on a changing perspective (a black dot on the horizon becomes four-legged and then two men) symbolizes how the protagonist's, John's, perspective changes from imaginative engagements with people, politics, and ideas, to engagements with small things or concrete objects, beginning with his discovery at the beach of a smooth, irregular fragment of glass. While Charles, John's friend, at the beach casts flat slate stones into the water, aware of objects only as a means of allowing physical action and release, John becomes attached to them with the child's and artist's fascination, which lures him away from the practical and pragmatic adult world of action and politics, in which he had a bright future. John thus becomes alienated from all those around him, including Charles. Symbolically during their last encounter, both end up conversing at cross purposes, neither person understanding the other.

"A Haunted House" and "Lappin and Lapinova" show, respectively, success and failure in human communion. The former story uses the convention of the ghost story and gothic fiction, almost satirically or ironically, to suggest the broader theme of the mystery of the human heart. Implicitly two kinds of mystery are contrasted: the mystery of ghosts, haunted houses, secret treasures, and so on, and the real, important mystery of what is most worthwhile in the universe—the ghostly couple's lesson at the story's close that the house's hidden treasure is love, "the light in the heart." The implicitly living couple presumably have love, paralleling the ghostly couple's bond. The cyclical repetitions in the story help convey, stylistically, the pulsation or beating of the human heart, the seat of this love. In contrast, the married couple in "Lappin and Lapinova" become alienated because the husband cannot genuinely share in the wife's imaginative fantasy of the two of them as rabbit and hare, reverting to his pragmatic and stolid family heritage and an arrogant masculine impatience.

Most of the nine stories constituting the Mrs. Dalloway party cycle ("Mrs. Dalloway in Bond Street," "The New Dress," "Happiness," "Ancestors," "The Introduction," "Together and Apart," "The Man Who Loved His Kind," "A Simple Melody," "A Summing Up") naturally deal, by their focus on a social occasion, with communion or alienation, as suggested by the title "Together and Apart." In "Mrs. Dalloway in Bond Street," the title character remains isolated or insulated from the surrounding world, symbolized by the gloves that she is going to buy (perhaps for the party), by her general disregard of traffic and other phenomena while she muses about the death of a recent acquaintance, and by her disregard of a literal explosion that ends the story (though paradoxically she communes with an acquaintance by remembering and uttering the name while ignoring the explosion). At the party itself, Mabel Waring, the protagonist of "The New Dress," is alienated because her new dress, owing to her limited means, seems a failure and source of embarrassment; Stuart Elton, protagonist of "Happiness," remains withdrawn in himself to preserve an egocentric equilibrium that is his happiness; Mrs. Vallance, protagonist of "Ancestors," is alienated by the superficial and undignified talk and values of the young around her, in contrast to her past. Woolf's feminist concerns about the unjust subordination and oppression of women (prominent in "Phyllis and Rosamond," "The Mysterious Case of Miss V.," "The Journal of Mistress Joan Martyn," "A Society," "A Woman's College from Outside," and "The Legacy") are suggested by the isolation and alienation of Lily Everit, who feels inadequate when introduced to Bob Brinsley, symbol of thoughtless male power and conceit. Despite Everit's esteemed essay writing (paralleling Woolf's), Brinsley negligently assumes that she must as a women write poetry, as his initial question shows. Everit feels crushed, stifled, and silenced by the weight of masculine accomplishment in the arts and sciences.

Two impromptu pairings in the Dalloway party cycle—Roderick Serle and Ruth Anning of "Together and Apart," and Prickett Ellis and Miss O'Keefe of "The Man

Who Loved His Kind"—achieve temporary communion: Serle and Anning when they imaginatively attune to each other, sharing profound emotions about experiences in Canterbury; Ellis and O'Keefe when the latter concurs with the former's concern about the poor excluded from affairs such as Mrs. Dalloway's party. These couples, however, driven apart at story's end by the evening's experience—Serle and Anning when the former is mockingly accosted by a female acquaintance, and Ellis and O'Keefe when the former fails, with some self-centered posturing, to appreciate the latter's understanding of the need for beauty and imagination in the life lived at all social levels. Only the protagonists of the last two stories of the cycle, George Carslake in "A Simple Melody" and Sasha Latham in "A Summing Up," achieve a transcendence over isolation and alienation. Carslake melds all the partygoers and himself through a blend of imagination, art, and nature by meditating on a beautiful painting of a heath in the Dalloways' house and imagining the various partygoers on a walk there that reduces them all to fundamentally decent human beings coalesced in a common enterprise. Like Carslake, Latham achieves wisdom by fixing on inanimate objects, the Dalloway's beautiful Queen Anne house (art) and a tree in the garden (nature), and meditating on them; like Carslake, Latham sees people admirably united in motion—in her reverie, adventurers and survivors sailing on the sea.

Other major works

NOVELS: *The Voyage Out*, 1915; *Night and Day*, 1919; *Jacob's Room*, 1922; *Mrs. Dalloway*, 1925; *To the Lighthouse*, 1927; *Orlando: A Biography*, 1928; *The Waves*, 1931; *Flush: A Biography*, 1933; *The Years*, 1937; *Between the Acts*, 1941.

NONFICTION: *The Common Reader: First Series*, 1925; *A Room of One's Own*, 1929; *The Common Reader: Second Series*, 1932; *Three Guineas*, 1938; *Roger Fry: A Biography*, 1940; *The Death of the Moth and Other Essays*, 1942; *The Moment and Other Essays*, 1947; *The Captain's Death Bed and Other Essays*, 1950; *A Writer's Diary*, 1953; *Letters: Virginia Woolf and Lytton Strachey*, 1956; *Granite and Rainbow*, 1958; *Contemporary Writers*, 1965; *Collected Essays, Volumes 1-2*, 1966; *Collected Essays, Volumes 3-4*, 1967; *The London Scene: Five Essays*, 1975; *The Flight of the Mind: The Letters of Virginia Woolf, Vol. I, 1888-1912*, 1975 (published in the United States as *The Letters of Virginia Woolf, Vol. I: 1888-1912*, 1975; Nigel Nicolson, editor); *The Question of Things Happening: The Letters of Virginia Woolf, Vol. II, 1912-1922*, 1976 (published in the United States as *The Letters of Virginia Woolf, Vol. II: 1912-1922*, 1976; Nigel Nicolson, editor); *Moments of Being*, 1976 (Jeanne Schulkind, editor); *Books and Portraits*, 1977; *The Diary of Virginia Woolf*, 1977-1984 (Anne Olivier Bell, editor, 5 volumes); *A Change of Perspective: The Letters of Virginia Woolf, Vol. III, 1923-1928*, 1977 (published in the United States as *The Letters of Virginia Woolf, Vol. III: 1923-1928*, 1978; Nigel Nicolson, editor); *A Reflection of the Other Person: The Letters of Virginia Woolf, Vol. IV, 1929-1931*, 1978 (published in the United States as *The Letters of Virginia Woolf, Vol. IV: 1929-1931*, 1979; Nigel Nicolson, editor); *The Sickle Side of the Moon: The Letters of Virginia Woolf, Vol. V, 1932-1935*, 1979 (published in the United States as *The Letters of Virginia Woolf, Vol. V: 1932-1935*,

1979; Nigel Nicolson, editor); *Leave the Letters Till We're Dead: The Letters of Virginia Woolf, Vol. VI, 1936-1941,* 1980 (Nigel Nicolson, editor); *The Essays of Virginia Woolf,* 1987-1989 (3 volumes); *The Essays of Virginia Woolf,* 1986-1992 (6 volumes).

Bibliography

Banks, Joanne Trautmann. "Virginia Woolf and Katherine Mansfield." In *The English Short Story, 1880-1945: A Critical History,* edited by Joseph M. Flora. Boston, Mass.: Twayne, 1985. In about twelve pages, the philosophical themes of several stories (imagination, perception) are briefly explored, plus the affinities of the two writers, deriving from feminist concerns and admiration of Anton Chekhov's short fiction.

Daiches, David. *Virginia Woolf.* Norfolk, Conn.: New Directions, 1942. Brief comments are offered on "A Haunted House," "The Mark on the Wall," "Monday or Tuesday," "A Society," "The String Quartet," and "An Unwritten Novel."

Dick, Susan, ed. Introduction and notes to *The Complete Shorter Fiction of Virginia Woolf.* 2d ed. San Diego: Harcourt Brace Jovanovich, 1989. Along with classification of stories into traditional ones and fictional reveries, with affinities in works of nineteenth century writers such as Thomas De Quincey and Anton Chekhov, invaluable notes are given on historical, literary, and cultural allusions, as well as textual problems, for every story.

Fleishman, Avrom. "Forms of the Woolfian Short Story." In *Virginia Woolf: Revaluation and Continuity,* edited by Ralph Freedman. Berkeley: University of California Press, 1980. In twenty-six pages, abstract theoretical issues concerning genre are discussed; then several stories are divided into the two categories of linear (for example, "The New Dress" and "Kew Gardens") and circular (for example, "The Duchess" and "Lappin and Lapinova") in form.

Guiget, Jean. "Stories and Sketches." In *Virginia Woolf and Her Works.* Translated by Jean Stewart. London: Hogarth Press, 1965. In fourteen pages, the stories are divided into several groups by style (such as the impressionistic ones) or theme (such as the observer studying another person), with perceptive comments on specific symbols.

Meyerowitz, Selma. "What Is to Console Us? The Politics of Deception in Woolf's Short Stories." In *New Feminist Essays on Virginia Woolf,* edited by Jane Marcus, Lincoln: University of Nebraska Press, 1981. In fourteen pages, in contrast to formal aspects or general philosophical themes such as the quest for reality, the political and social content of several stories is stressed, particularly feminist issues of subordination and powerlessness, alienation, negative male traits, class conflict, and oppressive social institutions.

Norman Prinsky

RICHARD WRIGHT

Born: Natchez, Mississippi; September 4, 1908
Died: Paris, France; November 28, 1960

Principal short fiction

Uncle Tom's Children: Four Novellas, 1938; *Uncle Tom's Children: Five Long Stories*, 1940; *Eight Men*, 1961.

Other literary forms

Although Richard Wright is best known for his novel *Native Son* (1940), his nonfiction works, such as the two volumes of his autobiography *Black Boy: A Record of Childhood and Youth* (1945) and *American Hunger* (1977) along with books such as *Twelve Million Black Voices* (1941) and *White Man, Listen!* (1957), have proven to be of lasting interest. He developed a Marxist ideology while writing for the Communist *Daily Worker*, which was very influential on his early fiction, notably *Native Son* and *Uncle Tom's Children*, but which culminated in an article, "I Tried to Be a Communist," first published by the *Atlantic Monthly* in 1944. Although he abandoned Marxist ideology, he never abandoned the idea that protest is and should be at the heart of great literature.

Achievements

Wright is often cited as being the father of the post-World War II African-American novel. The works of James Baldwin and Ralph Ellison owe a direct debt to the work of Wright, and his role in inspiring the Black Arts movement of the 1960's is incalculable. Further, he was one of the first African-American novelists of the first half of the twentieth century to capture a truly international audience. Among his many honors were a Guggenheim Fellowship in 1939 and the Spingarn Award from the National Association for the Advancement of Colored People (NAACP) in 1941 for his novel, *Native Son*. This novel, which James Baldwin said was "unquestionably" the "most powerful and celebrated statement we have had yet of what it means to be a Negro in America," along with the first volume of his autobiography and the stories in *Uncle Tom's Children*, constitute Wright's most important lasting contributions to literature. His plots usually deal with how the harrowing experience of racial inequality transforms a person into a rebel—usually violent, and usually randomly so. The more subtle achievement of his fiction, however, is the psychological insight it provides into the experience of oppression and rebellion.

Biography

The poverty, racial hatred, and violence that Richard Nathaniel Wright dramatizes in fiction come directly from his own experience as the child of an illiterate Mississippi sharecropper. Richard was six years old when his father was driven off the land and the family moved to a two-room slum tenement in Memphis, Tennessee. The father deserted the family there. Richard's mother, Ella Wright, got a job as a cook, leaving Richard and his younger brother Alan alone in the apartment. When his mother became ill, the brothers were put in an orphanage. An invitation for Ella and the boys to stay with a more prosperous relative in Arkansas ended in panic and flight when white men shot Uncle Hoskins, who had offered the Wrights a home. The family lived for some time with Richard's grandparents, stern Seventh-day Adventists. In this grim, repressive atmosphere, Richard became increasingly violent and rebellious.

Although he completed his formal education in the ninth grade, the young Richard read widely, especially Stephen Crane, Fyodor Dostoevski, Marcel Proust, T. S. Eliot, and Gertrude Stein. The family eventually migrated to Chicago. Wright joined the Communist Party in 1933, and, in 1937 in New York City, became editor of the *Daily Worker.* The publications of *Uncle Tom's Children, Native Son,* and *Black Boy* brought Wright fame both in the United States and in Europe. In 1945, at the invitation of the French government, Wright went to France and became friends with Jean-Paul Sartre, Simone de Beauvoir, and other existentialists. His next novel, *The Outsider* (1953), has been called the first existential novel by an American writer. Wright traveled widely, lectured in several countries, and wrote journalistic accounts of his experience in Africa and Spain. He died unexpectedly in Paris of amoebic dysentery, probably contracted in Africa or Indonesia under conditions his friend and biographer Margaret Walker, in *Richard Wright: Daemonic Genius* (1988), believes indicate at least medically questionable decisions, or, possibly, homicide.

Analysis

"Fire and Cloud" in *Uncle Tom's Children* is perhaps the best representative of Richard Wright's early short fiction. It won first prize in the 1938 *Story* magazine contest which had more than four hundred entries, marking Wright's first triumph with American publishers. Charles K. O'Neill made a radio adaptation of the story that appeared in *American Scenes.*

Unlike the later works concerning black ghetto experience, "Fire and Cloud" has a pastoral quality, recognizing the strong bond of the Southern black to the soil and the support he has drawn from religion. Wright reproduces faithfully the Southern black dialect in both conversation and internal meditations. This use of dialect emphasizes the relative lack of sophistication of rural blacks. His protagonist, Reverend Taylor, is representative of the "old Negro," who has withstood centuries of oppression, sustained by hard work on the land and humble faith in a merciful God.

Wright's attitude toward religion, however, is ambivalent. Although he recognizes it as contributing to the quiet nobility of the hero, it also prevents Taylor from taking effective social action when his people are literally starving. The final triumph of Reverend Taylor is that he puts aside the conciliatory attitude which was part of his religious training and becomes a social activist. Instead of turning the other cheek after being humiliated and beaten by white men, he embraces the methods of his

Marxist supporters, meeting oppression with mass demonstration. Strength of numbers proves more effective and appropriate for getting relief from the bigoted white establishment than all his piety and loving-kindness. Early in the story Taylor exclaims "The good Lawds gonna clean up this ol worl some day! Hes gonna make a new Heaven n a new Earth!" His last words, however, are "Freedom belongs t the strong!"

The situation of the story no doubt reflects Wright's early experience when his sharecropper father was driven off the plantation. Taylor's people are starving because the white people, who own all the land, have prohibited the blacks from raising food on it. No matter how Taylor pleads for relief, the local white officials tell him to wait and see if federal aid may be forthcoming. When two Communist agitators begin pushing Taylor to lead a mass demonstration against the local government, white officials have Taylor kidnapped and beaten, as well as several deacons of his church. Instead of intimidating them, this suffering persuades them to open confrontation. As the Communists promised, the poor whites join the blacks in the march which forces the white authorities to release food to those facing starvation.

The story's strength lies in revealing through three dialogues the psychological dilemma of the protagonist as opposing groups demand his support. He resists the Communists initially because their methods employ threat of open war on the whites—"N tha ain Gawds way!" The agitators say he will be responsible if their demonstration fails through lack of numbers and participants are slaughtered. On the other hand, the mayor and chief of police threaten Taylor that they will hold him personally responsible if any of his church members join the march. After a humiliating and futile exchange with these men, Taylor faces his own church deacons, who are themselves divided and look to him for leadership. He knows that one of their number, who is just waiting for a chance to oust him from his church, will run to the mayor and police with any evidence of Taylor's insubordination. In a pathetic attempt to shift the burden of responsibility that threatens to destroy him no matter what he does, he reiterates the stubborn stand he has maintained with all three groups: he will not order the demonstration, but he will march with his people if they choose to demonstrate. The brutal horse-whipping that Taylor endures as a result of this moderate stand convinces him of the futility of trying to placate everybody. The Uncle Tom becomes a rebel.

Critics sometimes deplore the episodes of raw brutality described in graphic detail in Wright's fiction, but violence is the clue here to his message. Behind the white man's paternalistic talk is the persuasion of whip and gun. Only superior force can cope with such an antagonist.

Wright's best short fiction is "The Man Who Lived Underground." Although undoubtedly influenced by Dostoevski's underground man and by Franz Kafka's "K," the situation was based on a prisoner's story from *True Detective* magazine. The first version appeared in 1942 in *Accent* magazine under the subtitle "Two Excerpts from a Novel." This version began with a description of the life of a black servant, but Wright later discarded this opening in favor of the dramatic scene in which an unnamed fugitive hides from the police by descending into a sewer. This approach allowed the story to assume a more universal, symbolic quality. Although racist issues are still significant, the protagonist represents that larger class of all those alienated from their society. Eventually the fugitive's name is revealed as Fred Daniels, but so completely is he absorbed into his Everyman role that he cannot remember his name when he returns to the upper world. His progress through sewers and basements becomes a quest for the meaning of life, parodying classic descents into the underworld and ironically reversing Plato's allegory of the cave.

Although Plato's philosopher attains wisdom by climbing out of the cave where men respond to shadows on the cave wall, Wright's protagonist gains enlightenment because of his underground perspective. What he sees there speaks not to his rational understanding, however, but to his emotions. He moves among symbolic visions which arouse terror and pity—a dead baby floating on the slimy water whose "mouth gaped black in a soundless cry." In a black church service spied on through a crevice in the wall, the devout are singing "Jesus, take me to your home above." He is overwhelmed by a sense of guilt and intuits that there is something obscene about their "singing with the air of the sewer blowing in on them." In a meat locker with carcasses hanging from the ceiling, a butcher is hacking off a piece of meat with a bloody cleaver. When the store proprietor goes home, Fred emerges from the locker and gorges on fresh fruit, but he takes back with him into the sewer the bloody cleaver—why he does not know.

When Fred breaks through a wall into the basement of a movie house, the analogy to Plato's myth of the cave becomes explicit. He comes up a back stair and sees jerking shadows of a silver screen. The Platonic urge to enlighten the people in the theater, who are bound to a shadow world, merges with messianic images. In a dream he walks on water and saves a baby held up by a drowning woman, but the dream ends in terror and doubt as he loses the baby and his ability to emulate Christ. All is lost and he himself begins to drown.

Terror and pity are not the only emotions that enlarge his sensibilities in this underground odyssey. As he learns the peculiar advantages of his invisibility, he realizes that he can help himself to all kinds of gadgets valued by that shadow world above ground. He collects them like toys or symbols of an absurd world. He acquires a radio, a light bulb with an extension cord, a typewriter, a gun, and finally, through a chance observation of a safe being opened by combination, rolls of hundred dollar bills, containers of diamonds, watches, and rings. His motivation for stealing these articles is not greed but sheer hilarious fun at acquiring objects so long denied to persons of his class.

In one of the most striking, surrealist scenes in modern literature, Fred delightedly decorates his cave walls and floor with these tokens of a society which has rejected him. "They were the serious toys of the men who lived in the dead world of sunshine and rain he had left, the world that had condemned him, branded him guilty." He glues hundred dollar bills on his walls. He winds up all the watches but disdains to set them (for he is beyond time, freed from its tyranny). The watches hang on nails along with the diamond rings. He hangs up the bloody cleaver, too, and the gun. The unset diamonds he dumps in a glittering pile on the muddy floor. Then as he gaily tramps around, he accidentally/on purpose, stomps on the pile, scattering the pretty baubles over the floor. Here, indeed, is society's cave of shadows, and only he realizes how absurd it all is.

When the euphoria of these games begins to pall, Fred becomes more philosophical, perceiving the nihilistic implications of his experience. "Maybe *any*thing's right, he mumbled. Yes, if the world as men had made it was right, then anything else was right, any act a man took to satisfy himself, murder, theft, torture." In his unlettered, blundering way, he is groping toward Ivan Karamazov's dark meditation: "If there is no God, then all things are permissible." Fred becomes convinced of the reality of human guilt, however, when he witnesses the suicide of the jewelry store's night watchman, who has been blamed for the theft he himself committed. At first, the scene in which police torture the bewildered man to force a confession strikes Fred as hilariously funny, duplicating his own experience. When the wretched man shoots himself before Fred can offer him a means of escape, however, Fred is shocked into a realization of his own guilt.

The protagonist ultimately transcends his nihilism, and like Plato's philosopher who returns to the cave out of compassion for those trapped there, Fred returns to the "dead world of sunshine and rain" to bear witness to the Truth. Like the philosopher who is blinded coming out of the light into cave darkness, Fred seems confused and stupid in the social world above ground. When he is thrown out of the black church, he tries inarticulately to explain his revelation at the police station where he had been tortured and condemned. The police think he is crazy, but because they now know they accused him unjustly, they find his return embarrassing. Fred euphorically insists that they accompany him into the sewer so that they too can experience the visions that enlightened him. When he shows them his entrance to the world underground, one of the policemen calmly shoots him and the murky waters of the sewer sweep him away.

This ironic story of symbolic death and resurrection is unparalleled in its unique treatment of existential themes. Guilt and alienation lead paradoxically to a tragic sense of human brotherhood, which seems unintelligible to "normal" people. The man who kills Fred Daniels is perhaps the only person who perceives even dimly what Daniels wants to do. "You've got to shoot this kind," he says. "They'd wreck things."

Other major works

NOVELS: *Native Son*, 1940; *The Outsider*, 1953; *Savage Holiday*, 1954; *The Long Dream*, 1958; *Lawd Today*, 1963.

PLAY: *Native Son: The Biography of a Young American*, 1941 (with Paul Green).

NONFICTION: *Twelve Million Black Voices: A Folk History of the Negro in the United States*, 1941; *Black Boy: A Record of Childhood and Youth*, 1945; *Black Power: A Record of Reactions in a Land of Pathos*, 1954; *Pagan Spain*, 1957; *White Man,*

Listen!, 1957; *American Hunger*, 1977; *Richard Wright Reader*, 1978 (Ellen Wright and Michel Fabre, editors).

Bibliography
Fabre, Michel. *The Unfinished Quest of Richard Wright.* New York: William Morrow, 1973. Although this volume is one of the most important and authoritative biographies available on Wright, readers interested in Wright's life should consult Margaret Walker's biography as well (see below).

_____. *The World of Richard Wright.* Jackson: University Press of Mississippi, 1985. A collection of Fabre's essays on Wright. A valuable resource, though not a sustained, full-length study. It contains two chapters on individual short stories by Wright, including the short story "Superstition." Supplemented by an appendix.

Felgar, Robert. *Richard Wright.* Boston: Twayne, 1980. A general biographical and critical source, this work devotes two chapters to the short fiction of Wright.

Kinnamon, Kenneth. *The Emergence of Richard Wright.* Urbana: University of Illinois Press, 1972. A study of Wright's background and development as a writer, up until the publication of *Native Son.*

_____, ed. *A Richard Wright Bibliography: Fifty Years of Criticism and Commentary: 1933-1982.* Westport, Conn.: Greenwood Press, 1988. A mammoth annotated bibliography (one of the largest annotated bibliographies ever assembled on an American writer), which traces the history of Wright criticism. This bibliography is invaluable as a research tool.

Walker, Margaret. *Richard Wright: Daemonic Genius.* New York: Warner Publishing, 1988. A critically acclaimed study of Wright's life and work written by a friend and fellow novelist. Not a replacement for Michel Fabre's biography but written with the benefit of several more years of scholarship on issues that include the medical controversy over Wright's death. Walker is especially insightful on Wright's early life, and her comments on Wright's short fiction are short but · pithy. Includes a useful bibliographic essay at the end.

Katherine Snipes
(Revised by *Thomas J. Cassidy*)

WILLIAM BUTLER YEATS

Born: Sandymount, near Dublin, Ireland; June 13, 1865
Died: Cap Martin, France; January 28, 1939

Principal short fiction

John Sherman and Dhoya, 1891, 1969; *The Celtic Twilight*, 1893; *The Secret Rose*, 1897; *The Tables of Law. The Adoration of the Magi*, 1897; *Stories of Red Hanrahan*, 1904; *Mythologies*, 1959.

Other literary forms

William Butler Yeats, a prolific writer, composed hundreds of lyrical, narrative, and dramatic poems. It was not unusual to find characters from his short stories appearing in his poems; *Michael Robartes and the Dancer*, a collection of poems published in 1920, is one example. In addition to writing poetry, he contributed to the Irish dramatic movement, which culminated in the establishment of the Abbey Theatre in Dublin. His *Cathleen ni Houlihan* (1902) and *Deirdre* (1906) are typical plays of that early period. Yeats was a prolific and accomplished essayist and also produced various works of autobiography (collected in one volume entitled *Auto-biographies*, 1926, 1955) as well as an ambitious philosophical treatise entitled *A Vision* (1925, 1937), which details his cosmology.

Achievements

Yeats's reputation as one of the major poets of the twentieth century is unassailable, and his influence, particularly on the course of American verse, as practiced most notably by Robert Lowell, is equally well attested. His adaptation of native Irish materials for poetic ends, his mythic projection in verse of his life and times, his conception of art as an antidote to history have exerted a powerful imaginative influence on poets succeeding him. In a more narrowly Irish context, his ideological pronouncements and cultural commitments—the latter culminating in the establishment of the Abbey Theatre—have constituted an overwhelmingly important instance of the relationship of the artist to society.

Yeats received honorary degrees from Queen's University (Belfast) and Trinity College (Dublin) in 1922. Receipt of the Nobel Prize in Literature followed in 1923, as well as honorary degrees from the University of Oxford in 1931 and the University of Cambridge in 1933.

Biography

Born in Dublin to the painter John Butler Yeats and Susan Pollexfen of Sligo, William Butler Yeats was of Irish Protestant background. His childhood was spent in London, Dublin, and Sligo. He was educated at the Godolphin School, Hammersmith, Dublin High School, and the Metropolitan School of Art, where he fell under the spell of George Russell (Æ) and other Dublin mystics. John O'Leary, the Fenian leader, and Maud Gonne, the passionate actress and patriot, were two Irish friends, while Arthur Symons and Lionel Johnson of the Rhymers' Club were London friends. When Maud Gonne and later her daughter Iseult rejected his marriage proposals, Yeats married Georgie Hyde-Lees, an Englishwoman, in 1917. They had one son and one daughter. After the Irish Civil War, he served as Senator for the Irish Free State, 1923-1928. Yeats traveled extensively, including lecture tours to the United States. In 1899, Yeats with Lady Gregory, Edward Martyn, and George Moore established an Irish theater which led to the Abbey Theatre. With George Bernard Shaw and George Russell (Æ), Yeats founded the Irish Academy of Letters in 1932. His complex life experiences were literary source material for his works. Acutely aware of the religious and philosophical conflict facing the world, he believed that a viable literature was an alternative resolution until religion and philosophy offered another solution.

Analysis

With the exception of "John Sherman," William Butler Yeats's short stories mirror his attraction to the spirit world and reflect his fascination with good and evil. Since they were written during the *fin de siècle* period when literary and graphic artists, epitomized by the French symbolists, were expressing a world-weariness and pessimism that celebrated the triumph of evil, it is understandable that Yeats's tales articulate that prevailing mood. These early fictional works also identify the themes which were to occupy Yeats's poetic genius for the remainder of his life.

An integral part of the Irish literary movement, the tales have a dual purpose: to revitalize ancient Irish myths for modern Ireland and to serve as a model for artists attempting to write in Irish about Irish subjects. In the stories, Yeats celebrates the exploits of fairies and pagan Irish heroes which he discovered in the oral and written literary traditions; his tales thus become source material for other storytellers. Yeats's *The Celtic Twilight*, a collection of folklore gathered from local storytellers, became important source material for Yeats's later work. In recording the fantastic behavior of the various spirits and their relationship to the country people, Yeats stored information which he used later to dramatize his belief in communication between the material and the immaterial worlds. "Dhoya" is an excellent example of a revitalized myth, and "The Twisting of the Rope" illustrates Yeats's role as a mentor for others.

In "Dhoya," Yeats writes about a local Sligo legend. He had recently edited *Fairy and Folk Tales of the Irish Peasantry* (1888), and his imagination was stimulated by the living nature of these expressions of the conflict between the natural and preternatural worlds. "Dhoya" honors an ancient Celt who lived before the time of the Pharaohs, Buddha, and Thor. In predating the time of known heroes, Dhoya, the Celt, exists before recorded history. It follows then that Yeats's native Sligo has indeed an ancient history, for Dhoya is deserted at the Bay of Ballah, the fictional name of Sligo Bay. The Formorians, an ancient Irish tribe, abandon Dhoya, a giant of tremendous strength, because he cannot control the violent rages which come over him. While enraged, he kills those around him and destroys whatever he can touch. He is believed to be possessed by demons, and a plan is concocted to exile him to the Bay of Ballah.

Dhoya, living alone in the forests and along the beaches, experiences more frequent attacks, but they are directed against his shadow or the halcyon, the beautiful and peaceful legendary bird. Years pass, and a quality of timelessness adds to the mystical nature of the tale, for Dhoya is hundreds of years old. One day he kills a great bull, and the herd chases him until he eludes it by running into the deepest part of the bay, a spot called Pool Dhoya. To this day, and in Yeats's day, the deepest part of Sligo Bay is known as Pool Dhoya, a fact which Yeats incorporates into the story to create a living legend.

Yeats also introduces legendary characters. Dhoya ranges over the mountains where Diarmuid and Grania, pagan lovers of the written Irish literature of pre-Christian Ireland, traveled. In time, Dhoya also experiences a love like Diarmuid. It comes to Dhoya as a gentle breeze upon his forehead, nothing more; but he longs for that touch, which remains only a touch for an untold number of years. Eventually, he develops a depression which he plans to shake off by building a huge bonfire at the rising of the moon. The unhappy lover prays to the moon and makes all kinds of sacrifices—strawberries, an owl, a badger, deer, swine, birds, and whatever else he can find to appease the moon. Soon thereafter, a voice calls "Dhoya, my beloved." Trembling, Dhoya looks into the forest, sees a white form which becomes a flowering plant as he touches it. Dazed, the giant returns to his cave where he finds a beautiful woman cleaning and rearranging the spears and skins.

She throws her arms about his neck, telling him that she yearns for his love. Having left her happy people from under the lake where age, sorrow, and pain are unknown, she desires love in the changing world, a mortal love which her people cannot experience. Dhoya loves her with a mad passion which is not matched by the beautiful fairy, unnamed by Yeats. Then a man from under the sea appears to reclaim the lady. Holding a spear tipped with metal, he challenges Dhoya, whose rage returns as he fights to keep his love. He wins that battle only to lose to the fairy who reappears and challenges him to a game of chess. Before she leaves Dhoya, the fairy sings a strange love song which was part of "The Wandering of Oisin" (1889):

> My love hath many evil mood
> Ill words for all things soft and fair
> I hold him dearer than the good
> My fingers feel his amber hair.

This stanza is central to "Dhoya" and to the great poems which follow. The happy spirit is unhappy and seeks human love which is neither perfect nor perpetual—a paradox which haunts Yeats.

"John Sherman," a realistic story which Yeats called a short romance and wanted to be judged as an Irish novel, is a variation of the Dhoya theme. Although the story lacks the cultural unity of the Irish novels of William Carleton, John Banim, and Gerald Griffin, it does demonstrate the great influence upon Yeats of William Blake, whose poetical works Yeats had recently edited.

The story takes place in Ballah and London, two contrary locations representing the virtuous countryside and the villainous city. There is also a set of contrary characters who, even if they were merged, would not represent the ideal character. John Sherman of Ballah and William Howard of London have different views on almost everything, yet they become engaged to the same woman. Mary Carton of Ballah and Margaret Leland of London are different, but both are very confused about their love for John Sherman. Sherman's mother and Margaret's mother really represent the country mother and the city mother; neither has a life beyond motherhood. Such artificial characterizations doom the plot of "John Sherman," which—although intended as a love story—with a little revision could have become a comedy or farce. Certainly, it is the lightest piece of work that Yeats produced; but unlike other Irish writers, Yeats lacked a comic sense.

"Proud Costello, MacDermot's Daughter, and the Bitter Tongue," from *The Secret Rose*, is a love story which exhibits the intensity of Dhoya's love for the fairy, but the lovers are mortals of the sixteenth century. Costello loves Una, daughter of MacDermot, who is promised by her father to MacNamara. Una loves Costello and sends a message to him by Duallach, the wandering piper. Costello must appear at her nuptial feast, at which she will drink to the man she loves. At the betrothal drink, to the amazement of all, she drinks to Costello; he is then attacked by the members of the wedding party and barely escapes with his life. Una dies without seeing Costello again, but at her funeral procession he sees the coffin and is considered her murderer. Loving her still, Costello swims to the island where Una is buried, mourning over her grave for three days and nights. Confused, he tries to swim back to the mainland but drowns in the attempt. His body is brought to the island and buried beside his beloved; two ash trees are planted over their grave site. They grow tall and the branches, like lover's arms, entwine themselves, symbolic of the undying love between Costello and Una. This motif, common in folklore, appealed to Yeats's sensibility because of the implied relationship between the natural world and the affairs of mortals.

From another perspective, Yeats writes again about that relationship in "The Twisting of the Rope." This story is one of the six connected stories grouped as the *Stories of Red Hanrahan* which tell of the plight of Hanrahan, a hedge schoolmaster enchanted by a spirit on Samhain Eve, the night (the equivalent of Halloween) on which the Celts believed spirits roamed the earth searching for mortals. Since his enchantment, Hanrahan becomes a traveling poet of the Gael who sings of the past heroic age when the ancient Irish kings and queens ruled Ireland. The people, although they welcome Hanrahan into their cottages, fear him because he is of the other world and is able to charm others, especially young and impressionable women.

One night Hanrahan is observed casting his spell over Oona, an attentive listener of his tales; but her mother and a neighbor woman, watching Oona drift into the spirit world, plan to thwart Hanrahan's influence. They cannot order the poet out of the house because he might cast a spell over their animals and fields, destroying cattle and corn, so they devise a scheme whereby Hanrahan is asked to twist a rope from the bundles of hay which the women bring to him. Feeding him more and more rope and praising him for the fine job of rope-making, they eventually get Hanrahan to the door and out of the cottage. Realizing that he had been tricked, he composes a song, "The Twisting of the Rope." Douglas Hyde, who wrote the first Irish play for the new Irish dramatic movement (*Casad-an-Sugan*, 1901), selected Yeats's short tale for production. His success in revitalizing Irish myth and encouraging the continuation of the written Irish literary tradition assures Yeats a prominent place in Irish letters.

Another aspect of Yeats's personality was his fascination with the occult, an attraction which led him to explore Christian, Jewish, and Oriental mysticism in his writings. As John O'Leary made Yeats conscious of the past political Irish culture, George Russell (Æ), to whom *The Secret Rose* was dedicated, indoctrinated Yeats into the Dublin Theosophist Circle, which was occupied with the study of Rosicrucianism. It was a subject about which Yeats could never learn enough, and in "Rosa Alchemica" he approaches the topic through the story of the life of Michael Robartes. Yeats says in an explanatory note to the collection of poems known as *Michael Robartes and the Dancer* (1920) that Robartes had returned to Dublin from Mesopotamia where he "partly found and partly thought out much philosophy."

This knowledge, which Robartes wants to share with his old friend, is revolutionary. It consists of an understanding that modern alchemy is not concerned with simply converting base metal to gold. On the contrary, the new science seeks to transform all things to the divine form; in other words, experiential life is transmuted to art. The process involves rituals through which novices are initiated gradually into the sect. Robartes brings his friend into a temple, but in order to proceed, he must first learn a series of intricate dance steps; then he is dressed in a costume of Greek and Egyptian origin for the mad dance. At this point the friend, fearing for his sanity, flees from the phantasmagoria.

"The Tables of the Law" and "The Adoration of the Magi" are two other short stories that deal with religious mysteries. In "The Tables of the Law," Owen Aherne, like Michael Robartes, returns to Dublin after studying mysticism and alchemy. He hates life and cherishes a medieval book with its secrets of the spirit. Jonathan Swift, Aherne thinks, created a soul for Dublin gentlemen by hating his neighbor as himself. A decade later, the narrator sees Aherne again at a Dublin bookstore; his face is a lifeless mask, drained of the energy to sin and repent as God planned for mortal man. God's law tablets make mankind commit sin, which is abhorrent to Aherne.

Michael Robartes, appearing again in "The Adoration of the Magi," promises the return of the Celtic heroes. Three men in the tale, perhaps demons, watch the death of the Wise Woman. Civilization has not progressed; Christianity has not fulfilled its mission. The hope of nations lies in the reestablishment of the aristocratic order of the Celtic civilization. To a greater degree, Yeats develops this theme in later verse, essays, and plays with a blurring of the character of Cuchulain, the pagan Irish hero, with Christ and Saint Patrick.

Yeats's reputation as a poet and a dramatist overshadows his renown as a story-teller. His tales have intrinsic worth nevertheless, and can be read as a prelude to his later great works.

Other major works

PLAYS: *The Countess Cathleen*, 1892; *The Land of Heart's Desire*, 1894; *Cathleen ni Houlihan*, 1902; *The Pot of Broth*, 1902; *The Hour-Glass*, 1903; *The King's Threshold*, 1903; *On Baile's Strand*, 1904; *Deirdre*, 1906; *The Shadowy Waters*, 1906; *The Unicorn from the Stars*, 1907; *The Golden Helmet*, 1908; *The Green Helmet*, 1910; *At the Hawk's Well*, 1916; *The Player Queen*, 1919; *The Only Jealousy of Emer*, 1919; *The Dreaming of the Bones*, 1919; *Calvary*, 1921; *Four Plays for Dancers*, 1921 (includes *Calvary*, *At the Hawk's Well*, *The Dreaming of the Bones*, *The Only Jealousy of Emer*); *The Cat and the Moon*, 1924; *The Resurrection*, 1927; *The Words upon the Windowpane*, 1930; *The Collected Plays of W. B. Yeats*, 1934, 1952; *The King of the Great Clock Tower*, 1934; *A Full Moon in March*, 1934; *The Herne's Egg*, 1938; *Purgatory*, 1938; *The Death of Cuchulain*, 1939; *Variorum Edition of the Plays of W. B. Yeats*, 1966 (Russell K. Alspach, editor).

POETRY: *Mosada: A Dramatic Poem*, 1886; *Crossways*, 1889; *The Wanderings of Oisin and Other Poems*, 1889; *The Countess Kathleen and Various Legends and Lyrics*, 1892; *The Rose*, 1893; *The Wind Among the Reeds*, 1899; *In the Seven Woods*, 1903; *The Poetical Works of William B. Yeats*, 1906, 1907 (2 volumes); *The Green Helmet and Other Poems*, 1910; *Responsibilities*, 1914; *Responsibilities and Other Poems*, 1916; *The Wild Swans at Coole*, 1917, 1919; *Michael Robartes and the Dancer*, 1920; *The Tower*, 1928; *Words for Music Perhaps and Other Poems*, 1932; *The Winding Stair and Other Poems*, 1933; *The Collected Poems of W. B. Yeats*, 1933, 1950; *The King of the Great Clock Tower*, 1934; *A Full Moon in March*, 1935; *Last Poems and Plays*, 1940; *The Poems of W. B. Yeats*, 1949 (2 volumes); *The Collected Poems of W. B. Yeats*, 1956; *The Variorum Edition of the Poems of W. B. Yeats*, 1957 (P. Allt and R.K. Alspach, editors); *The Poems*, 1983; *The Poems: A New Edition*, 1984.

NONFICTION: *Ideas of Good and Evil*, 1903; *The Cutting of an Agate*, 1912; *Per Amica Silentia Lunae*, 1918; *Essays*, 1924; *A Vision*, 1925, 1937; *Autobiographies*, 1926, 1955; *A Packet for Ezra Pound*, 1929; *The Autobiography of William Butler Yeats*, 1938; *Essays, 1931-1936*, 1937; *On the Boiler*, 1939; *If I Were Four and Twenty*, 1940; *The Letters of W. B. Yeats*, 1954; *The Senate Speeches of W. B. Yeats*, 1960 (Donald R. Pearce, editor); *Essays and Introductions*, 1961; *Explorations*, 1962; *Ah, Sweet Dancer: W. B. Yeats, Margot Ruddock—a Correspondence*, 1970 (Roger McHugh, editor); *Uncollected Prose by W. B. Yeats*, 1970, 1976 (2 volumes); *Memoirs*, 1972; *The Collected Letters of William Butler Yeats: Volume I, 1865-1895*, 1986.

MISCELLANEOUS: *The Collected Works in Verse and Prose of William Butler Yeats*, 1908.

Bibliography

Bloom, Harold. *Yeats.* New York: Oxford University Press, 1970. An influential work by a leading contemporary critic. The emphasis is on Yeats's Romanticism. The poet is seen as the English Romantic poetry's heir. The prosodic, aesthetic, and imaginative implications of the inheritance is the subject of much intense and sophisticated discussion.

Donoghue, Denis. *Yeats.* London: Fontana, 1971. The best brief survey of the subject. Yeats's life, works, and thoughts are clearly presented in their many complex interrelations. The study's unifying argument is the author's conception of Yeats's understanding of, and identification with, power. Contains a useful chronology and succinct bibliography.

Ellmann, Richard. *W. B. Yeats: The Man and the Masks.* New York: Macmillan, 1948. The first biography to avail of unrestricted access to Yeats's posthumous papers. The poet's doctrine of the mask is adopted as a biographical trope. Life and work are perceived as being mutually reinforcing. In many ways, the most satisfactory biographical treatment of Yeats.

Jeffares, A. N. *W. B. Yeats.* London: Hutchinson University Library, 1988. To some extent a redaction of the same author's *W. B. Yeats: Man and Poet* (1949). The earlier work made more extensive use of Yeats's papers than the Ellmann work cited above. Here the author adds more information from the same source. The overall effect, however, is one of narrative deftness.

_____. *A New Commentary on the Poems of W. B. Yeats.* London: Macmillan, 1984. This commentary was published in order to be in alignment with the 1983 edition of Yeats's poems. Otherwise the approach is the same as in the previous edition. The contents of Yeats's *The Collected Poems* are comprehensively annotated. Dates of composition are supplied, difficult allusions clarified, links to other works by Yeats made. An indispensable student's guide.

McCormack, W. J. *Ascendancy and Tradition in Anglo-Irish Literary History from 1789 to 1939.* Oxford, England: Clarendon Press, 1985. A study that lives up to the broad range of its title. Contains a crucial culminating section on Yeats, conceived of as poet and playwright, and more importantly, as ideologue. Essential for an appreciation of Yeats in his Irish context. An important example of the realignment of Yeats's achievement and significance.

Torchiana, Donald. *Yeats and Georgian Ireland.* Evanston, Ill.: Northwestern University Press, 1966. One of the major ways in which Yeats derived myth from history was through his reading of the works of major Irish writers of the eighteenth century. This study analyzes Yeats's knowledge of Jonathan Swift, Bishop George Berkeley, Oliver Goldsmith, and Edmund Burke. The influence of these thinkers on Yeats's poetry and prose is then assessed. An illuminating study of the impact of the Irish context particularly on the poet's later work.

Eileen A. Sullivan
(Revised by *George O'Brien*)

YEVGENY ZAMYATIN

Born: Lebedyan, Russia; February 1, 1884
Died: Paris, France; March 10, 1937

Principal short fiction
Povesti i rasskazy, 1963; *The Dragon: Fifteen Stories*, 1966.

Other literary forms
Yevgeny Zamyatin's most important piece of fiction was his novel *My* (1952; *We*, 1924), which was written in 1920-1921. A satirical examination of a future utopian state, the novel affirms the timeless value of individual liberty and free will in a world which places a premium on conformity and reason. This work exerted a significant influence on George Orwell's *Nineteen Eighty-Four* (1949). Zamyatin also wrote plays, adaptations, and film scenarios. His early dramatic works are historical plays—*Ogni svyatogo Dominika* (1922; *The Fires of Saint Dominic*, 1971) and *Attila* (1950; English translation, 1971)—while a later work, *Afrikanskiy gost* (1963; *The African Guest*, 1971), provides a comic look at philistine attempts to cope with Soviet reality. The author's most successful adaptation for the screen was a version of Maxim Gorky's *Na dne* (1902; *The Lower Depths*, 1912), which Zamyatin transformed into a screenplay for Jean Renoir's film *Les Bas-fonds* (1936; *The Lower Depths*, 1937).

Achievements
Although Zamyatin is best known in the West for his novel *We*, it has been his short fiction that has been most influential in the Soviet Union, since *We* was not published there until 1987. In his short fiction, Zamyatin developed an original prose style that is distinguished by its bold imagery and charged narrative pacing. This style, along with Zamyatin's writings and teachings about literature in the immediate postrevolutionary period, had a decisive impact on the first generation of Soviet writers, which include such figures as Lev Luntz, Nikolay Nikitin, Venyamin Kaverin, and Mikhail Zoshchenko. In addition, Zamyatin's unswerving defense of the principle of artistic and individual freedom remains a vivid element of his literary legacy.

Biography
Yevgeny Ivanovich Zamyatin was born on February 1, 1884, in Lebedyan, a small town in the Russian heartland. The writer would later point out with pride that the town was famous for its cardsharpers, Gypsies, and distinctive Russian speech, and he would utilize this spicy material in his mature fiction. His childhood, however, was a lonely one, and as the son of a village teacher, he spent more time with books than with other children.

After completing four years at the local school in 1896, Zamyatin went on to the *Gymnasium* in Voronezh, where he remained six years. Immediately after he was graduated, Zamyatin moved to St. Petersburg to study naval engineering at the Petersburg Polytechnic Institute. Over the next few years, Zamyatin became interested in politics and joined the Bolshevik Party. This political involvement led to his arrest late in 1905, when the student was picked up by the authorities who were trying to cope with the turbulent political agitation that swept the capital that year. Zamyatin spent several months in solitary confinement, and he used the time to write poetry and study English. Released in the spring of 1906, Zamyatin was exiled to Lebedyan. He soon returned to St. Petersburg, however, and lived there illegally until he was discovered and exiled again in 1911.

By this time he had been graduated from the Institute and had been appointed a lecturer there. He also had made his debut as a writer: in 1908, he published the story "Odin" ("Alone"), which chronicles the fate of an imprisoned revolutionary student who kills himself over frustrated love, and in 1910, he published "Devushka," another tale of tragic love. Although neither work is entirely successful, they both demonstrate Zamyatin's early interest in innovative narrative technique. A more polished work of his was *Uezdnoe* (1913; *A Provincial Tale*, 1966), which Zamyatin wrote during the months of renewed exile in 1911 and 1912. Zamyatin's penetrating treatment of ignorance and brutality in the Russian countryside was greeted with warm approval by the critics. On the other hand, his next major work, *Na kulichkakh* (1914; at the end of the world), provided such a sharp portrait of cruelty in the military that the publication in which the story appeared was confiscated by the authorities.

In 1916, Zamyatin departed Russia for Great Britain, where he was to work on seagoing icebreakers. His experience abroad provided the impetus for two satires on the British middle class—*Ostrovityane* (1918; *The Islanders*, 1972) and "Lovets chelovekov" ("The Fisher of Men"). Zamyatin returned to Russia after the abdication of Czar Nicholas in 1917 and embarked upon a busy course of literary endeavors. The period from 1917 to 1921 was a time of remarkable fecundity for the writer: he wrote fourteen stories, the novel *We*, a dozen fables, and a play. This body of work evinces an impressive diversity of artistic inspiration. Zamyatin's subjects range from the intense passions found in rural Russia ("Sever," "The North") to the dire conditions afflicting the urban centers during the postrevolutionary period ("Peshchera," or "The Cave"; "Mamay"; and "Drakon," or "Dragon") to ribald parodies of saints' lives ("O tom, kak istselen byl inok Erazm," or "How the Monk Erasmus Was Healed").

In addition to his own literary creation, Zamyatin dedicated himself to encouraging the literary careers of others. He regularly lectured on the craft of writing to young writers in the House of Arts in Petrograd, and he took part in numerous editorial and publishing activities. Among those whose works he helped to edit were Anton Chekhov and H. G. Wells. For many of these editions, he also wrote critical or biographical introductions, and such writers as Wells, Jack London, O. Henry, and George Bernard Shaw received Zamyatin's critical attention. As a result of this editorial work and his involvement in such literary organizations as the All-Russian Union of Writers, which he helped to found, Zamyatin's own productivity began to decline after 1921, particularly his prose.

At the same time, Zamyatin found himself in the awkward position of having to defend himself against those who perceived something dangerous or threatening in the ideas his work espoused. In his prose fiction and in numerous essays, Zamyatin consistently articulated a belief in the value of continual change, innovation, and renewal. Seizing upon the thermodynamic theory of entropy—the concept that all energy in the universe tends toward stasis or passivity—Zamyatin warned against the dangers of stagnation in intellectual and artistic spheres. Exhorting writers to be rebels and heretics, he argued that one should never be content with the status quo, for satisfaction with any victory can easily degenerate into stifling philistinism. By the same token, Zamyatin denounced conformist tendencies in literary creation and decried efforts to subordinate individual inspiration to predetermined ideological programs.

Given the fact that one of the ideological underpinnings of the new Soviet state was a belief in the primacy of the collective over the interests of the individual, Zamyatin's fervent defense of individual freedom could not help but draw the attention of the emerging establishment. The writer was arrested in 1922 along with 160 other intellectuals and became subject to an order for deportation. Yet without his knowledge, and perhaps against his will, a group of friends interceded for him and managed to have the order withdrawn. After Zamyatin's release in 1923, he applied for permission to emigrate, but his request was rebuffed.

During the latter half of the 1920's, the political climate in the Soviet Union became more restrictive, and Zamyatin was among a number of talented writers who were singled out for public denunciation and criticism. He found that the doors to publishing houses were now closed to him and that permission to stage his plays was impossible to obtain. Zamyatin did not buckle before the increasingly vituperative attacks directed toward him. Indeed, he had once written that "a stubborn, unyielding enemy is far more deserving of respect than a sudden convert to communism." Consequently, he did not succumb to pressure and make a public confession of his "errors," as some of his fellow writers were forced to do. On the contrary, he stood up to this campaign of abuse until 1931, when he sent Joseph Stalin an audacious request for permission to leave the Soviet Union with the right to return "as soon as it becomes possible in our country to serve great ideas in literature without cringing before little men."

With Gorky's help, Zamyatin's petition was granted, and he left the Soviet Union with his wife in November, 1931. Settling in Paris, he continued to work on a variety of literary projects, including translations, screenplays, and a novel entitled *Bich bozhy* (1939; the scourge of God). Because of his interest in film, he envisioned a trip to Hollywood, but these plans never materialized. He died on March 10, 1937.

Analysis

Perhaps the most distinctive feature of Yevgeny Zamyatin's short fiction is its charged, expressive narrative style. The writer characterized the style of his generation of writers in a lecture entitled "Contemporary Russian Literature," delivered in 1918. Calling the artistic method of his generation Neorealism, he outlined the differences between Neorealist fiction and that of the preceding Realist movement. He states:

> By the time the Neorealists appeared, life had become more complex, faster, more feverish. . . . In response to this way of life, the Neorealists have learned to write more compactly, briefly, tersely than the Realists. They have learned to say in ten lines what used to be said in a whole page.

During the first part of his career, Zamyatin consciously developed and honed his own unique form of Neorealist writing. Although his initial experimentation in this direction is evident in his early prose works (and especially in the long story *A Provincial Tale*), this tendency did not reach its expressive potential until the late 1910's, when it blossomed both in his satires on British life and in the stories devoted to Russian themes. The stories *The Islanders* and "The Fisher of Men" provide a mordant examination of the stifling philistinism permeating the British middle class. The former work in particular displays the tenor and thrust of Zamyatin's satiric style. The first character introduced into the tale is a minister named Vicar Dooley, who has written a *Testament of Contemporary Salvation*, in which he declares that "life must become a harmonious machine and with mechanical inevitability lead us to the desired goal." Such a vision raises the specter of death and stasis, not energy and life, and Zamyatin marshals his innovative narrative skills to expose the dangers that this vision poses for society.

One salient feature of Zamyatin's style is the identification of a character with a specific physical trait, animal, or object that seems to capture the essence of the character being depicted. Through this technique, the writer can both evoke the presence of the character by mentioning the associated image and underscore that character's fundamental personality type. What is more, once Zamyatin has established such an identification, he can suggest significant shifts in his characters' moods or situations by working changes on the associated images themselves. In *The Islanders*, this technique plays a vital role in the narrative exposition, and at times the associated images actually replace a given character in action. Thus, one character's lips are compared at the outset of the story to thin worms, and the women who attend Dooley's church are described as being pink and blue. Later, a tense interaction between the two is conveyed in striking terms: "Mrs. Campbell's worms twisted and sizzled on a slow fire. The blues and pinks feasted their eyes." Similarly, the central protagonist is compared to a tractor, and when his stolid reserve is shattered by feelings of love, Zamyatin writes that the tractor's "steering wheel was broken." Through this felicitous image Zamyatin not only evokes his hero's ponderous bulk but also suggests the unpredictable consequences which follow the release of suppressed emotion.

As striking as his satires on British conservatism are, however, it is in the stories that he wrote on Russian subjects that Zamyatin attained the apex of his vibrant expressionistic style. In his lecture on contemporary Russian literature, he spoke of his desire to find fresh subjects for literary treatment. Contrasting urban and rural settings, he declared: "The life of big cities is like the life of factories. It robs people of individuality, makes them the same, machinelike." In the countryside, Zamyatin concludes, "the Neorealists find not only genre, not only a way of life, but a way of life concentrated, condensed by centuries to a strong essence, ninety-proof."

As if to illustrate this premise, in 1918 he wrote the long tale entitled "The North." This story celebrates the primal forces of nature: In a swift succession of scenes, Zamyatin depicts a passionate yet short-lived affair between a true child of the forest—a young woman named Pelka—and a simple fisherman named Marey. Pelka is perhaps the closest embodiment of the ideally "natural" character in all of Zamyatin's works. She talks with the forest creatures, keeps a deer for a pet, and loves with a profound passion that cannot understand or tolerate the constraints imposed by civilized man. Sadly, her brief interlude of love with Marey is threatened by his foolish obsession with constructing a huge lantern "like those in Petersburg." Marey's desire to ape the fashions of the city destroys his romantic idyll with Pelka. After she vainly tries to stir Marey's emotions by having a short fling with a smug, callous shopkeeper named Kortoma, Pelka engineers a fatal encounter between herself, Marey, and a wild bear: the two lovers die at the hands of the natural world.

To illuminate this spectacle of extraordinary desire and suffering, Zamyatin utilizes all the tools of his Neorealist narrative manner. Striving to show rather than describe, Zamyatin avoids the use of such connectors as "it seemed" or "as if" in making comparisons; instead, the metaphorical image becomes the illustrated object or action itself. Especially noteworthy in "The North" is Zamyatin's use of charged color imagery. By associating particular characters with symbolic visual leitmotifs, the writer enhances his character portrayals. Thus, he underscores Pelka's naturalism by linking her to a combination of the colors red (as of flesh and blood) and green (as of the vegetation in the forest). Zamyatin compared his method to Impressionism: the juxtaposition of a few basic colors is intended to project the essence of a scene. At times, Zamyatin allows the symbolic associations of certain colors to replace narrative description entirely. Depicting the rising frenzy of a Midsummer Night's celebration, Zamyatin alludes to the surging flow of raw passion itself when he writes: "all that you could see was that . . . something red was happening."

Zamyatin's attention to visual detail in "The North" is matched by his concern with auditory effects. He thought that literary prose and poetry were one and the same; accordingly, the reader finds many examples of alliteration, assonance, and instrumentation in his work. He also gave careful consideration to the rhythmic pattern of his prose, revealing a debt to the Russian Symbolist writers who emphasized the crucial role of sound in prose. Seeking to communicate his perceptions as expressively and concisely as possible, he tried to emulate the fluidity and dynamism of oral speech. One notes many elliptical and unfinished sentences in Zamyatin's prose at this time, and his narratives resemble a series of sharp but fragmentary images or vignettes, which his readers must connect and fill in themselves. Zamyatin explained: "Today's reader and viewer will know how to complete the picture, fill in the words—and what he fills in will be etched far more vividly within him, will much more firmly become an organic part of him."

Zamyatin's other works on the deep recesses of the Russian countryside reflect his calculated attempt to evoke deep emotions and passionate lives in elliptical, allusive ways. The story "Rus'" ("In Old Russia"), for example, is narrated in a warm colloquial tone in which the neutral language of an impersonal narrator is replaced by language that relies heavily on the intonations and lexicon of spoken Russian. This technique, called *skaz* in Russian, was popularized by writers such as Nikolay Leskov and Alexey Remizov, and Zamyatin uses it to good effect in this tale. His narrator's account of the amorous activities of a young married woman named Darya is accented with notes of sly understanding and tolerance. As the narrator describes her, Darya cannot help but give in to the impulses of her flesh. At the very outset, she is compared to an apple tree filling up with sap; when spring arrives, she unconsciously feels the sap rising in her just as it is in the apple and lilac trees around her. Her "fall," then, is completely natural, and so, too, is the ensuing death of her husband only a few days later. Again, Zamyatin's narrator conveys the news of the husband's death and the gossip that attended it in tones of warm indulgence. In the deep backwaters of Russia, he indicates, life flows on; such events have no more lasting impact than a stone which is dropped into a pond and causes a few passing ripples.

While Zamyatin was drawn to rural Russian subjects, he did not ignore urban themes: two of his most striking works of 1920—"The Cave" and "Mamay"— exhibit his predilection for expressive imagery and his nuanced appreciation of human psychology. In "The Cave," Zamyatin depicts the Petrograd landscape in the winters following the Russian Revolution as a primordial, prehistoric wasteland. This image dominates the story, illustrating the writer's own admission that if he firmly believes in an image, "it will spread its roots through paragraphs and pages." Yet while the overarching image of Petrograd's citizens as cave dwellers creates a palpable atmosphere of grimness and despair in "The Cave," the images with which Zamyatin enlivens "Mamay" are more humorous. This story continues a long tradition in Russian literature of depicting the life of petty clerks in the city of St. Petersburg. The protagonist here is a meek individual who bears the incongruous name of Mamay, one of the Tatar conquerors of Russia. Mamay's wife is a stolid woman so domineering that every spoonful of soup eaten by Mamay is likened to an offering to an imperious Buddha. The sole pleasure in little Mamay's life is book collecting, and it is this mild passion that finally stirs the character into uncharacteristic action. He had been gathering and hiding a large sum of money with which to buy books, and at the end of the story he discovers with dismay that his stockpile has been destroyed by an enemy. Enraged, he is driven to murder. This contemporary

Mamay, however, is only a pale shadow of his famous namesake: the intruder proves to be a mouse, and Mamay kills it with a letter opener.

Zamyatin's pursuit of a charged, expressive narrative manner reached a peak in the early 1920's, and in at least one work, "Rasskaz o samom glavnom" ("A Story About the Most Important Thing"), the writer's ambition resulted in a work in which stylistic and structural manipulation overwhelm semantic content. Zamyatin creates a complex narrative structure in which he shifts back and forth among three plot lines involving the life of an insect, revolutionaries in Russia, and beings on a star about to collide with the Earth. The tale forcefully conveys the writer's sense of the power of the urge to live and procreate in the face of imminent death, but in certain passages, his penchant for hyperbole and intensity of feeling detracts from the effectiveness of the work as a whole.

Later in the decade, however, Zamyatin began to simplify his narrative techniques; the result can be seen in the moving story "Navodnenie" ("The Flood"), perhaps the finest short story of this late period. Written in 1928, "The Flood" reveals how Zamyatin managed to tone down some of his more exaggerated descriptive devices, while retaining the power and intensity of his central artistic vision. One finds few of his characteristic recurring metaphors in the story, but the few that are present carry considerable import. The work's central image is that of flooding, both as a literal phenomenon (the repeated flooding of the Neva River) and as a metaphorical element (the ebb and flow of emotions in the protagonist's soul). The plot of the story concerns a childless woman's resentment toward an orphaned girl named Ganka, who lives in her house and has an affair with her husband. Sofya's rising malice toward Ganka culminates on a day when the river floods. As the river rises and a cannon booms its flood warning, Sofya feels her anger surging too: it "whipped across her heart, flooded all of her." Striking Ganka with an ax, she then feels a corresponding outflow, a release of tension. Similar images of flooding and flowing accompany Sofya's childbirth, the feeding of her child, and the rising sensation of guilt in her heart. In the final scene of the story, the river again begins to flood, and now Sofya feels an irrepressible urge to give birth to her confession. As she begins to reveal her murderous secret, "Huge waves swept out of her and washed over . . . everyone." After she concludes her tale, "everything was good, blissful . . . all of her had poured out."

The recurring water images link all the major events in "The Flood," and Zamyatin achieves further cohesiveness through additional associations such as birth and death, conception and destruction. The tight austerity of his later fiction endows that body of work with understated force. The writer himself commented on the conscious effort he made to achieve this kind of effective simplicity: "All the complexities I had passed through had been only a road to simplicity. . . . Simplicity of form is legitimate for our epoch, but the right to simplicity must be earned."

The oeuvre that Zamyatin left behind provides an eloquent testament both to the man's skill as a literary craftsman and to the integrity and power of his respect for human potential. His innovations in narrative exposition exerted a palpable influence on his contemporaries, and his defense of individual liberty in the face of relentless repression holds timeless appeal for his readers.

Other major works

NOVELS: _Uezdnoe_, 1913 (novella; _A Provincial Tale_, 1966); _Na kulichkakh_, 1914 (novella; _A Godforsaken Hole_, 1988); _Ostrovityane_, 1918 (novella; _The Islanders_, 1972); _Bich bozhy_, 1939; _My_, 1952 (_We_, 1924).

PLAYS: _Ogni svyatogo Dominika_, 1922 (_The Fires of Saint Dominic_, 1971); _Attila_, 1950 (English translation, 1971); _Afrikanskiy gost_, 1963 (_The African Guest_, 1971); _Five Plays_, 1971.

SCREENPLAY: _Les Bas-fonds_, 1936 (_The Lower Depths_, 1937; adaptation of Maxim Gorky's novel _Na dne_).

NONFICTION: _Litsa_, 1955 (_A Soviet Heretic_, 1970).

MISCELLANEOUS: _Sobranie sochinenii_, 1929; _Sochineniia_, 1970-1972.

Bibliography

Brown, Edward J. "Zamjatin and English Literature." In _American Contributions to the Fifth International Congress of Slavists_. Vol. 2. The Hague: Mouton, 1965. Within general comments on Zamyatin, Brown discusses his interest in, and debt to, English literature stemming from his two-year stay in England before and during World War I.

Collins, Christopher. _Evgenij Zamjatin: An Interpretive Study_. The Hague: Mouton, 1973. In this ambitious study, Collins advances a rather complex interpretation of Zamyatin, mostly of _We_, on the basis of Carl Gustav Jung's idea of the conscious, unconscious, and individualism.

Kern, Gary, ed. _Zamyatin's "We": A Collection of Critical Essays_. Ann Arbor, Mich.: Ardis, 1988. A collection of essays on Zamyatin's magnum opus, _We_, covering the Soviet view, mythic criticism, esthetics, and influences and comparisons. It includes one of the best essays on the subject, Edward J. Brown's "_Brave New World, 1984_, and _We_: An Essay on Anti-Utopia."

Mihailovich, Vasa D. "Critics on Evgeny Zamyatin." _Papers on Language and Literature_ 10 (1974): 317-334. A useful survey of all facets of criticism of Zamyatin's opus, in all languages, through 1973. Good for gaining the introductory knowledge of Zamyatin.

Richard, D. J. _Zamyatin: A Soviet Heretic_. London: Hillary House, 1962. A brief overview of the main stages and issues in Zamyatin's life and works, paying some attention to his short fiction. An excellent, though truncated, presentation of a very complex writer.

Shane, Alex M. _The Life and Works of Evgenij Zamjatin_. Berkeley: University of California Press, 1968. The most comprehensive work on Zamyatin in English, covering, exhaustively but pertinently, his life and the most important features of his works, including short fiction. Using secondary sources extensively, Shane analyzes chronologically Zamyatin's works, in a scholarly but not dry fashion and reaches his own conclusions. Supplemented by an extensive bibliography of works by and about Zamyatin.

Julian W. Connolly
(Revised by *Vasa D. Mihailovich*)

ZHANG JIE

Born: Beijing, China; April 27, 1937

Principal short fiction

Ai, shi buneng wangj de, 1980 (*Love Must Not Be Forgotten,* 1986); *Zhang Jie's Collection of Short Stories and Movie Scripts,* 1980; *On a Green Lawn,* 1983; *Fang-zhou,* 1983; *Emerald,* 1985; *Zhang Jie chi,* 1986 (*Zhang Jie's Literature,* 1986); *As Long as Nothing Happens, Nothing Will,* 1988; *A Chinese Woman in Europe,* 1989; *You Are a Friend of My Soul,* 1990.

Other literary forms

Besides her short stories, Zhang Jie has written novels, poetry, screenplays, and literary criticism. She has also published her experience abroad in a book entitled *On a Green Lawn.* Although no major collections of her poetry and critical essays have been published, her novels *Chen zhong de chi bang* (1981; *Heavy Wings,* 1989) and *Only One Sun* (1988) are quite successful.

Achievements

Although Zhang started writing fiction in her early forties, she has become one of the best-known Chinese women writers in the world today. Her first novel *Heavy Wings* won the Maodun National Award for novels in 1985 (an award granted once every three years), and it has been translated and published in a dozen countries: Germany, France, Sweden, Finland, Norway, Denmark, Holland, Great Britain, the United States, Spain, Brazil, and the Soviet Union. Her second novel, *Only One Sun,* was translated and published in Holland in 1988. Zhang, however, is better known as a short-story writer. In 1978, she began publishing numerous stories and subsequently won various prizes. Two collections of her stories, *Love Must Not Be Forgotten* and *As Long as Nothing Happens, Nothing Will,* are widely studied in European and American college classrooms. *As Long as Nothing Happens, Nothing Will* won the Malaparte Literary Prize (Italy), a prize that has been won by famous writers such as Anthony Burgess and Saul Bellow.

Zhang's work has received considerable critical attention both in China and abroad. A feminist writer, she has forged a distinctive style that blends well her utopian idealism with social reality in her exploration of women's problems concerning love, marriage, and career. A social critic, she exposes China's hidden corruption and stubborn bureaucracy and vehemently champions the causes of democracy and reform through her literary forms. For her integrated concern for women and society, Zhang can be compared with Western writers such as Doris Lessing, Marge Piercy, and Ursula K. Le Guin. Her sentimental idealism and militant tone, however, have sometimes irritated critics and readers.

In her biographical note, "My Boat," Zhang made a modest statement: "A life still unfinished, ideals demanding to be realized. Beautiful, despondent, joyful, tragic. . . . All manner of social phenomena weave themselves into one story after another in my mind. . . . Like an artless tailor, I cut my cloth unskillfully according to old measurements and turn out garment factory clothes sold in department stores in only five standard sizes and styles." Although her statement applies to most of her stories, a few, with skillful innovations, cannot be judged by any "old measurements."

Biography

Zhang Jie was born in Beijing, China, on April 27, 1937. During the War of Resistance against Japan, her father left, and her mother, a teacher, brought her up in a village in the province of Liaoning. From childhood, she showed a strong interest in music and literature, but she was encouraged to study economics in order to be of greater use to new China. After she was graduated from the People's University of Beijing in 1960, she was assigned to one of the industrial ministries. Her novel *Heavy Wings* and the short story "Today's Agenda" definitely benefit from her acquaintance with industrial management and bureaucracy. Later, Zhang transferred to the Beijing Film Studio, where she wrote the film scripts *The Search* and *We Are Still Young.* She started to write fiction at the age of forty, which coincided with the end of the Cultural Revolution. In 1978, her story "The Music of the Forest" won a prize as one of the best short stories of the year. In 1979, she won the Chinese national short-story award again for "Who Lives a Better Life." Meanwhile, her story "Love Must Not Be Forgotten" became widely read and controversial. With the success of her stories, Zhang became a full-time fiction writer. In 1985, she reached the climax of her literary career by winning the Maodun National Award for *Heavy Wings* and the National Novella Award for *Emerald.* Zhang, who actively participates in international creative activities, has traveled to West Germany and the United States and was a visiting professor at Wesleyan University from 1989 to 1990. She has been a council member of the Chinese Writers' Association and the vice chair of the Beijing Association of Writers.

Zhang is known as a determined woman and a political activist. She took part in many political movements and joined the Chinese Communist Party at an early age. Although she mercilessly dissects the cause of China's backwardness and attributes it to feudal ideology as well as to the corruption of the Communist Party, she firmly defends the socialist system as that best suited to China. In spite of her support for socialism and genuine Marxism, however, she is often criticized inside China for her liberal tendencies. She proudly admits that she loves to read Western novels, particularly those of the eighteenth and nineteenth centuries. Like Dai Houying, Wang Anyi, and other contemporary Chinese writers, she believes that the humanism in classical Western literature is something that Chinese people should learn and promote. She was influenced by Western Romanticism as well as social critical realism. She stresses love and sacrifice, conscience and responsibility in all of her writings.

Zhang Jie is a pioneering feminist writer. She has one daughter and was divorced twice because she could not tolerate men who attempted to dominate women. From her bitter experience of social discrimination against women, especially those who are divorced or unmarried, Zhang attacks male supremacy and patriarchal ideology in Chinese social structure as well as in the consciousness or subconsciousness of every man, villain or hero. She staunchly insists on a woman's right to remain single and not to be discriminated against. Like early feminist writers in the West, however, she denies a woman's sexuality in order to achieve female autonomy.

Zhang Jie is fully aware that fiction writing in China is never separated from political reality. Partly because of her age and frail health and partly because of political risk, she envisages herself as an old, tattered boat sailing in the raging sea:

> . . . I renovate my boat, patch it up and repaint it, so that it will last a little longer: I set sail again. People, houses, trees on shore become smaller and smaller and I am reluctant to leave them. But my boat cannot stay beached for ever. What use is a boat without the sea?
> In the distance I see waves rolling toward me. Rolling continuously. I know that one day I will be smashed to bits by those waves, but this is the fate of all boats—what other sort of end could they meet?

Analysis

Zhang Jie writes on a variety of themes and subjects, ranging from the national political and economic reform to an individual's daily problem (such as Professor Meng's obsession with finding a bathroom abroad), from an unmarried girl's idealistic pursuit to a divorced woman's alienation and hard struggle, and from doctors' housing problems to intellectuals' vicissitudes. Her short fiction, written in a vigorous, fresh, romantic style, can be divided into three groups: feminist stories, social stories, and fabulous animal stories.

"Ai, shi buneng wangj de" ("Love Must Not Be Forgotten") and the novellas *Emerald* and *Fangzhou* (*The Ark*) represent the best in the first group. "Love Must Not Be Forgotten" portrays a thirty-year-old woman who wonders whether she should accept a marriage proposal. Like Ding Ling's Sofia, in her "The Diary of Miss Sophia," the protagonist finds her tall, handsome suitor to be a philistine who lacks spiritual substance and intelligence. Encouraged by the example of her mother, a widow who has lived all of her life in platonic love with an ideal man who has married another woman out of moral responsibility, she decides to remain single rather than waste her life in a loveless marriage. Although Zhang emphasizes love above all else in the story, she has said that "it is not a love story, but one that investigates a sociological problem." In the light of Chinese society by the end of the 1970's, the story obviously protests discrimination against "odd women"—that is, either women from the countryside who return there "educated" or professional women who fail to find men whom they can admire. To Zhang, love is actually the spiritual and creative pursuit of the self. By insisting on love, she strongly rejects the increasing commercialism and demoralization of Chinese society. As a feminist story, "Love Must Not Be Forgotten" explores the female tradition through the mother-daughter relationship and advocates female autonomy by setting women free from marriage-bound traditional life. Zhang is brave enough to declare in the story that "a solitary existence" may manifest a "progress in different aspects of social life such as culture, education and taste."

Emerald further creates the image of a strong single woman. The story involves two women's sacrifices for one incompetent man named Zuowei. When Linger is in college, she falls in love with Zuowei. She nurses him when he suffers tuberculosis, helps him catch up in his studies, rescues him from a whirlpool, and serves as his scapegoat in his political crisis. When Linger is labeled a rightist and is sent to reform in a remote area, however, Zuowei abandons her and marries Beihe. Linger has an illegitimate son by Zuowei, and, in spite of humiliation and ostracism, she bravely brings him up in the role of father-mother. Although Beihe has a so-called happy marriage, her husband weighs upon her like a burden. The story begins with Beihe's scheming to make use of Linger, a brilliant mathematician, to support her husband as a newly promoted head of a computer research group; it ends with Linger's acceptance to join the group, not as a sacrificial act for any man, but for the need of society as well as for her own self-fulfillment. As a result of being abandoned twenty-five years earlier, Linger remains active and intellectually keen, whereas Beihe is dragged down by a dull married life. In spite of Beihe's realization of the slave/master relationship between man and woman, husband and wife, there seems no escape for her. Through the characterization of Linger, Zhang further stresses the correlation between female self-fulfillment and liberation from marital bondage.

The Ark exposes prejudices against women at all levels of leadership, especially man-created obstacles such as political discrimination against, and sexual harassment of, single women. The story portrays a community of spinsters and divorcées who struggle desperately for equality with men in work, human respect, and professional advancement. Not even one man appears to be free from patriarchal influence. The only hope is pinned on a little boy who lives in the community of women and shares their feelings and language.

Although Zhang wrote these three stories separately, they become particularly significant when viewed together. Through her use of an eccentric, idealistic mother who passes the message of life to her daughter, Zhang shows how an individual woman can achieve autonomy by flouting social codes. By using two boats (a sumptuous, white, pleasure boat and an old wooden tub) to embody women running on opposite life tracks, Zhang breaks through the traditional jealous relationship between two women in love with one man to achieve a mutual understanding and a new female consciousness. By employing the image of the ark to represent the women's community, she demonstrates how female collective power, drawn from women's shared suffering, is needed to confront the combined patriarchal forces and transform the existing society.

"What's Wrong with Him?," "The Other World," and "Today's Agenda" are Zhang stories on social subjects. The title of the first story should have been "What's Wrong with Her?," "What's Wrong with Them?," "What's Wrong with Me?," and ultimately "What's Wrong with the Society?" Unlike her earlier stories, Zhang here discards the conventions of narrative strategies. The story contains no unifying plot, chronological order, or psychological details. What links all characters and phenomena together are the theme of madness and the space of a mental hospital. The pervasiveness of madness reminds the reader of Lu Hsün's "K'uang-jên jih-chi" ("The Diary of a Madman"). Unlike Lu Xun's madness, however, which is Kafkaesque paranoia caused by fear of persecution, Zhang's madness is schizophrenia, developed from repression of perversion or violence. Repressing his rage at the authority's corruption, Grandpa Ding turns to burning a tract of cotton that he has grown and becomes a Peeping Tom. Driven by insomnia and political discrimination, Doctor Hou Yufeng engages himself in a bloody fight with his roommate, a young carpenter, and finds his freedom only in becoming a madman. In order to get a decent room for receiving his foreign friends, a doctor in an eight-square-meter cell dreams day and night of a larger room. Finally, he finds three big rooms in his spitting imagination and goes to the leadership to offer his two imaginary rooms for those in extreme want of housing.

This world of madness is patriarchal. Though women are not Zhang's sole concern, the exposure of sexual discrimination pervades the story. She perceives that men want to marry not women but vaginal membranes and that men call any woman of independent thought "neurotic." A sexually objectified woman is passed like a ball from an ex-convict to a thief, to a rogue, then to a nameless ugly man. The specter of the victim leads her mad daughter to rape the father.

To heighten the madness, Zhang adopts violent verbal expressions, weird imagination, and stylistic fragmentation. For all these features, her self-image of a "witch" is recognized by Chinese critics. Xu Wenyu actually pictures her as a witch spitting incantations and says that "there must be something wrong with **her.**" The author is indeed mad; her madness lies in her unscrupulous power to snap off the evil of socialist China and penetrate into its dark consciousness.

"The Other World" is a humorous satire reminiscent of Mark Twain's *The Prince and the Pauper* (1881), only more savage and absurd. The protagonist, Rong Changlan, is an unknown painter. When his talent is discovered by a foreigner and he is invited to go abroad, he is showered with overwhelming attention from politicians, writers, painters, reporters, and women. Because of Yi Yang, a conventional painter, Rong's authorization to go abroad is revoked, and he suddenly becomes a nobody again. Upon returning to the county, he finds countless lice and their eggs in the seams and throughout the fibers of his clothes, which obviously stand for corruption, nepotism, and hypocrisy at large in Chinese society.

When reading "The Other World," one is completely unaware of its narrator. In the absence of a narrator, irony functions as the most effective weapon. Yi Yang appears as the most ardent supporter of young artists such as Rong Changlan. Knowing that Rong cannot drink, Yi Yang offers him one drink after another until Rong gets drunk, barking at the dinner table like a dog. Consequently, Mrs. Hassen revokes her invitation to Rong because of his deceptive (Rong had told her that he does not drink) and barbarous behavior. Comrade Ke, the Party authority of the International Cultural Exchange who first insisted on accompanying Rong abroad, now imposes on Mrs. Hassen a delegation of three—Ke, Ke's son, and Yi Yang.

Another melodramatic device in the story is Zhang's use of comic-strip characters. Through this device, Zhang lashes out most fiercely at conventional women. Unlike her other stories, "The Other World" contains not even one positive image of women throughout the whole farce. Women writers and reporters, in order to go abroad by marrying Rong, fight bloodily. More absurd, a woman who calls herself Yu Ping comes to the hotel to force Rong to admit that he is the father of her illegitimate child. When the woman is challenged, she suffers an epileptic seizure.

The title of the story "The Other World" is particularly significant. The city, full of corruption and absurdity, is the other world to Rong Changlan. He is fooled by this world and finds his freedom again upon his abandonment by the city. In Zhang's view, Rong Changlan is an artist with a soul. His painting *A Ruined Pagoda* reminds the reader of T. S. Eliot's vision of the wasteland. Europe, which could have been the other world of artistic inspiration for artists such as Rong Changlan, is abused as the other world that only spurs Chinese selfishness and political corruption. To some extent, the story is also a caricature of the demoralized China, following its open-door policy.

"Today's Agenda" is a satirical story against bureaucracy. Jia Yunshan, the bureau chief, cannot have breakfast because of the irresponsibility of the Water Bureau. When he drops dead at his routine meeting, readers learn that the day's agenda concerned the building of a new block of flats for high-ranking intellectuals and the tracing of a robbery case that took place during the Cultural Revolution. After tedious trivial arguments over Jia's funeral expense and fighting for the position left by the dead man, the new cabinet continues to dwell on the old questions. The old agenda of the bureau remains forever today's agenda. In this story, Zhang uses a repetitive narrative structure to echo its thematic monotony and tediousness. Although it is a good story, probing problems in the process of China's industrial reform, for a more artistic and insightful treatment of the subject one must read her novel *Heavy Wings.*

Among Zhang Jie's fabulous tales, "Nobby's Run of Luck" and "Something Else" are the most significant. The former portrays the life of Nobby, a prodigious circus dog. Nobby not only can do arithmetic, algebra, geometry, and trigonometry but also has all the noble qualities: he remains a bachelor in order to devote all of his energy to the circus show, he is never arrogant and domineering, and he shares any extra food with his colleagues. Yet when Nobby loses his mathematical brilliance as a result of constant political slandering, he is kicked around. He suffers from insomnia and eventually finds consolation in the majestic scene of the sea and the waves. The story ends with Nobby swimming into the ocean, in spite of the calling of love from Feiffer, a female dog. The reader is left to ponder whether Nobby drowns himself or commits a symbolic action to submerge into the world of nature and imagination.

"Something Else" is the story of a cat and his master, a bully. The cat is fed the heads and tails of fish eaten by the master and is beaten and kicked at the master's will. Even so, the cat thinks that he should stay with the master and be content, because the neighbor is rumored to eat cats and because the grass is not always greener on the other side.

These two well-written fables are also political satires. Nobby's luck can be everybody's fate, particularly that of an intellectual in China, while the cat's philosophy reveals an enslaved psychology and a conservatism that hold back the nation from rebelling against its tyranny and catching up with the Western world.

Other major works

NOVELS: *Chen zhong de chi bang*, 1981 (*Heavy Wings*, 1989); *Only One Sun*, 1988. NONFICTION: *Fang mei sanji*, 1982; *Zongshi nanwang*, 1990.

Bibliography

Bailey, Alison. "Travelling Together: Narrative Technique in Zhang Jie's *The Ark.*" In *Modern Chinese Women Writers: Critical Appraisals*, edited by Michael S. Duke. Armonk, N.Y.: M. E. Sharpe, 1989. Bailey analyzes Zhang Jie's narrative technique according to Western theories and compares her "narrated monologue" with European writers of the nineteenth century. Bailey believes that Zhang's effacement of the narrator ensures the reader's identification with, and sympathy for, the three unconventional single women in the story.

Dillard, Annie. *Encounters with Chinese Writers.* Middletown, Conn.: Wesleyan University Press, 1984. Dillard, in her chapter on Zhang Jie, vividly presents her, to Chinese and Americans, as a woman and a writer, through different images of the author. Dillard believes that Zhang always retains her trim bearing, while in China she is considered a nonconformist in dressing; Dillard also observes Zhang's conservative reactions to political issues as well as to sexual allusions, while in China she is actually a most controversial, outspoken writer both in the matter of love and the question of political reform. The gap between the two images of Zhang points to the cultural and political distance between the United States and China.

Hsu, Vivian Ling. "Contemporary Chinese Women's Lives as Reflected in Recent Literature." *Journal of the Chinese Teachers' Association* 23, no. 3 (1988): 1-47. Hsu analyzes several of Zhang Jie's stories about women. She particularly notes the two women's realization of their enslaved status in relation to the man whom they love in *Emerald.*

Louie, Kam. *Between Fact and Fiction.* Sydney, Australia: Wild Peony, 1989. In chapter 5, "Love Stories: The Meaning of Love and Marriage in China, 1978-1981," Louie treats Zhang's story "Love Must Not Be Forgotten" as a social commentary against the background of China's present problems concerning love and marriage. He points out that the story aims at China's problem of "old maids" and that Zhang's shouting at the end of the story is truly significant because her heroine remains single, "in defiance of aspersions inevitably cast upon her desirability." Louie also discusses love stories by other Chinese writers published in the early 1980's. Includes an excellent bibliography.

Zhang, Jie. "My Boat." *Chinese Literature* Summer, 1985, 51-54. Zhang Jie provides autobiographical information as well as her views on literature in relation to life, society, and the self. She believes that it is quite tragic for Chinese writers that the Chinese cannot separate fiction from real politics, thus persecuting writers endlessly.

Qingyun Wu

ÉMILE ZOLA

Born: Paris, France; April 2, 1840
Died: Paris, France; September 29, 1902

Principal short fiction

Contes à Ninon, 1864 (*Stories for Ninon,* 1895); *Esquisses parisiennes,* 1866; *Nouveaux Contes à Ninon,* 1874; *Les Soirées de Médan,* 1880 (a contributor); *Le Capitaine Burle,* 1882 (*A Soldier's Honor and Other Stories,* 1888); *Naïs Micoulin,* 1884; *Contes et nouvelles,* 1928; *Madame Sourdis,* 1929.

Other literary forms

Émile Zola is principally remembered as a novelist and also as the flamboyant journalist who took up the defense of Captain Alfred Dreyfus during the celebrated trial of the young Jewish officer which transfixed French society at the end of the nineteenth century. In addition to novels and journalistic essays, he is the author of numerous plays, essays, literary and artistic criticism, and an early youthful attempt at poetry.

Achievements

Zola will always be associated with the school of naturalism in France. He became the most widely read author at the beginning of the twentieth century, in part because of the sensationalism of his subjects, in part because of his early training as a public relations clerk. Because of his immense success, his aesthetic ideas were widely circulated, and a group of disciples was formed at Zola's country home outside Paris at Médan. Inspired by the medical advances made possible by scrupulous observation combined with precise analytical techniques, Zola proposed literature as a means of experimenting on humans. He specifically was interested in determining what happens when their environment is changed or their heredity tampered with; what would be the result of humans' gradual addiction to certain chemical compounds? When the literary subject matter was the lower class, envisioned is the unhealthy and the immoral side by side. One of his best known novels, *L'Assommoir* (1877; English translation, 1879), attempts to examine the effects of alcohol on the working class. Other works examine prostitution, political power, industrial power (the locomotive), and capitalism.

Biography

The son of an Italian engineer, Émile Zola grew up in Aix-en-Provence with a friend who was to become equally famous in the world of art, Paul Cézanne. Both came from modest families, and Zola learned early to resent the ordered and comfortable life of the bourgeoisie around him. The early death of his father prompted the family move to Paris, where his mother could find work, and where Zola attended the *lycée.* Failing to pass his *baccalauréat,* Zola gave up his studies and took a position in the civil service, then another with the distinguished Hachette publishing house, where he rose through the ranks to become head of public relations. During this time he made various attempts to write poetry and to penetrate the world of journalism, and he succeeded in establishing himself as an author with his collection of short stories *Contes à Ninon*. The following year, his novel *La Confession de Claude* (1865; *Claude's Confession*, 1882), attracted so much attention because of its sordid details that it aroused police interest. The unhappy management of Hachette ordered Zola to choose between publishing and writing, and the young author, already in the public eye, set out to earn his livelihood by his pen.

With his flair for publicity Zola was able to exploit both his public and his art with great success. Even his ideas of naturalism were tempered by what he realized the public wanted to hear. Inspired by Honoré de Balzac, he determined to develop a *comédie humaine* on his own terms; and this time he determined not only to make the cycle of novels a coherent whole but also to ensure that the cycle would be complete and accurate in every detail, with no contradictions. His early exposure to his father's scientific career prepared him for a lifelong fascination with science and its theoreticians, and his humble origins made him especially sympathetic to the lofty position accorded the *savant*. As a result, the organizing principle for his series of novels became the aesthetic of naturalism, which he carefully defined in a series of essays inspired by scientific and particularly medical treatises. Adopting the realists' idea of a "slice of life," Zola sketched out a family tree, and then proceeded to write a novel about the major members of that family, whose name would form the title of the twenty-volume series: *Les Rougon-Macquart* (1871-1893; *The Rougon-Macquart Novels*, 1885-1907). The first volume, *La Fortune des Rougon* (1871; *The Fortune of the Rougons*, 1886), was a good novel, but it did not spark popular imagination. Five other volumes appeared in the next five years, but it was the appearance of *L'Assommoir*, an epic about alcohol's effect on the worker, that notoriety— and hence financial success—came to Zola. From that point on he became the most talked-about and widely read author in France. It was not that he could do no wrong: ten years later, the appearance of *La Terre* (1887; *Earth*, 1954) so outraged the critics that Zola's then-disciples publicly repudiated him, declaring that his penchant for the sordid and the gruesome had betrayed the aesthetic of naturalism. The newspapers, however, eagerly printed the work, and the public eagerly bought it.

Zola attempted to soften this criticism of his work by writing novels and stories that erred in the other extreme: they were highly idealistic. Not only were some of *The Rougon-Macquart Novels* written in this more positive vein, but also, at the conclusion of the series, Zola embarked on two new series of novels, the romance *Les Trois Villes* (1894-1898; *The Three Cities*, 1894-1898) and what he called *Les Quatre Évangiles* (1899-1903; English translation, 1900-1903), the gospels of population, work, truth, and justice (which at his death was incomplete and published posthumously). This idealistic bent heightened Zola's outrage when he became increasingly convinced that the Dreyfus affair was, in fact, a vast conspiracy by the established government and military to denigrate a talented young Jewish officer.

With his usual lack of tact, Zola published his findings on the front page of the newspaper *L'Aurore* in a public letter whose first words were "J'accuse." Promptly prosecuted for libel, Zola fled to England and worked there until he learned that public opinion favored his position and that a retrial was imminent. His vindication helped to establish Zola as the leading author of France at the beginning of the twentieth century; nevertheless, his reputation as a pornographer in fact prevented him from achieving his cherished goal: election to the Académie Française. He died of asphyxiation from a defective fireplace flue (some seriously consider that there may have been an assassination plot involved), on September 29, 1902, and was accorded a hero's public funeral, at which Captain Dreyfus was present.

Analysis

Émile Zola's talent as a short-story writer is evident from the first sentence of "La Mort d'Olivier Bécaille" ("The Death of Olivier Bécaille"), included in the volume *Naïs Micoulin* of 1884. In this work the reader's curiosity is immediately piqued over the question of how a first-person narrator can deal with his own death. At first, the reader feels that Zola is perhaps presenting us with an example of a fleeting moment of consciousness after the physical body has died, as though he were presenting a distinction between body and soul, which, for a naturalist, would be an intriguing concept. As the narrative unfolds, however, the reader understands that Zola is instead exploring one of the most traditional of literary themes: the return from the dead. At age thirty-nine Zola is developing a theme that Guy de Maupassant would exploit in his story "En Famille" ("A Family Affair"). In contrast to Maupassant's objective narrative used for comic effect, Zola's first-person narrative not only captures interest but also develops it to a different effect: the reader understands, comes to sympathize with the narrator, and shares with him his experience of death.

At the moment of death which begins the story, the narrator thinks back over his life and over the lifelong obsession that death has held for him. The story gives a rapid flashback of his youth, marriage, and move to Paris, then returns to the present moment in a seedy hotel, where the narrator is taken ill and dies. The reader shares the narrator's outburst of affection for his young wife and the aroused interest of the neighbors and especially their children. As he did so successfully in *L'Assommoir*, Zola excels in capturing the atmosphere of the crowd. His pictures of unhealthy children are particularly moving; as aware as adults, their observations are all the more startling because they are true. Thus, when the first child cries out, "Il est mort, oh! maman, il est mort," her unsophisticated breach of social etiquette adds a moment of poignancy and accentuates the verisimilitude of the plot.

At first the reader wonders if the narrator is not simply dreaming, and Zola has the narrator ask himself the same question to heighten the tension. When a neighbor refers to the imminent arrival of the coroner, however, the question is answered. The cursory examination revolts the narrator, for he is conscious of being alive, in spite of the coroner's judgment; yet, like the condemned poets in Dante's *Inferno* (c. 1320), there is no outlet by which these frustrations can be expressed. Agonizing at his inability to summon help or attention, the narrator witnesses his own body being prepared for the funeral, observes the mourning of his wife, sees himself being enclosed in his own coffin, and hears the lid being nailed down. He experiences the funeral ceremony, the horror of being buried alive, and the climactic silence of an abandoned cemetery.

In spite of a perhaps unnecessary touch of scientific determinism, the story accelerates to its dramatic conclusion. Through superhuman effort the narrator manages to pry open his coffin, claw his way out of the ground, and stumble about on the street at night, before being overcome by exhaustion and emotion and injuring his head as he falls unconscious. When he regains his senses weeks later, he quickly realizes what has happened, that he has still not been able to make contact with his young wife in order to let her know that he is in fact alive. He escapes from his benefactors to rejoin his wife, only to find that she already has settled into a new life with a new man. Zola presents this absorbing tale with the control and economy required of an effective short story. The ordinary details of one's mundane existence take on a new proportion when viewed from beyond the tomb, and Zola does not hesitate to use imagery and symbolism to enhance the primitive and religious qualities of his story.

Perhaps the best known of Zola's short stories is "L'Attaque du Moulin" ("The Attack on the Mill"). It is the lead story in the collection *Les Soirées de Médan*, and along with Maupassant's "Boule de Suif," is largely responsible for the success of the collection that satirizes the Franco-Prussian War of 1870. Zola's contribution is a powerful account of humans' inhumanity to other humans, as war interrupts a pastoral romance and prompts its protagonists to actions of heroism and patriotism, only to leave them bloodied, nature devastated, and the windmill—a symbol rich in associations—laid waste. Humans' hubris ravishes both nature and humanity in this pacifist tale in which Zola demonstrates his characteristic poetic quality, which he retained despite his obsession with science. Like the Parnassian poets, his inability to follow rigorously his own aesthetic saved Zola and made possible his greatest writing. A visionary Romantic in the tradition of Victor Hugo, Zola's ability to evoke vast tableaux, both of human beings and of nature, along with his lyrical vision of people lend epic proportions to his work.

Other major works

NOVELS: *La Confession de Claude*, 1865 (*Claude's Confession*, 1882); *Le Vœu d'une morte*, 1866 (*A Dead Woman's Wish*, 1902); *Les Mystères de Marseille*, 1867 (*The Flower Girls of Marseilles*, 1888; also as *The Mysteries of Marseilles*, 1895); *Thérèse Raquin*, 1867 (English translation, 1881); *Madeleine Férat*, 1868 (English translation, 1880); *Les Rougon-Macquart*, 1871-1893 (*The Rougon-Macquart Novels*, 1885-1907; includes *La Fortune des Rougon*, 1871 [*The Rougon-Macquart Family*, 1879; also as *The Fortune of the Rougons*, 1886]; *La Curée*, 1872 [*The Rush for the Spoil*, 1886; also as *The Kill*, 1895]; *Le Ventre de Paris*, 1873 [*The Markets of Paris*, 1879; also as *Savage Paris*, 1955]; *La Conquête de Plassans*, 1874 [*The Conquest of Plassans*,

1887; also as *A Priest in the House*, 1957]; *La Faute de l'abbé Mouret*, 1875 [*Albine: Or, The Abbé's Temptation*, 1882; also as *Abbé Mouret's Transgression*, 1886]; *Son Excellence Eugène Rougon*, 1876 [*Clorinda: Or, The Rise and Reign of His Excellency Eugène Rougon*, 1880; also as *His Excellency*, 1897]; *L'Assommoir*, 1877 [English translation, 1879; also as *The Dram-Shop*, 1897]; *Une Page d'amour*, 1878 [*Hélène: A Love Episode*, 1878; also as *A Love Affair*, 1957]; *Nana*, 1880 [English translation, 1880]; *Pot-Bouille*, 1882 [*Piping Hot*, 1924]; *Au bonheur des dames*, 1883 [*The Bonheur des Dames*, 1883; also as *The Ladies' Paradise*, 1883]; *La Joie de vivre*, 1884 [*Life's Joys*, 1884; also as *Zest for Life*, 1955]; *Germinal*, 1885 [English translation, 1885]; *L'Œuvre*, 1886 [*His Masterpiece*, 1886; also as *The Masterpiece*, 1946]; *La Terre*, 1887 [*The Soil*, 1888; also as *Earth*, 1954]; *Le Rêve*, 1888 [*The Dream*, 1888]; *La Bête humaine*, 1890 [*Human Brutes*, 1890; also as *The Human Beast*, 1890]; *L'Argent*, 1891 [*Money*, 1891]; *La Débâcle*, 1892 [*The Downfall*, 1892]; *Le Docteur Pascal*, 1893 [*Doctor Pascal*, 1893]); *Les Trois Villes*, 1894-1898 (*The Three Cities*, 1894-1898; includes *Lourdes*, 1894 [English translation, 1894]; *Rome*, 1896 [English translation, 1896]; *Paris*, 1898 [English translation, 1898]); *Les Quatre Évangiles*, 1899-1903 (English translation, 1900-1903; includes *Fécondité*, 1899 [*Fruitfulness*, 1900]; *Travail*, 1901 [*Work*, 1901]; *Vérité*, 1903 [*Truth*, 1903]).

PLAYS: *Thérèse Raquin*, 1873 (adaptation of his novel; English translation, 1947); *Les Héritiers Rabourdin*, 1874 (*The Rabourdin Heirs*, 1893); *Le Bouton de rose*, 1878; *Madeleine*, 1878; *Théâtre*, 1878; *Renée*, 1887 (adaptation of his novel *La Curée*); *L'Ouragan*, 1901 (libretto, music by Alfred Bruneau); *L'Enfant-Roi*, 1905 (libretto, music by Bruneau); *Lazare*, 1921 (libretto, music by Bruneau); *Violaine la chevelue*, 1921; *Sylvanire: Ou, Paris en amour*, 1921 (libretto, music by Robert Le Grand); *Poèmes lyriques*, 1921.

NONFICTION: *Mes haines*, 1866; *Le Roman expérimental*, 1880 (*The Experimental Novel*, 1893); *Les Romanciers naturalistes*, 1881; *Documents littéraires*, 1881; *Le Naturalisme au théâtre*, 1881 (*Naturalism on the Stage*, 1894, best known as *Naturalism in the Theater*, 1968); *Nos auteurs dramatiques*, 1881; *Une Campagne*, 1882; *Nouvelle Campagne*, 1897; *La Vérité en marche*, 1901.

Bibliography

Baguley, David, ed. *Critical Essays on Émile Zola*. Boston: G. K. Hall, 1986. A collection of essays by noted scholars on Zola, including Philip D. Walker. Covers a wide variety of topics, including biographical and critical essays and articles. "The Experimental Novel" and "Zola's Ideology: The Road to Utopia" are two valuable entries from this collection. Contains a select bibliography of works on Zola for readers of English.

Lethbridge, Robert, F. W. J. Hemmings, and Terry Keefe, eds. *Zola and the Craft of Fiction*. Leicester, England: Leicester University Press, 1990. A collection of essays published in honor of F. W. J. Hemmings. Six of the ten essays are written in English by notable Zola scholars such as David Baguley, Philip D. Walker, and Joy Newton.

Nelson, Brian. *Zola and the Bourgeoisie.* New York: Macmillan, 1983. Illuminates the specific aspects of Zola's writing that demonstrate the nineteenth century's class structure and the results of the burgeoning bourgeoisie that had replaced the aristocracy and had come to hold the bulk of the country's wealth. Explores how the bourgeoisie vilified the artist who uncovered the base side of that class's nature through his social vision.

Schom, Alan. *Émile Zola.* London: Queen Anne Press, 1987. This eleven-year research effort considers Zola the journalist, the novelist, and the man himself and his values. Places Zola in the context of the artist as crusader against nineteenth century France and its societal ills. This modern look at the whole man includes photographs, illustrations, and a select bibliography.

Walker, Philip D. *Zola.* London: Routledge & Kegan Paul, 1985. A biography drawn from this professor of French literature's own studies, as well as those of many other critics, historians, and biographers. With a select bibliography.

Robert W. Artinian
(Revised by *Leslie A. Pearl*)

MIKHAIL ZOSHCHENKO

Born: Poltava, Russia; August 10, 1895
Died: Leningrad, U.S.S.R.; July 22, 1958

Principal short fiction

Rasskazy Nazara Ilicha, gospodina Sinebryukhova, 1922; *Uvazhaemye grazhdane,* 1926; *Nervnye lyudi,* 1927; *O chem pel solovei: Sentimentalnye povesti,* 1927; *Siren' tsvetet,* 1929; *Lichnaya zhizn',* 1933; *Golubaya kniga,* 1935; *Russia Laughs,* 1935; *The Woman Who Could Not Read and Other Tales,* 1940, 1973; *The Wonderful Dog and Other Tales,* 1942, 1973; *Scenes from the Bathhouse, and Other Stories of Communist Russia,* 1961; *Nervous People and Other Satires,* 1963; *A Man Is Not a Flea: Stories,* 1989.

Other literary forms

Although the fame of Mikhail Zoshchenko rests almost entirely on his short stories, the produced a few works in other genres that are often discussed as important facets of his opus, most notably longer stories (*povesti*), which are almost invariably treated as short novels outside Russia. Two of these, *Vozrashchennaya molodost'* (1933; *Youth Restored,* 1935) and *Pered voskhodom solntsa* (1943; 1972; *Before Sunrise,* 1974), show a different Zoshchenko from that seen in his short stories—an author who is attempting to rise above the everyday reality of his stories. The first of these novels is a variation on an age-old theme—a desire to regain lost youth, with a humorous twist in that the old professor renounces his restored youth after failing to keep up with his young wife. In *Before Sunrise,* Zoshchenko probed deeper into his own psyche, trying to discover his origins, going back even to the prenatal time. In order to achieve this, he employed the psychoanalytical methods of Sigmund Freud and Ivan Pavlov, which were and still are a novelty in Russian literature. His other longer stories (a few occasional pieces written at the behest of Soviet authorities in order to conform with the political trends of the time) and playwriting attempts do not enhance his stature; on the contrary, they detract from his reputation so much that they are generally ignored by critics and readers alike.

Achievements

Zoshchenko was fortunate to enter literature in the 1920's, when Russian writers were relatively free to choose their subject matter and to express themselves. His kind of writing—humorous stories and satire—seems to have been possible only in that decade. One of Zoshchenko's most significant achievements is making his brand of humor and satire unmistakably his, not an easy task in a nation known for its exquisite sense of humor. With an ear to the ground, he demonstrated an infallible understanding of human habits and foibles. He was able to see humor in almost every situation, although his humor is often suffused with sadness deriving from the realization that life is not as funny as it often seems. He frequently spoke for the

Soviet people when they were not permitted to speak freely, yet he did it in such a way that it was very difficult to pin on him a political bias or hidden intentions until very late in his career. Just as important was his ability to reproduce the language of his characters, a curious concoction of the language of the lower classes and the bureaucratese of political parvenus trying to sound politically sophisticated or conformist. As a consequence, his several hundred short stories serve as a gold mine for the multifaceted study of the Soviet people in the first decades after the revolution. In this respect, Zoshchenko's writings resemble those of Damon Runyon, Edward Lear, and perhaps Art Buchwald. That he was able to achieve all this without sinking to the level of a social or political commentator of the period reveals his artistic acumen, which has not been equaled before or after him.

Biography

Mikhail Mikhailovich Zoshchenko was born on August 10, 1895, in Poltava, Russia, to a lower-gentry, landowning family. His father was a painter of Ukrainian origin, and his mother was a Russian actress. Zoshchenko was graduated in 1913 from a high school in St. Petersburg, the city where he spent most of his life; one of the worst grades he received was in Russian composition. Later, he studied law at the University of Petersburg. World War I interrupted his studies, and he volunteered for service in the czarist army, became an officer, and was injured and gassed in 1916. In 1917, he volunteered again, this time for the Red Army, although his military duties were limited because of his former injuries. After the revolution, Zoshchenko settled in St. Petersburg (later Leningrad), trying several professions and not settling on any of them until he decided to be a free-lance writer. For short periods of time he was a railroad ticket agent, a border-guard telephone operator, an instructor in rabbit- and poultry-raising, a militiaman, a census taker, a detective, a carpenter, a shoemaker, a clerk-typist, and a professional gambler, among other professions. This plethora of jobs served Zoshchenko later as a source of material for his stories; it also explains the authenticity of his fiction as well as his deep understanding of human nature. In 1921, he joined the famous literary group of writers calling themselves the Serapion Brothers, who gathered periodically to discuss their own works. His affiliation with this group would have far-reaching effects on him, lasting long after the group had ceased to exist. Being apolitical and having as its main goal the purely artistic improvement of its members, the society contributed significantly to the development of Russian literature at that time; it also left a stigma on its members, however, that would especially haunt Zoshchenko two decades later.

Zoshchenko wrote his first story in 1907 but did not publish anything until 1921. His first book, a collection of short stories, was published in 1922. He immediately became one of the most popular Soviet writers, publishing several additional collections and hundreds of stories. He continued as a free-lance writer in the 1930's, his output unabated and his reputation high. Yet the new political and cultural climate, manifested especially in the demand on the writers to follow the dictates of Socialist Realism, forced him to alter his style. His fiction from that time consequently suffered in quality. He tried his pen in new genres, such as psychological and documentary fiction, with varying success. During World War II, he was active during the siege of Leningrad and was decorated for his performance. Later, he was evacuated to Alma-Ata, where he spent the rest of the war, mainly writing *Before Sunrise*. In 1946, the enmity between Zoshchenko and the regime, which had been simmering below the surface throughout his writing career, burst into the open when the party cultural czar, Andrei Zhdanov, viciously attacked him, together with the poet Anna Akhmatova, for their "antisocial" and "dangerous" writings. The attack meant removal from the literary scene—a punishment from which Zoshchenko never fully recovered. He disappeared until Joseph Stalin's death in 1953, and even then he was able to publish only a few anemic stories, from which the old spark and power were gone. He died in Leningrad on July 22, 1958. Since then, his reputation has been restored, and his stories are republished regularly. His works, though somewhat dated, are still held in high esteem, especially among literary critics.

Analysis

A typical Zoshchenko story is a four- to six-page sketch about a seemingly unimportant event in the lives of ordinary Soviet citizens. Most of his stories take place in Leningrad, and most of his characters come from the lower-middle class— managers, clerks, workers, artists—and the intelligentsia of both sexes, although peasants often appear as well. The episodes usually involve an exaggerated conflict in which the characters reveal their thoughts and attitudes about everyday reality. This dramatic conflict is presented in humorous tones that endear the characters to the reader; its resolution makes the reader chuckle, sometimes laugh aloud, but it seldom leaves him bitter, angry, or demanding decisive action.

This outward innocence, however, quickly dissipates after a closer look at the characters and their vexing problems. The reader realizes that the author does not always mean what he says and does not say what he means, and that much more lurks beneath the surface. In the story "Spi skorei" ("Get on with the Sleeping"), for example, a traveler has difficulties finding a suitable room in which to sleep, and when he does, his problems begin to unfold: a window is broken and a cat jumps in because it mistakes the room for a rubbish dump, a pool of water lies in the middle of the floor, there is no light ("you're not thinking of painting pictures in it?" he is asked both innocently and sarcastically by the innkeeper), the traveler has to use a tablecloth for a blanket and slides down the bed as if it were an iceberg, and, finally, the room is infested with bedbugs and fleas. At the end of the story, a woman's passport is returned to him by mistake. This comedy of errors, neglect, and incompetence is mitigated by the traveler's last words that the passport's owner "proved to be a nice woman, and we got to know each other rather well. So that my stay at the hotel had some pleasant consequences after all."

The inconveniences portrayed in Zoshchenko's tale are not tragic but rather amusing, and the author's habit of soothing conclusions—whatever their motives—tends to smooth over the rough edges. In "Melkii sluchai iz lichnoi zhizni" ("A Personal

Episode"), the protagonist, after realizing that women no longer notice him, tries everything to become attractive again, only to discover that he has grown old. It is all lies and Western nonsense, anyway, he consoles himself. "Semeinyi kuporos" ("The Marriage Bond") shows a young wife who leaves her husband following a fight; after failing to find a suitable place to live, she returns to him. The author again moralizes, "There is no doubt, though, that this question of living accommodation strengthens and stabilizes our family life. . . . The marriage bond is rather strong nowadays. In fact very strong." The husband in the story "Rasskaz o tom, kak zhena ne razreshila muzhu umeret'" ("Hen-Pecked") falls ill and is about to die, but his wife will not let him die, as they have no money for a funeral. He goes out and begs for money and, after several outings, regains his health. "Perhaps, as he went outside the first time, he got so heated from excitement and exertion, that all his disease came out through perspiration." In another story, "Bogataia zhizn'" ("The Lucky Draw"), a married couple win a huge sum in a lottery but become very unhappy because they have nothing to do afterward. In "Administrativnyi vostorg" ("Power-Drunk"), an assistant chief of the local police is so overzealous in his off-duty efforts to punish a poor woman who allowed her pig to roam the streets that he arrests his own wife because she interceded for the woman. In story after story Zoshchenko makes seemingly insignificant events so important to his characters that they find in them the moving force of their lives. The reader, however—usually a person who has been exposed to such chicanery at one time or another—cannot help but understand that there is something basically wrong with one's life when such trivial events, against which one feels so helpless, are often repeated in various forms, that such occurrences are not really trifles, and that the primary aim of Zoshchenko's satire is not only to amuse or to exercise social criticism but also to point, rather subtly, at the philosophical meaning of existence.

Zoshchenko's reputation primarily as a social satirist is still perpetuated by both the connoisseurs of his stories and the Soviet authorities who condemn him, the former saying that Zoshchenko's criticism of the Soviet reality is justified and the latter that it is too harsh and ideologically motivated, even if sugarcoated with humor. There is no doubt that such an interpretation of his approach to reality is possible. Bureaucrats in particular are singled out for scorn. In "Koshka i liudi" ("The Stove"), a committee in charge of maintenance for an apartment building refuses to repair a fuming stove, pretending that nothing is wrong, even though one of them falls unconscious from the fumes. In "Bania" ("The Bathhouse"), checks for clothing are issued after the clothes are taken away, wrong clothes are returned, and there are not enough buckets. In the story "Butylka" ("Bottle"), a bottle lies broken on the street and nobody picks it up. When a janitor sweeps it aside, he is told by the militiaman to remove it altogether. "And, you know," the author chimes in, "the most remarkable thing is the fact that the militiaman ordered the glass to be swept up."

In perhaps Zoshchenko's harshest criticism of bureaucracy, "Kamennoe serdtse" ("A Heart of Stone"), a director demands of his business manager a truck for his personal needs. When the manager tells him that no truck is available, the director threatens to fire him, but the manager retorts, "Now, if you were a product of the old order, an attitude like that toward your subordinate would be understandable, but you are a man of the proletarian batch, and where you got a general's tone like that I simply can't understand." Nevertheless, the director succeeds in getting rid of the stubborn manager. The not-so-subtle implication here is that the revolution has changed little and that vulgarity (*poshlost'*) is as strong as ever. In all such stories, the bureaucrats, who seem to run the country, are satirized for their unjustified domination and mistreatment of their fellowmen.

Seen through such a prism, Zoshchenko's attitude toward social problems in his country two decades after the revolution can be seen as direct criticism. In fact, Zhdanov used exactly such an interpretation to attack Zoshchenko in 1946 for his alleged anti-Soviet writings. Singling out one of the stories written for children, "Prikliucheniia obeziany" ("The Adventures of a Monkey"), Zhdanov excoriated the author for writing that a monkey, after escaping from a zoo in Leningrad during the war and experiencing many troubles with human beings, decides to return to the zoo because it is easier for him to live there. The question of whether Zoshchenko wrote this story simply to amuse children or as an allegory of the inhumane (or perhaps too human) conditions in the Soviet society remains unanswered. It is quite possible that the author meant to say the latter. Yet he refused to admit political ulterior motives or an ideological slant in his writings:

> Tell me, how can I have 'a precise ideology' when not a single party among them all appeals to me? . . . I don't hate anybody—there is *my* precise ideology. . . . In their general swing the Bolsheviks are closer to me than anybody else. And so I'm willing to bolshevik around with them. . . . But I am not a Communist (or rather not a Marxist), and I think I never shall be.

If one is to believe his words, one must assume that the political or ideological criticism was not foremost on his mind. As for social criticism, he saw no crime in it; on the contrary, he believed that it was his duty to try to remedy ills and shortcomings by poking fun at them, as all satirists have done throughout history.

It is more likely that Zoshchenko was primarily interested in criticizing the morals of his compatriots, and in this respect he is no better or worse than any other moralist. He himself said that for the most part he wrote about the petty bourgeoisie, despite the official claims that it no longer exists as a separate class: "For the most part I create a synthetic type. In all of us there are certain traits of the petty bourgeois, the property owner, the money grubber. I write about the petty bourgeoisie, and I suppose I have enough material to last me the rest of my life." When some of the stories containing such criticism are examined, it is hard to disagree with Zoshchenko and even harder to see them as simply political criticism of the new regime. It is the moral behavior of his characters rather than what the government tells them to do that fascinated Zoshchenko. As a natural satirist, he was attracted mostly to the negative traits in human nature. Foremost among these traits is marital morality or, rather, the lack thereof. Infidelity seems to be rampant among

Zoshchenko's marriage partners and, what is even more interesting, they have few qualms about it. In one example of a marital merry-go-around, "Zabavnoe prikliuchenie" ("An Amusing Adventure"), three couples are intertwined through their infidelity, somewhat incredibly, to be sure, but in a way symptomatic of the loosening of moral fiber within Soviet society. Dishonesty and cheating also seem to be rampant. In "Ne nado spekulirovat" ("The Greedy Milkwoman"), a young milkmaid, eager to pocket a large reward, recommends her husband to a widow seeking a new husband, mistakenly believing that after the marriage ceremony things will return to normal. The husband, however, likes the new arrangement and refuses to return to his lawful wife. Hypocrisy is revealed by workers who praise a deceased fellow worker even though they had not said a kind word about him when he was alive in "Posledniaia nepriiatnost'" ("A Final Unpleasantness"). Bribery is still abundant despite the official disclaimers, and thievery seems to be as common as winter snow. In two stories, "Telefon" ("The Telephone") and "Dobrorozhelatel'," the occupants of an apartment building are called away on urgent business only to find upon their return that their apartments have been robbed and ransacked. In "Akter" ("The Actor"), a reluctant actor is robbed right on the stage by fellow performers who pretend that their crime is part of the play.

Zoshchenko hints at an explanation for such behavior in the persistent discrepancy between the ideal and the real, between official façade and reality, and between appearance and substance. Another explanation can be found in the perpetual clash between an individual and the collective. In a charming one-page sketch, "Karusel'" ("The Merry-Go-Round"), the author destroys the myth that everything can be free in a society by having a young fellow ride a wooden horse, simply because it is free, until he almost dies. Another likely explanation can be found when untenable living conditions require several people to share not an apartment but a single room: those who live in the room are packed like sardines; all the tenants rush to the scene whenever even the smallest incident happens, and the room's occupants have completely lost any sense of privacy. How, it is implied, can a person preserve his own dignity and respect for others when he is given a bathroom for an apartment, in which his wife, a small child, and a mother-in-law struggle to live while thirty-two other tenants use the same bathroom ("Krizis"; "The Crisis")? Or when the tenants collectively pay the electricity bill until they almost come to blows because some use more and some use less electricity ("Letniaia peredyshka"; "Electricity in Common")? Similarly humiliating struggles are presented in "Istoriia bolezni" ("History of an Illness"), in which a person prefers to be ill at home rather than in a hospital because there he is thrust in the same bathtub with an old, deranged woman and contracts whooping cough while eating from the same plate that the sick children next door have used. Regardless of whether the Soviet citizens will ever learn to adjust to this omnipresent communal life, they are paying a terrible price in overwrought nerves and general misanthropy.

Perhaps the best explanation for the immorality portrayed in Zoshchenko's stories, however, is simply the imperfection of human nature. Many of Zoshchenko's characters display the same weaknesses found in all ages and societies, which a political system can only exacerbate. His characters are egotistical and selfish to the core, as in the story "Liubov'" ("Love"), in which a young man declares his undying love for a girl on a night stroll, but when they are attacked by a robber he protests when the girl is not robbed at all. Zoshchenko's characters are also often insensitive toward one another: a man on a train mistreats his woman companion; when people protest, he is surprised, saying that it is only his mother. Other characters are greedy, taking advantage of others; an innocent man is arrested by the secret police, and his relatives sell all of his possessions, even his apartment allotment; he returns, however, in a few hours. In another story, "Vodianaia feeriia" ("A Water Ballet"), when a man comes to a city, all of his acquaintances pay him a visit mainly to take a bath in his hotel. The characters are jealous (an illiterate woman finally agrees to learn how to read only after she stumbled upon a fragrant letter her husband had received from a teacher urging him to arrange for his wife's reading classes), and they are vain (a woman defends her moonshining husband before the judge but balks when the husband reveals that she is older than he). All these traits demonstrate that Zoshchenko's characters are normal human beings sharing the same weaknesses and problems with people everywhere. One can read into these traits the corroding impact of a repressive governmental system, but more likely, these characters would behave the same way regardless of the system under which they lived. Nor does Zoshchenko believe them to be beyond salvation. In one of his best stories, "Ogni bol'shogo goroda" ("Big-City Lights"), a peasant father visits his son in Leningrad with the intention of staying there permanently. When everyone makes fun of his peasant ways, however, the old man becomes irritated and starts to cause problems for everyone, until one day he is treated with deep respect by a militiaman. This causes the old man to change his ways, and he returns happily to his village. In the words of an intellectual in the story, "I've always been of the opinion that respect for individuals, praise and esteem, produce exceptional results. Many personalities unfold because of this, just like roses at daybreak." Whether Zoshchenko is revealing his naïveté here or is adding a didactic touch to mollify the ever-present censors is immaterial; in these few words he diagnoses one of the gravest ills of any totalitarian society.

There is another strain in Zoshchenko's storytelling that, again, sets him apart from other humorists and satirists: his penchant for the absurd and grotesque. Many of his characters and situations lead to a conclusion that in essence life is absurd more often than one thinks. As a result, some of his stories are paragons of an absurd set of circumstances that no one can fathom or untangle. In "Ruka blishnego" ("My Brother's Hand"), for example, a nice person, wishing to shake hands with all people, finds out belatedly that one person who was extremely reluctant to shake hands is a leper. The best story depicting this absurdity shows a shipwrecked man during the war unknowingly holding on to a floating mine, happy about his salvation and making plans about his future ("Rogul'ka"; "The Buoy"). The pessimism and pervasive sadness of Zoshchenko's fiction break through in stories such as these despite the humor, proving the old adage that often there is only one step between laughter and tears.

There are other facets of Zoshchenko's short story repertoire that are less significant, stories that are simply humorous without any pretense or deeper meaning, parodies of other famous literary pieces, stories showing the Russians' veneration of everything foreign, and others. They contribute to a multicolored mosaic of a life rich in human idiosyncrasies, in emotions and weaknesses, in lessons for those who need or seek them which offers plain enjoyment to connoisseurs of good literature. In this respect, Zoshchenko made a significant contribution to the wealth of both Russian and world literature, ranking among those first-rate humorists and satirists—Nikolai Gogol, Nikolay Leskov, and Anton Chekhov—who influenced him.

Other major works

NOVELS: *Vozvrashchennaya molodost'*, 1933 (*Youth Restored*, 1935); *Pered voskhodom solntsa*, 1943, 1972 (*Before Sunrise*, 1974).

Bibliography

Domar, Rebecca A. "The Tragedy of a Soviet Satirist: Or, The Case of Zoshchenko." In *Through the Glass of Soviet Literature*, edited by E. J. Simmons. New York: Columbia University Press, 1953. Domar begins her essay with Zoshchenko's excommunication from literary life by the political powers in 1946, then proceeds with the analysis of his stories and other works. Her conclusion is that conflict was inevitable given the nature of Zoshchenko's satire, and that satire cannot survive in a totalitarian atmosphere as that ruling Soviet literature. Domar considers the breaking of Zoshchenko's spirit a heavy loss for Russian literature.

McLean, Hugh. Introduction to *Nervous People and Other Satires*. New York: Random House, 1965. McLean attributes Zoshchenko's popularity with the readers to his making their hard life easier to bear through laughter. Life has not changed at all in the Soviet society and Zoshchenko capitalized on that in his stories.

Mihailovich, Vasa D. "Zoshchenko's 'Adventures of a Monkey' as an Allegory." *Satire Newsletter* 4, no. 2 (1967): 84-89. Mihailovich's contention is that this seemingly innocuous story published in 1946 is anything but that. It is basically un-Soviet and the authorities' alarm was justified, from their point of view, leading directly to Zoshchenko's ostracism and to the end of his career.

Monas, Sidney. Introduction to *Scenes from the Bathhouse, and Other Stories of Communist Russia*. Ann Arbor: University of Michigan Press, 1961. An informative introduction to the stories. Monas makes some interesting remarks, such as those about Zoshchenko's lack of development as a writer.

Titunik, Irwin R. "Mikhail Zoshchenko and the Problem of *Skaz*." *California Slavic Studies* 6 (1971): 83-96. Titunik examines the *skaz* technique as individualized speech and how Zoshchenko practiced it differently than other writers, leading to a conclusion that there are no safe assumptions about *skaz* and that it will continue to be evaluated by critics.

Von Wiren-Garczynski, Vera. "Zoshchenko's Psychological Interests." *Slavic and East European Journal* 11 (1967): 3-22. Zoshchenko's interest in psychological problems was brought on by his own neurasthenia and by his desire to understand the domain of the subconscious. Von Wiren traces the results of his exploration in *Youth Restored, Before Sunrise*, and some short stories. She believes that Zoshchenko would have developed into a much deeper writer than the one he is usually seen as, had his career not been cut short.

Vasa D. Mihailovich

ESSAYS

SHORT FICTION IN ANTIQUITY

The urge to tell stories, and the concomitant desire to listen to them, are ancient and universal in human beings. Because stories are pleasurable, they require no motive beyond that of entertainment, but for the same reason they are extremely useful in celebrating the past, in inculcating moral principles, in explaining religious doctrine, and in various other endeavors. As far back as narrative storytelling can be traced, it has been used for such purposes, as well as for pure pleasure.

A story told for the purpose of keeping alive the memory of past events—a purpose that predates literacy—will inevitably be altered in the process of retelling as the teller perceives ways of improving it. We may doubt that it really took anyone ten years to return home from the Trojan War, as it took Odysseus, or that such a person was diverted and detained by supernatural beings such as Circe and Calypso, but there probably was a Trojan War, and there may well have been an Odysseus who had great troubles arriving home again afterward. Because scholars now attempt to preserve carefully the distinctions between history and fiction with a historical setting, they tend to regard the *Odyssey* (c. 800 B.C.) as a good story but as bad history. Such generic distinctions would not have occurred to audiences in antiquity. Long after Thucydides, the first rigorous historian, wrote his *History of the Peloponnesian War* late in the fifth century B.C., storytellers saw no harm in altering history for artistic purposes. They altered freely the kinds of facts now regarded as worthy of respect; they were much less likely to tamper with the legendary characters of their heroes. Homer was more interested in preserving the truth of Odysseus' shrewdness and resourcefulness than in the chronology of his travels.

What the modern world regards as literature—the very word implies writing—invariably has its origins in an oral culture. Stories existed long before anyone devised a way to write them down. Even after a people become literate, they are much more likely to use their newfound language for nonliterary purposes, most often for business; later, they may begin to write down their poetry and fiction. Because people today think of "real" literature as written, they often suppose the efforts of preliterate people to be primitive and unworthy of attention. The preliterate people with whom we are familiar, after all, are young children and the culturally deprived. The idea of preliterates including sophisticated artists and mature audiences now seems odd—but it is nevertheless true.

Folktales

Probably the earliest form of fiction is the folktale in its various forms, including ballad and folk song. A folktale is a short narrative that is transmitted orally, with various tellers introducing modifications as the tale is passed along to a contemporary audience and down to succeeding generations. It is clearly impossible to come into direct contact with this oldest form of narrative as it existed in antiquity, but it is possible to know with considerable assurance what ancient folktales were like. For one thing, folktales still persist; for another, a comparison of extant folktales from around the globe reveals striking similarities and suggests that paleolithic audiences doubtless enjoyed the same fictive themes and patterns that continue to engross their descendants.

Fairy tales, myths, fables, and legends are forms of folktale distinguishable by their purposes and emphases. In literate cultures, folktales are likely to pass into written form, thus ceasing to be folktales. When the Brothers Grimm, early in the nineteenth century, collected and published the fairy tales with which their name has become synonymous, they were both preserving and destroying the tales in the process. When the tales are written down, they become standardized, they do not change with tellers, and they come to their audiences in a different form. Even a very young child, listening to a parent read a fairy tale, knows that it is coming from the pages of a book. Only since the time of the Brothers Grimm, or roughly a half century earlier in the case of folk ballads, have printed texts competed with and, in most cases, replaced oral transmission. When educated people such as Bishop Thomas Percy, the first great ballad collector, and the Brothers Grimm become involved, folktales become contaminated by the literary culture—much more so in the twentieth century with its radio, television, and recording and playback devices from the gramophone through the compact-disc recorder. Children will not listen to grandmother's stories if they can listen to (and watch) video presentations, and her stories die with her. Meanwhile, the entertainment media choose, reject, and edit folk materials for their own, usually commercial, purposes, a process quite unlike the one that brought the folk material down through the centuries.

Myth

"The narratives of literature," wrote Northrop Frye in *Words with Power* (1990), "descend historically from myths, or rather from the aggregate of myths we call a mythology." While perhaps too sweeping a generalization, this statement by a major critic demonstrates how important the study of myth has become. Myths are stories about gods, which humans devise to explain creation, existence, death, and natural phenomena of all sorts. From one point of view, myths are religious truths; from another, they are fictions. These viewpoints are often assumed to conflict, although they do not if it is conceded that fictions can convey truths. Some of the most profound truths can perhaps be conveyed only indirectly. It is sometimes alleged that myths recede as scientific explanations of natural phenomena advance.

Greek mythology permeates Western literary forms as far back as they can be perceived, though differently in different genres. Epics, for example, allude to myths, but rather than retell familiar myths they tend to employ mythological characters, with their well-known attributes, to interact in various ways with human characters, as to assist them in crises or thwart them if they turn impious. Thus, in the *Iliad* (c. 800 B.C.), Achilles' goddess mother Thetis restrains him from imprudent retaliation against Agamemnon, who has appropriated a woman whom Achilles earlier gained as a prize during the Trojan War, while in the *Odyssey*, the sea god Poseidon frustrates Odysseus' attempt to reach his homeland of Ithaca after the war because the latter has blinded Poseidon's son Polyphemus the Cyclops. In later romances, the gods continue to perform such functions, less often by direct intervention in human shape, more often through the prayers of the hero or heroine, characteristically directed to icons in sacred places.

The first collector of Greco-Roman myths to endow them with high literary polish was the Roman poet Ovid in his *Metamorphoses* early in the first century A.D. This work weaves together a large number of more or less unrelated stories in one continuous narrative. He begins with an account of the ordering of a primal Chaos and continues by describing an early golden age from which the earth has declined, after which he proceeds to the doings of the Olympian gods. In the eleventh of his fifteen books, Ovid turns his attention to "history," especially the legendary events leading to the establishment of the Roman Empire under Augustus in Ovid's own time. In unifying this disparate material, he used the technique of seizing upon a frequent, though not inevitable, feature of the old myths—the transformations or metamorphoses of characters into other forms of being: trees, animals, springs of water, and the like. In addition to this thematic unification, Ovid links the myths by associative devices, by stories within stories, and sometimes by quite arbitrary but ingenious transitions. Ovid avoids monotony by a modulation of tone from eloquently grand all the way to quietly informal. Enormously popular in the Middle Ages and Renaissance, Ovid influenced writers of fiction for centuries.

Fables and Parables

Of the ancient narrative forms devised to serve a nonliterary purpose, the fable is perhaps the most ingratiating. The fable is usually short, often features animals that portray human weaknesses and vices, and is told to illustrate a moral truth, which may or may not be explicitly stated at the beginning or end. Fables have been found on Egyptian papyruses, among the birth tales of Buddha, and in Sanskrit literature. The fables best known in the Western world, however, come chiefly from Greece, the earliest known one being the story of the hawk and the nightingale in Hesiod's *Works and Days* (c. eighth century B.C.). About two centuries later, a slave named Aesop composed fables, according to Herodotus (a Greek historian who himself told wonderful stories, sometimes of dubious factual value). Subsequently, Aesop came to be regarded as the originator of virtually all ancient fables, the charm of which, along with their utility in promoting virtuous and sensible behavior, earned for them a popularity that they have retained throughout the centuries. It is a rare child who does not know the story of the fox and the grapes or that of the dog in the manger. Many proverbs are essentially fables in outline form.

Fables have been cultivated by professional writers since classical times, though Greek and Roman writers were inclined to work them into larger literary contexts, an example being the Roman poet Horace who, as part of his book of satires in the first century B.C., gave posterity the story of the town mouse and the country mouse. The medieval Persian poet 'Ubaid Zakani told a cat-and-mouse fable with a satiric twist. A cat, conscience-stricken after eating mice, finds religion. All the mice in the neighborhood rejoice but later find that the cat devours more of them than ever—as a religious duty. Fables persist in Europe in Geoffrey Chaucer's "The Nun's Priest's Tale," and notably in the fables of Jean de la Fontaine and in the characteristically modern ones of James Thurber.

Another type of story with a nonliterary purpose is the parable. The details of a parable, such as Christ's parable of the laborers in the vineyard, present a moral lesson, usually implicitly but nevertheless pointedly. Parables are common in religious prose around the world; they are, for example, a frequent feature of Hindu scriptures. The famous thirteenth century Persian poet Sa'di of Sheraz in his *Gulistan* (1258; *The Rose Garden*, 1806) combines poetry and prose parables. One of the latter tells of a great wrestler who teaches a young protégé all of his holds except one. The overconfident protégé challenges the master to a match, but the latter of course uses that one hold to throw him. Parables are usually considered a species of allegory, in which the characters and actions make literal sense but point to another, usually moral, level of meaning. As a fictional form, allegory did not otherwise develop very far in antiquity but became extremely popular in the Christian Middle Ages.

Although fables and parables are created for nonliterary purposes, they hold a secure place in the hearts of story lovers. Furthermore, since fables such as Aesop's and the parables of Christ are so well known, many subsequent writers have used them both structurally and allusively in making longer fictional works.

Epic

Modern readers often think of Homer as standing at the beginning of Western literature; anthologies of ancient classics usually begin with those extended heroic narratives, the *Iliad* and the *Odyssey*, traditionally assigned to the blind poet. In an important way, however, the Homeric epics represent the end of a literary tradition, or at least an important turn in the literary road, for they came into being (or at least into the form familiar to posterity) around the time that the Greek alphabet was being devised and Greek literacy was becoming possible. A long oral tradition lies behind these folk epics. They could be written down not long after they were composed, but initially they were listened to, not read, and they were transmitted orally like any other type of folk narrative.

There are important differences between the kind of story that Homer told and the others mentioned above. Anyone can learn a ballad or song or short fable, but the development of longer oral narratives required the memorization of stories as long as some modern novels. Inevitably, professional performers arose to meet this need. These rhapsodists, as they were called, accomplished the remarkable feat of memorizing whole epics. They would not have been able to achieve these mnemonic feats, however, without the assistance of techniques such as systematic meter and verbal formulas that could be plugged into metrical lines at strategic points. Thus epic narratives were embodied in beautiful rhythms that became available to reading audiences of later times only if they could read Homeric Greek, but skillful translators can imitate the effects of the original poems to a certain extent.

The many repeated lines and phrases and the fixed epithets attached to the names of characters in Greek epics are not affectations or signs of imaginative weakness but essential features both for rhapsodist and audience. Although later "literary" epic poets such as Vergil had considerably less need of such devices, the attractiveness of the hexameter line used in the *Iliad* and *Odyssey* led him and other Roman poets to adapt it to Latin, as well as other features originally devised for practical purposes in an oral culture. Vergil wrote his epic, the *Aeneid* (c. 29-19 B.C.; English translation, 1553), and expected people to read it, but in an age when people did not often have the privilege of holding that rare and expensive thing, the book, these oral features continued to enhance the memorability of the epic.

The Homeric epics purport to treat of a heroic era several centuries before the time of their composition (around the eighth century B.C.). Scholars disagree over whether the same poet actually composed both poems, but each is, in its own way, a narrative masterpiece. The *Iliad* focuses on a struggle of wills between two stubborn Greek kings, the commander in chief, Agamemnon, and the great warrior Achilles, whose refusal to take part jeopardizes the effort to seize Troy and return Helen, Agamemnon's sister-in-law, to her Greek husband. The story develops systematically to the point at which the Trojan prince Hector's killing of Achilles' close friend Patroclus and subsequent dishonoring of his body drives Achilles to exact revenge on Hector. The fact that the *Iliad* does not deal at all comprehensively with the war but ends with the Trojan king Priam's reclaiming of his son's body from Achilles suggests the likelihood of other epics detailing other aspects of the conflict, especially its climax, which the *Iliad* stops short of recounting. Indeed, fragments of Trojan War epics from a somewhat later period do exist.

Whereas the *Iliad* focuses on the events of a few days outside the gates of Troy, the *Odyssey* covers ten years and takes its hero all over the Mediterranean world. It too is admirably constructed, paralleling the simultaneous experiences of son and father, Telemachus and Odysseus, then allowing Odysseus to describe his decade of adventures to a friendly people with whom he has taken temporary refuge, and finally bringing Odysseus and Telemachus together to plan and execute retaliation against the suitors of the former's wife (Penelope), who have invaded Odysseus' house and besieged her relentlessly during his absence. The device of allowing Odysseus to tell his own, often improbable, story serves the important purpose of preserving Homer from charges of lying—a handy protection that other writers of fiction were not slow to imitate. From the reader's perspective, Odysseus' narrative, covering four of the twenty-four books, fills in the prior adventures that the *in medias res* beginning (that is, the beginning in the middle of things) has left hanging; it also delays and thus enhances the climax.

The lost Greek epics include a cycle on the legends of Thebes (given dramatic treatment by the Greek tragedians) and a *Persica*, or epic on the Persian Wars of the early fifth century B.C., by Choerilus of Samos. Extant is a third century *Argonautica* by Apollonius of Rhodes, an Alexandrian Greek whose narrative of Jason and the

Argonauts takes the gods and religion much less seriously and puts a new emphasis on love, relatively unimportant in Homeric epic but central in the romances to come.

Roman writers imitated the Greek achievement in epic as in other forms of both literary and nonliterary art. The earliest original Roman writer of an epic, Gnaeus Naevius, composed an epic on the First Punic War (254-241 B.C.), in which he served as a young man, but only a few lines survive. Quintus Ennius wrote a more ambitious epic on the history of Rome up to his time, the *Annales*, in eighteen books, of which about six hundred lines survive. The most important Roman epic poet, of course, was Vergil (70-19 B.C.), who took as his subject the legendary career of Aeneas, one of the numerous sons of King Priam, who gathered remnants of the defeated Trojans and set out for Latium, the site of the future Rome. The *Aeneid* is in twelve books, the first six of which have been called Vergil's *Odyssey*, or account of Aeneas' journey to Latium, while the last six resemble the *Iliad* in concentrating on the war that Aeneas and his companions must wage to secure this site of future Roman glory. Epics commonly celebrate the supposed virtues of a people, and Aeneas embodies the Roman ideal of piety and civic duty. Vergil paints an unforgettable picture of a man who relishes war not at all but is obliged to prosecute one. Vergil would doubtless have been amazed at the influence that book 4 of his *Aeneid* (his story of the love of the Carthaginian queen, Dido, expressed for Aeneas, and Aeneas' dutiful rejection of her offer of herself and share of her African kingdom) had on subsequent fiction.

After Vergil, the most important Roman epics are those of Lucan (A.D. 39-65), whose *Pharsalia* deals with the civil war between Julius Caesar and Gnaeus Pompey, and Statius (c. A.D. 45-96), who went back to the Theban legends for his *Thebaid* (c. A.D. 90). After these poets of what is called the Silver Age of Roman literature, the heroic ideal passed into prose romances as indicated below.

The folk epic reappeared in other cultures for centuries thereafter, usually with many features similar to those of the Homeric epics. The Old English *Beowulf*, composed around the eighth century, seems to derive in large measure from fairy tales like the *Odyssey*; the Old French *Chanson de Roland* (eleventh century; *The Song of Roland*, c. 1100) resembles the *Iliad* particularly in its magnification of a relatively small martial incident, in this case one from the conflicts between Carolingian barons, into heroic proportions; the German *The Nibelungenlied* (c. 1200), like both Homeric epics, shows signs of a long development from earlier oral narratives. All these epics memorialize feats of a heroic age from the perspective of a people who are tacitly confessing that the era of heroes has ended. Between these epics and the Scandinavian sagas, the chief difference is formal: the latter are normally in prose rather than in verse. Of the many sagas, one of the best is the Icelandic *Grettis Saga* (*The Saga of Grettir*, 1914), which dates from about 1300 in its present form. It incorporates many folklore motifs, including the hero's battles with ghosts and trolls. Literary epics generally persist longer in a culture, with John Milton's *Paradise Lost* (1667) arguably the last great epic in English.

Eastern peoples also have their epics. Iranians, for example, treasure the *Shahna-*

mah of Firdusi, who composed his epic around the year 1010. It begins with the creation of the universe and proceeds through forty thousand lines to the rise and subsequent glories of the Iranian people. The great epics of India, the *Rāmāyana* and *Mahābhārata*, while resembling the Homeric ones in a number of respects, are, unlike the *Iliad* and *Odyssey*, sacred books. Only about one fifth of the *Mahābhārata* is taken up by the main story, but the narrative portions are still longer than the two great Greek epics combined. Long as such works are, they incorporate many episodes and incidents, which are in effect short stories.

Comic and Satiric Fiction

Satire, which ridicules individuals, institutions, and sometimes other literary works for the sake of promoting better ones, also took narrative form in antiquity. Often, satire seems clearly allied with fables and parables in that the story is not told for its own sake, but some satirists are accomplished storytellers. In fact, Northrop Frye, in his influential *Anatomy of Criticism* (1957), identifies Menippean satire as one of the four characteristic forms that fiction has taken in Western literature. It is named for a Greek writer of the third century B.C., Menippus, whose works influenced a succession of Greek and Roman writers. The *Saturae Menippeae* of the Roman author Varro (116-27 B.C.) exists only in fragmentary form. It is the work of a moralist who viewed Roman life critically in the tumultuous era leading to the establishment of the Empire. The chief Greek follower of Menippus, Lucian (c. A.D. 120-after 180), wrote *Alethes historia* (*A True History*, 1634), which parodies travelers' tales, including the *Odyssey*, by describing a voyage that begins on the sea, continues in the sky, and even visits the Elysian Fields. Doubtfully ascribed to Lucian is *Onos* (*The Ass*, 1684), important as the basis of Apuleius' masterpiece described below.

The Satyricon of Petronius Arbiter (c. A.D. 20-c. 66) is a long prose narrative interspersed with verse; only a substantial fragment survives. It is regarded as the ancestor of the picaresque fiction that arose in sixteenth century Spain, spread quickly over Europe, and remains viable today. Encolpus, the narrator, and Ascyltus are two young men wandering about the Italian peninsula living by their wits. In the most famous section, that of Trimalchio's dinner party, the two take part in an elaborately ridiculous party given by a tasteless rich man. In the Trimalchio episode, Petronius is not primarily a satirist but a devotee of the art of purely entertaining fiction—an activity that professional writers of the ancient world scorned. Not only is the party, marked by a drunken brawl and even a dogfight, one of the liveliest works of the Latin Silver Age, but also Petronius even manages to incorporate two ghost stories for good measure.

A century after Petronius, Rome produced its other genius of comic prose, Lucius Apuleius (fl. A.D. 155). His *Metamorphoses* (also known as *The Golden Ass*) alone among Latin prose narratives has survived the centuries complete. Like so many Roman artistic achievements, it imitates an earlier Greek work, but Apuleius' adaptation is superior to its original. The hero, Lucius, fascinated by sorcery and enchantment, is by a miscalculation transformed into an ass, in which shape he remains for most of the eleven books. Apuleius greatly expands the episodes of his source and adds numerous stories of his own: adventure stories, tragedies, fairy tales, erotica—an enormous variety of types. Sometimes they support the main narrative, sometimes they are tonally inappropriate; they are there because Apuleius recognized them as good stories. He missed no opportunity to add action and surprises, and he excelled at vivid and dramatic details. Of the interpolated narratives, his story of Cupid and Psyche is the most celebrated. Psyche is a woman so beautiful that the jealous goddess Venus orders Cupid to make her fall in love with an ugly creature, but instead Psyche and Cupid become lovers. After a string of adventures brought on by Venus' vindictiveness, Psyche, deified, becomes Cupid's bride. Here Apuleius has reworked mythological material freely to produce a highly original narrative.

Even when incongruous in their context, Apuleius' stories increase the pleasure of the literary journey and prolong the suspense. Eventually, of course, Lucius finds an opportunity to eat roses, the one act that will return him to human form. As a whole, *The Golden Ass* foreshadows the rogue or picaresque novel, but in its particulars this work can be seen as one of the earliest collections of short—and not so short—stories. Because Apuleius could in his time exploit comically the mythological characters and motifs that Ovid, an exploiter himself by temperament, still took with relative seriousness, he created a highly original fictive work that would open new vistas for later satirists and comic writers.

Romance

Epic was "displaced"—to use W. P. Ker's term (*Epic and Romance*, 1897)—by romance in the medieval world, but the distinction between them sometimes blurs, especially in the transitional romances of the early Christian era. The hero of a romance is likely to rival the epic warrior in such traits as strength, courage, and resourcefulness, but he is unlikely to serve as an idealized representative of a people or nation in the manner of, say, Vergil's Aeneas. Rather, he is a private individual whose adventures do not culminate in the establishment of a state or the winning of a war but in winning a beautiful heroine—herself a character not found in epic. The titles of the early Greek romances—*Chaereas and Callirhoe, Leucippe and Clitophon, Daphnis and Chloë*—signify the emergence of a female character equal in interest to the male hero. Although Vergil might accurately have titled the fourth book of his epic "Aeneas and Dido," Dido disappears thereafter, only turning up briefly in the underworld after her suicide. Dido is not a woman to win or to please but an obstacle to be overcome. Although Odysseus does strive to be reunited with Penelope, neither Homer nor his audience would have dreamed of reducing even this less serious of his epics to *Odysseus and Penelope.* The later romances blend the beauty and passionate spirit of Dido with the loyalty and perseverance of Penelope to make heroines who become the be-all and end-all of the heroes' existence.

Whereas epics perpetuate legends and old traditions and thus are bound in certain respects by what their devisers understood as history, romances are historical only in the manner of their modern counterparts; the authors are free to invent characters and adventures to suit their plot and, with the same end in mind, to devise fictional roles for their "historical" characters. Insofar as romancers work clear of allegiance to legend and create an unhistorical milieu, they create a distinctive genre. Another important difference is formal: the Greco-Roman epics are in verse—the literary form of the time—while the early romances are in prose.

The surviving Greek romances, which, in suitable modern translations, have finally been gathered conveniently by B. P. Reardon (*Collected Ancient Greek Novels*, 1989), feature lovers who are buffeted about in an alien world. Though normally of noble blood, they are often reared as foundlings. The heroine is likely to retain her virginity through a succession of captivities by pirates, lustful potentates, and others yet more savage. These romances' concern with chastity often seems no more than deference to respectability of the sort that constrained Victorian novelists. In the face of Fortune, both hero and heroine often remain passive, and Fortune remains stubbornly bad until the happy ending. Prescient dreams, strange coincidences, presumed deaths (later explained away either naturally or supernaturally), and escapes from seemingly impossible predicaments abound. The hero and heroine are always ready to die rather than confront the prospect of the other's extinction or marriage to someone else. Unlike both epic and satire, romance has no moral or historical lessons to inculcate, but it aspires to spiritual edification in its idealization of character.

Although fragments of earlier Greek romances exist, the first complete specimen is the *Chaereas and Callirhoe* of Chariton, written probably late in the first century A.D. It begins simply and straightforwardly: "My name is Chariton, of Aphrodisias, and I am clerk to the attorney Athenagoras. I am going to tell you the story of a love affair that took place in Syracuse." Actually this narrative, slightly more than one hundred pages in modern translation, jumps briskly around the Mediterranean world. The hero and heroine, actually married early in the story, are separated by Callirhoe's presumed death, and both she and her husband endure many perils before their reunification. Despite many quotations from, and allusions to, Homer, this work was probably scorned by intellectuals of the day. It is well constructed, however, and uses dialogue effectively. Although it exists in but a single manuscript, scattered fragments found on Egyptian papyruses suggest popular appeal. (It must be remembered that even a "popular" reading public was tiny compared to that of today.)

In *An Ephesian Tale of Anthia and Habrocomes*, attributed to one Xenophon of Ephesus, roughly contemporary with Chariton, a similar plot draws in several episodes of folk origin. Graham Anderson, in *Ancient Fiction: The Novel in the Greco-Roman World* (1984), has shown similarities between Greek and oriental tales in this and other romances, which illustrate how widely such folktales were disseminated. Stylistically, *An Ephesian Tale of Anthia and Habrocomes* is rather crude and monotonous.

A more miscellaneous romance is *Leucippe and Clitophon*, composed by Achilles Tatius, probably late in the second century A.D. In the first few pages, the author describes a meeting with his hero, Clitophon, who is then allowed to tell his story in the first person—though Clitophon becomes more or less omniscient in the process. Clitophon is unusual among romantic protagonists in failing to remain completely loyal to Leucippe during their lengthy separation; circumstances force her to become the consort of a foreign potentate for a time, but their goal is nevertheless eventual reunion. The style ranges from poetic to prosaic. Achilles can manage realistic descriptions of a storm at sea, psychological portraits of his characters, elaborate puns, and melodramatic incidents.

Around A.D. 200, a writer known as Longus composed the pastoral romance *Daphnis and Chloë*, thus blending elements from a poetic tradition whose monuments are the eclogues of Theocritus and Vergil with prose narrative. Longus shows considerable ingenuity in accomplishing the difficult feat of combining features from the static, halcyon world of pastoral with the mobile and frequently menacing milieu of romance. The young lovers' staunch relationship is traced from the time of their childhood as goatherds and shepherds through their sexual awakening and ultimate union. The story does not leave the island of Lesbos, famed as the home of the first great lyric poet (certainly the first great woman poet) Sappho. Whereas the innocent Daphnis and Chloë must prevail over the wiles of more sophisticated enemies and even well-intentioned friends, this plot keeps them close to home, and unlike the noble lovers of other romances, these two desire nothing more than a fruitful marriage and the opportunity to continue tending their flocks.

The longest and best known of the Greek romances, Heliodorus of Emesa's *Ethiopica* (A.D. 225; *An Ethiopian History*, 1569; also known by several other titles, including *The Story of Theagenes and Charikleia*, after its protagonists), dates from the third or fourth century. It is an ambitious work by a sophisticated writer who was obviously eager to put romance on a footing with the still venerated epics. Whether or not he succeeded, at times he loses interest in Theagenes and Charikleia as a result of his preoccupation with elaborate stories within stories and the fierce battles he stages among Egyptians, Persians, and Ethiopians. There is also a mystery to be solved about Charikleia's parentage; she turns out to be an Ethiopian, although an extremely light-skinned one. Heliodorus is one of the greatest of Greek prose stylists, and he influenced such towering figures as Miguel de Cervantes, Sir Philip Sidney, and Jean Racine.

An excellent general account of the Greek and Roman romances is Ben Edwin Perry's *The Ancient Romances: A Literary-Historical Account of Their Origins* (1967).

Romance is a form that has flourished in many parts of the world. An Arabic example that has become especially well known in Europe and the United States is *Alf Layla wa Layla* (*The Thousand and One Nights*), better known as *The Arabian Nights' Entertainment*. Transmitted orally for centuries, it is a collection of stories that has existed in some form for more than a thousand years. Like many later literary works, the tales themselves (not always a thousand) are set within a frame story, in this case one about a misogynist king who has vowed to kill all women. Two young women avoid his wrath by telling him a different unfinished story each evening, thus postponing their fate until he hears the end. Immediately upon finishing, they launch upon another story; the tactic goes on until the king finally abandons his homicidal program. The stories themselves—those of Aladdin, Ali Baba, and Sinbad the Sailor, for example—have spread all over the world since publication in various languages in the eighteenth and nineteenth centuries. Clearly the work of various hands, they have been traced to India, Iran, Iraq, Egypt, and even Greece. The interested reader may consult M. I. Gerhardt, *The Art of Story-Telling: A Literary Study of the Thousand and One Nights* (1963).

Medieval Persian poets developed a verse form called *mathnavi* for long narratives. Nizami of Ganja, who flourished late in the twelfth century, composed several of these, including *Laili and Majnun,* a tragic poem akin to the courtly European romances of the same era.

Murasaki Shikibu (c. 978-c. 1030) prevails as the most illustrious of early Japanese romancers. Her *Genji monogatari* (*The Tale of Genji,* 1925-1933), composed early in the eleventh century, has been called the oldest novel in the world. It includes a series of delicately crafted love stories and depicts forcefully Japanese court life of her time, an atmosphere that Murasaki knew well. Since its translation into English by Arthur Waley in 1935, it has gained recognition in English-speaking countries.

Lo Kuan-Chung (c. 1330-1400) gave coherent form to cycles of legends long popular in China. His *San kuo chih yen-i* (*Romance of the Three Kingdoms,* 1925) is based on historical events of the third century A.D., while *Shui-hu chuan* (translated as *All Men Are Brothers* by Pearl Buck, 1933) also has gained a following in the West.

Columbia University Press has done much to introduce English-speaking readers to Asian fiction, as well as other literary forms, with a series of translations and "approaches." One example is *Approaches to the Oriental Classics: Asian Literature and Thought in General Education,* edited by William Theodore De Bary (1959).

Robert P. Ellis

THE FABLE TRADITION

Although it is impossible to trace the genre of the fable to a single source or a first writer, it is known that the fable tradition has its roots far back in ancient history; in fact, the fable is perhaps one of the earliest forms of the short story. Although readers have most often come to associate the fable with Aesop, even to the extent of attributing to Aesop fables written at a much later time, the fable tradition actually flourished in many cultures other than that of ancient Greece, as proven by the existence of fables in diverse ancient writings.

From the time of its very inception, the fable seems to have entailed the notion of allegory. According to the definition of the ancient Greeks, whose fables are most familiar to the Western world, the fable is a story, a tale, a narrative; the Greeks made clear the fable's fictional nature by terming it μυθος (from which comes the word "myth") and thus distinguishing this sort of tale from the historical tale, which was termed λόγος, or ἱστορία. Nevertheless, although the tale was fictive, its intent was to portray allegorically a reality of some kind, and this basic assumption concerning the fable's nature has characterized the fable throughout centuries of varied treatment.

As it most commonly appears, the fable personifies animals, or occasionally plants, or sometimes even the elements of nature, so as to reveal some truth; ordinarily that truth concerns a particular aspect of human behavior, although some fables which are etiological (such as how the turtle got its shell) have come to be attached to the genre. The use of animals to represent human truth may have come about in part because people are familiar with animals, often living in close association with them. Moreover, certain animals have been perceived as displaying various attributes or patterns of behavior which have come to be associated with them, such as the wiliness of the fox and the rapaciousness of the wolf. Although it is difficult now to determine whether the animals actually possess such traits or whether the fable has taught the reader to perceive the animals as possessing such traits, the fact is that certain animals have come to embody an identifiable symbolic meaning. Human familiarity with both the animals themselves and with their distinguishing characteristics makes them particularly well suited to metaphorical or allegorical uses.

Even though the early fables occasionally included gnomic lines, the fables were not written with specific morals attached but relied instead on implication and inference. The practice of adding epimythia, statements which overtly present the fable's moral purpose, became very popular in the Middle Ages when the fables were used for moral instruction. Since these medieval fables are the ones that are known best, the fable has come to be identified with moral didacticism; in its genesis, however, the fable's purpose seems to have been merely to contain wisdom.

The most famous writer of fables is, of course, Aesop. By the time of the Middle Ages his fables existed in many variant forms—in verse and in prose, and in many languages such as French, German, Latin, and English. Although Aesop was not the only source of medieval fables, many of the most popular are traceable ultimately to

Aesop, by means of such redactors as Demetrius Phalereus, Phaedrus, Babrius, Avianus, and Gualterus Anglicus. Since Aesop probably did not write his fables down, the reader is obliged to rely on the testimony of these later writers who claim that their collections are based on Aesop's work. The extent to which Aesop is responsible for all the fables attributed to him cannot be finally determined, but it is known that he is associated with the beginning of the genre as it developed in Greece.

There were earlier users of the fable than Aesop, but their work, for the most part, has been lost. Archilochus, a Greek poet believed to have lived on the island of Paros in the seventh century B.C., composed a number of fables concerning the fox and the monkey, the fox and the eagle, and the fox and the hedgehog, but unfortunately his work survives only in fragments. Another early fable is that of Hesiod, a Greek poet who lived in Boeotia and who wrote around 700 B.C. His fable of the hawk and the nightingale, contained in the poem "Works and Days," is one of the oldest known of the Greek fables:

> A hawk catches a nightingale and carries her in his claws high up to the clouds. In response to her pitiful wailing the hawk asks why she screams, since her master has her and she will therefore go wherever he wishes to take her; if he wishes to eat her he will, or if he wishes to let her go, he may do so. The hawk points out that one who tries to match strength with someone stronger will not only lose the battle but will be hurt as well by shame.

Hesiod claims that his fable is for the barons, who will understand it.

Even older is the fable in Judges 9:8-15, concerning the trees who seek a king:

> The olive tree, when asked to reign over the other trees, responded by inquiring if it should leave its rich oil, which honors gods and men, so as to sway over the trees. The fig tree, also asked, similarly inquired if it should leave its good fruit in order to reign. In like manner the vine inquired if it should leave its good wine, which cheers gods and men. The bramble, when asked, responded that if the trees were in good faith anointing it as king they should take shelter in its shade, but if they were not, that fire should come out of the bramble and burn up the cedars of Lebanon.

Despite such earlier fables as these, however, it is with Aesop, who is believed to have lived in the sixth century B.C., whom the fable has come to be most closely associated. Much of Aesop's life remains a mystery, although tradition has it that he was a Phrygian slave who was owned by Iadmon of the island of Samos, that he was ugly and deformed, and that he was killed by the people of Delphi. How much of this legendry is true one cannot know. From the testimony of Herodotus, Aristophanes, Xenophon, Plato, and Aristotle, scholars today have concluded that Aesop did exist and that he was known as a fabulist who concerned himself with moral and satirical lessons; Plato, for example, tells of Socrates amusing himself during the last days of his life with Aesop's tales. Beyond this, however, there is no real way of verifying "facts" about Aesop's life.

Similarly there is a lack of absolute information about Aesop's canon. The first collector of Aesop's fables of whom there is knowledge is Demetrius Phalerus, who was reported to have assembled Aesop's fables in prose in the fourth century B.C.

This collection is not available, although it was, apparently, the source used by the later fabulists Phaedrus and Babrius. Phaedrus, a Roman who lived in Greece in the first century A.D., wrote a collection of fables in Latin verse which included Aesopic tales as well as new fables which Phaedrus himself wrote concerning contemporary social and political events. While Phaedrus states in his Prologue that he is merely putting into verse stories which Aesop invented, he does in some instances attribute a particular fable to Aesop, such as the tale of the dog and the meat:

A dog carrying a piece of meat in his mouth while crossing a river sees his reflection in the water; believing that he sees another dog also carrying meat, he snatches for the reflection, letting fall the meat he held in his mouth. In addition to failing to get that which he coveted, he also loses that which he already had.

In its simplicity, its brevity, and its implied meaning, this fable is typical of the early Aesopic tradition.

Babrius, like Phaedrus, was a Roman who is believed also to have lived in the second half of the first century; like Phaedrus, Babrius added to the Aesopic fables tales of his own composition, in the collection he wrote in Greek verse. Again like Phaedrus, Babrius refers to Aesop in his Prologue, explaining that his intent is to soften and sweeten Aesop's sometimes hard or stinging iambic lines. One of the best known of the Aesopic fables is that of the fox and the grapes, which is included in the Babrius collection:

A fox, seeing several bunches of grapes hanging from a vine, leaped in vain to pick the fruit, which was ripe and purple. Being unable to reach the grapes he went away, remarking as he went that the grapes were sour, and not ripe at all as he had thought.

To these two sources, Phaedrus and Babrius, and through them to Aesop, are traceable most of the fables which were popularized in the Middle Ages and which have become part of our fable lore.

Along with Phaedrus and Babrius, another writer of the first century A.D. to whom readers are indebted for a particular popular fable is Horace, a Roman poet who included in his *Satires* (35, 30 B.C.) the fable of the town mouse and the country mouse. Horace explains that this fable's purpose is to illustrate the care that accompanies wealth:

When the country mouse entertains his city friend, the city mouse scorns the meal of peas, oats, and bacon rinds. Since life is so short, the city mouse explains, one should seek pleasure, which can be found in the city. Once there, the country mouse finds that indeed luxuries abound and delicious food is available, but when the watchdogs are let loose, frightening the country mouse half to death, he decides that his quiet home and simple food are quite sufficient for him.

This fable was used repeatedly by later writers to demonstrate the virtue of the simple life and the wisdom of keeping one's proper place in the social hierarchy.

Both the Phaedrus and the Babrius collections were used extensively by later writers. The Babrius collection was put into Latin verse, perhaps around A.D. 400, by

Avianus, a Roman writer of whom little is known. The Avianus fables, because of their simplicity, were popular in medieval schools as exercises in grammar and composition; fables had been recommended for this purpose as early as the first century A.D. by Quintilianus, a rhetorician who prized the Aesopic fables as aids in memorizing, reciting, and composing. The Avianus fables were also used by Alexander Neckham for his *Novus Avianus* of the late twelfth century, on which a number of later French versions rely. The Phaedrus translation of the fables was the basis for the tenth century *Romulus* collection in Latin prose, which circulated widely in manuscripts of varying contents. This collection, which was said to be directly derived from Aesop, was extremely popular. In the twelfth century, Gualterus Anglicus (Walter the Englishman) translated this *Romulus* collection into Latin verse; it is also from Walter's translation, known in the Middle Ages as *Esopus, Ysopet,* or *Isopet* (or the *Anonymous Neveleti,* since the collection was published anonymously by Nevelet in 1610), that many later French and Italian versions are derived.

Also writing fables in the twelfth century was Marie de France, who drew on both the *Romulus* collection and the *Roman de Renart* (c. 1175-1205), the tales of Reynard the fox, for her fables, many of which referred to contemporary society. Another French writer, whose fables were influenced by the work of Marie, by the *Romulus* collection, and by Hebrew lore, was Rabbi Berechiah ben Natronai ha-Nakdan, who, toward the end of the twelfth century, wrote his *Fox Fables.* In spite of the title, however, not all the fables concern the fox, as, for example, the fable of the mouse who overeats:

> A mouse who was black and thin went through a hole into a granary where he ate until he was immensely fat. When he was ready to leave he discovered he could not fit through the hole. A cat informed him that unless he vomitted up what he had eaten and grew thin, he would never be able to leave and would never see his father again. This story is for one who covets the wealth of others but who eventually loses what he gains.

Like other writers and collectors of fables in the Middle Ages, Berechiah attached an epimythia, a brief concluding passage which made explicit the fable's moral application.

This custom of using fables specifically for didactic purposes became in the Middle Ages part of the fable tradition. Fables were used by medieval preachers as exempla, to illustrate Scriptural or doctrinal points and to portray moral and immoral behavior. Such churchmen as Jacques de Vitry, who included fables in his collection of exempla, and Odo of Cheriton, who collected fables specifically to be used in sermons, helped to popularize the moralization of fables. As a consequence, the fables possessed today almost uniformly have a moral attached.

In addition to being used by medieval preachers as exempla and by medieval teachers as exercises in language and composition, fables were used by medieval poets for both didactic and aesthetic ends. Geoffrey Chaucer, writing in the last half of the fourteenth century, immortalized in "The Nun's Priest's Tale" the fable of Chauntecleer, the proud cock who lets himself be tricked and captured by the fox, but who then in turn tricks the fox into permitting him to escape. This same fable was also used by Robert Henryson, a Scots poet working approximately a century later, who reworked a number of well-known tales for his volume of *Morall Fables of Esope* (1621). In Henryson's hands the fable was a vehicle not only to point out a moral but also to convey social and political commentary. Typical of Henryson's treatment of the genre is his fable of the sheep and the dog:

A dog who is poor falsely claims before the ecclesiastical court that a sheep owes him a loaf of bread. The court, composed of the sheep's natural enemies, is presided over by a wolf as judge. Although the sheep makes a noble defense, pointing out the prejudicial atmosphere and the unfairness of the court, he loses the case and must sell his wool to pay the dog.

The *Moralitas* which follows explains the fable's allegorical significance: the poor shivering sheep is like simple folk who are oppressed on all sides but who suffer particularly from the corruption in the civil and ecclesiastical courts. The sheep plaintively asks God why He sleeps so long and permits such evil to go unchecked in the world. The large part which the *Moralitas* plays in Henryson's fables is evident in such poems as this, wherein Henryson devotes sixteen stanzas to the fable itself and nine stanzas to the explanation of the moral. Henryson's collection of thirteen fables, to which are appended such extended *Moralitates*, perhaps develops to its poetic extreme the convention of the epimythia.

Working at approximately the same time as Henryson in the fifteenth century was Heinrich Steinhöwel, who, using the prose *Romulus* collection, published a reworking of the Aesopic fables around 1480. Steinhöwel added to the fables promythia, statements at the beginning of the fables concerning their moral purposes. It is believed that Steinhöwel's *Äsop*, or a French translation of Steinhöwel by Machaut, or both, were used by William Caxton when he began, in 1483, to print his *Aesop*, which was one of the first of the fable collections printed in English.

The Middle Ages was clearly one of the great periods of growth and popularity for the fable, a time during which the form was widely and successfully used for such diverse purposes as instruction and entertainment. The fable experienced similar major revivals of interest in the late seventeenth century and in the eighteenth century, when it was taken very seriously as a literary genre.

The seventeenth century revival of interest in the fable was due in large part to the work of the Frenchman Jean de La Fontaine, who published twelve books of fables between 1668 and 1694. He is perhaps more responsible than anyone else for moving the fable into the realm of poetry. Although he claimed to be unoriginal, to be merely translating and adapting from Aesop and Phaedrus, his originality was made manifest in the lyrical and dramatic verse with which he transformed his material. Followers of La Fontaine included such writers as John Gay and Robert Dodsley, the Spanish writer Tomás de Iriarte, the German writer C. F. Gellert, and Ivan Krylov, a Russian writer of the late eighteenth and early nineteenth centuries.

La Fontaine's innovative treatment of the genre did, however, provoke a counter movement. In response to what he perceived as La Fontaine's revolutionary and inappropriate poeticizing of the form, Gotthold Lessing, writing in Germany in the eighteenth century, initiated an opposing trend for fabulists. His intent, as indicated in his 1759 collection, *Fabeln*, was to return to the original conventions of the Aesopic fable, to make the fable not poetic but philosophical. His fables, accordingly, were short, simple, and pithy. An interesting example is that of the nightingale and the lark:

> What can be said to poets who go on flights above their readers' understanding? As the nightingale inquired of the lark, does one soar so high deliberately, so as not to be heard?

The controversy in the eighteenth century over the nature of the fable was of great interest to writers and critics; in contrast to scholars of other times who dismissed the form as suitable primarily for the purposes of teaching and preaching, eighteenth century scholars considered the fable to possess genuine literary respectability. After this great flowering of interest, however, the fable fell into disuse as a literary form.

Nevertheless, in the twentieth century the genre may be experiencing a revival, or perhaps a rebirth in a new form; the work of such writers as Donald Barthelme, John Barth, Kurt Vonnegut, Jr., Jorge Luis Borges, and Gabriel García Márquez has been said to be, in various ways, akin to the fable. These writers may, however, be redefining the genre as they explore, through it, the notion of story. For the most part, fabulists prior to the twentieth century used the fable as a vehicle for transmitting a specific message and kept its form discrete. In contrast, some twentieth century writers of short fiction employ the fable not because of the form's didactic abilities but because of the form's magical essence—its enchantment as an older form of story. Such contemporary writers frequently blend the fable form directly into a narrative and do not, in consequence, make a clear definition between the two genres. In such works there often results a mix of the fantastic and the realistic; fabulous narrative elements which abrogate scientific laws are blended with firmly realistic narrative elements. Other contemporary writers, however, keeping the form of the fable discrete, include fable segments within a larger narrative framework; John Barth, for example, in a self-conscious use of the form, uses wisdom figures within a narrative to tell tales within tales, and García Márquez uses fablelike short-story elements within his narrative form.

While many contemporary writers of short fiction do not use the fable form didactically—Kurt Vonnegut, Jr., for example, seems to indicate that the moral is that there is no moral—other conscious fabulists such as James Thurber have deliberately sought a didactic end. Part of the appeal of Thurber's satire is that the form serves as a commentary upon the content; part of his fables' humor and irony depends upon his use of what many see as a childish form to convey sophisticated ideas. Consequently, in contrast to those contemporary writers of short fiction who use the fable to convey a nebulous worldview and who move into the fable's magical world as a retreat from the realistic world, Thurber is more in the tradition of Aesop in using the fable form purposefully to convey a sharply satiric commentary upon human behavior.

The tradition of the fable, then, persists in the twentieth century world, although in a seemingly changing form. Originally a "short story" which usually depended upon elements of narrative, drama, and dialogue, the form in its infancy used fantasy, usually in the shape of personified animals, to convey human reality. The form's roots were thus firmly located in the psychological desire to remove human truths to a simpler realm, specifically the world of animals. This desire to simplify and simultaneously mythify human experience is surely basic to much imaginative writing. At the same time, the early form of the fable was concise and pithy, readily engaging the mind and achieving the immediate effect of an understanding on one plane— that is, on the plane of the supernatural or the extraordinary—which could be transferred to and which would inform another plane—the plane of reality and human experience. The form's ability to achieve this immediate understanding made it perfectly suited to didactic ends.

In the twentieth century, however, except when used by such consciously traditional fabulists as Thurber, the fable seems to be changing in two important ways: one rarely sees a direct one-to-one correspondence wherein the fabulous world and the real world are juxtaposed, wherein a fictive creature reveals truth about real human beings; and similarly one rarely finds a direct moralization. Whereas the fable developed as an apologue, a fiction created to edify, in contemporary usage the fable has become primarily a device of fantasy, a fictional technique used to evoke a magical world. The contemporary fabulist, then, in refocusing the genre upon fantasy, uses the form for the effect of creating enchantment, thereby preserving and continuing one of the earliest purposes of the story.

Evelyn Newlyn

THE SAGA AND THÁTTR

The term "saga" (pl. "sögur") is Old Norse in origin and means "a saw" or "saying." After written language supplemented oral language in the North, the word "saga" was extended to include any kind of legend, story, tale, or history written in prose. As a literary term, "saga" refers more specifically to prose narratives written in medieval Iceland. The sagas are traditionally classified according to their subject matter. The main types of sagas are *Konungasögur* (Kings' Sagas), *Íslendingasögur* (Sagas of the Icelanders or Family Sagas), *Sturlunga saga* (Saga of the Sturlungs), *Byskupasögur* (Bishops' Sagas), *Fornaldarsögur* (Sagas of Past Times), *Riddarosögur* (Sagas of Chivalry), and *Lygisögur* (Lying Sagas). In general, Family Sagas and Kings' Sagas are of highest literary merit. Their excellence ranks them among the finest work of the European Middle Ages.

Closely associated with the saga in medieval Icelandic literature was the tháttr (pl. thættir), a shorter prose form which is related to the saga in roughly the same fashion as a short story is to a novel: the most evident difference between the two is length. Tháttr literally means "a single strand," as of rope. The Icelanders early extended this meaning metaphorically to refer to parts of written works. Episodes of narratives, chapters of histories, or sections of law were thus known as thættir. Icelandic short stories came to be called thættir because many of them are preserved as anecdotes or strands in sagas, particularly in the Kings' Sagas.

While the term "saga" has made its way into popular modern nomenclature as a label for an epiclike narrative, the word "tháttr" has no cognate descendant in English and has but recently been accorded attention as a genre with its own governing rules. The common habit of embedding short stories in the sagas suggests why the Icelandic thættir have either been overlooked or absorbed into a general discussion of saga literature. Enough versions of single stories exist both as separate manuscripts and as episodes in the sagas to indicate that the stories had a recognizable identity of their own, more or less independent of the host texts. Genre distinctions in medieval Icelandic writing were not particularly definitive. Terms such as "frásaga" (story, narrative), "æfentyri" (adventurous exploits), and "hlut" (part) mingle with "saga" and "tháttr" as reference terms in the literature. On occasion a narrative referred to in one place as a tháttr is called a saga in another. Although more sophisticated and telling differences between saga and tháttr were established through practice of the arts, the boundary between stories and sagas remained fluid.

Evidence of the strong ties and shifting boundaries between the saga and tháttr forms has provoked ongoing speculation about the original relationship between the two. The once-held belief that tháttr were oral tales recorded by scribes and then linked into sagas has been discarded. Sagas and thættir represent a sophisticated confluence of numerous sources both written and oral, and are dependent as well on the genius of their individual authors. While the origin of saga and tháttr writing is a matter of speculation, it can be said that the two are related emanations of the deeply rooted storytelling traditions of Northern Europe.

Storytelling, poetry recitation, and their descendant written forms have historically been the most favored of all arts in Scandinavia and particularly in Iceland. This affection for and mastery of the literary arts in Iceland has been attributed to strong urges of an emigrant culture to preserve knowledge of its European ancestral history. Medieval Icelandic manuscripts are the single preserve of certain heroic Germanic myths and tales which were part of a shared tradition of the Northern peoples. The old literature was lost in Germany and England, where Christianity arrived early. In Scandinavia, where Teutonic mythology and religion held sway for centuries longer (Sweden did not have a Christian bishop until the twelfth century), some of the old myths and stories were preserved, mainly in two Icelandic texts known as the *Eddas*. The *Poetic Edda* (ninth to twelfth century; English translation, 1923) contains heroic, didactic, and mythological poems which allude to events, legends, and beliefs of the Teutonic tribes. The *Prose Edda* (c. 1220; English translation, 1916) relates mythological and heroic stories of the pre-Christian North and provides an elaborate poetics for the poetry associated with the legends.

Medieval Icelanders had material as well as patriotic motives for their literary efforts. Those who note the preponderance of writing and the relative absence of other artistic endeavors in Iceland point out the lack of native materials necessary for practicing other arts.

Those who engaged themselves in such vigorous literary activity on a remote and rural island several hundred miles from the European mainland were by majority Norwegian emigrants who came to Iceland during the reign of Harald Fairhair. Harald's ambitious rise to power during the later decades of the ninth century clashed with the Norwegian landed gentry whose livelihoods and properties were threatened by the young monarch's expansion. Rather than suffer servitude or death many chose emigration westward. Various other causes, including hope for a better life and need to escape the law, brought more settlers.

From all accounts, the Icelanders were industrious and enterprising farmers, exceptionally literate and particularly skilled in self-government and law. Those who could argue the law and bring cases to just settlement were highly regarded. The Icelandic pioneers organized assemblies called "Things" which ruled the country by democratic process. They elected to their head not a monarch, but a lawspeaker, part of whose job it was to recite the entire body of law each three years. The first law of the land was a customary one, added to and refined at the annual assembly and passed by memory between generations. An old law formula recited in *Grettis Saga* (c. 1300; *The Saga of Grettir*, 1914) gives evidence that alliterative techniques aided in memorization and so rendered law into a poetry of sorts. This law system, suggested by district assemblies in Scandinavia, was unlike any other the world had known. Democratic assemblies ruled the entire country of Iceland for more than eight hundred years before such an idea began to infect Western history on a larger scale. Although the system was far from utopic in practice, it commanded the respect and loyalty of the people. Words were the recognized bond of the body democratic; they were to replace force as the *modus operandi* of government. Against this vision of rational and peaceable government struggled old revenge codes from the heroic tradition. Conflicts between law and violence and the law's frequent incapacity to stop violence became major themes in the Family Saga literature.

Christianity was adopted by assembly vote in the year 1000. One of the most important legacies of the new faith was the access its missionaries provided to written language. Icelanders quickly learned the Latin the churchmen brought and became familiar with its texts. They also put the new alphabet to most vigorous use in the practice of vernacular and sometimes secular literatures. Young Icelanders furthered their educations in Europe or at home. By the early twelfth century there were two bishoprics in Iceland, at Skalaholt and Holar. Both sees supported schools where chieftains sent their sons. At Holar, Icelandic farmboys learned Gregorian chant and Latin versification from a French clergyman. Class distinctions were few, thus allowing the new learning to spread rapidly.

Christianity, with its attendant teachings and written language, initiated Iceland into European traditions. Biblical lore and Christian ethics were added to the Icelanders' stock of old Germanic stories and myths without replacing the older literature. Confident of the value of their own history, Icelanders gave over their enlarged knowledge to the service of the stories of their own peoples. Possibilities for preservation became virtually unlimited. Stories, law, and history had found their harbor on vellum. Before the era closed, Iceland produced a prodigious amount of hagiography, historiography, homiletics, astronomy, grammars, laws, romances, and story, much of it in Icelandic.

The oldest manuscripts which are preserved in Iceland are from the twelfth century; the earliest text is thought to have been a legal code. Ari Thorgilsson (c. 1067-1148) is regarded as the father of Icelandic vernacular history. His *Libellus Islandorum*, commonly called *Íslendingabók* (c. 1120; *Book of the Icelanders*, 1930), comments on the settlement of Iceland, on exploration voyages to Greenland and Vinland (America), and on other important political data associated with the founding of the island republic. *Book of the Icelanders* well reflects the respect for historical data and interest in biography which continued to be evident in the later Kings' Sagas and Family Sagas; it is written in a style free from embellishment; it is sober and thorough but not without touches of human interest.

Of more central importance to the evolution of the distinctly literary sagas and thættir is *Landnámabók* (c. 1140; *Book of Settlements*, 1973), which was also first written in Ari Thorgilsson's time and is sometimes attributed to him. *Book of Settlements* is a rich depository of historical and legendary anecdotes about four hundred of Iceland's first settlers. The work documents land claims, describes farmsteads, and gives accounts of feuds, law cases, and marriages. It lavishes special care on genealogy, naming the pioneers' descendants and ancestors as fully as the author's knowledge allows. The author weaves dramatic incident and brief character sketches in with the more sober demographic and historical data. About Ingolf, who was Iceland's first settler, *Book of Settlements* reports that as soon as he saw Iceland he threw his high-seat pillars into the sea and made settlement where they landed.

Details of ordinary life, both comic and domestic, interlace the carefully prepared documentary. One section describes a dale named for a cow, and another tells about a man who lost his life in battle when his belt broke and his britches fell. In the *Thórdarbók* version of *Book of Settlements*, the author justifies his compilation, noting that civilized peoples are always eager "to know about the origins of their own society and the beginnings of their own race." Historians continued to expand and revise *Book of Settlements*, issuing it in various editions during the thirteenth and fourteenth centuries.

The first document to which the name "saga" is attached is the fragmentary *Oldest Olafs saga helga* (*St. Olaf's Saga*) from the late twelfth century. Although primarily a hagiographic account of King Olaf Haraldsson (St. Olaf, c. 995-1030), the saga does contain several thættir made lively by verbal exchanges. *St. Olaf's Saga* was likely composed at the Benedictine monastery in northern Iceland. Such monasteries carried on a wide range of literary activities, not all of them religious in nature. Translations of European histories were undertaken and biographies of kings were written with an eye to more than the kings' saintly virtues. Most of these early works are lost.

The popularity of sagas about kings is evidenced by the compilation of the *Morkinskinna* ("rotten skin") in c. 1220. *Morkinskinna* is a collection of biographies of eleventh and twelfth century Norwegian kings which incorporates thirty thættir, among them "Halldor Snorrason," "Ivar's Story," and the most famous tháttr, "Audun and the Bear," one of the most beautiful pilgrimage stories in world literature.

When the Icelandic biographers of kings set to documenting the lives of long dead Norwegian monarchs, they turned to the skaldic verse which celebrated their subjects. The fixity of the verse patterns and the conventionality of the kennings (elaborate metaphors) made the poetry a more reliable medium for accurate preservation of the kings' lives than oral tales.

Skaldic verse had its origins in Norway, but Icelanders became its greatest practitioners. Several of Iceland's pioneers were skalds, including the most famous of all skaldic poets, Egil Skallagrimsson, whose two beautiful poems, "Hö fudlausn" (*"Head Ransom"*) and *"Lament for My Sons,"* are centerpieces in *Egil's Saga* (c. 1220; English translation, 1960). Many Kings' Sagas are liberally interspersed with skaldic poems, but it would be a mistake in most cases to think of Kings' Sagas as merely prose expansion of the tighter verse forms. The numerous histories which grew out of the skaldic tradition seem to have directed attention to the art of biography for its own sake. These Kings' Sagas, especially those found in the *Morkinskinna* and *Flateyjarbók* manuscripts, are also host to dozens of thættir which feature as their subject a meeting between an Icelander and a Norwegian or Danish king. These short stories probably gave rise to techniques, characters, and themes more purely fictional than the histories which embody them. The subject matter of the thættir is not often traceable to skaldic verse.

Practitioners of skaldic poetry became favorite subjects for both saga and tháttr writers. A number of heroes of the great Family Sagas—Egil, Gisli, Grettir, and

Gunnlaug among them—are also famous poets. The Kings' Sagas contain many stories which feature a Norwegian king and his skald. Even heroes who are not poets can grace a scene with a skaldic verse when the occasion warrants.

Side by side with the newer written forms, stories continued to be recited; such performances also provided subject matter for the writer of sagas and thættir. In *Morkinskinna* is recorded the story of a young Icelander visiting a European court. It is Yuletide and the boy makes the court company merry each night with his stories. As Christmas draws near the boy's spirits fall, for his stock of stories is nearly spent. He tells King Harald he has but one final story, the story of Harald's own adventures abroad. The king is delighted by this unexpected attention and arranges it so the story lasts for the twelve nights of the festival.

Medieval Icelanders told stories about stories and stories about poems. They recorded poems about past events which were made into stories with poems embedded in them; they celebrated those who recited and wrote verse and tale. Clearly the literary arts and its practitioners were accorded a position of honor, and what the bards praised in their ancestors they put into practice themselves.

The medieval Icelander who has most clearly come to embody the Icelandic desire to preserve antiquarian literature is Snorri Sturluson (1179-1241), a historian and poet who simultaneously practiced the more pragmatic arts of law and diplomacy. Snorri's work is impressively diverse. He is the author of the so-called *Prose Edda*, which is a compendium of Germanic mythology, a catalogue of kennings and a poem of more than one hundred stanzas authored by Snorri. The poem is accompanied by a commentary on the stanzaic and metric forms of each verse. Other works attributed to Snorri include the masterful collection of Kings' Sagas known as *Heimskringla* (c. 1230-1235; English translation, 1964), one part of which is the distinguished *St. Olaf's Saga*. Snorri has been called the author of *Egil's Saga*, although that is a matter of conjecture.

During the thirteenth century, the powerful Sturluson family dominated Icelandic political affairs. Snorri undertook diplomatic missions to Norway and was powerful in Icelandic politics, serving twelve years as Lawspeaker. His talents as historian, literary critic, antiquarian, sagaman, and poet rank him as the most prominent literary figure of his age. He was also an influential and wily chieftain who was deeply involved in the internecine struggles of the day and who was neglectful of family obligations. It was his own estranged son-in-law who, leading sixty men, murdered Snorri from ambush in response to an order from the Norwegian king.

This incident serves to point up the state of general lawlessness which plagued the Icelandic Republic in the thirteenth century. (The Saga of the Sturlungs gives lurid account of these days.) While the old democratic system of assembly rule had never matched in practice what it held in theory, legend at least had it that for several generations the country was, for the most part, at peace. The prestigious assemblies had continued to function, and respect for the law had kept violent family feuds from turning into general lawlessness. By the first decades of the thirteenth century, however, Iceland's political and social life had become a welter of competing factions. The Norwegian crown, the assemblies, and the church bishops vied to impose a gaggle of rules and counterrules. The lines of authority were so indistinct that no group hesitated to use force to advance its position.

It was during these last chaotic days of the Icelandic Republic (Norway assumed jurisdiction over the country in 1262) that the most sophisticated of all the sagas, the Family Sagas, were written. These Sagas of Icelanders owe important debts to the centuries of interest in law, history, and kings' lives which preceded them. Yet the blend of national history, genealogy, local legend, and character anecdote gathered into stories with structures and aesthetic values of their own is quite unlike earlier sagas or Continental literature of the same period.

Nowhere else in Europe (excluding the British Isles) had prose been adopted for such clearly literary purposes: the medium of the Continent's literature was still verse, and the subject matter was heroic and traditional when it did not take up prevailing Christian motifs. In Europe, the thirteenth century was the age of scholasticism, and its literature was written mainly under the inspiration of the Christian faith. Dante's *La divina commedia* (c. 1320; *The Divine Comedy*, 1802) stands as the age's crowning achievement.

The Icelanders knew the heroic tradition well. This hoard of common experience, which found voice in works as diverse as *Beowulf* (c. 1000), the *Poetic Edda*, and *The Nibelungenlied* (c. 1200; English translation, 1970-1971), was kept alive mainly by Icelanders. Nor were the Icelanders unaffected by the Christian literature or courtly romance. Thomas of Brittany's *Tristan* (c. 1160) was translated into Old Norse as *Tristrams saga ok Ísöndar* in 1226, and numerous other translations followed.

Such material engaged the imaginations of the Family Saga writers and supplied them with a storehouse of conventional stories, cosmological schemes, and codes of heroic behavior, but the subject matter and the ethos of the Family Sagas spring from a native source. Sagamen took their ancestors' history and their own knowledge of the Icelandic landscape and transformed the Icelandic experience into narratives and stories which, in retrospect, read remarkably like novels and short stories. The high literary merit of the Family Sagas has made them widely known outside of Iceland and linked the name "saga" with their particular subject matter. The more than one hundred and twenty sagas and þættir thought to have been written during the thirteenth century provide a remarkable fictional portrait of the tenth and the first third of the eleventh centuries. The sagamen rendered their histories in human terms. They were interested in individual men and women and the drama their lives provoked. By aesthetically arranging these incidents, which often range over a century and involve scores of characters, the sagamen aroused interest in the moral dimensions of their ancestors' acts and the larger questions which they raised about human destiny in general.

The saga writer's techniques are those which are often associated with modern realistic fiction. Verisimilitude is of primary importance. Characters are not drawn as types but are faithful portraits of individuals. Characters speak as people do to one another and are revealed through action. Description is minimal and lyrical effusion is absent. The imagery is spare, homely, and solid, free of affectation and exaggeration.

Presumably the authors of the Family Sagas did not have in mind a literary experiment when they wrote their stories. More likely they sought to reduplicate the actual features of life as they thought it had existed for their ancestors and as they had come to know it. For a long time it was thought that the sagas provided reasonably accurate histories of the Icelandic pioneers and their descendants. Research conducted in the past thirty years, however, has shown that the sagas are not reliable as histories nor as indices to local geography, although they take historical events and lives of historical persons as their subject. It is far more accurate to describe the sagas as well-composed fiction. The manner of presentation is the historian's but the effect is literary. Pertinent genealogies are recorded, local customs explained, and place names accounted for as the stories unfold. Use of the authorial "I" is almost totally absent, and point of view is established by selection of detail and juxtaposition of scenes rather than by interpretive commentary.

Saga language also suggests the historian's objective tone. Concrete nouns are its hallmark. Verbs tend to be generalized and clauses strung loosely by means of parataxis. Interpretive adverbs and adjectives are avoided, and, when employed, they are determining rather than descriptive. Descriptions of landscapes or of persons are consequential. If a river is filled with floating chunks of ice, someone will surely jump from one to another or swim between them. When fantastic elements or dreams break into a realistic account, verisimilitude is not lost. For example, the same language is employed in *Grettis Saga* when the monster Glam attacks Grettir as when the opponent is human or the scene less dramatic.

Language spoken in the Family Saga is terse and laconic. It is never rhetorical or stylized. Dialogue typically occurs at dramatic moments and so increases tension and reveals character. Forceful and felicitous language is accorded the highest respect: lawspeaker, poet, and wit have the day. To die with a quip on one's lips is a measure of heroic stature. Vesteinn dies complimenting his assailant on his effective blow and Attli falls noting that "broad spears are becoming fashionable nowadays."

Family Sagas tend to be episodic. Individual scenes begin and end in rest. They are related to one another by movement through time as well as by cause and effect patterns generated by the action. Characteristically a saga closes decades or even centuries after it begins, and this remorseless passage of time is often associated with fate. The saga's episodic structure attains its unity through juxtaposition and symmetry among its lesser parts. Reliance on techniques of short fiction is apparent: the scene is the basic unit of the Family Saga, and the larger effects of the narrative rely on the successful realization of each scene and the arrangement of those scenes.

Although bound into a close family by the commonality of the Icelandic historical milieu and shared method of construction, the Family Sagas support a range of character types and thematic interests broader than other medieval literatures. *Laxdœla Saga* (c. 1200; English translation, 1899) has as a main theme the decline of the generous habits which prevailed during the pioneer generations. Unn the Deep Minded, who gave wise counsel until the day of her death, is mother of the Laxdaela clan and emblem of pioneer largesse. _Laxdæla Saga_'s central story is of the imperious Gudrun who forces her third husband to kill Kjartan, her former lover and her husband's cousin. Kjartan is a hero in the old tradition and also one of the first to practice Christianity in Iceland. His death ushers in a more violent era; Gudrun takes control and sets off revenge killings which disrupt the entire district. Peace is finally won, but in an atmosphere less luminous and expectant than that of the pioneer age. _Eyrbggja Saga_ (c. 1200) also has a district's history as its subject and shares some characters with _Gísla Saga Súrssonar_ (c. 1200; _The Saga of Gisli_, 1963). The powerful Snorri godi, known for his strength and wiliness in a number of sagas, figures in many scenes, and his attempts to advance his career by means of shrewd planning and outright trickery provide focus in the otherwise diffuse history of the Snaefelsness region. _Eyrbggja Saga_'s author had a strong antiquarian interest. Hauntings and old religious rites figure prominently in the saga. Strict adherence to the heathen viewpoint does not admit the romantic and heraldic details which decorate the latter half of _Laxdæla Saga_.

Several of the finest sagas are biographies. _Egil's Saga_ preludes the story of the famous warrior-poet with a long and well-wrought section about Egil's father, grandfather, and uncle and their conflicts and alliances with Harald Fairhair. Egil himself is portrayed as a Viking with a lusty appetite for brawling and ransacking. He has a series of confrontations with European royalty, managing in the most extreme situation to save himself from Eirik Bloodaxe's wrath by composing and reciting a poem in praise of the king. In his mature years, Egil settles in Iceland and is one of the few saga heroes to die of old age. In his last years Egil becomes old and blind and is mocked by servants, but his contrariness exerts itself to the last. He takes his treasure and buries it without a trace.

The Saga of Gisli and _Grettis Saga_ are biographies of Iceland's two great outlaws. Both heroes are poets. Gisli is a man obsessed by the desire to protect family honor; he kills his sister's husband to avenge the killing of his wife's brother. He is found out and outlawed, and his enemies pursue him and drive him to take up undignified poses and disguises to save his life. He is also terrorized by bloody, prophetic dreams which appear in the saga as verses given him by dream women, one bright and one dark. Gisli makes brave defense and is portrayed as a far greater man than those with whom he does battle. _The Saga of Gisli_ distinguishes itself by its intensely concentrated telling. A foreboding and tragic tone sounds throughout.

Grettir's outlawry is longer and less ominous than Gisli's. Like Egil, Grettir is a precocious and taciturn child. After a brilliant youthful career as a land-cleanser, Grettir's great strength is arrested by a curse placed on him by the monster Glam. The battle scene between Grettir and Glam is one of the finest in saga literature. The reckless young hero hears how Glam has ravaged the Vatnsdale district and is anxious to test his strength against such an opponent. He is warned from such opportunism but he pays no heed. Grettir defeats Glam but is cursed by the dying monster to a life of fear and solitude. Grettir's outlawry, which follows this battle, is the result of a false charge. He is eventually forced into the interior of the island where he lives as a solitary, fending off those who come to kill him for bounty. Despite his perilous situation, Grettir becomes a gentler and more dignified man during his nineteen years of outlawry. He dies a tragic death, but the saga ends with the lucky adventures of Grettir's half-brother, which are presented in the "Spés tháttr."

Njál's Saga (c. 1300; *The Story of Burnt Njal*, 1861) is called the greatest of all the Family Sagas. It encompasses the two biographies of Gunnar of Hlidarendi and Njal, which are followed by the story of Kari's vengeance. This intricately designed triptych is woven into a whole by the author's imaginative grasp of every feature of his narrative. Gunnar lives his life within the framework of the old heroic code, but he is not a lucky man. He arouses the envy of lesser men and has a wife who steals. He is unable to stop a chain of events which leads him to kill three members of the same family, a situation which Njal has predicted will lead to his death. Gunnar is hunted down and murdered in his own house, a victim of lesser men. His wife, Hallgerd, a sinister force in the saga, betrays him. Gunnar's friend and mentor, Njal, is a lawyer and a prophet of sorts who devotes his life to an attempt to replace the old revenge codes with justice and law. His attempts are insightful and trusting but finally fruitless. His own sons kill Njal's foster son, and after other violent developments, Njal and his family are burned in their house by Flosi. Njal's son-in-law Kari takes revenge. Reconciliation is finally achieved after Kari and Flosi are both absolved in Rome. The reconciliation is confirmed when Kari marries Flosi's niece, the young woman who instigated the burning of Njal. On a larger plane this saga takes as its subject the upheaval and redefinition of values associated with the coming of Christianity to Iceland. Njal himself has certain characteristics of the Christian martyr. *Laxdæla Saga* and *Grettis Saga* contemplate this same theme from different points of view.

The great age of Family Saga writing seems to have ended about 1300, a time just postdating the passing of the Icelandic Republic into Norwegian control. Of the major Family Sagas only *Grettis Saga* is thought to have been written later. Authors of the later era turned their attention to mythic and heroic themes drawn from the Germanic heritage. They wrote what are known as Sagas of Past Times, which have as their subjects fantastic, heroic, and supernatural events of the remote past.

The most notable of the Sagas of Past Times is the *Völsunga Saga* (c. 1200-1300; *Saga of the Volsungs*, 1965), which opens by recounting the earliest days of the tribe of the Völsungs. The flower of the clan is Sigurd, the most popular of all Northern heroes. Sigurd kills the dragon Fafnir and comes into possession of the Nibelungen wealth. Later he is betrothed to the Valkyrie Brynhild, but the affair comes to tragedy when Sigurd, under a witch's spell, forgets Brynhild and marries another woman. Brynhild is married into the same family and eventually urges her husband to kill Sigurd. When the deed has been accomplished, Brynhild throws herself on Sigurd's funeral pyre. The remainder of the saga follows the life of Sigurd's widow, Gudrun, and the revenge killings her children carry out. Stories and characters of the *Völsunga Saga* are common to all Germanic peoples; *The Nibelungenlied* is based on the same tales which also form the basis for Wagner's Ring cycle.

The author of the *Völsunga Saga* relied heavily on the eddic poems which include all the elements of his story. The prose in *Völsunga Saga* is notably passionless and lacks the verisimilitude which the solid presence of the Icelandic landscape and historical personages gave to the Family Sagas. The Sagas of Past Times in general do not retain the high literary standards of their predecessors, although sagas such as *Ragnar Lodbrook's Saga*, *Orvar Odd's Saga*, and *Hrolf Kraki's Saga* are popular as swashbuckling adventure stories. Icelandic romances of chivalry (*Riddarasögur*) and the fairy tale or Lying Sagas (*Lygisögur*), which were based on foreign models, captured the interest of fourteenth and fifteenth century writers. These outlandish adventures are written in an ornate and verbose style. The day of the Family Saga had passed; although Family Sagas were collected and copied during the fourteenth and fifteenth centuries, and were doubtlessly read, they were no longer written.

Away from the European mainstream, Icelandic writers created a literature of psychological realism worthy of comparison to nineteenth and twentieth century fiction. At the same time, the Family Sagas found a unique place within the humanistic tradition of the Middle Ages. Sagamen were, of course, Christian. The importance of an individual life, the emphasis on selflessness, forbearance, and conciliation as well as other Christian values exert quiet force when they appear as qualities of fine men and women, whether they are pagan or Christian. The pagan heroic code, with its stringent and violent demands, comes to clash with these gentler ideas. Such conflicts may be within an individual, between family members, or argued in the courts. Whatever the dramatic forum, the importance of the immediate conflict is never sacrificed to point up an abstract principle. Family Sagas are primarily good stories well told. The best of them retain allegiance to district history and genealogy without allowing antiquarian interests or Christian creed to obscure their aesthetic designs.

The Family Sagas number around thirty-five and are anonymous. They vary in length from a few pages to more than four hundred. *Njál's Saga* is the longest, and both *Egil's Saga* and *Grettis Saga* are more than three hundred pages long. Most of the longer sagas deal with heroes and families in the Northern and Western regions of Iceland. *Njál's Saga* is set in the South. The sagas which are set in Eastern Iceland are fewer in number and they are shorter. Among them are two fine sagas, *The Vapnfjord Men* and *Hrafnkel's Saga* (c. 1200; English translation, 1935). *The Vapnfjord Men* is the story of a friendship between two brothers-in-law which disintegrates when they are alienated by a Norwegian merchant and quarrel over a box of silver. After one friend casts off his sick wife, who is the other friend's sister, a feud opens and continues into a second generation. Reconciliation is achieved only after a young man kills his best-loved uncle in answer to an earlier killing. Half-hearted battles between the inheritors of the quarrel convince them that it is more honorable to end the fighting.

Hrafnkel's Saga is a masterpiece of short fiction. It relates the story of the precocious son of an Icelandic pioneer who rises quickly to district prominence. Hrafnkel kills his shepherd for riding his horse and is brought to trial by the shepherd's family. Judgment is passed against Hrafnkel, and he loses his wealth and is tortured at the confiscation trial. Later, after abandoning his heathen practices, Hrafnkel rises again to district renown. He takes revenge on his opponents by killing an innocent man, and this time there is no retort. Hrafnkel remains in control and enjoys great prestige. The saga makes exceptionally fine use of landscape features to forward its plot, and the dialogues spoken at the National Assembly are among the best in Family Saga literature. Characters in this tightly woven saga are finely and individually drawn.

Short sagas stand midway between the saga and the tháttr genres. *Hrafnkel's Saga*, for example, is a saga, although in the main it tells a single strand story. In English collections it is often placed among Icelandic stories. At thirty-five pages, it is longer than a tháttr and much shorter than the generational sagas. Such commonality of subject matter and similarity of technique do bind saga and tháttr and might well indicate that they are shorter or longer redactions of the same prose form. As noted earlier, boundaries between saga and tháttr are not explicit. Despite the wide common ground, however, certain provinces belonging only to the tháttr reveal its closer affinities to the modern short story.

One hundred short stories are usually named as thættir. Approximately forty-five of these fall into a group which features an Icelander as protagonist, and among this group are the most distinguished of the stories. Tháttr length runs from a single page to about twenty-five pages, the average being between ten and twelve standard printed pages.

While the Family Sagas typically take as heroes famous men or families, the thættir usually choose a common man. Thættir about Icelandic farmers cluster around the lives of saints, historic heroes, folklore heroes, or kings. By far the most popular subject matter is the Icelander who travels to the court of a European king; these thættir outnumber all others by approximately five to one. Such a predominance of one sort of short story may be an accident of preservation, but it is more likely that the Kings' Sagas, which host them, provided a kind of yeast for the development of such short stories. One suspects they are fictional and imaginative, even fanciful outgrowths associated with the serious business of relating kings' biographies.

A tháttr tends to focus on a single character. At first the hero may appear to be a fool, who later proves himself to be inventive and insightful. Many tháttr heroes are poets, and some are simple, anonymous travelers. These protagonists are usually young men strayed away from home, equipped with a native wit or goodness which is hidden under an offhanded ingenuousness. In a typical tháttr of the King and Icelander type, the Icelander speaks with one or more monarchs, often alienates himself in the initial meeting, and leaves court intent on proving his true worth to the king. The moments of recognition and reconciliation tend to be complimentary to both king and Icelander; a spirit of equality unites the common man from the North with the powerful monarch. The effect is clearly patriotic, revealing the pride the Icelanders took in the most ordinary among their ancestors.

Hreidar the Fool is one such story. Hreidar is the younger of two brothers and said to be barely able to care for himself, but it is apparent almost immediately that he is a very canny fool. Hreidar traps his brother into taking him abroad with him, where he manages to meet King Magnus. Magnus is charmed by his eccentricity and invites Hreidar and his brother to stay at court. The king predicts that Hreidar will lose his even temper and learn to be clever with his hands.

When he is rudely teased by some of King Harald's men, Hreidar does lose his temper and kills a man. He seeks asylum with an upland farmer, and while in hiding, tries his hand at metalsmithing. When Harald and his men arrive to capture Hreidar, he is well enough hidden to escape detection. He is willing to risk his life for a joke, however, and bursts into Harald's presence handing him a gilded silver pig he has made. Before Harald realizes the pig is an insult, Hreidar races away and returns to King Magnus, for whom he recites a poem and is rewarded with an island. Hreidar gives the island back at Magnus' suggestion and returns to Iceland where, as the text says, he put aside his foolishness and became a successful farmer.

In brief, the lowly Icelander has his way with everyone. His foolish cleverness reveals Harald to be a harsh and tempestuous man and Magnus to be a good ruler and counselor. For his own part, Hreidar has an entertaining series of adventures and returns home a wise and more mature man.

The tone in such a story is noticeably lighter than in the Family Sagas. Thættir are infused with the optimistic outlook of the Christian Middle Ages, in contrast to the Family Sagas, whose scope tends to be epic and serious. While there are many comic moments in the Family Sagas, the burden of bringing alive the ethos of an age imposes epic obligations on an author. The tháttr writer is free from such weighty obligations. While a character like Hreidar shares nobility of spirit with a saga hero like Hrafnkel, the tháttr author is not burdened with the long-term consequences of his hero's deeds except in the most general way. The tháttr writer, for example, need not confront his hero's death. The tháttr form may well have encouraged writing stories which were more fictional than historical. The interchange between Icelander and king typically has far more moral and psychological consequence than historical importance. Ivar in *Ivar's Story* is an Icelandic poet residing at the court of King Eystein. Ivar asks his brother to tell Oddney back in Iceland that he wishes to marry her. Ivar's brother does not deliver the message; instead he marries Oddney himself. Ivar hears the news and becomes downcast. The King cannot understand his sorrow and calls Ivar to him and offers him land, gifts, and other women, but Ivar is not solaced. The King can think of nothing else to offer except his companionship. Ivar accepts Eystein's offer of friendship. Each day before the tables are cleared, Ivar joins the King and speaks of Oddney to his heart's content. Soon the poet's happiness returns and he remains with King Eystein.

The tháttr writer seems to have enjoyed a greater imaginative freedom because he was not bound to make aesthetic sense of a vast amount of time. Since he wrote about a moment often unmarked in history and about an Icelander whose life was not particularly noteworthy, he could turn his attention to the creation of a fictional environment. The thættir are not analyses of historical deeds whose consequences are national in scope; they are tributes to the characters of kings. The stories also celebrate the characters of common Icelanders who call forth the true natures of the kings they visit. Likely the Icelandic writers knew little about life in Norway or about its landscape, so focus tended to remain on character and dialogue, which were explored and exploited to the exclusion of other features. The thættir characters found themselves in realistic dilemmas and extricated themselves through dint of their imaginations, or, as in the famous case of Audun, by innocence and goodness. The story is called *Audun and the Bear.*

Audun is a Westfjord man of very modest means who gives all of his money for a Greenland bear which he wishes to present to King Svein of Denmark. When Audun lands in Norway, King Harald, having heard about the precious bear, invites Audun to court, hoping to buy it or have it given to him. In a graceful show of honesty and naïveté, Audun tells Harald he wishes to deliver the bear to Svein. Harald is so startled by the man's innocence that he sends him on his way even though Norway and Denmark are at war. Audun finally makes his way to Svein, but not without begging for food and selling half of the bear to do so. Svein is pleased and supplies Audun with silver for a pilgrimage to Rome. When Audun returns to Svein's court after his journey south, he is reduced to a beggar and the kings' men mock him. Svein recognizes Audun and richly rewards him, praising him as a man who knows how to care for his soul. Audun refuses a position in Svein's court in order to return to Iceland to care for his mother. On his way home, he visits once more with Harald and at the Norwegian monarch's request tells him about the gifts Svein has given him. Among those gifts is an arm ring which Svein has instructed Audun to keep unless he can give it to a great man to whom he was obligated. Audun gives the ring to Harald, because, as he says, Harald could have had his bear and his life but took neither. Audun sails back to Iceland and is considered a man of great luck. In the few scenes of this story, the tháttr author gathers peace, goodwill, generosity, and integrity around this modest Icelander, who, without consciousness, becomes a model of the medieval pilgrim.

The thættir as a group, although they are restricted in subject matter, tend to take the shape of modern short stories; they develop character swiftly and pointedly through action. They are dramatic rather than narrative. Genealogy is curtailed if it is used at all. The ominousness of fate and the burden of history are usually dispensed with. Language is terse and witty, often with a lightness appropriate to its subject.

During the fourteenth century, the themes of the Sagas of Past Times were also taken up by tháttr writers. These stories tend to lack the tension, the energy, and the comic juxtaposition of earlier thættir. The old patterns are visible but without the solidity that the stories of Icelanders in the kings' courts have. The setting shifts to prehistoric Europe and the plots often read as bawdy folktales. In the story *Gridr's Fosterling, Illugi* (c. 1300), for example, the young prince's playmate, Illugi, wins royal favor by killing a revenant and is allowed to accompany the prince on an ocean voyage. When Illugi swims to shore for fire to save the ship's crew from freezing, he wanders into the cave of an ogress who tests his courage before allowing him her daughter's favors. The monster is a queen under an evil spell. Illugi destroys the spell and marries the daughter. The queen marries the prince and all live happily ever after.

When this sort of subject matter replaced the realistic action and individual characters of the earlier thættir, the stories became less distinguishable as a genre and certainly less akin to modern fiction.

This shift in subject matter indicates a stronger bonding with the European literatures. The popularity of the adventure and the fantastic tale were prompted by the Continental interest in romance. Certain of the later thættir are strong and resemble the best *fabliaux*. The strongest stories of this group are usually reliant on historical matter and the learned tradition, as their predecessors were, rather than on folktale. "Spes Tháttr" which concludes *Grettis Saga*, is an example. Because of their optimistic character, thættir do have natural affinities to *fabliaux*, but the tháttr's strengths are particularly its own. The use of realistic characters, few and vividly dramatized scenes, vigorous dialogue, and definitive imagery give the medieval Icelandic short story a distinct place in the history of European short fiction.

Helen Menke

FORMS OF SHORT FICTION
IN THE EARLY MIDDLE AGES

The early Middle Ages (for the purposes of this discussion, c. 476-1050) represent a time of transition and readjustment from the declining Roman, classical era to a culture that more and more clearly defined itself as a new age in the West (medieval scholars considered themselves modern men). This period saw the gradual development of the romance languages from Vulgar Latin and, especially as social conditions stabilized in the late eighth and early ninth centuries, the development of an increasingly varied body of literary work.

It is only fair and necessary to assume literary continuity in this transitional time. The great Latin writers, Ovid for example, were recopied as well as imitated, and Latin versions of the fables of Aesop continued to be produced and read. There was, of course, a considerable body of oral fiction, but this study will be confined to such exemplars of short fiction that have survived in written form. It will be necessary, especially for the early centuries of the period, to abstract our exemplars from works that are not fictional per se. Many of the writings of the late classical and early Christian periods were grammatical or historical, and early Christian writings were primarily dogmatic treatises. Furthermore, the Church Fathers tended to distrust pagan literature even when their own writings betrayed their classical educations in every sentence, as an examination of the works of St. Jerome or St. Augustine easily shows. Later, although the Church was responsible for the suppression of much pagan literature, notably the Germanic heroic works, remnants of which survive in Old Icelandic (Old Norse) versions, the accommodation of the literary impulse to the Christian ethos would produce a significant body of hagiographical literature and, in the later Middle Ages, the various romance cycles in which the didactic element does not overwhelm real literary merit.

The *Etymologies* (622-623) of Isidore, Bishop of Seville, provides us a contemporary definition of story (*fabula*): story does not speak of things done (*res factae*) but of things created in speech (*res fictae de loquendo*). The emphasis in this study will be on the latter point, "things created," because even in historical or quasi-historical works, authors such as Pope St. Gregory the Great or Bishop Gregory of Tours would break the flow of their narratives to develop or expand upon a striking episode, making of it more a vignette than a mere recital of details. What one finds, in other words, are coherence of focus and intensity of presentation that make of such an episode a totality of intrinsic narrative interest. One looks for fictive *form* and not necessarily fictive *content*. The writer imposes his or her creative skill upon the incidents, factual or not, so that they become almost independent of the historical, narrative matrix in which they are found.

These early works of "short fiction" should possess as well the sharp, intense focus of the lyric or the *lai* as opposed to the broader scope and grander scale of the epic or extended romance. Most of the works considered in this study will range from 250 to 500 words, but length is less of a concern than focus, scale, or ambiance: *Beowulf* (early eighth century?) is not lengthy, but it fits the definition of epic very obviously when compared to the unity of conflict to be found in the late ninth century *Waltharius* or the Irish tale *The Exile of the Sons of Uisliu*, also written in the ninth century. These two works are better termed heroic lays or tales than epics. Other generic categories of short fiction include the vignette or anecdote, both of which tend not to be found independently from some larger narrative framework; the saint's life or miracle tale whether in verse or prose; and, at the end of our time period, the romantic tale, even when it still possesses a strong heroic or mythic content.

The period under discussion extends from A.D. 476, the date of the deposition of the last Roman emperor in the West, to c. 1050, a time when it was manifest that political and economical stability, along with an influx of new knowledge and the rise of the great cathedral schools, had led to the beginnings of the high Middle Ages. As chart 1 indicates (see end of essay), the historical events relevant for this study go back to 375, the death of Ermanaric, the Ostrogothic emperor whose deeds, filtered through the lost chronicle of Cassiodorus and its condensation written by Jordanes, figure in the Old Icelandic *Hamðismál* (tenth century; *Poem of Hamðir*, 1923). A similar process occurred with the stories of Attila the Hun and Theodoric the Ostrogoth as history was transmuted into heroic legends that spread from their places of origin near Rome or the Rhine as far west as Iceland.

As important to this study as historical personages are events marking the development of European national units, such as the Treaty of Verdun (843) that created France and Germany, and of the major European languages, such as the Strasbourg Oaths (842), which testify to the necessity of using both Old French and the Germanic dialects so that all witnesses of the proceedings might understand the oaths of peace between Charles the Bald and Louis the German. A history of literary development in the early Middle Ages is also a history of the development of the major European languages as tools of creative expression as well as of day-to-day communication. Indeed, for some time, many of the works to be discussed in this study were analyzed chiefly as linguistic monuments rather than as literary exemplars. Twentieth century studies, however, have repeatedly established their literary merits.

The chronological arrangement of chart 2 (see end of essay) illustrates the increasing variety of forms in the literature of the early Middle Ages as well as the linguistic variety that characterizes the latter part of the period. The apparent consistency of literary forms of the pre-Carolingian period is somewhat misleading since the vignettes and anecdotes found in the various works differ widely in content and presentation. Consider, for example, the Munderic episode in Gregory of Tours's *History of the Franks* (c. 575-594) and one of the dialogues from the first book of the *Dialogues* (c. 593) of Gregory the Great.

The story of Munderic is actually an episode in the reign of Thierry I (511-534), son of Clovis (466?-511). Munderic, a relative of Thierry I, revolts against his king, claiming that his blood makes him equally entitled to the throne. He gains followers and is besieged by Thierry I. His defense is strong enough that Thierry I resorts to guile, luring Munderic from his stronghold with false pledges of good faith and having him executed once he is vulnerable.

This episode has multiple functions in Gregory's narrative: it is one of the historical events he is bound to include in his work, but it is also one of a series of episodes portraying the ruthlessness and administrative ingenuity of Thierry I. Although Gregory deplores Thierry I's tactics, this attitude is mixed with some admiration for Thierry I's strength of character. Furthermore, the Munderic episode offers an opportunity for Gregory to exercise his skill as a storyteller. The events are not complicated, but the episode stands out because of Gregory's use of two motifs—good faith and bad faith—that are intensified by repetition. Munderic is a traitor, but he has a loyal following; Thierry I, the rightful ruler, does not hesitate to use deceit, and his envoy, Aregyselus, is able to persuade the strangely guileless Munderic that Thierry I will honor the oath sworn on the altar in his name. Aregyselus promptly betrays Munderic to Thierry I's forces and Munderic, finally aware of treachery, kills the messenger and dies, honorably defending himself. With no real description of his personality, one still can perceive a rather simple, straightforward man who is destroyed as much by his ambition as by the machinations of his opponent. The techniques of fiction, especially the coherence provided by the emphasis of two major motifs, elevate the episode from a mere sequence of events to the status of story.

The anecdotes of Gregory the Great are more easily identified as fiction because the narrator himself describes them as tales he has heard from others and will now relate to his interlocutor, Peter. One such story, found in book 1 of the *Dialogues*, is a conventional exemplum describing the powers of a holy man and the chastising of a thief. The latter has stolen vegetables from the monastery garden, so the prior commands a snake to guard the path. The thief, startled by the snake, tries to escape but finds himself entangled in the fence, hanging head downward. The prior dismisses the snake with a blessing and rebukes the thief, giving him the vegetables he had tried to steal.

Many scholars have commented on the naïveté Gregory shows toward these stories. He relates tale after tale, seeming to give critical acceptance to even the most preposterous. This may be, but Gregory saw as a function of the anecdote or exemplum the edification through pleasure of the least sophisticated of his audience. What appears to be naïveté, a quality one can ascribe to a politician and religious leader such as Gregory only with difficulty, is actually an absence of ironic overtones. The snake obeys a command made in the name of Christ; this is simply one of the conventions of the miracle tale. The miracle is the focus and *raison d'être* of the story and is the one element that cannot be called into question if the tale is to succeed.

The anecdotes and miracle stories told by Bede the Venerable in his *Ecclesiastical History of the English People* (731) are of a more sober variety than those of Gregory the Great. They are generally biographical, such as the story of Caedmon, and the forces of the miracles is on personal help—healing or the conferring of some special gift such as Caedmon's gift of song. A good example of Bede's narrative skill is his description of Caedmon's painful reluctance even to remain in the hall when others were drinking and singing lest he be required to sing; this realistic touch heightens the effect of the miraculous bestowal of musical talent. Likewise, Bede's usual narrative restraint enhances the effect of such stories as one comes upon them as gems in a plainer matrix.

Bede and Gregory have in common their use of hagiography as the controlling convention for the stories they incorporate into their works. With Paul the Deacon, readers return to the more secular, heroic cast of story that was observed in the work of Gregory of Tours. One much-praised episode, the story of Alboin, was reworked in various versions as late as the Elizabethan period. Alboin's career is developed at length in the first two books of Paul's *History of the Lombards* (after 787), but it is the story of his winning his weapons and a man's place in his society that deserves critical consideration. Alboin must receive his weapons from the king of a foreign nation, and the king he chooses, Turisind, is the father of a man Alboin has just killed. Turisind, mindful of the oath of peace extended to all guests, restrains his men, gives Alboin his weapons, and allows him to depart unharmed. It is the tension between Alboin's audacity and Turisind's honorable restraint that gives the episode its power. Paul allows the story to stand on its own merits, which are considerable, but in other instances such as the story of Lamisso, he feels free to comment if the details of the story strain the readers' credulity too much. His doubts and disclaimers appear as storyteller's asides which do not hamper the progress of the narrative; the asides do not prevent him from giving all the details of the story, however improbable.

To suggest that the most prominent literary monuments of the sixth through the eighth centuries were, for the most part, Latin secular histories that incorporated short tales rather misrepresents the fictive activity of that period. Much has been lost, for example, of stories in Old High German. It is also safe to assume oral versions for the stories that have been dated as eighth century or later. When stories are connected, however tenuously, with historical events, one can assume that some version of those events entered the storyteller's realm soon afterward. One of the best sets of examples involves the heroic tales concerning the Huns, the Burgundians, and the Goths; there is enough of the historical to tempt scholars to link each character with a historical personage and enough events that are patently contrary to established fact that one is forced to see the storyteller's hand and judgment at work.

The first example of the evolution of story from history concerns the death of the Ostrogothic ruler, Ermanaric, in 376, an event attested by a contemporary historian Ammianus Marcellinus and in the later histories of Jordanes and thus presumably in the lost history of Cassiodorus. Ermanaric had executed Sunnilda, the wife of a treacherous member of his following, having her torn apart or trampled by wild horses. Her brothers attempted to avenge her death but succeeded only in wounding Ermanaric so that he was permanently incapacitated. Later, this story becomes linked with the legends of the Nibelungs and the Völsungs and forms the background for the Old Icelandic *Hamðismál*. Gudrun, a well-known figure in the Nibelung and Völsung legends, urges her sons, Hamðir and Sþrli, to avenge the death of Svanhildr, their sister. As in the earlier account, the death of the sister is not part of the action of the story proper but forms a powerful motivation for her brothers. The *Hamðismál* departs from its sources in the introduction of Erpr, an illegitimate half-brother, killed by Hamðir and Sþrli when he offers, with taunting speeches, to accompany them. The brothers succeed in mutilating Jǫmunrekkr (Ermanaric) but they are destroyed by his men, realizing too late that, if they had allowed Erpr to assist them, they would have killed Jǫmunrekkr and survived the encounter. The focus of the lay has shifted from simple revenge to a tragedy of hubris and folly as the brothers' wrongful violence against Erpr destroys them. The *Hamðismál*, an excellent example of the stark narrative of the lays in the collection known as the *Poetic Edda*, is brief and tightly constructed, with no word or incident that is irrelevant to the plot. The author has as well a gift for understatement, especially in Sþrli's rebuke to Hamðir: "You'd have had a brave heart [Erpr's], Hamðir/ if you'd had a wise one:/ a man lacks much/ when he lacks a brain" (*Hamðismál*, stanza 27).

Ermanaric figures in several heroic tales such as the *Völsunga Saga* (c. 1200), the *Widsith* Old English (seventh century?), and the Old Icelandic *Þiðreks saga* (seventh century?). He is usually depicted in negative situations, although some versions of the Ermanaric stories show some sympathy for his plight. The *Þiðreks saga* links him, in a totally nonhistorical fashion, with another figure of history and legend, Theodoric the Ostrogoth, who was known in legend as Dietrich von Bern (Dietrich of Verona) and as Þiðrek. Theodoric's literary development is much more involved than that of Ermanaric; his fame as a conqueror and a ruler made him the focus of many legends. One of the earliest tales in which he figures, although not as a character, is one of the best, the fragmentary *Hildebrandslied* (c. 800), the only extant example of Old High German heroic tale.

Hildebrand, returning to Italy with Dietrich from exile, is confronted by the army of his enemy, Odoaker (Odovacar). The conflict is to be decided by a duel, and Hildebrand's opponent is his own son, Hadubrand, who had been a very young child when his father was exiled. Hildebrand identifies himself, but Hadubrand, convinced that Hildebrand had died long before, refuses to believe him. Hadubrand insists on fighting, even when his father begs him to reconsider. The poem breaks off but the outcome is certain to be tragic: either the father will kill the son as in the case of Rustum and Sohrab, or the son will kill the father as Oedipus does Laius. In fewer than seventy lines, however, the poet has presented an episode that is powerful and deeply moving—almost a drama since much of the poem is in dialogue. The two characters reveal their personalities in their speeches. Hadubrand is all adolescent pride and truculence; Hildebrand is desperate as he realizes the futility of his pleading, seeing that his paternal affection must yield before the demands of his honor as a warrior.

Although events in the *Hildebrandslied* can be located in the historical context of Theodoric's conflict with Odovacar, the poet has chosen the father-son conflict as the focus of his work and has even altered historical fact for the sake of his story. Theodoric defeated Odovacar; the latter did not drive him out of his kingdom. This nonhistorical detail is a kind of "name-dropping," a storyteller's device to attract and hold the attention of his hearers as he proceeds to tell a story of his own making. Furthermore, the motif of exile works well for the conflict in the *Hildebrandslied* and, in fact, becomes a part of the Theodoric legend. Theodoric's and Hildebrand's exile also allow the poet to allude to another character, Attila the Hun, with whom they presumably resided for a time.

The impact of Attila on Western civilization is undeniable, and the legends of the races he encountered attest to his impact on their fiction as well. The "Scourge of God" was also the benevolent patron of Walther in the ninth century *Waltharius* and received positive treatment as Etzel in the thirteenth century *The Nibelungenlied* (c. 1200). The negative portraits of Attila are to be found in the Old Icelandic tales of the Nibelungs and the Völsungs such as the *Atlakviða* (ninth century?; *Lay of Atli*, 1923). Later medieval stories would link him with the other legendary figures from the time of the migrations, making him the contemporary not only of Theodoric, born twenty years after his death, but also of Ermanaric, who lived and died long before Attila's time. These complexities are of less importance than the tales themselves, two of which, the *Waltharius* and the *Atlakviða*, will be discussed here.

The *Waltharius* contains the stuff of epic. Attila has taken hostages from three of the kingdoms he has encountered: Walther, a prince of Aquitaine; Hildegund, a Burgundian princess; and Hagen, a Frankish nobleman. The *Waltharius*, however, is not the story of war but of the ingenuity and martial prowess of Walther himself as he extricates himself from various dilemmas. Moreover, Walther is not an Odysseus; his struggles are with men, not with gods. He wishes only to free himself and Hildegund, his beloved, from the benevolent captivity of Attila, who considers him one of his best warriors. The lovers escape when Attila and his men are all intoxicated after a feast given by Walther. They reach the kingdom of the Franks only to be attacked by Gunther, the Frankish king who covets the treasure Walther has brought from his Hunnish captivity. Among Gunther's men is Hagen, who had escaped earlier from Attila. Hagen is forced by his allegiance to Gunther to join him in a two-against-one combat with Walther, who before this was his friend, but he rationalizes his acquiescence to Gunther's demand by means of the vengeance he must seek for a nephew killed by Walther during the battle. All three fighters survive the conflict, although Walther loses his right hand, Gunther loses a leg, and Hagen loses one eye; at the end, Walther mocks Hagen for joining Gunther against him.

The poet uses all the techniques of the epic—scholars have suggested the influence of Vergil's *Aeneid* (c. 29-19 B.C.)—while maintaining his focus on personal conflicts, especially that between Walther and Hagen. In this respect, the poet of the *Waltharius* resembles the poet of the *Hildebrandslied*. The great events and personages of the migrations and the fall of the Roman Empire are simply contest and background for the central conflicts of the tales. Both the *Hildebrandslied* and the *Waltharius* are heroic lays that achieve their narrative power by concentrated focus on potentially tragic confrontations.

In the *Atlakviða*, Attila is given the negative role which is more familiar to most readers. Gunther and Hagen appear as the brothers of Gudrun, the wife of Atli (Attila). Atli has persuaded the brothers to come to his court, and, once they are there, he tortures them to force from them the location of the great treasure of the Nibelungs. Hǫgni (Hagen) is killed, and Gunther eventually dies in a pit of snakes. Gudrun takes vengeance in Aeschylean fashion; she kills her sons by Atli and serves him their flesh. She then sets fire to the hall and all perish. The *Atlakviða* is as terse and stark as the other example of the Eddic lay, the *Hamðismál*. The poet attends to the basic matter of the conflicts—Atli's avarice, the heroic resistance of the brothers, and the total vengeance of Gudrun.

The tales of the Goths, the Burgundians, and the Huns are primarily interesting because of their literary style, which combines narrative simplicity with compelling, dramatic situations that in and of themselves serve the purposes of characterization. The other aspect of their importance involves the way in which important figures and events of history find their way into fictional narrative, a process much more complex than this study can indicate, but one which demonstrates the interaction between fact, tradition, and the creative impulse.

History and fable (or story) come together also in one of the major Old English heroic works, the *Battle of Maldon* (c. tenth century). The poem has been much admired for the clarity with which it illustrates both the glory and the tragedy of the heroic ethos in confrontation with the reality of war. Byrthnoth, the leader of an English troop, permits an invading party of Norwegians to cross, at low tide, a causeway that at any other time would be impassable. His heroic and hubristic generosity dooms him and his men in the subsequent battle. They die to a man, one of the last survivors rendering in epigrammatic fashion the code by and for which they lived and died: "Heart must be braver, courage the bolder/ Mood the stouter as our strength grows less!"

The *Battle of Maldon* exists for us without the opening lines, but the point at which the story begins is nevertheless lyrical in force: a young knight frees his falcon and this, the poet says, is a sign that he will not fail his leader; the poem maintains this elegiac note throughout. Scholars have established nearly all the details concerning the historicity of the battle, but it is the work of the poet—his skill in depicting Byrthnoth's *ofermoð*, hubris, and the dogged courage of his men—that makes the *Battle of Maldon* unequaled in tragic impact within its scope except by the *Hildebrandslied*.

An early passage in this study mentioned the accommodations that Christian literary sensibilities made to some of the modes of secular literature. The various hagiographical stories of the early Middle Ages are a good index to this accommodation. One might argue that the tales of saints and martyrs are not, strictly speaking, fiction, yet their narrative form quickly becomes standardized—miraculous birth, early piety, many miracles, much self-denial, fortitude under oppression, and painful martyrdom or blissful death—and, of greater significance, these tales participate in one of the major fictional modes, that of romance. No matter how gruesome the details of a martyrdom might be, the tale has, in the Christian context, the requisite "happy ending" of romance. The saint's life or miracle is yet another aspect of the wish fulfillment that underlies the mode of romance.

One must make distinctions among the various forms of medieval hagiography. The Old English *Andreas* (eighth century?) or the *Elene* (750-785), or the Irish *Voyage of St. Brendan* (ninth century, written in Latin), are quite different from such Old French works as the *Cantilena of St. Eulalia* (c. 880) sequence or the *Life of St. Alexis* (1040). The Old English tales have a strong heroic element and have a wider scope of action than the Old French tales. The *Voyage of St. Brendan* takes the form of a quest and has been linked with the Old Irish voyage tales (*Imramma*) such as the *Voyage of Bran* (seventh century) or the *Voyage of Maeldune* (seventh-ninth century). It is as much a tale of the wonders witnessed by St. Brendan and his companions as it is the story of a holy ascetic.

The *Voyage of St. Brendan* relates the quest of the abbot St. Brendan and several of his monks for a fabled "Promised Land of the Saints," an earthly Paradise. The journey is a series of encounters with strange creatures and enchanted places, but it is also a spiritual journey. Some scholars have argued that the various islands or sailing conditions, such as the Coagulated Sea (the Sargasso?), can be identified and that the *Voyage of St. Brendan* suggests actual journeys perhaps even to the Americas. This hint of possible veracity accounts in part for the popularity of the work all through the medieval period, but its popularity resulted as well from the writer's descriptions of the beautiful and the strange, from the way in which monastic spirituality is unified with the quest for marvels (centuries before the Old French *Quest of the Holy Grail*, 1225-1230), and from the person of St. Brendan himself. His calm faith sustains his monks through all of their fantastic adventures, and even the presence of a sea monster, the leviathan Jasconius, does not disrupt the tranquil tone of the work.

In contrast to the *Voyage of St. Brendan*, the spirituality and piety of the *Andreas* and the *Elene* seem more vigorous and active. Andreas (the apostle Andrew) must rescue his fellow-apostle Matthias from a race of cannibals. The poem graphically describes the torments suffered by Andreas once he rescues both Matthias and the youth of the cannibal race chosen to die in Matthias' stead. Among the best passages of the poem are those that describe Andreas' sea journeys with a mysterious boatman who catechizes him on matters of faith and who is, as Andreas slowly realizes, Christ himself. Andreas' role as deliverer and missionary crystallizes in the image of the water from the rock, a flood Andreas invokes to destroy his enemies. He relents so much as to pray for the resurrection of the youths of the cannibals, and, having converted them to Christianity, he departs. For all of his passivity, Andreas is a fighter, a thane of Christ, and a Moses figure. He is timid when first confronted with his task, but the dominant impression left by this heroic miracle tale is the forceful personality of its protagonist.

The same evaluation applies to Cynewulf's *Elene*, the story of the recovery of the

True Cross by St. Helena, mother of the emperor Constantine. Confronted by the obstinacy of the elders of Jerusalem, she incarcerates a wise man who is known to hold the key to the mystery of the rebel teacher executed in that city. The wise man, named, oddly enough, Judas, yields before Elene's harshness and reveals not only the identity of the rebel but also the place of His crucifixion. Only one of the crosses found there can resurrect a dead youth, and Elene claims it as the long-sought relic. Judas converts to the Christian faith and receives the name Cyriacus, and Elene returns to her son in a triumph of healing miracles.

The *Elene* and the *Andreas* have been described here as heroic miracle tales because they emphasize the power of their protagonists (and their protagonists' Patron). Andreas, although broken by torture, can nevertheless invoke an enemy-destroying miracle, and Elene uses the power of her imperial rank, usually a negative element, in the service of the Faith. Indeed, the *Elene*, from its first episode, the triumph granted Constantine by the sign of the Cross, deals with the *power* of the new Faith. This emphasis on militant Christianity is in marked contrast to the hagiographic narratives of the *Cantilena of St. Eulalia* and the *Life of St. Alexis.*

The *Cantilena of St. Eulalia* is the first literary monument of the French language. In addition to its linguistic significance it also attests to the adaptation of the liturgical sequence (an extended embellishment of a line of text) to the uses of lyric poetry. The poem is very brief and tells the story of Eulalia's martyrdom in the simplest manner. Eulalia, a young Christian noblewoman, refuses to give up her faith; brought before Maximian, she persists in her resistance and is given over to be burned. When the flames do not harm her, Maximian orders her beheaded. Her soul flies to heaven in the form of a dove.

For all its brevity, the *Cantilena of St. Eulalia* presents a complete dramatic action that builds in intensity from Eulalia's resistance through the torturing and martyrdom, and is resolved in her soul's flight. As stated above, this tale differs from the Old English tales here described in its emphasis not on Eulalia's active power but on her endurance and her helplessness to resist, physically at least, her tormentors. Also, the focus of the tale is on the personal rather than the social effects of the miracles.

The *Life of St. Alexis*, another early French monument, deals again with the struggles of an individual. Alexis, a wealthy young man, decides on his wedding night to reject all—wife, riches, and family—to devote himself to prayer and self-denial. After a lengthy self-exile, he returns to his home and lives, unrecognized by his family, as a poor holy-man under the staircase of his former home. His family only learns of his true identity by means of a letter that they find after his death. The poem ends proclaiming Alexis' joy in Heaven where he is reunited with his maiden bride. The *Life of St. Alexis* follows the conventions of the flight-from-the-world, which is one of the many varieties of saints' lives. Its compact narrative and careful handling of rhythm and assonance show the French language in the process of becoming one of the major literary languages of the West.

The saints' lives have been described as participating formally in the mode of romance in a period in which, for the most part, heroic tales dominated. The great age of medieval romance would begin in the early decades of the twelfth century, but as early as the ninth century and possibly even earlier, there were Celtic precursors to many of the major romances. The Irish *Exile of the Sons of Uisliu* has been linked with the development of the Tristan legend, and the *Wooing of Etain* (ninth century), also Irish, with the legend of Lancelot and Guinevere at least insofar as the abductions of Guinevere are concerned.

The *Exile of the Sons of Uisliu*, sometimes called the story of Deirdre, describes the fate of those sons of Uisliu who accompany Noisiu, their brother, into exile after he elopes with Deirdre, who has been promised to Conchobar, king of Ulster. The outcome is tragic for both lovers: Noisiu is treacherously slain, and Deirdre, who sings two poignant laments for her lover, later commits suicide rather than be given to one she despises. One can see the details that later became part of the Tristan story—the illicit love affair, the lovers' flight, and their tragic demise—but the work has its own inherent interest. One sympathizes with Deirdre, fated from before her birth to cause dissension among men, when she chooses Noisiu in defiance of the arrangement that makes her the property of the aging Conchobar. Likewise, Noisiu draws the reader's sympathy as he is taunted by Deirdre into accepting her, an act that seals his fate.

The *Wooing of Etain* is the story of how King Eochaid Airem wins Etain, a princess of the fairy-folk, loses her to her former mate who is also of Faery because of a rash boon, and regains her by besieging the fairy-mounds and eventually succeeding in the trials set before him there. This tale reappears in many guises, not only in the *Lancelot* (c. 1168) of Chrétien de Troyes but also in *Pwyll, Prince of Dyred*, one of the tales included in *The Mabinogion*, a group of Welsh tales dating from the very end of the period under discussion here. Like the *Exile of the Sons of Uisliu*, the *Wooing of Etain* is important as a good piece of fiction in its own right, from the lavish description of Etain with which it begins to the moment of surprise when Etain is magically abducted despite the hapless Eochaid's attempts to guard her.

In bringing together an extended discussion of the forms of short fiction in the Middle Ages, a danger exists of oversimplification or of a too-pat schematic view of diverse developments. The period of the early Middle Ages was an unsettled time. Necessary social and economic adjustments to the collapse of Roman domination in the West threatened the preservation of the classical tradition of education. The number of surviving works of fiction seems small beside the compendiums of rhetorical, historical, or doctrinal works, but at no time did the art of fiction lapse, certainly not as far as oral transmission and development was concerned, as the complicated history of the Goths, Burgundians, and their heroes clearly shows. Often, however, "story" was put to work in sermons or in histories without losing the essential crafted nature that sets a work of fiction apart from mere sequential reportage. Many of the independent stories never ceased to engage their audiences, and storytellers adapted them by retelling or forging ever more complex combinations of the tales, some with the range and scope, for example, of the Theodoric stories.

Although many of the gems of early medieval fiction remain buried in little-read histories or in collections primarily of interest to scholars, others, some of which have been discussed here, are now receiving the scholarly and critical attention they have deserved as literary works.

Amelia A. Rutledge

CHART I

Historical		Literary	
375	Death of Ermanaric	520	Cassiodorus' *History of the Goths* (lost)
435	Defeat of Gundaharius by the Huns	c. 591	Gregory of Tours's *History of the Franks*
451	Defeat of Attila by the Burgundians	c. 550	Jordanes' *Getica* (abbreviated version of Cassiodorus' work)
453	Death of Attila		
476	Odovacar king in Italy (deposition of the last Roman ruler)	593	Gregory the Great's *Dialogues*
		622-623	Isidore of Seville's *Etymologies*
493	Theodoric the Ostrogoth conquers Italy	731	Bede's *Ecclesiastical History of the English People*
		750-785	Cynewulf; *Elene*
			Andreas
		eighth century	
		after 787	Paul the Deacon's *History of the Lombards*
768-814	Reign of Charlemagne	c. 800	The *Hildebrandslied*
842	The Strasbourg Oaths	ninth century	Irish tales: *Exiles of the Sons of Uisliu; Wooing of Etain*
843	The Treaty of Verdun	c. 850-890?	The *Waltharius*

987	Hugh Capet crowned	c. 880	The *Cantilena of St. Eulalia*
		ninth and tenth centuries	Icelandic tales: *Atlakviða; Hamðismál*
991	The Battle of Maldon (poem composed soon afterwards)	tenth century	Welsh tales: *The Mabinogion*
		1040	The *Life of St. Alexis*

CHART II

Author	Work	Date	Language	Form
	PRE-CAROLINGIAN c. 500–750			
Cassiodorus	*History of the Goths* (lost)	520	Latin	History/Vignettes
Jordanes	*Getica*	c. 550	Latin	History/Vignettes
Gregory of Tours	*History of the Franks*	c. 575–594	Latin	History/Vignettes
Gregory the Great	*Dialogues*	593	Latin	History/Vignettes
Bede	*Ecclesiastical History*	731	Latin	History/Vignettes
Paul the Deacon	*History of the Lombards*	after 787	Latin	History/Vignettes

CHART II

Author	Work	Date	Language	Form
	CAROLINGIAN AND ANGLO-SAXON c. 750-1000			
Cynewulf	*Elene*	750-785	Old English	Heroic miracle-tale
	Andreas	eighth century	Old English	Heroic miracle-tale
	Hildebrandslied	c. 800	Old High German	Heroic verse-narrative
	Waltharius	late ninth century	Latin	Heroic verse-narrative
	Cantilena of St. Eulalia	c. 880	Old French	Verse hagiography
	Battle of Maldon	early tenth century	Old English	Heroic verse-narrative
	Life of St. Alexis	mid-tenth century	Old French	Verse hagiography
	CELTIC AND ICELANDIC c. 800-1050			
	Voyage of St. Brendan	ninth century	Latin	Prose hagiography
	Exile of the Sons of Uisliu and Wooing of Etain	ninth century	Old Irish	Heroic/romantic prose narrative
	Atlakviða; Hamðismál	ninth/tenth centuries?	Old Icelandic	Heroic verse-narrative
	The Mabinogion	tenth century?	Welsh	Heroic/romantic prose-narrative

THE ROMANCE FORM IN THE LATE MIDDLE AGES

The Middle Ages witnessed the flowering of one of the most important predecessors of the modern short story, the romance. By the late Middle Ages, this genre had become an extremely popular literary form. During the genre's inception in the eleventh century, the term "romance" referred exclusively to a composition written in French—a "Romance" language. During the literary history of the Middle Ages, however, the term came to denote a fictional narrative of a particular type: the romance focused upon love and/or adventure, but it relied on conventional plots to achieve this focus; it was daringly unrealistic in conception and frequently employed remote settings, but nevertheless strove for psychological realism; and it contained characters who were usually stylized but, by being types, were universal and therefore readily and uniquely understandable.

Although this sort of literature assumed a generic identity and acquired a defined form during the Middle Ages, it had its roots in much earlier tradition. Classical epics such as the *Odyssey* (c. 800 B.C.) and the *Aenied* (c. 29-19 B.C.); sagas such as *The Nibelungenlied* (c. 1200); *chansons de geste* such as *The Song of Roland* (c. 1100); and the early chronicle accounts of Arthur all contain the elements of love, mystery, adventure, and psychology that have now come to be associated with romance. These earlier works, however, differ from romance in being consciously nationalistic and either historical or pseudohistorical, whereas romance, even while striving for verisimilitude, is nevertheless consciously and deliberately fictional.

During the Middle Ages the romance became a distinct literary type in part because writers wished to free themselves from the restrictions of the epic form and in part because the developing interest in new themes and ideas required new modes of expression. The treatment accorded the story of Arthur, surely one of the most famous figures in English literature, well exemplifies the change in literary expression from epic to romance. Whereas the earliest accounts in which Arthur appears portray him as a historical hero who comes to assume national importance, by the time of the Middle Ages he has been transformed by courtly writers from a historical and national hero to a hero of romance. Apparently the first historian to mention Arthur is Nennius, whose ninth century *Historia Britonum*, a redaction of previous chronicles from the seventh and eighth centuries, describes Arthur as "the leader of battles" who slaughters many pagans, and notes Arthur's use of Mary's image to assist him in combat; Arthur is said to have singlehandedly slain 960 men in one day. A similar but much briefer account of Arthur's prowess in battle is found in the *Annales Cambriae*, the tenth century work of a Welsh writer who states that Arthur, having carried the cross of Christ on his shoulders for three days and three nights, was victorious in the Battle of Badon. Around 1125, William of Malmesbury, in his *Gesta Regum Anglorum* (*The Deeds of the Kings of the English*, 1847), attests Arthur's historicity while he simultaneously acknowledges that mythmaking concerning Arthur is taking place; he differentiates between the Arthur of truthful histories and the Arthur of false myths produced by the Bretons. In fact, the Arthurian legend expanded greatly during this time, both in England and on the Continent; with every crossing of the English Channel the legend accumulated more and more material, so that the actual historicity of Arthur became increasingly difficult to verify.

These historical and pseudohistorical accounts provided the basis for the more deliberately imaginative Arthurian writings, which are the major sources of contemporary Arthurian legendry and which begin to appear in the twelfth century. In that century there is a shift from treatment of Arthur as a historical figure to treatment of him as a figure of mythic proportion. Geoffrey of Monmouth's *Historia Regum Britanniae* (c. 1136; *The History of the Kings of Britain*, 1903) consciously builds upon the scant writings of Nennius to create a national hero for England; to do this Geoffrey added to Arthur's primary historical characterization as a fighter and a leader of warriors the coloration of chivalry, thus combining in his work, and in the figure of Arthur, both epic and courtly traditions. Geoffrey adds to the legend the descent of Arthur from Aeneas of Troy, the begetting of Arthur by Uther Pendragon, the figures of Merlin and Mordred, and the courtly entourage which was necessary in order to reshape Arthur from a local chieftain into a great king. Indications of courtliness are displayed in the notions that a woman could be an incentive for the knight to excel and that the knight's bravery and nobility could be an incentive for the woman to be pure.

This transformation of the Arthurian story from epic to romance was continued in Wace's *Roman de Brut* of 1155; Wace adds to the written legend the tradition of the Round Table, dramatizes the Arthurian story through the addition of dialogue and action, and portrays Arthur as more courtly and less barbaric, as possessing other than martial attributes and abilities. Layamon's *Brut*, written around 1200, makes further additions to the legend of an extraordinary and supernatural nature, such as the fays who nurture the infant Arthur and the mysterious ladies who take Arthur away to Avalon. As other writers drew upon and developed the Arthurian material, the story of Arthur, the national hero, eventually became merely a backdrop, or a departure point, for stories which focused on such corollary themes as the quest for the Holy Grail and on such other knights as Perceval, Lancelot, and Gawain. By the time *Sir Gawain and the Green Knight* was written late in the fourteenth century, Arthur had been completely transformed from the epic hero he had been at his inception to the chivalric hero of romance.

This transformation of Arthurian material represents only one reflection of that radical shift in literary interest from epic to romance which occurred in the Middle Ages. Prior to this time literary expression had taken the epic form of such works as the *Iliad* (c. 800 B.C.), the *Aeneid*, *Beowulf* (c. 1000), and *The Song of Roland*, works which had a national character and which presented a hero who represented national ideals and virtues. By the time of the twelfth century, however, it became evident that national traditions were no longer so clearly separate and distinct, that cultural interpenetration was causing traditions to blend, and in consequence that themes and ideas, and modes of expressing those themes and ideas, were held in common by writers of many nations.

In addition to the diminishing nationalism in literary themes, other trends also contributed to the maturing of the romance form in the Middle Ages. The genre's development was significantly aided by the infusion of material from classical sources, particularly such Latin works as Ovid's *Metamorphoses* (A.D. 2) and *Ars Amatoria* (c. 1 B.C.; *The Art of Love*, 1612), and of Celtic materials, many of which may have provided substance for the Arthurian legend. An additional influencing factor was the formation of a new perspective on women; in the Middle Ages women came to assume a position of greater importance in society than they had previously enjoyed, in part because of the popularity of the cult of the Virgin, which venerated Mary and through her all womankind, and in part because of the dissemination of chivalric and courtly ideals which similarly respected and exalted women. Although debate continues as to whether or not a "system" of courtly love was recognized as such in the Middle Ages, we do know for certain that courtly attitudes existed, that people aspired to courtly ideals, and that those courtly attitudes and ideals influenced people's conduct. In conjunction with, and perhaps as a result of, the cult of the Virgin, the courtly mystique elevated women to positions of morally and spiritually superior beings who could inspire admirers to transcend human limitations and rise to new heights of nobility; courtly love made a religion of male devotion to his lady, and courtly idealism demanded a high degree of civilized and sophisticated behavior in its adherents.

Medieval romance, then, can be seen to differ from epic—a term which includes saga and *chanson de geste*—in content, form of presentation, and emphasis. Whereas the epic usually concerns a serious subject of national importance and a warrior-hero whose actions have national implications, the romance often has a weak and insignificant plot which concerns a matter of personal importance, such as a love affair and its attendant problems or a chivalric adventure; the plot of the epic serves to reveal the hero's character and to establish his national importance, while the plot of the romance serves to reveal motivation, to delineate psychological processes and responses, and to explore intellectual and emotional dilemmas. Although many romances deal with the four "matters" of Rome, France, Britain, and England, which would lead one to believe they were historical in nature, their purpose was nevertheless primarily entertainment, and they often contained elements of the mysterious and the supernatural. Further contrasting the epic, which is usually sharply focused and unified, the romance is often of much looser structure; the plot is often episodic, and the episodes are both undeveloped and yet usually embellished by picturesque and detailed descriptions. Moreover, whereas the epic usually focuses on the character of the hero, the romance often relies upon stylized types or faintly drawn characterization, focusing instead on the hero's generally exaggerated adventures, which often lack real purpose. The romance hero fights for the sake of fighting, while the epic hero ordinarily fights only for a highly significant or exalted purpose. Finally, while the epic very often is tragic, ending with the hero's death, the romance frequently has a happy ending.

The courtly idealism so characteristic of the romance form during the Middle

Ages first appeared in members of the French aristocracy and in the poetry of the Troubadours and Trouvères. From France the courtly ideal spread to England, advanced in part by the enormously influential work of Andreas Capellanus. A chaplain to the French court, Capellanus, in the latter quarter of the twelfth century, codified the system of courtly love in his work *De Arte Honeste Amandi* (*The Art of Courtly Love*, 1941). The work's first two books define love, establish its rules, and detail the appropriate conduct for its devotees, while the third book, curiously, serves as a retraction which seems to contradict everything said before. The first two books, emphasizing the ennobling nature of passionate love, explain the incompatibility of love and marriage; in fact, Capellanus states that love has no place in marriage since love requires secrecy, jealousy, apprehension, and difficulty in attainment. Marriage is not, however, an excuse for not loving, but of course the beloved must be someone other than one's spouse. Capellanus also states that the lover's whole mind is on the beloved and, in consequence, the lover will suffer greatly, will exhibit paleness, and will experience sleeplessness, heart palpitations, and loss of appetite.

The influence of this codification of courtly love on medieval romance, on the later romance tradition, and indeed on Western society, is immeasurable, since the work of Capellanus is both descriptive in recording existing attitudes and prescriptive in establishing those attitudes as the ideal. The emotional concept which we now call "romantic love" is thus "born" during the Middle Ages, when love was separated from marriage; marriage, after all, was based on such things as property and politics and was therefore practical and mundane, whereas courtly love, as depicted by Capellanus, is spiritual and passionate. Thus, in its establishment of love as an ennobling social influence, in its systemization of the rules for the conduct of love, and in its development of the notion of feminine worth, the work of Capellanus influenced to a very great extent both literature and society. Many of the deepest patterns of behavior which today govern relations between the sexes have their genesis in the code which Capellanus describes.

If Capellanus provided a formulization of the rules of courtly behavior, two other French poets of the latter part of the twelfth century, Marie de France and Chrétien de Troyes, provided extremely influential artistic celebrations of the courtly system. The approximately fifteen extant lais which are attributed to Marie are all short, simple, and direct, and were probably intended to be sung to harp accompaniment; emphasizing love rather than warfare, the poems reflect courtly sentiment in their focus upon courtesy, chivalry, and loyalty in love. Typical of Marie's themes and treatments is the lai of "Lanval." In disfavor with his king, Lanval one day rides into the country; lying down to rest, he is approached by two beautiful maidens who take him to their lady in a nearby pavilion. The lady, obviously a supernatural being, gives Lanval her love and a bottomless purse but warns him that if he speaks of her to anyone he will never see her again. When Guinevere accuses Lanval of being false to his lord, of having secret sins, and of despising women, he defends himself by stating indignantly that in fact he has a lover and that the lowliest of her servants excels Queen Guinevere in every way. Denounced by Guinevere to Arthur, Lanval is directed to produce his lady and prove his statement but he is, of course, unable to summon her. Saved from prison only by the surety of his friends, he is about to be sentenced to exile when a procession of beautiful maidens arrives, the last of whom is Lanval's mistress. When Arthur agrees that she is indeed more beautiful than the queen, Lanval's supernatural lover takes him away with her to Avalon.

Marie claimed that her intent in her work was merely to turn traditional tales into romance, and clearly she uses in her lais many conventional topoi: the woman scorned motif draws upon the theme of Potiphar's wife; the idea of the supernatural lover comes either from Celtic fairy lore or from the classical myth of Cupid and Psyche; and the bottomless purse and the outcast who becomes favored above all are elements common in folktale. Marie has, however, imbued these thematic strands with the coloration of courtly love, so that the lai serves as an exemplum illustrating one of the courtly love tenets—the necessity of keeping love secret.

Chrétien de Troyes, also writing in the last half of the twelfth century, produced several romances for the French court. Of those five extant, the unfinished *Perceval* (c. 1180) is notable as a spiritual romance concerning the quest for the Holy Grail which was used by Wolfram von Eschenbach for his romance *Parzival* (c. 1200), and which inspired as well a number of later romances concerning the Grail legend; this romance overtly links chivalry and religion in the romance form. Chrétien's *Lancelot* (c. 1168) is significant for its development of the ideas that love between a husband and wife is impossible and that love requires an absolute and unhesitating devotion. Although Chrétien undoubtedly received the material for this romance from Marie de France, his emphasis on psychological analysis, and his examination of the parameters of human commitment to a code of conduct, make his treatment of the material unique. In the course of the romance Lancelot sets out to rescue the queen who, as a result of Arthur's rash promise, has been taken captive. Having been unhorsed by the captor, Lancelot is walking disconsolately behind a cart when the driver tells him to get in if he wishes to learn about the queen. Although Lancelot's love for Guinevere is great, his pride and his dismay at having to ride in so unknightly a fashion cause him to take two more steps behind the cart before getting into it. After this act, although he triumphantly passes a number of tests of his devotion to his queen which require him, among other things, to resist a seduction attempt, to crawl painfully over a bridge made of swords, to fight backward so as to keep his eyes fixed on the tower where his lady watches, and to play the coward in a tournament, Lancelot is nevertheless treated disdainfully by the queen because of the incompleteness of his devotion, indicated by those two additional steps which he had taken behind the cart before climbing in. This romance clearly demonstrates the absolute necessity of total commitment to the loved one.

In the twelfth century, then, and beginning with such writers as Chrétien de Troyes and Marie de France, the romance tradition began to flower. Writers at that time, engaged in freeing themselves from the limiting confines of the epic tradition, were exploring new ways of expressing new ideas and themes. Many of these new ideas and themes concerned the four "matters" we have come to associate with romance:

the matter of France, which focuses upon the adventures of Charlemagne and his peers; the matter of Rome, which consists of romances based upon classical material, whether legendary or historical; the matter of Britain, which concerns stories from Arthurian legend; and the matter of England, which treats native English heroes or heroes whose lives and adventures in some way concerned England.

Those romances concerned with the matter of France—the Charlemagne romances—are closest in kind to the epic form. They concern themselves less with love and psychology and more with warfare and heroism. Just as the matter of Britain romances derive ultimately from the epic treatment of Arthur, the Charlemagne romances have as their ultimate source *The Song of Roland*, the Old French epic detailing Roland's heroism, Oliver's wisdom, Ganelon's treachery, and Archbishop Turpin's bravery and piety. The Charlemagne romances (early fourteenth century) fall roughly into two groups; one group, concerning the story of Otuel, contains such romances as *Otuel, The Sege of Melayne,* and *Roland and Vernagu,* while the other group, concerned with the story of Ferumbras, contains such romances as *The Sowdone of Babylone* and *Sir Ferumbras.* The earliest Charlemagne romance in English, *Otuel,* is a tale which contrasts the original Old French epic in diminishing the stature of Roland in order to elevate that of the hero Otuel. After detailing Otuel's conversion to Christianity in the midst of his combat with Roland, who had killed Otuel's uncle Vernagu, the romance describes Otuel's performance as a Christian knight in battles against the Saracens. *The Sege of Melayne,* another romance in the Otuel group, is notable for its depiction of Archbishop Turpin as a heroic figure in battle and for its presentation of religious visions and miracles. *Roland and Vernagu* makes use of the Latin legend that Charlemagne went to the Holy Land and received there such relics as St. Simeon's arm, Mary's smock, and the crown of thorns; the romance also tells of the invasion of Spain and of Roland's battle with Vernagu. Unfinished, the romance was perhaps intended as an introduction to *Otuel.* The Charlemagne romances, in their treatment of the religious conflict between Christians and infidels, are in some ways akin to Arthurian romances concerned with the Grail theme, in that in both sorts of romances religious faith provides a significant motivating force.

In the second group of romances, which concern the Ferumbras theme, *The Sowdone of Babylone* tells of Laban, Sultan of Babylon, and his twenty-foot-tall son Ferumbras who sack Rome and, having obtained the relics of the Passion—the cross, the crown of thorns, and the Crucifixion nails—remove them to Spain. When Charlemagne's army comes to recover the relics, many adventures ensue. Oliver meets Ferumbras in single combat, conquers him, and converts him, after which Ferumbras fights with the Christians against the Saracens. This romance has a noteworthy love story which concerns Floripas, the Sultan's daughter, who falls in love with Guy of Burgundy, one of Charlemagne's knights. Her ingenuity and determination, which are inspired by her love, are ultimately significant in the victory of Charlemagne's forces and the rescue of the relics; consequently, after being baptized, she is married to her lover. A number of the incidents in the second part of this romance form the substance of another romance titled *Sir Ferumbras*, which is consciously and carefully crafted and which is perhaps therefore one of the best of the English Charlemagne romances.

Although medieval romances concerned with the matter of Rome had as possible subjects the adventures of Alexander the Great, the Trojan War, the siege of Thebes, and the adventures of Aeneas, stories of Alexander and of Troy seem to have been the most popular. *Kyng Alisaunder* (fourteenth century), the best of the Alexander romances, first tells of Alexander's begetting through the magical powers of the Egyptian king Nectanebus, who contrives to mate with Olympias, the wife of Philip of Macedon, and thereby fathers Alexander. The romance also details Alexander's rise to power and his various military accomplishments, particularly his wars with Darius, King of Persia. The second part of the romance, treating Alexander's conquest of India and the many adventures he experienced in the Far Eastern countries, relies heavily on the excitement of the unknown and the distant in its description of mythical beasts and other wondrous sights.

The Alexander romances, although concerned with a historical figure, had little basis in history, as did the romances based upon the Troy theme. Since Homer was unknown to Western Europe in the medieval period, Troy romances were based not on the *Iliad* but on two later accounts of the Trojan siege by Dictys Cretensis and by Dares Phrygius, whose works concern the story of Jason and the Argonauts in their quest for the Golden Fleece, the siege of Troy, and the Greeks' return home. Among the Troy romances that make use of these accounts is *The Gest Historiale of the Destruction of Troy* (thirteenth century), which details Jason's adventures; the history of Troy; the kidnaping of Helen; the story of Cassandra; the Greeks' preparation for the journey and the journey itself; the siege, the battle, and the destruction of Troy; the departure of Aeneas; and the return adventures of Ulysses. Other romances on the Troy theme include the *Laud Troy Book* (c. 1400), which selectively treats the material of the *Gest Historiale*; John Lydgate's *The Hystorye, Sege and Dystruccyon of Troy* (1513); and, of course, Geoffrey Chaucer's poem *Troilus and Criseyde* (1382), which is considered by many to be among the finest executions of this theme. Chaucer uses the Trojan War, however, merely as a backdrop for an examination of chivalric love and the complex psychologies of his two main characters; his concern is with human love, human relations, and human idealism, and the student of romance could do no better than to study Chaucer's poem in order to obtain a thorough understanding of the genre of romance.

One of the most popular of the four matters was the Arthurian theme, the matter of Britain, which was treated extensively by writers in England and on the Continent. As time passed, and as more and more material accrued to the legend of Arthur, several other personages came in their own right to be the focus of romances; Gawain, Tristan, Lancelot, Galahad, and Perceval are all the subject of stories in which Arthur is only a minor or a corollary figure. Sir Thomas Malory, one of the most influential writers of Arthurian material, pulled together for his *Le Morte d'Arthur* (1485) much of the legendary and many of the romances into a more or less unified whole; although Malory's work is certainly a redaction of earlier writings, it is much more than that, in large part because of Malory's reshaping of the material into a body of writing which has coherence and purpose. Many later treatments of the story of Arthur are based upon Malory's work. The enduring popularity of the Arthurian theme is evident in such twentieth century works as Thomas Berger's *Arthur Rex* (1979), Richard Monaco's *Parzival: Or, A Knight's Tale* (1977), T. H. White's *The Once and Future King* (1958) and *The Book of Merlyn* (1977), and the several treatments of the theme by Mary Stewart.

The romances said to concern the matter of England for the most part differ in some important ways from the other medieval romances here discussed; they are often much less courtly and less sophisticated than the other romances, and they advance and support humble and simple virtues rather than the aristocratic virtues of chivalry and the courtly life. The inherited material of these romances, whether of native or foreign origin, having been adapted to the lower-class taste, is consequently often spare and realistic, with little of descriptive set pieces and other courtly elements. Action is preferred to introspection and analysis, and the poems are usually vigorous and balladlike in their concision.

Among these romances concerning the matter of England are *King Horn* (c. 1250), which uses the exile and return theme; *Bevis of Hampton* (1622), which begins with a variation on the Hamlet theme; *The Tale of Gamelyn* (c. 1350), from which Shakespeare drew for *As You Like It* (1599-1600); and *William of Palerne* (early fourteenth century), which uses the popular werewolf theme. Perhaps most reflective, however, of the spirit and the values of England's peasantry and its growing middle class is *Havelok the Dane* (c. 1350), a romance concerning a hero who is wrongly excluded from his kingdom in Denmark by an untrustworthy guardian. When the poor fisherman who reared Havelok can no longer support him, Havelok obtains work as a kitchen-helper, soon earning renown locally for his ability to putt the stone; while such activities seem the very antithesis of courtly endeavor, they are nonetheless solidly representative of middle-class virtues. In time Havelok marries an orphaned English princess, Goldeboru, who, like Havelok, was betrayed by a guardian; when one night Goldeboru sees a luminous mark on Havelok's shoulder which indicates his royalty, she is overjoyed. After returning to Denmark and claiming his throne, Havelok conquers England and rewards all who have treated him well. The emphasis throughout the poem is on adventure, justice, and homely but traditional virtues, an emphasis which clearly distinguishes this romance, and the other romances on the matter of England, from those romances of the period which emphasize courtliness.

In sum, then, medieval romances can be seen to encompass a wide variety of subjects and to represent various cultural attitudes. In the medieval age the form drew upon a broad spectrum of sources, including history, legendry, folktale, saint's life, exemplum, fairy lore, and classical materials. After its beginning in the twelfth century, the romance was widely adapted throughout the next three centuries by writers of many countries whose works cross-influenced one another to the extent that establishing direct lines of descent for particular themes or subjects is generally impossible. The pervasiveness of those ideas in later fiction results in part from the genre's use of themes which transcend temporal limitations; the motifs of the wicked guardian, the disinherited hero, the scorned admirer, the wronged lover, and the love-triangle, which are found in such abundance in medieval romances, continue to inform later works of short and long fiction. The medieval romance, like myth and folktale, thus draws on archetypal situations and figures for the presentation of its themes, but at the same time it satisfies the reader's desire for the unusual, the strange, and the alien.

Romance also transcends time in its presentation of the idealized world; the impulse to depict such a world, seen continually in medieval romances, persists in contemporary fiction. Similarly, the medieval romance's insistence on seeing women as admirable creatures and as sources of inspiration enabled the genre to posit the validity of love as a motive for and a cause of nobility, an idea which continues to govern much twentieth century writing. Clearly, the importance of medieval romance in contributing form, material, and attitude to the development of modern prose fiction can hardly be overestimated; the romance provided a broad imaginative scope while it simultaneously bequeathed a legacy of rich material for plot and characterization.

In the late seventeenth and early eighteenth centuries the romance as a literary form declined in popularity, making way for neoclassical forms. In the late eighteenth century the Gothic romance became popular, but this was a variation on the traditional romance form which relied heavily on sensational material and the evocation of emotions heightened to a painful degree. In the nineteenth century, romance ceased to be primarily a generic distinction and became instead an attribute, or a characteristic, or an attitude, which was frequently juxtaposed to realism; whereas realism meant the objective literary consideration of ordinary people in ordinary situations, romance came to mean the subjective literary consideration of the unusual. Nathaniel Hawthorne, in his preface to *The House of the Seven Gables* (1851) illustrates this perception of the genre as he states that romance implies for the author a latitude in content and expression which permits the manipulation of the atmosphere and the delicate and judicious inclusion of the marvelous.

In modern times, romance has undergone yet further alterations. When hearing the term in the twentieth century, one usually thinks either of "confessional" love stories found in pulp magazines or of popular love stories in novel form, of the sort sold in dime stores. The *form* of romance has clearly deteriorated from that of the Middle Ages, but the *characteristics* of romance are deeply ingrained in our literary heritage. Any literature which is other than firmly realistic, which strives for psychological analysis, which establishes a world as it ought to be rather than as it is, which sees love as a motive force for nobility, or which is imaginative in simultaneously portraying an unreal world with unreal characters who nevertheless reveal human truths, owes its very essence to the romance tradition.

Evelyn Newlyn

SHORT FICTION IN THE SIXTEENTH
AND SEVENTEENTH CENTURIES

Modern scholars have disagreed sharply over whether Renaissance prose fiction can best be seen as taking tentative steps toward the eighteenth century novel or whether it marks the end of a medieval tradition. As with most academic debates, both approaches are useful and depend on the critic's perspective. In fact, in some limited but important ways, the state of prose fiction between the first use of movable type in England (1485) and the last decades of the seventeenth century is comparable to that in modern times. It was an era of deep-rooted sociocultural change: a traditional mode of literature was slowly dying or being adapted to an apparently less discriminating audience; also, a bewildering variety of literary experiments, many of which were uncertain or outright failures, was accompanied by an uncertainty about the conventions and the value of prose fiction. To read the works of George Gascoigne, Thomas Deloney, or Aphra Behn is certainly to have received notions about the nature of prose fiction radically challenged. Yet a useful comparison of their strangeness to the modern reader can be made to the reader's increasing familiarity with the postmodern experiments in fiction of today. There is also the awareness that although the world they describe is, largely, one that is now lost, they do nevertheless articulate important aspects of modern cultural heritage and so of modern self-understanding.

The period marked by the English revolution, the Restoration, and the Settlement of 1688 makes one of the vital watersheds in history, and its effects can be sensed in the age's prose fiction. By the late seventeenth century, many of the European literary fashions which England had belatedly adapted were taking root, and as socioeconomic balance shifted radically, so a new form of prose fiction developed. Historical changes of such magnitude, however, rarely occur overnight, and the whole era, in particular between 1570 and 1640 when the period's social, intellectual, and cultural turmoil was at its most concentrated, provides anticipations and experiments of enormous interest. In any period of unusual turbulence, writers and texts tell the reader more than they know, and the role of the critic is more than usually that of deconstructing the obvious surface referentiality of texts, as the reader searches for evidence for deeper implicit, but eventually enormously important, changes in a society's culture.

So far as "short" fiction is concerned, the Renaissance, unlike later centuries, had no coherent theory of prose fiction in general, let alone for distinguishing between shorter and longer forms. The period inherited a huge variety of shorter forms from its past—jests, anecdotes, fables, exempla, romances, *fabliaux*, homilies, folktales, *récits, novelle*—but few writers seem to have given conscious attention to questions of length. Instead, they seem to have been anxious to justify the art of fiction-making itself—"poetry" was their usual term—alongside other human activities. Much Renaissance fiction is uneasily claimed to be "history" and contains elaborate justifications of the teller's veracity. Although George Gascoigne and John Barth are worlds apart in sophistication of technique, both show a self-conscious uneasiness about their craft that points not merely to the uncertain quality of fiction but, beyond, to the nature of their societies. If one looks to France, Italy, or Spain, one finds evidence for a more self-conscious concern with shorter as opposed to longer forms of fiction and, indeed, in France between about 1560 and 1600 and again between 1660 and 1700, various short forms dominated fashions in prose fiction. In England, however, no such self-consciousness seems to have existed, and in order to get an adequate sense of what forms of short fiction did exist, it will be necessary to stretch and at some points to ignore the limits of the topic.

Notwithstanding uncertainty over the nature of prose fiction (and this is not simply an English phenomenon), an increasing amount was written and published as the new technology of moving type coincided with the expansion of the reading public. Among the earliest books printed by William Caxton and Wynkyn de Worde were editions of medieval romances, and by 1600, approximately one-quarter of the books printed in England were prose fiction. The expansion of a literate, book-buying class was a complex business, and one of its most relevant aspects was the growing fear observable among the dominant and educated classes that the more the reading public grew, the more literary standards and—by association—social and political order, would be threatened. Authors who preferred the traditional role of court entertainer slowly adapted to the new commercial market, often with some reluctance, as new economic relationships developed between authors, entrepreneurs, and readers that would eventually radically transform the nature and status of the craft. Whereas Sir Philip Sidney's primary audience was his sister, his family, and his friends, and John Lyly saw his fiction as a means of social advancement, Robert Greene, Thomas Nashe, Deloney, and, by the mid-seventeenth century, most writers of fiction had abandoned the traditional role. While still archaically addressing their readers in continual parentheses as "gentles" and "fayre ladies" in approved courtly manner, writers increasingly found themselves related commercially to their audiences and usually conceived their role as purveying and reinforcing what they saw as their audience's normative values. Any emergent values or techniques observed, in hindsight, in Nashe, Deloney, or Behn are expressed indirectly in their works.

The major emergent literary form in the period was, of course, the drama of the public theater. Like prose fiction, the drama went through a period of uncertainty and experimentation and had to reconcile a long tradition of communal entertainment with new intellectual pretensions and the new demands of the marketplace. A brief comparison is instructive. While the best of Elizabethan prose fiction is manifestly the expression of the same energies that produced the Elizabethan drama, it is striking that while in the theater an art form developed which expressed the energies of the period in a remarkable fusion of popular entertainment and philosophical and psychological profundity, fiction-writing remained a minor and peripheral form. One cannot simply say that the energies that later ages gave to the novel and short story were directed into the drama: the theater seems uniquely equipped to explore the bewildering variety of problems the age felt within experience of contingency and change. The role-playing of the theater, its inherent relativism, its juxtapositions of opposing philosophies and moods, and its fierce demands on emotional involvement, all seem, in hindsight, to have captured the needs and confusions of the age— better, perhaps, than the age itself knew.

The theater had, as well, the advantage of developing subtle forms of independence of court values (although not of court patronage or censorship). By making the fascination of human actions its central interest, it opened the possibilities for audiences to contemplate themselves, their society, their world. More than any other literary or art form, the drama articulated the age's struggle to free itself from archaic and residual intellectual, social, and political forces and to release the emergent drives of a new world. Readers look back to *Hamlet* (c. 1600-1601), *Doctor Faustus* (1588), *The White Devil* (1612), and *The Tempest* (1611) as embodiments of energies and insights that were—and often despite the immediately succeeding age—to come through as forming and directing subsequent history. By contrast, the greatest work of prose fiction in the age, Sidney's *Arcadia* (1590), looks back nostalgically to an earlier world of order and stasis. What seemed to Sidney's contemporaries to be the shoring up of standards was eventually to be seen as retrogressive and nostalgic, and so far as prose fiction is concerned, the real growing points—for the eighteenth century novel and beyond—were peripheral and obscure parts of Renaissance culture.

Having identified somewhat the place of prose fiction in the sociocultural dynamic of the age, it is now appropriate to examine specifically the characteristics of short prose fiction. Notwithstanding the difficulty of defining "short" forms for the period, there are a variety of interesting works and points of potential growth for later ages. First to be dealt with will be those forms of fiction to which Renaissance authorities would have given greatest approval, those directly associated with the aesthetic demands of the court—adaptations of medieval romances, translations, and imitations of Continental modes (especially the *novella*, the *conte*, and the various picaresque forms). Second, the counterdominant forms of prose fiction which, explicitly or not, modified or challenged the dominance of the court will be covered. These included the middle-class adaptation and eventual transformation of romance, fiction which bore the marked impact of Protestantism, and the various forms of short fiction that emerged from sociopolitical realities on the periphery of or outside the dominant culture. These forms—folk stories, anecdotes, jests, tales of ordinary and seemingly trivial experience—however excluded by the hegemonous forms, nevertheless constitute a crucial part of the cultural life of England and point beyond to the life and literature of later periods.

During the sixteenth century, literature and the arts generally became increasingly subject to the control and values of the age's dominant institution, the court. As the Tudor state took a more confident shape, it systematically—although on a European scale, belatedly—attempted to use the arts as an instrument in its policy of centralization and control. Epic and lyric poetry and the masque particularly felt its pressure, and the development of these modes especially show the power of the court over its subjects. The most important works of prose fiction in the European Renaissance—those by François Rabelais, Miguel de Cervantes Saavedra, and Sidney—all articulate directly or in reaction the new buoyancy and aggressiveness of the Renaissance court. Most writers of any kind were either courtiers or financially dependent on court patronage; until late in the sixteenth century, most conceived of themselves as court entertainers. As the court hegemony broke down over the succeeding century, writers were forced to find alternative social roles and audiences and to change their modes of writing to express the new social realities.

The dominance of the court in the Tudor period meant that the works written or translated were heavily influenced by court taste. The majority of early works of prose fiction drew on traditional medieval chivalric material—stories of romantic love, Arthurian adventures, and the like. Even as early as 1500, their values were fast becoming archaic so far as actual social practices are concerned, but their increasingly escapist aura continued to appeal to readers for the next two centuries by means of an intriguing mixture of nostalgia and practicality. Their settings, characters, and actions are essentially escapist—enchanted islands, captured ladies, gallant knights, monsters, miracles, coincidences—but they are invariably heavily moralistic.

Indeed, it is one of the strengths of the late Elizabethan flowering of prose fiction that even the most tedious and confused tale can suddenly break into an earnest moral argument between the author and his readers. Prompted by marginal notes and directly addressed by the author (who in the most unpredictable and seemingly postmodernist manner can drop his seeming objectivity at any moment), one may be asked to enter an intense moral debate. Walter R. Davis has argued that central to Elizabethan romance is an attempt to test traditional moral and intellectual beliefs, embodied in the romance world of pure, idealized motives opposed to reminders of a harsher reality in which the readers uncomfortably lived. He points further to the higher interest in ideas in English romances than in their European counterparts; one witnesses the earnest adaptation to pragmatic ends of a set of values essentially idealistic, escapist, and archaic.

In most cases, however—the earliest signs of a countermovement are not found before the works of Deloney in the 1590's—the reified values of the romances are the traditional chivalric ones, and any real possibility of debate, like that afforded by the drama—*Hamlet, Troilus and Cressida* (c. 1601-1602), *The White Devil*, say—is lost. Nevertheless, aristocratic readers of the typical romance tale in 1590 make a fascinating case history: surrounded by the uneasiness of a world increasingly threatened by strange new sociocultural forces, they turned to prose fiction as they turned to Edmund Spenser's *The Faerie Queene* (1590-1596) or, a decade after, to the Jacobean court masque, for the reassurance of values and habits long archaic and unlike the reality outside their chambers. Perhaps a few miles away, however, in a dank public theater, a new play about a German necromancer was alluring or disturbing audiences from very different social groups with the thrill of blasphemy, ambition, and the possibility (reassuringly, to most of the audience, unsuccessful) of avoiding a just damnation.

When turning to the examples of short prose fiction from which the Renaissance reader had to choose (especially those few occasions when writers seemed more conscious writing "short" forms), one discovers that the prose fiction of the English Renaissance was, as in so many other fields, dominated by continental models. Most important for the period's short fiction was the Italian *novella*, best exemplified by Giovanni Boccaccio in the fourteenth century, a form able to use a variety of serious, romantic, and satiric elements within a framework of transmitting a sense of vivid, immediate life from teller to hearer. Various *novelle* by Boccaccio himself were translated or imitated and published in sixteenth century England, including, quite early, the anonymous, lively *Frederyke of Jennen* (1509), derived through various intermediaries from Boccaccio's *Decameron: O, Prencipe Galeotto* (1349-1351; *The Decameron*, 1620). Later in the period, many of the 214 *novelle* by Matteo Bandello, richly melodramatic stories of love and violence, were translated or imitated. In 1567, William Painter published *The Palace of Pleasure*, taken from François de Belleforest's French version of Bandello. Subtitled "tragicall Novells and dolorous Histories," Painter's work was described rather disapprovingly by the humanist educator, Roger Ascham, in *The Scholemaster* (1570) as "fond books, of late translated out of Italian into English, sold in every shop in London." Painter includes more than one hundred short tales, including the contemporary story of the Duchess of Amalfi (later adapted by John Webster), all combining rich melodrama and dogged, simplistic moralization. Painter offers them as demonstrations that the world is "a stage and theatre" providing "diversitie of matter pleasant and plausible" as well as being "for example and imitation good and commendable." Titillating scandal exists side by side with moral lectures—a typical combination in the English collections of *novelle*.

A similar combination, even more diverse in its elements, can be found in Geoffrey Fenton's adaptions of Belleforest and Bandello in his *Certain Tragicall Discourses* (1567), thirteen short tales, mainly about the evils of lust, combining prurient details and long moralizing harangues on the inevitability of divine punishment. George Pettie's *A Petite Palace of Pettie His Pleasure* (1576) also adapts twelve *novelle*, but their direct brevity is swamped, again, by coy moralizing and also—a new element which shows how the form was being adapted to genteel courtly taste—by a self-consciously elegant prose style, heavy-handed allegory, stylized debates, stolid abstractions, and sly asides to members of the courtly audience. Despite the sycophantic tone, however, Pettie's work does show a strong sense of its audience, as does Barnaby Rich's *His Farewell to Militarie Profession* (1581), eight stories adapted from various *novelle* and addressed to the "righte courteous Gentlewoman" of the court with the usual mixture of titillation and moral commonplaces. All these examples of framed *novelle* and others—Edmund Tilney's *Flower of Friendship* (1568) or George Whetstone's *An Heptameron of Civill Discourses* (1582)—seem unaware that the *novella*'s power lies precisely in its brevity and directness; they aspire to longer, leisurely, more courtly forms of prose fiction. It was left to later dramatists such as William Shakespeare and Webster to use the concentration of the *novella* in a different medium.

Similarly, sophisticated in its handling of a short form—and providing an instinctive contrast with England—is the tradition in France. Until the reign of François I, France, like England, remained dominated by Italian or Spanish models. From the 1530's, however, and as part of the sudden rebirth of secular and religious literature associated with the Pléiade and the court *salons*, there grew up an impressive tradition of prose fiction. Its longer forms were dominated by Rabelais, its shorter forms (the *conte*, *novella*, or *récit*) by Marguerite de Navarre in the *L'Heptaméron* (1558) and her circle, including Bonaventure Des Périers, Henri Estienne, and Belleforest. The vogue for short fiction, either as part of a collection told by a variety of *dévisants*, or storytellers, who frequently offered diverse interpretations of similar situations and so involved the readers in a moral debate, or else in separate unlinked examples, resulted in great advances in the art of short fiction. One can see a dramatic thematic widening, an unprecedented sophistication of style and technique, and an important contribution to the expressive powers of French prose. By the end of the century, short fiction in France was not merely highly popular but had become a major literary form in a way that English prose fiction did not until the eighteenth century. English writers adapted material from the French collections of stories but seemed to learn little about the sophisticated possibilities of the form.

The third major source—and, again, it provides a contrast with English fiction writers—is Spain. As in Italy and France, the Iberian peninsula developed a varied tradition of fiction, seen at its greatest in Cervantes' *Don Quixote de la Mancha* (1605, 1615; English translation, 1612-1620). Sentimental novels, pastoral romances, picaresque tales, and rogue fiction, are all evidence of vigorous interest in shorter forms of fiction in Spain and Portugal. David Rowland translated the *Lazarillo de Tormes* (1554) in 1576, "strange and mery reports, very recreative and pleasant," and James Mabbe in 1622 *The Rogue* or *The Life and Adventures of Guzmán de Alfarache* (1599, 1604), thus bringing two notable examples of the picaresque into English. Margaret Tyler's *The Mirror of Princely Deeds* (1578) and Anthony Munday's *Palmerin of England* (1581) and many others adapted the rambling, idealized adventure-romance. These chivalric works—which Cervantes attempts to "demolish" for their "ill-founded structure" and absurdities—were enormously popular in England, but as long works, they need not detain us, except to underline how the English taste turned inevitably to such leisured, essentially escapist, fiction.

One further foreign influence, although one hardly contemporary with Sidney, Lyly, and their fellows, should be mentioned. English writers were usually aware that their literary inheritance included a number of distinctive stories written in pre-Christian Greece. Usually referred to as "the Greek romances," these included Heliodorus' *Aethiopica*, Longus' short tale *Daphnis and Chloë*, and Achilles Tatius' *Clitophon and Leucippe*, all of which were translated into English in the 1560-1590 period. All are elaborate in incident, intricate in plot, and held together by a graceful, sensual melancholy, and all stress the fickleness of human affairs. Greene's prose romances and Shakespeare's dramatic romances are among English works which show a careful study of their attractive atmosphere and incident-packed plots.

Between about 1570 and 1610, then, occurred what can justly be seen as a most interesting flowering of prose fiction. A great variety of short and long fiction—much derived from Italian, Spanish, and French sources—was translated, adapted, or imitated. Medieval romances, English and continental alike, were revived in prose versions; the new writers of the Elizabethan younger generation—Gascoigne, Sidney, Greene, Thomas Lodge, Nash, Deloney, Emmanuel Forde—produced a variety of native examples. Although it is, once again, difficult to sort out distinctively "short" forms—and in some cases impossible if one wishes to get a rounded picture—one can nevertheless note some of the most important trends and illustrate them largely from short examples. Interestingly, one of the best pieces of prose fiction in English was written early in the period and is sufficiently contracted—about 32,000 words long—to almost qualify as "short" fiction. It is the court poet-translator George Gascoigne's *The Novel of Master F. J.*, first published in 1573 and ostensibly set in some unnamed Northern castle, and then republished in 1575, somewhat rewritten, retitled, and set in a typical Italianate court, accompanied by a denial that the early version had been, as had been alleged, a *roman à clef*. The work appeared as part of a miscellany of court entertainments by Gascoigne entitled *A Hundred Sundrie Flowres Bound Up in One Small Poesie* and included poems and translations, all "gathered partely . . . in the fyne outlandish Gardins of Euripides, Ovid, Petrarcke, Ariosto, and others: and partly by invention, out of our own fruitful Orchardes in Englande." *The Novel of Master F. J.* itself is described as "a pleasant discourse of the adventures of master F. J. conteyning excellent letters, sonnets, Lays, Ballets, Rondlets, Verlays and verses."

Alongside most other examples of prose fiction, short or long, between 1500 and 1700, *The Novel of Master F. J.* is an unusually coherent and skillful piece of fiction. Put in a European perspective, it appears as a typical product of a sophisticated court society, an antiromantic *novella*. It depicts the affair between a young man, saturated with the rhetoric of courtly love, learning something of his own naïveté and the archaic nature of his ideals, and a highly manipulative young married woman. *Amour courtoise* was, by the 1570's, long dead in practice, except in the archaic rituals revived in the Elizabethan court; Gascoigne's tale is an amusing scrutiny of its irrelevance to the actual experience of human love—as opposed to its value for social allegiance to the Queen. Within a very limited sphere, Gascoigne is doing for the courtly tale, and the ethos behind it, what Cervantes was to do for longer chivalric romances.

During the late 1570's and 1580's, there was a concentrated attempt, largely initiated by Sir Philip Sidney and his circle, to bring about a renaissance of English letters. Sidney's own *Astrophel and Stella* (1591), *The Defence of Poesie* (1595), his sister's *Psalms*, and Spenser's *The Faerie Queene* are all parts of this movement. In prose fiction Sidney also led the way with the age's most important prose work, *The*

Countesse of Pembroke's Arcadia (written 1579-1580; revised c. 1582-1584, first published 1590 under the title *Arcadia*). Sidney's work epitomizes the dominance of the court over Elizabethan culture but, interestingly, it also betrays something of the intellectual and sociocultural strains that were to challenge the hegemony of the court over the next fifty years. Unlike most other prose fiction of the period, the *Arcadia* presents a complex and challenging model for aristocratic living, for action in and comprehension of the world. The debate Sidney takes the reader into may, finally, be settled by archaic and regressive ideas, but it is infinitely more complex and disturbing than any other work of prose fiction, and far more interesting. Motivation and moral insight are rooted in actual cultural and intellectual values. Technically, too, Sidney's work is far in advance of any other work of prose fiction, short or long, before the eighteenth century. While the *Arcadia's* plot is appropriately elaborate (especially in the revised new *Arcadia*), it is nevertheless unified by a coherent and subtle vision, all the more interesting because one senses that, like Spenser, Sidney increasingly felt the pressure to explore and question the values of his class and age. It is arguable, indeed, that the new *Arcadia*, like *The Faerie Queene*, is an unfinishable work, its elaborate display and complexity an epitome of its author's uneasiness before the questions his work raised for him and his society, and one that he sensed would never be settled within his lifetime.

Sidney's work was the most admired piece of prose fiction in English before Samuel Richardson's *Pamela* (1740). It was imitated, completed, translated, summarized, and, in part, dramatized; it increasingly became regarded as a storehouse of lost moral wisdom. The *Arcadia* was a mine of plots and situations for dramatists and for later writers of prose fiction; only the collections by Pettie, Painter, and their like were used so much by the following century's writers. The most popular tale within the complex fabric of Sidney's work was that of Argalus and Parthenia, which was probably at least as familiar to English readers as the story of Romeo and Juliet and which inspired poems, plays, and a variety of cheap chapbook condensations or summaries of the *Arcadia*. Some versions, late in the seventeenth century, add characters such as a villainous mother and a tricky maid and vastly increase the melodramatic violence and suspense. None of the imitations, short or long, approach the intellectual richness or formal mastery of Sidney's work. Indeed, so great was the power of Sidney, as an ideal even more than as a person, that the *Arcadia* might well be seen as hindering developments in prose fiction over the next century or so.

The other major writer of the 1570's and 1580's who, although not strictly a writer of "short" fiction, nevertheless deserves mention is John Lyly. His works, *Euphues, the Anatomy of Wit* (1579) and *Euphues and His England* (1580), provide excellent examples of the pressure of the court upon the role of the fiction writing and the style and scope of his work. Whereas by his position as an aristocrat, Sidney had both the freedom and security to challenge or at least severely qualify court values, Lyly was an eagerly aspiring court-follower, anxious for preferment and happy to write according to court taste. *Euphues, the Anatomy of Wit* is court fiction *par excellence*, a courtly game designed primarily to provide stylish entertainment with a minimum of intellectual substance. Although occasionally ironical in intent, Lyly is concerned less with the substance of ideas than with their manipulation as part of a demonstration of wit and sophisticated cleverness. His audience is almost exclusively the ladies and gentlemen of the court, and his intention is to flatter, titillate, and reassure; what moral insights he offers are incidental to the use of stylistic devices as witty display. Yet beneath the glittering surface of Lyly's prose there can be clearly sensed the unresisted pressure of the court: contrary ideas are balanced to "prove" that moderation and judicious reasoning coincide with the commonplaces of the Elizabethan regime. Commonplace didacticism is presented, through the formal and mellifluous structure of the prose, as universal truth. In other words, Lyly is not simply offering his elegant style for admiration: he is asserting against the chaos of the world outside the mannered beauty of the court the order of the courtly ideal. His style creates an emblem of harmony, a sense of formalized security, completely controlled so that the harsher realities of the outside world cannot invade. The constant use of superlatives—"the sweetest wine turneth to the sharpest vinegar"—has often been commented upon for its formal beauty, but it is more than decorative: it is a device designed to suggest that the whole possible range of experience has been considered and, through art, is being controlled and ruled. Lyly's style is thus a flattering mirror of the court, and the readers of his books are invited to enter and take their places in that world. Almost as much space is given to such invitations, flattering the reader, as to dialogue: "Euphues had rather lye shut in a Ladyes casket, than open in a Schollar's studie" is Lyly's own gloss on his work.

Sidney and Lyly epitomize different aspects of the court aesthetic's hold over prose fiction—although, of course, it was not only over prose fiction, nor was it simply an aesthetic. Hardly any prose fiction, short or long, during the 1580's or early 1590's escaped their influence. Euphuism gave writers such as Greene, Lodge, Brian Melbancke, and William Warner an elegant mode of presenting characters and ideas as part of a tapestry of stylistic effects; Sidney gave his followers an emphasis on moral seriousness and, interacting with the influence of Greek romance and Spanish chivalric romances, an emphasis on the unpredictability and the infinite complexity of human events.

It is with Lodge and Greene that one can see the romance tradition being adapted to shorter fictional forms. Although Stephen Gosson's *The Ephemerides of Phialo* (1579), Anthony Munday's *Zelauto* (1580), and Brian Melbancke's *Philotimus* (1583) are all medium-length adaptations of Lyly's mode, with exemplary dialogues and debates and a self-conscious elegance of style, Greene and Lodge provide readers with the best evidence for the popularity and the adaptability of the court-dominated forms. Lodge is the more influenced by Sidney. In *Rosalynde* (1590), for example, the major source for Shakespeare's *As You Like It* (1599-1600), the typical (although not exclusively) Arcadian motif of the contrast between court and country is used to test charmingly the ideals of conduct and style on which the court prided itself. *A Margarite of America* (1595) is similarly Sidneian in its mellifluous pastoral atmosphere and delicate moral touches. Between 1579 and 1592, Greene (who was probably the best-selling short-fiction writer of the whole period, with some seventy editions of his romances published before 1640), published about thirty pieces of fiction and, in fact, derived much of his income from what he termed his "trifling Pamphlets . . . and vaine fantasies." He continually adjusted his work to prevailing fashion, writing Euphuistic fiction (*Mamilius*, 1583), love-tales, low-life and criminal stories, moral exempla—*The Myrrour of Modesty* (1584) shows that "the graie heades of dooting adulterers shall not go with peace into the grave"—and adventure stories. Of his shorter works, *Pandosto, the Triumph of Time* (1588) is an especially interesting use of the Greek romance tradition. Used by Shakespeare for the main source of the plot of *The Winter's Tale* (1610-1611), it is a tale of lost love, unpredictable fortune, and unexpected joy and sorrow all designed to stress the illogicality and unpredictability of fortune, but unlike Shakespeare's play, revealing, in Walter Davis' words, an "almost cynical or Calvinistic assumption of the inconsequentiality of human purposes." Another example of Greene's adaptability in a brief form is *A Quip for an Upstart Courtier* (1592), a calculated criticism of the waste and self-deception of pretentious gentility, written from the conservative viewpoint of a cautious bourgeois. The ethos of this and of his lively "conny-catching" rogue-fiction pamphlets, which display something of the vigorous anarchy of the lowlife and the criminal subculture of London, show the gradual adaptation of the romance to a wider audience and, eventually, to anticourt sentiments. As Davis comments, Greene "began his career as the staunchest of the young Euphuists, but by the end of it he had neglected everything Lyly stood for." As such he epitomizes the revolution that was coming over much of the literature of the age by the time of his death in 1592.

Before looking in some detail at the distinctive features of the short fiction of the 1590's, it is perhaps important to sense something of an overview of the courtly fiction that dominated the 1570's, 1580's, and early 1590's, and which in increasingly adapted forms continued to be overwhelmingly popular through the seventeenth century. As can be seen from looking at its two dominant writers, Sidney and Lyly, courtly fiction is essentially conservative in intellectual outlook: originating in the values of the court, it harks nostalgically back to a world of order, harmony, and mystery. Essentially escapist in its values, it therefore tends to avoid or else to romanticize the pressures and contradictions of material life. Its characters are abstractions and types. Its settings are exotic and romantic, its plots episodic, coincidental, melodramatic, and unsurprising in their continual unexpectedness. Its style, if rarely as explicitly as in Lyly, tends to reinforce the ethos of nostalgia. It is rhetorically heightened, static and emblematic, and self-conscious in its use of rhetoric and ornament to convey the experience of participation in a ritual of comfort and wish fulfillment. In its origins, courtly fiction grew from a tradition of oral entertainment, its tellers subservient (although aspiring) members of the court whose values it espoused. Its narrative techniques go back to those courtly origins. They still show marks of the storyteller, the court entertainer, conscious always of the audience before him and of the roles he must therefore play. Although there is no clear break with the writers of the 1590's, readers do start to become aware of new forces threatening and disconcerting the dominance of the court. Even Lyly betrays something of an unease before a crucial transition that had, in fact, been under way since the invention of printing: the creation of a larger, more impersonal, and more diverse audience created by the printing press. This was a literate although not necessarily a learned audience eager for entertainment and the reinforcement of its own very different and rapidly changing values and experiences.

In many areas of literature, the 1590's saw disturbing formal and thematic developments—in satire, in a pared-down rhetoric in both poetry and prose, in the public theater, in the influx of new ideas, and in the virtual invention of new literary forms. So far as prose fiction is concerned, the developments have often been described as the surfacing of a new strain of realism, anticipating, clumsily, developments in the eighteenth century novel. The confusions and the achievements of the 1590's deserve better than that. They are both important crystallizations of the enthusiasms and anxieties of their time and indicative of wider and more long-term cultural changes. Erich Auerbach's observation that "courtly culture was decidedly unfavorable to the development of a literary art which should apprehend reality in its full breadth and depth" has real point here. It is seen, very clearly, the ways in which the public theater of Shakespeare's time responded to and in part created the tastes and self-consciousness of a new audience, and how its new modes of perceiving reality were in part dependent on its growing independence and rejection of the values of the court—paradoxically even while it was ostensibly responsible to and dependent on the court. Only spasmodically does one see such possibilities develop in prose fiction.

The 1590's show some of the few signs. The later works of Greene, written just before his death in 1592, show him turning to the raw energies of contemporary London life for the material of fiction, and the possibilities of a new, disturbing realism can be seen in another transitional writer, Thomas Nash. Like Greene, Nash adapted his considerable talents to both traditional courtly tastes and to a new, wider, less discriminating audience. He attacked the "idle pens," "fantasticall dreams," and "worne out impressions of the feyned no where acts" of the chivalric romances and saw his *The Unfortunate Traveller: Or, The Life of Jack Wilton* (1594) as written in a "cleane different vaine." Using an impressive range of satire, parody, burlesque, and realistic observation, Nash's work is a picaresque biography of one Jack Wilton, an adventurer who observes warfare, travel, and various aspects of contemporary life. Nash's plot is unsophisticatedly episodic, and the straightforwardness of his hero, a roguish outsider able to inhabit a variety of recognizable milieux, affords him an unusual degree of realistic observation. *The Unfortunate Traveller* is a typical 1590's work, akin to experiments in poetry and drama, mixing the characteristics of a variety of traditional literary modes, held together by the restless persona of its author, and betraying signs of emergent cultural experiences straining at the restrictions of older artistic forms.

Some of Nash's other works, including *Nashe's Lenten Stuffe* (1599) and *Have with You to Saffron Walden* (1596), are on the boundary (not easy to draw in the 1590's) between fiction and disputation. In these two works, he fictionalizes his enemy Gabriel Harvey, pouring scorn on his learning and affectations and complaining that true learning and wit go unrewarded. In his complaint, one senses less the iconoclast than the aspiring court entertainer, harking back to older, more traditional ways, idealized in *Pierce Penniless* (1592) by the Sidneys. He bewails that a gentleman like himself should have to make himself "a gazing stock and a publique spectacle to all the world for nothing." Like many of his generation—restless, ambitious, Inns of Court or University men—Nash is self-indulgent, insecure, and despite his astringent style, still seeing his fiction as a means to preferment in a world where advancement seems increasingly denied. While he has the true performer's delight in rhetoric and a vivid sense of his audience—"Readers, be merry; for in me there shall want nothing I can doo to make you merry," he cries in *The Unfortunate Traveller*—his qualities of realistic observation and pointed commentary remain incidental to his residual conception of the role of fiction, and they point forward to later developments despite his own intentions.

Nash, Greene, and Lodge all show signs of a vital transition in the nature and function of prose fiction. Even in the *Arcadia*, in so many pivotal ways the age's most significant work, there are signs of the incipient breakdown, even at its apparent height, of the cultural hegemony of the court. Any culture contains, as has been shown, residual elements of an earlier phase of society—frequently embodied in the dominant and therefore more conservative tastes of society—and emergent cultural values and experiences, which often appear unbeknown to authors and which the modern reader identifies as culturally significant. The confusion and experimentation of the 1590's is not unique to prose fiction writers, but in their searches for social and literary identity one can certainly sense something of the age's most important cultural shifts.

Raymond Williams, commenting on the *Arcadia*, points to the irony that the work which gave its name to a central facet of the English pastoral tradition should have been written on a real country estate whose wealth had been created by upsetting traditional bonds between people and their land, and then ruthlessly exploiting the enclosures thus acquired. Sidney certainly seems unaware of the irony, and the reader may notice, perhaps a little uncomfortably, that he seems supremely indifferent to the pressures of the real-life values or problems of tenants, peasants, or any class below the level of his admirable, if erring, heroes and heroines. What, as was seen with Greene and Nash, the 1590's bring is a gradual transformation of the forms and function of traditional fiction by an audience and an incipient structure of values, beliefs, and habits that would eventually transform not only prose fiction but also the sociocultural fabric of England. It is therefore fascinating to see the court romance invaded and subverted increasingly in the years following the 1590's. What are usually termed "bourgeois romances" can be seen as early as the 1580's. At first they are simply adaptations of the traditional fantastic adventures, except that their heroes are not aristocratic but middle-class knights errant. In works such as Lodge's

The Life and Death of William Longbeard (1593), Henry Roberts' *Pheander the Mayden Knight* (1595), and Richard Johnson's *The Most Pleasant History of Tom a Lincolne* (1607), the quests of the heroes are to protect values that express the world not of Arcadia but of Southwark or Eastcheap.

The bourgeois romances are cautious and decorous to the point of incongruity, however, calling into question their courtly antecedents by implication only and explicitly intent on appealing still to the values of "the gentleman reader," although the term is taking on a meaning far broader than Baldassare Castiglione, Sidney, or even Nash would have approved. The most successful writers of this form of fiction are Emmanuel Forde and Thomas Deloney, whose works, like Gascoigne's or Greene's, are somewhat awkwardly located between "long" and "short." Forde's enormously popular *The Most Pleasant History of Ornatus and Artesia* (1595?) and *Parismus* (1598-1599) are works of moderate length which add to an explicitly although romanticized bourgeois setting an interest in the motivation of humble people exploited by overbearing aristocrats. Deloney was almost as popular a writer and even more interesting in his mixture of realism and traditional romance. In 1596 he was accused of "bringing in" the Queen to one of his works, "to speak with her people in dialogue in very fond and undecent sort," which would never have done for Sidney (or Spenser). His heroes typically rise from being lowly apprentices or servants to becoming wealthy clothiers or Members of Parliament. His settings are still idealized, but are recognizably related to England rather than Arcadia and are peopled with a variety of merchants, shoemakers, citizens, and goodwives, whose natural loyalties are more patriotic, Deloney constantly asserts, than those of the aristocracy. In *Thomas of Reading* (c. 1600) after an especially jovial interview with the King, Hodgekins the clothiers' spokesman "affirmed on his faith that he had rather speak to the king's majesty than to many justices of peace." With such a revolution in the content of his work, Deloney is, however, disappointingly traditional, even archaic, in the structure and mode of his fiction. His work is still chivalric romance, adapted for a new class anxious to see its newfound respectability and power idealized in the way its superiors continued, more uneasily, to idealize theirs.

One can, however, find fiction (and significantly, specifically short fiction) that escapes the dominance of the residual court modes if one looks even further from Whitehall than Hodgekins and his like afford. The recovery of popular, especially lower-class, literature in the period is beset with extraordinary difficulties. Much, if not most, has been lost simply because it was not or could not be written down and printed; much that has survived in print has been laundered for a more genteel audience. From various written sources, often very indirect ones, however—commonplace books, letters, and the like, as well as some printed sources—one can piece together a vivid tradition of folk and popular art that never escaped the force of the dominant sociocultural pressures, but which nevertheless constituted a rich tradition in its own right and which surfaced, increasingly, in the seventeenth century in the Commonwealth and in works such as John Bunyan's *The Pilgrim's Progress* (1678). Difficult as it may be to pin down a visible tradition of folk stories actually published in the period, one can nevertheless from indirect sources (letters, brief mentions in plays, and other works) see how the stories of traditional folk heroes, such as Robin Hood, served as outlets for the frustrations and ambitions of the underprivileged and unlettered.

Indeed, perhaps the most pervasive form of short fiction, written or oral, in the period is the short, homely anecdote or tale. Hundreds of examples are found, often tucked away in other literary forms (in Shakespeare's *Henry IV*, 1597-1598, for example) or assembled in the enormously popular collections of jest-books. Jest-books were accumulations of varying length of tales and jokes, most centered on a clinching or witty *riposte* designed to provoke laughter or admiration (or a free drink); the tales used a variety of typical characters—faithless wives, rapacious clergy, corrupt lawyers—that simultaneously drew on traditional wisdom and sharp observation. A typical example is the anonymous *The Sackful of News* (1558), a collection of twenty-two miscellaneous jests, some with dialogue, some with brief, pithy morals, but all meant for entertainment. Some of the jests are developed into short capsule-biographies and become picaresque tales of a rogue or practical joker whose exploits demand the reader's sympathy. Examples include George Peele's *Merry Conceited Jests of George Peele* (1607), *Dobson's Dire Bobbes* (1607), and *Long Meg of Westminster* (published 1620, probably written thirty or more years earlier). The atmosphere is usually colloquial and vulgar, and the basic narrative structure is episodic, with a rapid focus on a succession of individual incidents.

Anecdotes, jest-books, and jest-biographies all bring us much closer to the world that court romances were deliberately written to exclude and control. They constitute an undercurrent of short fiction that, while surfacing as much indirectly in other forms of literature as in their own right, nevertheless constitute a genuine alternative to the dominant cultural forms. The sources of energy in key works of the age—again, Bunyan provides an important example—coincide with and reinforce the tradition the reader must next consider. That tradition, Protestantism, on the surface seems antithetical to the dominant characteristics of prose (or any) fiction, and it is usually ignored in histories of the prose fiction of the period. This neglect is unfortunate, since in many ways Protestantism constituted the most important forward-looking movement of the whole age.

Except for occasional references, one group of Renaissance writings neglected as examples of prose fiction are the popular theological tracts. Many, admittedly, are among the most memorably unreadable works ever written—with exceptions such as John Foxe's *The Book of Martyrs* (1563), which is a masterwork of propaganda, of religious devotion, and, it might be suggested, of fiction. At its greatest moments—in the account of the deaths of Latimer and Ridley, for example—Foxe sets the reader down as an eyewitness (even ear- and nostril-witnesses) to events purportedly historical, revealing the details of which only the victims themselves could have been aware. Facts are redoubled, hearsay becomes fact, rumor is given tongue, and Foxe's rhetoric above all else directs his readers to participate in the revulsion against the persecutions of Bloody Mary.

In short, Foxe, self-consciously or otherwise, takes over the rhetorical duplicity and inherent depravity that pious Protestants mistrusted in literature, art, and above all prose fiction. During the 1570's, indeed, as the new movement in prose fiction gathered impetus, Protestant moralists shifted their traditional attacks on medieval verse romances to the new prose examples. Ascham, no extremist, regretted that the Bible was banished from the court and "Morte Arthure received into the Princes Chamber." Philip Stubbes, Gosson, and Perkins described the prose romances as "idle tales," "dreams merely to amuse the idle," "bookes of love, all idle discourses and histories," "nothing else but enticements and baites unto manifold sinnes." In the 1630's, the sophisticated Nicholas Ferrar spoke for a century of Protestant condemnation when he stated that romances and tales could not be allowed "to passe for good examples of vertue among Christians." Protestant theologians such as William Prynne in the 1630's or John Milton a decade later saw prose fiction as "profane discourses," or "baits for sin and corruption."

Behind such condemnations lies a suspicion of the autonomy of the human imagination, expressed in Saint Augustine's oft-cited definition of a tale or fable as "a lie, made for delectation sake." Yet, although Protestants attacked their society's increasing tolerance of books "whose impure Filth and vain Fabulosity, the light of God hath abolished utterly," as one Puritan pamphleteer put it, there is nevertheless a sense of the gradual fusion of fiction writer and theologian in a tradition of popular theological pamphlets heavily influenced by Foxe. Of course, as C. S. Lewis noted, while most of the attacks on prose fiction were by Protestants, so were most of the defenses. Sidney's *Arcadia* was praised by such stern moralists as his friend Fulke Greville for its moral seriousness, and it has been made apparent how consistently English readers and writers alike were most comfortable when their fiction was reassuringly moralized. In Europe, the Council of Trent was attempting to create a religious literature to replace the secular forms that dominated genteel and popular taste, and its influence can be seen in both the devotional lyric and in a fashion for explicitly Christian romances. The movement is especially associated with Jean Pierre Camus, Bishop of Bellay, whose *Dorothée* (1621) and *Palombe* (1624) are examples of the genre. Each is a Christianized pastoral romance designed to teach, respectively, the purity of marriage and the duties of parents. The typical romance features that have been observed are all present—dreamlike atmosphere, idealized characters, complicated plots—all held together by an explicitly theological drive.

Even more interesting are works that, while explicitly rejecting any fictional status, nevertheless show the marked influence of fictional techniques. Thomas Beard's *The Theatre of Gods Judgements* (1596, and many subsequent editions) is a case in point. Beard's aim is to survey the whole course of human history to demonstrate the inevitability of God's revenging judgments over a world which is "nothing else but an ocean full of hideous monsters or a thicke forest full of theeves and robbers." Apart from its highly colorful interpretation of God's nature, Beard's work is distinctive for its reliance on an endless succession of anecdotes, tales, and gossip— in short, on a variety of short fictions. Beard's style has the dash and crudity of

Greene's conny-catching pamphlets and the vividness of Nashe or Bandello: of the eighty-seven chapters in his first edition, eighteen are concerned with lust, whoredom, and uncleanness, twelve with the crimes of great men, and eleven with murder. Even within chapters dealing with offenses against less spectacular commandments—such as blasphemy (4), false witness (3), idolatry (3), and perjury (2)—his examples are chosen for their lurid powers of persuasion. Many of his examples are taken from Foxe and significantly elaborated by techniques which are drawn from the sources in popular culture which provided the strength of the best Elizabethan fiction. Yet another unusual hybrid is John Reynolds' *The Triumphs of God's Revenge, Against Murther* (1621), in which quite explicitly the enemy is not merely sin but fiction. Reynolds attacks the popularity of the amorous romance which, he says, panders to humankind's bare appetites by their "Perfuming, Powdering, Croping, Paynting, Amarous kisses, Sweet Smyles, Suggered speeches, Wanton embracings, and lascivious dalliance."

When one thinks of the importance of prose fiction in succeeding centuries, one might well look back to Beard and Reynolds (or to Bunyan's self-chastisement for reading lewd romances) as misguided opinions bypassed by history. Paradoxically, however, it was the Puritan dynamic, with its emphasis on self-understanding and the conscience of the individual before God, which came through into the eighteenth century to provide the intense moral concerns of Daniel Defoe, Richardson, and others. Protestant books of devotion and moral treatises turned inevitably to fictional portraits to exemplify worthy behavior. The classical genre of the character-book was revived and infused with a distinctive moralistic caste and again stressed not idealized characters in unrealistic settings but the temptations and contingencies of the world and the correct inner attitudes to cultivate. In short, the intense moral seriousness of the Protestant dynamic started, through the seventeenth century, to constitute a genuine countercultural movement which radically transformed the whole tone of English (and, by the 1620's, North American) life. Part of that transformation is the effect not only on forms of popular literature but also on the creation of a sensibility which would look to fiction with a new concentration on realistic motivation, recognizable settings, verisimilitude of characterization, and intense and complex moral dilemmas. Protestant polemics against fiction may have, in the period, distorted or helped prevent the maturing of an audience for prose fiction, but ultimately it provided crucial elements to make it possible.

The best short fiction in the sixteenth and seventeenth centuries, then, was written in this period of transition, between about 1570 and 1620, when it looked as if the tradition established by Sidney, Gascoigne, Lyly, Lodge, Greene, and Nashe and then modified by Deloney and Forde might produce a flowering in fiction akin to that in France, Italy, or Spain. This did not happen, however. R. A. Day has described the period between the death of Elizabeth and the early eighteenth century as a "wasteland" so far as fiction is concerned. It is a pardonable exaggeration. Continental fiction continued to dominate, especially the Spanish picaresque such as the old *La Celestina* (1499), which was first translated into English in 1631, and the long French heroic romance such as Honoré d'Urfé's *L'Astrée* (1607-1627), which was imitated in England in the 1640's and 1650's. Of the shorter works, Cervantes' *Exemplary Novels* (1613), one of the landmarks in the development of the European short story, was translated by James Mabbe but was not widely influential in England. Mabbe, in fact, translated only the romantic, melodramatic stories, not the more important and forward-looking low-life examples. Of the native works, the most popular were reprints of Sidney, Forde, Johnson, Munday, and Deloney. Overall, the fiction of the whole century presents a depressing picture.

Nevertheless, one can certainly pick out both interesting trends and a variety of fictional forms. Of the shorter kinds of fiction—tales of sentiment and love, collections of *novelle* in the manner of Boccaccio (who was first translated in 1620), didactic and exemplary fiction, jest-books, cautionary tales—all continued to be published. By and large, however, C. C. Mish's summary is an apt one: the course of short fiction during the years 1600-1660 was a "downward decline; the bright promise went down in sterile entertainment and preciousness." While (as Mish and others have shown) it is possible to put together an anthology of entertaining pieces from the period, most of the work is derivative, nostalgic, uncertain in style, and vitiated by inconsistency of technique and uncertainty of aim. The best continues to be translation—from the French, Italian, or Classical sources which continued to dominate European taste in fiction—or short, popular tales and anecdotes in the jest-book or jest-biography tradition such as Hugh Peters' *The Tales and Jests of Hugh Peters* (1660) and Nathaniel Crouch's *English Jests Refined* (1687), or picaresque fiction such as the anonymous *Murther upon Murther* (1684), *Sir John* (c. 1700), and *Bateman's Tragedy* (c. 1700). It is in the later seventeenth century, in fact, that the folklore and folktales of which there was only spasmodic evidence a century before start to surface in published works. Stories of Robin Hood, Fortunatus and his Magic Purse, and the like were clearly the main fictional diet of the lower classes, and had been for centuries. Only gradually were they becoming part of the mainstream of English culture. Other fiction remained firmly in the tradition of improbable, elaborate romance, often with exotic settings expressing the public's interest in newly discovered or fashionable parts of the world such as America, Turkey, or Surinam.

Major historical transitions do not occur overnight, and although in post-Restoration England there is little to change the picture of what short fiction was written there, nevertheless from the 1680's on there are signs of a new impetus in prose fiction that would lead to the re-creation of the genre as central to English culture during the following two hundred years. One sign is the indirect but crucial impact of the Protestant emphasis on soberly meeting and contemplating oneself as an individual and learning what it was, in this world, that might make for one's salvation. Indicative of this new importance of self-analysis was the gradual rise of epistolary fiction, stories in the form of letters, which was eventually to lead to Richardson's *Pamela*. In the seventeenth century, epistolary fiction was typically focused on the personal lives of wellborn or respectable women, and, while hardly (to modern taste) penetrating beneath the genteel surfaces, in retrospect these attempts represent an enormous breakthrough toward psychological realism. Telling a story in letters, as in the anonymous *Lettres portugaises* (France, 1669; translated as *Five Love-Letters from a Nun to a Cavalier* in 1678), allows the reader to focus on and partly inhabit the self-consciousness of the narrator. Gradually, prose-fiction writers were discovering what the dramatists had almost a century before—the need to let the reader participate in the making of the work's meanings. Another important change was the growing insistence, already anticipated by Nash or Deloney, on a degree of external verisimilitude in fiction. Details of setting became more functional, characters were introduced as part of the ongoing plot, motivation was more carefully linked by logic and circumstance, and speeches became more colloquial.

Particularly in France, there was a rapid growth in the variety and sophistication of short fiction. The long romance, *le roman de longue haleine*, gradually became less important in France and a variety of shorter, more realistic forms, became more dominant. The crucial difference between the earlier tales of Bandello, Cynthius, or Marguerite de Navarre and those of Madame de Lafayette (*La Princesse de Montpensier*, 1662, or *La Princesse de Clèves*, 1678) and others is precisely the movement toward some degree of *vraisemblance* in setting and, especially, in psychology. In England the development was slower, but a growing verisimilitude of setting at least appears in some of the tales of roguery such as John Davies' *Scarron's Novels* (1665), translated and adapted from the diverse short pieces in Paul Scarron's *Le Roman comique* (1651, 1657; English translation, 1651, 1657; also as *The Comical Romance*, 1665).

In the various kinds of fiction written after the Restoration, too, a new solution slowly developed for a problem that had clearly worried Elizabethan prose fictionists—the role of the narrator within the work. In collections such as Boccaccio's, Cynthius', or Painter's, there is usually a close relationship maintained between the narrator and the author in the introductory or "frame" material that links the individual tales together. At other times, as in Gascoigne or Sidney, the narrator will directly address his reader, at times be seemingly omnipotent, and at other times be disarmingly frank about his ignorance of his characters' motives, actions, or origins. In short, there is a shifting and often arbitrary relationship between the different narrative voices of the work; there is a characteristic opaqueness which continued into the eighteenth century in Laurence Sterne and which, interestingly, has reappeared in such fictionists as John Barth, Robert Coover, Raymond Federman, and Ronald Sukenick.

Gradually, however, especially after the Restoration, one can sense in fiction, first in France and then in England, the rise of fictional illusionism. The question of the author's access to the states of mind of his characters, especially if they were portrayed as historically real, which by the time of Jane Austen or William Makepeace Thackeray or Henry James was seen as jejune, was for Madame de Scudéry or Aphra Behn a most awkward one. The diverse solutions—the claims of having seen letters, read diaries, spoken to the persons involved—seem naïve to later eyes, but the questions being asked gradually produced the belief in the illusionism of fiction, the omnipotence of the narrator, and the self-contained autonomy of the world of the novel or tale. Without such developments, the so-called "realistic" novel of later centuries would not have been possible.

Of all the shorter fiction written in England after the Restoration, the most significant, and still readable, is that by the woman dramatist-novelist Aphra Behn, who wrote a dozen or so pieces of short fiction. Most are interesting mixtures of traditional romance with a few rather genteel hints of the new realism. Her stories are melodramatic, generalized, and elevated, but nevertheless—as in *The Perjur'd Beauty* (1688), *The History of the Nun* (1689), or the longer (posthumously published in 1688) *The Fair Jilt* and *Oroonoko*—reach unusual levels of intensity. *The Perjur'd Beauty* compresses into twenty-one pages the complicated love affairs of five men and women, including one, the beautiful and unpredictable Ardelia, who falls in love with three men, causing the death of all three men, the sister of one, and her own. Superficial, exploitative, and psychologically improbable, the work nevertheless has some energy and concentration that make it more approachable than the longer works of the period such as the Earl of Orrery's labored *Parthenissa* (1654-1669), which drags its reader lugubriously through six volumes nostalgically looking back to the world of Sidney's *Arcadia*.

In 1692, near enough to the end of this study's period to constitute a landmark, an indication at least of slowly changing tastes and of the deeper sociocultural currents beneath, William Congreve published his *Incognita*. Written when Congreve was twenty-two, the work—a charming, well-plotted, amusing Scarronian tale, a not altogether unsympathetic attack on the romance tradition—contains a preface which was to set out many of the issues for prose fiction in the next decades. He comments on the incredibility of the romance tradition: romances, he argues, are "generally composed of the Constant Loves and invincible Courages of Hero's, Heroins . . . where loftly Language, miraculous Contingencies and impossible Performances, elevate and surprise the Reader into a giddy Delight." Novels, by contrast, "are of a more familiar nature; come near us . . . with . . . Events but not such as a wholly unusual or unprecedented." Congreve's terminology was not new—Jean Regnault de Segrais in 1656 had distinguished the *nouvelle* from the *roman* by its greater *vraisemblance*—but in England, Congreve's explicit statement marks an important turning point in the development of fiction, as he bids farewell to the archaic world of romance and looks to the already emergent modes of short and long fiction that were to dominate the next century.

Looking back over this survey of short prose fiction between the impact of printing in the late fifteenth and the late seventeenth centuries, one can see that the changes in literary taste are inevitably the expressions of complex but definable structures of idea and feeling in the life of the whole society. In England the period was one of political and social energies for radical change, concentrated, thwarted, and then overwhelmed by forces closely tied to the new dominance of entrepreneurial capitalism. At the beginning of this period, the sociocultural power was slowly slipping from the older feudal aristocracy to classes more in harmony with the new forces of secularism, industrialism, and dominance over the world, nature, and one another. The cultural development of England between 1500 and 1700 is too complex to summarize thus, but one can see how the fiction of the period responds to and articulates such pressures—the slow replacement of an increasingly archaic mode of romance narrative, the slow growth of a confident new illusionism ("realism" is far too question-begging a term), an uncertainty not merely about the mode of fiction but about the very place of fiction in such a society, the spasmodic surfacing of repressed cultural modes of living in folktale, jest, or other popular forms—through the otherwise dominant cultural forms. Such changes can be discussed in literary terms, but they are not simply literary changes. In particular, this is the case with the so-called growth of realism. The triumph of realistic prose narrative in the eighteenth century is the triumph of a way of seeing the world, which provides an illusion that chosen events are linked causally, that details can be selected from human events and be perceived as inevitable, given, and irreducible. Realism, however, like the social system that it expresses, stresses the product and its consumption by the reader, not the production. Just as capitalist society represses the mode of production of any article and stresses the product's marketable value, so realism (produced, in fact, by a certain use of language) stresses only the final illusion of reality and the harmonious final effect on the reader-consumer. The writer's concern throughout this period with the place of the narrator in his text reflects more than a technical problem; in the eighteenth century, both Jonathan Swift and Laurence Sterne mercilessly satirize the notions that language is simply instrumental and reading is simply consumption. They look back, angrily or whimsically, to the earlier period when the writer-narrator was on more arbitrary but nevertheless intimate terms with his reader, and the writer did not feel obliged to believe that language was identical with the real world. The gradual triumph of the illusion of realism is undoubtedly the single most important development in this period—which, as we have seen, does contain (despite many modern scholars' opinions) a goodly variety of amusing, interesting fiction—but its triumph is not simply a passing fashion. Realism, with all its apparent naturalness, is the exact, and in many ways limited and limiting, articulation of the dynamic of a new age. In England (in America, a very different pattern was starting to emerge triumphantly) readers had to wait another two hundred years for an equivalent literary change—and for the complex cultural changes intertwining with and expressed by it.

Gary F. Waller

SHORT FICTION IN THE EIGHTEENTH CENTURY

The eighteenth century did not produce the first modern short story as it is known today as an art form, a clearly defined genre. Seldom during the century did a story have the firm story line and economy of effect that would justify labeling it a short story in the modern sense; a story was concerned with how an experience is valued and what difference it makes to someone, not merely what is said and done. A surprising number of literary historians agree that the birth of the genre did not occur until the early nineteenth century, in *The Sketch Book of Geoffrey Crayon, Gent.* (1819-1820), by Washington Irving.

As Benjamin Boyce states in his essay "Eighteenth-Century Short Fiction," however, for "the present discussion . . . 'short fiction' includes any kind of imaginative writing about people that contains or implies action and that does not exceed in length 12,000 words." Within this definition can be found the vast variety of forms of short fiction that were produced by writers of the eighteenth century. These include fairy tales, Oriental tales, satirical adventure tales, the *conte*, epistolary fiction, rogue literature, *sueño* (or dream) fiction, essays, moral tracts, character sketches, the German *Novelle*, and the *nouvelle* or novelette (considered by some critics to be merely a stepchild of the novel, simply a short, uncomplicated novel; for this essay's purposes, the novelette qualifies as eighteenth century short fiction). As will be seen, the great periodical of the eighteenth century, *The Spectator* (1711-1712, 1714), was the chief vehicle for the majority of these forms. In the latter part of the century, with the advent of Romanticism, gothic fiction and psychological tales became immensely popular.

It is quite apparent from the foregoing list that if the birth of the distinctly defined genre of the short story did not occur until the nineteenth century, then the eighteenth could fairly be said to be its gestation period. It saw a time in which fragmentary but excellent characteristics of the short story were refined until they coalesced into the superb whole. The seeds that allowed the growth of the genre were planted in the eighteenth century.

To appreciate fully the merits of authors or their writings, it is necessary to throw a searchlight on the period in which they wrote. The eighteenth century was, after all, one of the great pivotal and transitional eras of all time. It saw a severe dichotomy of thought. The century opened with the Enlightenment (also called the Age of Reason), then moved through the beginning of the Industrial Age with the invention of the steam engine in 1765, and then saw the American and French revolutions before closing under the strong and lasting influence of the age of passion, Romanticism. This essay will examine briefly the events of the age when considering each individual nation. The short fiction of the Western world is the focus here: England, America, France, Germany, Spain, and Italy.

England

England in 1700 was possibly the most advanced nation in Europe, yet the English scene of 1700 was darkened by political and religious corruption and injustice. Literature was strictly for aristocrats—those "to the manor born." Public schools were slowly being instituted, but they were few, and most people were unable to read or write. The cities, however, were growing, and the well-to-do were spending less time in their countryseats and more in the cities—more specifically, in the coffeehouses, discussing the latest news from abroad, from Parliament, from society.

Within these conditions was found the germ of the eventual short story proper. The need for a new social expression against the excesses of the Restoration created the personal essay, which attempted not only to address the conflicts of the time but also to chronicle the "talk of the town." Fictional "talkers" were created by the authors of periodicals. In *The Tatler* (1709-1711), created by Joseph Addison, and later in the superior *The Spectator*, created by both Addison and Richard Steele, were found the highest quality of fictional talkers, reflectors of their times. *The Spectator* was one of the most important periodicals of the century, greatly influencing writers throughout Western Europe and America. The best-known of the characters about whom Mr. Spectator "talks" in *The Spectator* is Sir Roger de Coverley, a good-natured gentleman who represents surviving feudalism and through whom the vehement opposition between town and country was expressed.

The mixture of fashionable contempt for book learning, blended with shrewd wit, is well represented in the character of amiable, simpleminded Will Wimble, one of Sir Roger's friends. His character is amazingly fleshed out with gentle satire in the de Coverley papers. Poor Will, younger brother to a baronet, has no estate and naturally no business sense, but he has mastered the craft of idleness. The depiction of English homebred life formed the basic nature of the early eighteenth century story: a graceful realism and the criticism of manners in an attractive satirical style, found especially in Addison's stories.

The Tatler and *The Spectator* were the first organs attempting to give form and consistency to the opinions rising out of the social context. Through Addison and Steele, public opinion was founded by a conscious effort of reason and persuasion. *The Spectator* and its predecessors (1690-1716), with their dual purposes to instruct and/or entertain, were true children of the Enlightenment. Reason and instruction were foremost considerations, and often this made for severe didacticism. Happily, though, the vehicle for instruction was fictional entertainment. That philosophy, consistently followed, is put best in Mr. Spectator's own words: "The mind ought sometimes to be diverted, that it may return to thinking better" (*The Spectator*, 102). Short fiction, still dubious and generally unfamiliar as a form of entertainment, played an important role in the success of *The Spectator*, and in a smaller way, *The Tatler* that preceded it.

Through character sketches such as those in the de Coverley papers, the short story began tentatively to detach itself from the essay. *The Spectator*, unlike earlier periodicals, presented dialogue not merely as a device to present two viewpoints but as a give-and-take between two generally believable characters. Although the short fiction in *The Spectator* is not always technically well drawn, it did provide embryonic examples of modern narration and developed characters.

Perhaps the best narrative is Addison's "The Vision of Mirza" (*The Spectator*, 159). Oriental tales became enormously popular after Antoine Galland's translation of *The Thousand and One Nights* (or *The Arabian Nights' Entertainments*) in 1704 and the later partial translation of Galland's version into English (1706). *The Spectator*, not surprisingly, capitalized on the form's influence in Oriental-flavored moral tales such as "The Vision of Mirza." Other forms of Oriental tales appeared as "letters" from the Orient, as in Charles de Montesquieu's *Lettres persanes* (1721; *Persian Letters*, 1722) and Oliver Goldsmith's *The Citizen of the World* (1762), and as romances—moral, philosophical, or satirical—such as Voltaire's popular *Zadig* (1748; English translation, 1749) and Samuel Johnson's similar *Rasselas, Prince of Abyssinia* (1759).

"The Vision of Mirza" displays a pleasing mixture of elements—Oriental material, allegory, and dream vision—and showcases Addison's ability to construct a narrative around a consistent mood and condensed action. A good narrator also controls a story by presenting a scene in its varied details. Addison excels in imaging a scene, and in "The Vision of Mirza," the reader is taken successfully by the second paragraph to enjoy the air on the mountaintops above Baghdad.

In Steele's sketch, "The Matchmaker" (*The Spectator*, 437), realistic details and several characters in motion make it a delightful narrative story. From the beginning words, the emphasis is on minute details of movement and gesture and on conversation with real people. "The Biter" (*The Spectator*, 504), though technically a simple character sketch, contains the record of actual spoken words, presented in such a way as to convey a conversational tone and the sting of wit, and is an excellent short narrative episode.

Whether directly by description or indirectly through action, the authors come close, in a number of cases, to achieving the conflict, unity of mood, and character interplay necessary for the short story proper, as in "The Envious Man" (*The Spectator*, 19). Sir Roger and his friends acted and talked in accordance with their imagined personalities. Human figures so naturally drawn had not appeared in English prose fiction before. The smooth, easy flow of words and natural conversational tone overlaid with brevity throughout *The Spectator* is worth a study for any short-fiction enthusiast.

The custom of didacticism restricted the range of short fiction in the eighteenth century to a certain extent. The tones in Samuel Johnson's didactic essays in *The Rambler* (1750-1752), though of high quality, approach dictatorial instruction. Anyone comparing the light and rhythmical periods of *The Spectator* to the ponderous sententiousness of *The Rambler* will perceive that the spirit of preaching was gaining ground on the genius of conversation. Hannah More's *Cheap Repository* tracts (1795-1798) also reflect the limitations of didacticism. Brought up from childhood on *The Spectator* and *The Rambler*, which introduced new and lofty conceptions of the principles of morality, the characters in More's tracts and her fifty tales and ballads are merely pegs on which to hang principles. The principles are stated with considerable skill in her case, but there is little development of character to help the case of short fiction at the time.

Didacticism of the period did reap benefits, though. The didactic morality influenced other writers such as Daniel Defoe and Jonathan Swift. The satire was generally directed against the upper classes, which, through writers such as Defoe, began a sympathetic understanding of poverty and travails of the underprivileged. Truth and realism were the watchwords of Defoe, a professed moralist. He brought to his short fiction a journalistic sense of truth and clarity. Indeed, Defoe's *A True Relation of the Apparition of One Mrs. Veal* (1706), long considered fiction, is merely a piece of expert reporting. His writing skills are evident, and the account has the same clear and simple delineation of scenes and the same lucid factual tone that compels the reader's belief, which Defoe's later famous works, such as *Robinson Crusoe* (1719), have.

Another English writer admired for his simplicity, lucidity, and reasonableness is Oliver Goldsmith, the most noteworthy successor of Johnson in the art of the didactic short story. He writes with a range of humor, from subtle irony to broad farce, and the impulse to tell a good story carried his imagination far beyond the scope of so-called "good sense." His writing contains a delightful balance of reason and imagination. In Goldsmith's work is found the essential conflict of the eighteenth century, the struggle between reason and passion. In his preface to *The Citizen of the World* (1762), he writes of this conflict: "I resemble one of those solitary animals that has been forced from its forest to gratify human curiosity. My earliest wish was to escape unheeded through life; but I have been set up, for halfpence, to fret and scamper at the end of my chain." In the story, the dichotomy of Goldsmith's mind is reflected by the reasonable and gay Chinese Philosopher and the gloomy, secretive Man in Black. Shades of the power of Romanticism are evident.

In the middle years of the eighteenth century, the novel is prominent among literary forms in England. Ultimately, the great novelists in England exerted a deep influence on Europe. Therefore, while the *nouvelle* in France emerged as a popular art form in the late seventeenth and early eighteenth centuries, the novelette and other similar fictional forms in England were quite overshadowed by the novel. Some of these included travel accounts, secret *histoires*, memoirs, and biographies (each of these forms were usually thinly disguised romances of passion). Eliza Haywood, who wrote, among other short fiction, *Secret Histories, Novels, and Poems* (1725), is an example of an author who acquiesced to the decreasing demand for the above fictional forms and wisely moved on to produce good quality novels.

Because of the emergence of the novel in England, then, the short story generally remained tied to the essay, chiefly in the periodical. Within this small range, its success was remarkable, and its impact kept the seeds of short fiction, though dormant in many ways by the end of the century, still alive.

America

In America during the eighteenth century, all roads did not lead to the novel, as in England. As literary historian Edward J. O'Brien (*The Advance of the American*

Short Story, 1931) theorizes, the answer lies in the difference of temperament and environment between the English (and Europeans) and the Americans. The more impatient and restless temperament of the pioneers, settling the relatively new and largely unexplored nation, and their view that there was little place for leisure in their rough and difficult environment (compare hardworking wealthy landowners in America to the Court and aristocracy of England and Europe in the 1700's) made the short story much more appealing—being brief and able to condense emotion into a figurative moment as it flies.

The essays of Benjamin Franklin covered a broad range of subject matter, in form and in purpose; it can be said that they kept short fiction creatively alive in the 1700's in America. He wrote gracefully and urbanely, yet could write equally well in the rough school of realism fathered by Defoe. The earthy realism of Franklin's style is vividly exemplified in one of his essays, "Reflections on Courtship and Marriage" (1749), in which he describes the picture that some women present in the morning, with "frowsy hair hanging in sweaty ringlets, staring like Medusa with her serpents . . . teeth furred and eyes crusted. . . ."

Influenced by the great periodicals in England, humor and satire were increasingly being given more stress in American essays. Franklin's "Dogood Papers" (1722) demonstrate his vivid imagination and his sense of the ridiculous. They resemble in style the colloquial manner of *The Spectator*, with one major difference, more typical of the aggressive pioneer spirit of America: the learned allusions and literary anecdotes of *The Spectator* were replaced by homely sayings and by comic, even earthy stories. They also show remarkable empathy for women and their problems, as Franklin sees through the eyes of the widow Silence Dogood; many are related to women's affairs and problems.

In 1732, Franklin wrote a series of three character sketches: of Anthony Afterwit, an honest tradesman with an extravagant wife; of Celia Single, a sketch with considerable dialogue as a forum to discuss women's rights; and of Alice Addertongue, whose words, through Franklin's pen, speak facetiously about scandal yet scrupulously avoid making his newspaper, *The Pennsylvania Gazette*, a scandal sheet as were some of the other papers of the day.

Franklin's "The Bagatelles" (1722-1784), lighthearted or humorous essays, are classics in short fiction that cover a great emotional range. Here, Franklin momentarily lays aside his constant watchword "utility." For once, his essay becomes not a mere means to an end. "The Elysian Fields" (1778), for example, is an excellent piece that shows considerable similarities to modern short stories—with a clearly discernible beginning, middle, and end, with elements of surprise and balanced irony. He was a writer clearly ahead of his time. Franklin established a tradition of humor and journalistic writing that was peculiarly American and that can be found in the best of modern short fiction.

France

In France, as well as America and England, the formal short story—with its exacting demands of narrative structure, content, and development—did not fully develop until well into the nineteenth century. From France, though, at the end of the seventeenth century and through the first half of the eighteenth, came the highest-quality short fiction in Europe and America. Voltaire and the Encyclopedists, leaders in Enlightenment thinking, were producing high quality *contes philosophiques*, and the *nouvelle* had replaced the heroic romance in popularity. A short fiction centered on a love intrigue, the *nouvelle*, though generally longer than most short fiction, showed the move toward shorter pieces and is considered integral to the development of the short story.

The first work of fiction in the 1700's actually to comply with the theory of the *nouvelle* is Robert Challes's *Les Illustres Françoises* (1713; *The Illustrious French Lovers*, 1727). The work is a collection of *nouvelles* or *histoires*, joined together within a narrative frame, so it belongs to the fictional genre that also contains Giovanni Boccaccio's *Decameron: O, Prencipe Galeotto* (1349-1351; *The Decameron*, 1620) and Geoffrey Chaucer's *The Canterbury Tales* (1387-1400). Challes's *nouvelle* is revolutionary in the way in which it focuses more closely on the texture of experience than earlier fictions, but at the same time it places heavy stress on the elements that restrain and shape emotional and impulsive elements in human character.

Montesquieu, a forerunner of Voltaire, deserves further mention in this essay for his vastly entertaining *Persian Letters*, fictional letters written home by two Persians traveling in France. One can enjoy them for their subtle irony and urbane style, and one can faintly hear the first criticisms of the artificiality of the French aristocracy.

Voltaire, in the early eighteenth century, stood as a symbol of the Enlightenment, and he is now considered an intellectual precursor of the French Revolution. He used—as did Franklin, who manifested the same spirit and ideals in America before the American Revolution—the weapon of humor to correct human folly. The bizarre adventures in *Candide* (1759) are the best examples of his skill in persuading with a smile to carry the reader along on an even flow, even while he uses satire's fierce energies to challenge readers' complacencies. He reveals the underside of the Enlightenment ideal of reason: that the much praised reason of human beings can also expose their weaknesses.

Voltaire at once invented the *conte philosophique* and brought it to such perfection that only few writers have dared to imitate him. *Le Micromégas* (1752; *Micromegas*, 1753), *Zadig*, and *Candide* all show Voltaire's ability to cover ground with complete lucidity in a small number of words. The first page of *Candide* offers a wonderful example. Without the slightest sense of haste or compression, the scene is set, the chief characters are introduced, and the tone and feeling of the story are established.

To complete a view of eighteenth century short fiction in France, it is necessary to observe the revolutionary effects, to observe how the disintegrating work of Voltaire and the Encyclopedists was followed by the constructive work of Jean-Jacques Rousseau, the dreamer. The earlier writers, such as Voltaire, worked to expose, even to destroy, the existing system; the later writers, such as Rousseau, were hopeful constructors, dreamers of ideal commonwealths and societies. Rousseau, at first alone, and seconded only later in life by the enthusiasm of a new school of Romanticists, imparts a touch of poetic fire to French thought in the latter half of the eighteenth century. Rousseau's *Julie: Ou, La Nouvelle Héloïse* (1761; *Eloise: Or, A Series of Original Letters*, 1761) marks the beginning of the new period. The essential idea is of life as an organic whole and human beings as creatures essentially connected with the rest of nature by virtue of their emotions—this is the very center of Romantic theory. Rousseau's *nouvelle* marked the shift in writing to an increase of subjectivity, which was ultimately painful and stressful (eventually, intense subjectivity became, as Johann Wolfgang von Goethe described it, a form of sickness). The new, free intensity of feeling of Romanticism, however, opened the floodgates of creativity, and the short story flourished in the nineteenth century because of it.

Even before Rousseau and full-blown Romanticism, there was an interest on the Continent in highly developed emotional responsiveness. In Germany, Goethe's work *Die Leiden des jungen Werthers* (1774; *The Sorrows of Young Werther*, 1779) was immensely influential in establishing the image of the introspective, self-pitying, melancholy Romantic hero. In fact, it was the German Romantic school that developed most quickly and thoroughly in Europe.

Germany

Although it was the novel that became the most popular fictional form in Germany during the "Romantic" end of the eighteenth century, excellent short fiction was produced as well because of the stronger emphasis on the narrative, rediscovered interest in fables, and the relaxed formal structures allowing increased freedom of expression.

The German *Novelle*, an original romance form of short fiction, was cultivated by the German Romanticists as well. Noteworthy is Goethe's *Unterhaltungen deutscher Ausgewanderten* (1795; *Conversations of German Emigrants*, 1854), with its escapist motif, written for the German periodical *Die Horen*. It is a framework series of stories intended primarily to entertain and to instruct, written much in the same manner as Boccaccio's *The Decameron*. As in the Italian work, there is a background of suffering and death contrasted with the relative calm among the small group of aristocrats involved in the storytelling.

The German Romanticist Ludwig Tieck was a prolific writer of *Novellen*, but his best work was in the realm of Romantic fairy tales. The excellent *Der blonde Eckbert* (1797; *Fair Eckbert*, 1828) is a product of dreams and fancies, which spin a web of varicolored moods and atmospheres. It delves into the depths of the subconscious. The awe-inspiring potency of Romantic writing is seen here at its best. Tieck succeeds quite well in giving poetic form to his mystic feeling for nature and in making nature a sort of allegory for the vague strivings and imaginings of humankind. True to his fatalism, which told him that human beings are at the mercy of higher powers, the horrible is seen as residing in nature itself and overpowering humankind.

The Romanticist's aversion to rationalism is exemplified in Tieck's famous short-fiction works in the three-volume *Volksmärchen* (1797), characterized by childlike feeling, unrestrained imagination, and satire against the Enlightenment. Here, Reason is held up to ridicule, and winsome miraculous happenings come into their own. Tieck and other early German Romantics sought the elements of wonder and horror in old fairy tales and in old German chapbooks and found far-off colorful lands of poesy, miracles, and dreams.

Spain

Both Romanticism and the Enlightenment came late to Spain, which was weakened from divisions and the loss of much territory at the beginning of the eighteenth century as a result of the War of the Spanish Succession (1714). Additionally, throughout the century, government censors and inquisitors were vigilant. As late as 1793, for example, a group of intellectuals who wanted to publish a periodical called *El Académico* made a promise that shows the power of censorship over the press at that time. They proclaimed, "We will say nothing, quote nothing, and become involved in nothing which might cause offence and would rather pass for ignorant in the eyes of some than for men of new ideas." It was a situation unique to the rest of the Western world at that time.

Although censors and inquisitors might have kept much of the Enlightenment out of print, however, they could not keep it out of Spain. For example, in the 1770's, the bishop of Plasencia complained to the king of the ease with which he had procured the irreligious and subversive writings of Voltaire himself. If such works could not be published in Spain, it was difficult to avoid their discussion at private gatherings and in the coffeehouses.

By the middle of the century, increasing contact with the rest of Europe led Spanish writers to explore international literary forms. One of the first to adopt an obviously European style was José Clavijo y Fajardo, whose periodical *El Pensador* began to appear weekly in 1762. The model for this was clearly *The Spectator*. Seven whole speculations are translated, and there are direct imitations of at least six others. Clavijo y Fajardo adopted many of *The Spectator*'s fictional forms. Some of his fictional devices, however, have purely Spanish sources.

The periodicals encouraged the development of short forms and rapid, even casual reading habits in readers. Enlightenment topics occupied the majority of space in Spanish periodicals and fueled such dangerous prose works as *Cartas marruecas* (1775), by José de Cadalso y Vásquez (the most original of the literary Enlightenment thinkers of the day), which accepts the morality of the Moors as well as the Christians in the central characters. Works such as Cadalso's often fell victim to the Inquisition into the nineteenth century.

A pre-periodical short fiction form that was to become a staple of Spanish periodicals in the late eighteenth and early nineteenth centuries was the fictional dream or *sueño*. Diego de Torres Villarroel's *Sueños morales* (1727 and 1728) and later those of Ramirez de Gongora are the best examples of the dream fiction that later found its way in the form of short *sueños morales* into the periodicals.

In the light of eighteenth century repression in Spain, it is understandable that through most of the century, Spanish writers restrained their imagination. Even Spanish satires were more closely related to the everyday in Spain than, say, Jonathan Swift's *Gulliver's Travels* (1726) or Voltaire's *Candide*. The Peninsular War in the middle of the century was instrumental in opening the way for Romantic thought with its non-*hidalgo* officers, which made the first real breach in the status system. The middle and lower classes had found a voice. Finally, in the 1790's, with the publication of Mor de Fuentes' *La Serafina* (1796)—a novel of love in the provinces told in the form of letters and singing the virtues of country life and simple people— it was obvious that Romanticism was arriving.

Italy

In Italy, if the seventeenth century, under the iron despotism of Spain, was a time of stagnation, then the eighteenth was a period of recovery, for Italy was one of the territories lost by Spain in the War of the Spanish Succession. The ancient luster of literature, indeed, was but feebly rekindled, but an invigorating breath pervaded the nation as Spanish dominion disappeared from Italy. People wrote and thought in comparative freedom.

The extinction of the free spirit of the Renaissance was the more unfortunate for Italy, as it arrested the development of speculative and scientific research, which had seemed to be opening up there. Therefore, it was natural that the thrust of Italian literature was toward those directions in the eighteenth century, not toward fiction in its many forms experienced throughout the Continent. Certainly no novelist of reputation wrote from Italy during the century. Italy could have easily degenerated into mediocrity but for the tremendous literary convulsions at the end of the century. Only in drama did Italy stand apart and supreme during nearly the whole of the age.

By the middle of the century, a strong wave of foreign influence, particularly from France, and more indirectly from England, aided markedly in the awakening of Enlightenment thinking reflected in Italian literature. As one might assume by now, it was the periodical that hurried the spread of liberal ideas in Italy and kept various forms of short fiction active. It should also be no surprise that *The Spectator* was the model for most Italian periodicals, such as *Il Caffe* (1764-1766) and Gaspare Gozzi's *La Gazzetta veneta* (1760-1761), which included imaginative original sketches and stories with acute but gentle satire and humor directed at the Venetian scene. Gozzi continued the tradition in 1761 and 1762 with *L'Osservatore venuto*, a journal of manners and customs very similar to Addison's *The Spectator*.

Gozzi's younger brother Carlo was a writer of note with considerable ability. The popularity of his works show the slow move to Romanticism that blossomed at the end of the century in Italy. Carlo Gozzi's best-known works are his fairy tales. The most successful one of his famous scenic stories is the exotic and fantastical *L'Amore delle tre malarance* (1761; the love of three oranges). His stories were intensely popular throughout the Romantic period and beyond.

Italy was one of the last countries to feel the effects of Romanticism, but as the cosmopolitan drift became more and more powerful toward the end of the century, writers such as Goethe and Sir Walter Scott excited the curiosity of Italian readers. Italy joined late but joined entirely the movement, impatient with the prosaic present and enamored of the neglected Middle Ages.

As the eighteenth century drew to a close, Spain and Italy were playing literary catch-up, while the focus in Germany, France, and England was on the novel. The geographic isolation of America made it a separate entity as far as literature was concerned, almost an anomaly. Given the state of short fiction in England and on the Continent by the end of the eighteenth century, perhaps it is not surprising that the short-story genre emerged strong and distinct in America. In England, great periodicals such as *The Spectator* had lost considerable influence in the face of the proliferation of low-quality magazines, penny dreadfuls, and chapbooks because of cheaper printing methods and a growing working-class readership.

The news for short fiction, however, was not all bad. Gothic themes were found not only in cheap magazines but also in high-quality novels. Also, the element of suspense and tension in the gothic theme found its way into the modern short story, elements that had been lacking throughout the eighteenth century. Additionally, the coming of the popular magazine established a market for brief prose pieces, however inferior those pieces might be. The way was kept open for the exceptional creativity of nineteenth century writers and for the emergence of the distinct short-story genre.

The debt that these writers owe to the Enlightenment periodicals is not small. The vast array of fictional forms produced in these publications paved the way for the cohesive short forms that evolved in the nineteenth century.

The Spectator was the model for most of the periodicals of the age. For good reason, it was the most widely read and the best periodical of the century. The purpose of *The Spectator* was not only to instruct but also—and this is perhaps its most significant contribution to the short-story genre—to entertain. The motto for *The Spectator* 1 was successfully followed by Addison and Steele and has the kind of staying power that makes it a worthy goal for fiction of any age: "Not smoke after flame does he plan to give, but after smoke the light, that then he may set forth striking and wondrous tales."

Marilyn Schultz

SHORT FICTION: 1800-1840

By the year 1800 various Western literatures could boast isolated examples of works which, if they were published today, would almost certainly be called short stories in the modern sense of the term. These works are in one sense rather like those hypothetical Phoenicians or Greeks or Vikings who stumbled onto America before Columbus. In the final analysis we celebrate Columbus not so much for being the first as for being the first to make much historical difference. By the same token, the originator of the modern short story is the writer whose first short story made the most dramatic difference to the genre and to subsequent literary history. By 1800, although well on the way, that person had not yet arrived. What was found then in short fiction throughout the Western world was a dizzying variety of forms, traditions, genres, and subgenres that sometimes approached quite closely the modern short story, which in fact seemed to have produced splendid isolated examples, as in Sir Richard Steele's *The Spectator* 113, but which—although generating fine literature according to other criteria—finally fell short of a consistent vision, a full conception of the short story as it is thought of today.

This short narrative current in the year 1800 can be arbitrarily divided in as many different ways as might a custard pie, but the most meaningful division would seem to be into the broad categories of work in the tale tradition on the one hand and in the essay-sketch tradition on the other.

The Tale Tradition

The tale tradition had by far a longer and more complex history than the essay-sketch tradition. Virtually every anthropologist, linguist, and literary historian would agree that tales in one form or another are approximately as old as language, and if language is the distinguishing feature of Homo sapiens, then tales must have originated at almost exactly the same time as human beings. Judging from what is known of human nature, one can assume that the first tales took the form of either lies or gossip, which remain among the most seductive categories of narrative today. People must have soon varied the literary fare with the sort of oral tales which seem to have flourished then and which still flourish today among preliterate peoples in just about every culture on the face of the earth: myths, legends, folktales, jokes, anecdotes, and so on—and subsequently with the sorts of refinements and variations of these forms which develop in diverse guises in various cultures at various times. Among the terms (often overlapping) for specifically oral tales with which Stith Thompson deals in his classic study, *The Folktale* (1851), are *Märchen*, fairy tale, household tale, *conte populaire*, novella, hero tale, *Sage*, local tradition, local legend, migratory legend, *tradition populaire*, explanatory tale, etiological tale, *Natursage*, *pourquoi* story, animal tale, fable, jest, humorous anecdote, merry tale, *Schwank*, and so on.

Of course, such genres invariably alter, sometimes quite subtly, sometimes fundamentally, when the means of transmission becomes not the more or less dramatic human voice (with accompanying facial expressions and physical gestures and so on) of a person immediately present, but impersonal pen and ink. Earlier sections of *The Folktale* describe some of the forms of written tale that have spanned the centuries since the paleolithic oral tale: Geoffrey Chaucer's *fabliaux*, saints' legends, beast fables, and Chivalric romances, for example.

About the year 1800, as for many decades before and after, there were basically three avenues by which these works in the tale tradition reached the public. The first is the oldest, the most widespread, and in many ways the most important—oral storytelling. It is safe to say that until television metastasized so dramatically in the 1950's almost everyone on the planet was introduced to literature by way of tales such as "Snow White" and "Jack and the Beanstalk" or stories of Spider or of Rabbit and Coyote or of Fox or Bear. Even the Saturday morning television programs so many children watch are fundamentally in the same tale tradition. The second means of transmission was books. European children had long enjoyed chapbooks like *Jack the Giant Killer*, and adults titillated their own imaginations with fare as varied as jest books and saints' legends. Countless European fairy tales had appeared in print, among them Charles Perrault's *Histoires et contes du temps passé, avec des moralités* (1697), but a powerful new influence entered in 1704-1717 with Antoine Galland's first European translation (into French) of *The Thousand and One Nights* (or *The Arabian Nights' Entertainments*). Something of the international character of these stories may be inferred from the fact that the English translated the French translation which was itself an Arabic (largely Persian) translation of stories primarily derived from India and China. Where the stories ultimately originated and how old they really are no one will ever know. The magnificent example of *The Thousand and One Nights* and the growing interest in the past and in primitives which helped stimulate the rise of Romanticism led to Jacob and Wilhelm Grimm's *Kinder- und Hausmärchen* (1812, 1815, 1822; *Grimms' Fairy Tales*, 1824-1826) and to a host of similar folkloric collections in the early 1800's.

The tales in books tended to be one step from the traditional oral tales, but by 1800 a third medium, periodical publications—chiefly newspapers and magazines— offered a bewildering variety of forms of tale. Many were quite traditional; magazines published forms such as fables, anecdotes, fairy tales, and legends. Many, however, were quite different forms; many were much closer to what would be recognized as the modern short story. James Louis Gray lists among the many subgenres of short fiction in late eighteenth and early nineteenth century periodicals forms he calls tales of character, moral tales, histories, dialogues, sentimental tales, adventure tales, and allegories of the heart.

By the year 1800 all these antecedent forms continued to exist—orally or in print— and inevitably had a tremendous impact on the mind of anyone concerned with short fiction.

The Essay-Sketch Tradition

The second grand tradition dominating short prose works in the year 1800 was that of the essay, especially the periodical essay or sketch. One can trace full-fledged tales back to the evolution of language, but the essay or sketch can hardly have existed before the creation of a fairly sophisticated system of writing. In one form or another essays must have existed from the time the first writer attempted (the word "essay" comes from the French word meaning to try or to attempt) to capture in prose thoughts or feelings about some subject; alternately the sketch must have begun when the writer attempted to characterize or to describe some subject in prose.

Most historians of Western literature recognize as the first great writer of sketches the Greek philosopher Theophrastus, who around 300 B.C. composed a book called *Characters*; the work was composed of several short prose pieces, each representing some basic character or personality type. Theophrastus' sketches had a tremendous influence on later writers of sketches, especially those in the seventeenth century: Joseph Hall, John Earle, Sir Thomas Overbury, and Jean de La Bruyère. These writers in turn influenced Joseph Addison and Sir Richard Steele, who in *The Tatler* and *The Spectator* developed a number of more or less typical characters; the most important was Sir Roger de Coverley, a good-natured provincial squire with whom the sketch approached the sort of sophistication with which subsequent novelists were to treat character. In the decades preceding 1800 various writers such as Benjamin Franklin and Oliver Goldsmith, inspired by the example of Sir Roger, carried the character sketch further and further from idealized abstraction, closer and closer to the sort of uniqueness and individuality associated with character in fiction. With the gradual waxing of Romanticism and the slow shift of emphasis from thought to feeling, the character sketch had evolved into a form only slightly removed from the modern short story.

The essay has a similar lengthy history. From the beginnings of the form, the subject discussed seems to have held precedence over the individual mind acting on that subject, but in 1580 a minor literary revolution occurred when the Frenchman Michel de Montaigne published his *Essais*. Wishing to explore the nature of humanity and convinced that each person was a microcosm of the whole, he determined to plumb his own mind in detail ("I myself am the matter of my book. . . . It is myself that I depict"). Few subsequent essayists ever achieved a style or tone approaching Montaigne's charming intimacy, but his intensive compelling introspection helped others, even writers such as the relatively formal Sir Francis Bacon, shift their own focus more in the direction of personality. Again Addison and Steele played a crucial role; in *The Tatler* and especially in *The Spectator*, they popularized what had been a relatively esoteric form and established a most successful model for a periodical series; these periodical series offered a variety of brief compositions on a dizzying miscellany of topics, unified by little but the persona of the essayist, the anonymous Tatler or Spectator. Benjamin Franklin and other followers cultivated a richer personality in the essayist; and by the year 1800, with the rise of sentimentality and Romanticism, the personality of the essayist became dramatically more important, to reach a plateau shortly in the familiar or personal essay as practiced by Charles Lamb and his contemporaries and followers.

Absolutely pure prose forms are approximately as rare as unicorns. Although the essay takes the natural form of exposition and the sketch inherently, irresistibly gravitates toward description, some narrative did invade both forms. We are familiar with narrative essays and with sketches which are almost stories; these were popular phenomena long before the birth of the modern short story.

Washington Irving: The Creation of the Modern Short Story

Precisely when did the modern short story begin? The question is like asking precisely where it is that the blue shades into violet in a rainbow. The more specific and dogmatic the answer the less reliable it is likely to be. It is known, however, that by the early 1800's in America, and in various degrees throughout the Western world, two distinct traditions existed side by side: one, the tale tradition full of narrative bursting with drama and incident, extraordinary situations and settings, and rather flat characters depicted for the most part externally; the other, the essay-sketch tradition, more subtly developed, largely ignoring striking incidents to focus on the vagaries of character, preferring the more normal and usual (in one sense more realistic) characters, situations, events, and settings, depending more on sharply observed detail, introspection, and thoughtfulness than on drama. The union of these two traditions was to mark the creation of the modern short story—but precisely when did that happen?

Literary historians, although less than unanimous, show a surprising degree of agreement that the modern short story began in America and that the American with whom it began was Washington Irving. The finest scholar of the American short story, Frederick Lewis Pattee, wrote that the form began in October, 1807, with Irving's publication in the periodical series *Salmagundi* of "The Little Man in Black." The piece is short and a story but has decidedly too little sophistication, too little psychological depth, and too little successful imagery really to succeed as a modern short story. At least as good, if not better, a case could be made for "Sketches from Nature" (perhaps by Irving or by his collaborator James Kirke Paulding, although in fact more likely by both), which appeared a month earlier in the same periodical series. Here we have a focus on mood and psychological subtleties, on sharply observed imagery, and on interior states. The problem is that finally the psychic change on which the piece ends does not add up to very much. The solution seems simple now: merely blend the virtues of "The Little Man in Black" (those of the tale tradition generally) and the virtues of "Sketches from Nature" (those of the essay-sketch tradition); but the evolution which had waited several thousand years after the introduction of writing to the Western world, tens and perhaps hundreds of thousands of years after the invention of storytelling, was in no hurry to occur.

No one with any degree of certainty can point to any given work as indisputably the world's first modern short story. We can with confidence, however, point out the first truly great modern short story produced in the Western world: "Rip Van Winkle," which appeared in the May, 1819, debut of Washington Irving's periodically published book, *The Sketch Book of Geoffrey Crayon, Gent.* Earlier writers had managed various blends of the tale and essay-sketch traditions before Irving, but none managed so brilliantly to blend the best of both traditions as to create from these two an irresistibly successful example of a wholly new form. How did Irving do it?

The most memorable parts of the story, the striking incident pattern involving Rip's experience with the dwarfish sailors of the *Half-Moon* and his two-decade-long nap, Irving based on a tale about a goatherd taken from Germanic folklore. In another bow toward the tale tradition, within the text itself, Irving's narrative persona, Diedrich Knickerbocker, relates that he heard the tale told orally by Rip himself and by other old Dutch settlers in the Catskills. The supernatural motifs of encountering the crew of Henrick Hudson's *Half-Moon*, who return every twenty years to tipple and to play ninepins in the mountains, and of course Rip's long sleep, also derive from the traditions of oral narrative.

In one form or another, however, all these elements existed long before Irving. His genius consisted in the brilliance with which he transmuted the elements which the tale tradition offered to him and to every other writer of his time. Irving transformed those basic elements by treating them as he might have treated the essential matter of a periodical essay or sketch. He developed Rip not as the flat character so common in tales, not as a kind of cardboard marker to be pushed from square to square in a board game, but as a rich, full, complete human being. Rather than merely assert certain abstract qualities in his character, Irving shows us through rich details a Rip who is good-natured, lovable, feckless, irresponsible, and (inevitably, given the above qualities and a wife too) terribly henpecked. The details with which Irving develops Rip are realistic, credible, and concrete—precisely the kinds of details with which the contemporary sketch-developed characters descended from Sir Roger de Coverley. Few if any previous prose tales could boast a character so effectively developed in terms of a credible human personality.

For many, the most characteristic aspect of the modern short story is its quality of psychological analysis, and of course the short prose form most inclined to intimate personal revelation came from the essay-sketch tradition, the familiar or personal essay. It is no accident that *The Sketch Book of Geoffrey Crayon, Gent.*, generally credited with containing the first great American successes in the personal essay, also contained a minutely detailed analysis of Rip Van Winkle's slowly dawning recognition of the immense changes twenty years made in himself and in his environment. Rarely if ever in a prose tale before Irving's masterpiece has the reader spent so much time minutely analyzing a character's mind.

Yet in "Rip Van Winkle," Irving pays quite as much attention to setting as to personality and psychology. With the rise of Romanticism, verbal sketches of nature achieved the same sort of popularity as those in the visual arts. Unlike almost any previous tale, "Rip Van Winkle" opens not by introducing a character or by outlining an incident or a situation, but with a subtle, sensitive, and thematically quite relevant description of a setting: the Catskills and a sleepy Dutch village within them. The careful arrangement and coloring, the sharp detail, and the attention to atmosphere in "Rip Van Winkle" help set it apart from earlier prose tales, which tended either to ignore setting or to dismiss it in brief idealized summary.

Some define the modern short story in terms of its realism, another quality much more characteristic of the essay-sketch tradition than of works in the tale tradition. For many readers the supernatural tipplers and Rip's incredible twenty-year sleep absolutely destroy any of the story's claims to realism—as they should if these elements reflect the mood of the story as a whole; but they do not, for three reasons. First, the great mass of the story (all but about six paragraphs) takes place in a densely realistic environment, in a setting developed with detail rich and credible enough to be all but photographic; few stories, for example, picture a scene more powerfully realistic than the long account of Rip's homecoming. Second, Irving gives us every reason to disbelieve that anything supernatural ever occurred. For one thing, most of the townspeople themselves refuse to believe Rip's story; for another, we learn that Rip himself told several versions of his story before finally fixing on one. A third point (one that cannot be appreciated if readers consult only various anthologies' butchered reprintings of the story) is that Irving chooses to tell the story *not* through an omniscient narrator, *not* through the reliable Geoffrey Crayon who supposedly authors *The Sketch Book of Geoffrey Crayon, Gent.* as a whole, but through the credulous dunderhead Diedrich Knickerbocker, purported author of Irving's ridiculous *A History of New York* (1809). In a note at the end we learn that even Knickerbocker realizes how unbelievable Rip's story is and feels obliged to offer corroborating evidence. The evidence: he has heard of equally incredible stories supposed to have occurred in the Catskills, and, for the clinching argument, he heard the story from Rip Van Winkle himself who even (and before a rural justice of the peace) signed, with an *x*, a document testifying to the tale's accuracy. In a technical strategy as old as time, Irving allows us our choice between alternative explanations: the story is literally true or, if we prefer, Rip ran away from his henpecking wife and, hearing that after twenty years she died in a fit of anger at a peddler, he promptly returned with an outrageous lie to explain his long absence, a lie which only the most naïve will believe in the least. For those inclined to look closely, behind the façade of fantasy Irving displays an architecture grounded in solid reality.

It was particularly the confluence of these elements from the tale (plot and striking incident) and from the essay-sketch (character, psychological depth, setting, realism) which created the modern short story. Certain other, rather more unique, factors of "Rip Van Winkle" pioneered various subsequent trends in the short story. The intense focus on a unique place—the physical surroundings, the habits and customs and peculiar modes of thought of a subculture—showed the way for the local color movement which dominated Western literature in the second half of the century. In the bookish outsider Diedrich Knickerbocker bamboozled by a backwoods native's outrageous tall tale (and in "The Legend of Sleepy Hollow" the outsider Ichabod Crane's unhappy experiences with the native frontiersman Brom Bones), there is found an early example of frontier humor, a mode that burst on the scene in the 1830's and eventually gave rise to Mark Twain and *The Adventures of Huckle-*

berry Finn (1884) and in the present time to much of William Faulkner's work. Other important aspects of "Rip Van Winkle" are the story's toying wth conventions of literary realism through its claim to truth based on a statement taken before a notary public; its layering of narrators—from Irving to Crayon to Knickerbocker who bases his version on Rip's oral tale; and its recycling of Knickerbocker from *A History of New York* and *Salmagundi* and reference to one of Rip's cronies, Peter Vanderdonk, and to his ancestor, Adriaen Van der Donck, who actually lived and who wrote an actual description of New Netherland (New York), to which Irving also refers in the story. This "deconstructive" technique of calling into question the essential "reality" of the narrative itself looks forward to O. Henry and beyond to the Postmodernists among our contemporaries.

Irving's literary earthquake, "Rip Van Winkle," was followed by a series of aftershocks that began the new decade of the 1820's for the short story. "The Spectre Bridegroom" and "The Legend of Sleepy Hollow" and "The Adventure of the German Student," all read with pleasure today, show an increasing tendency toward the Gothic mode which Nathaniel Hawthorne, Edgar Allan Poe, and Herman Melville were to employ to create some of the finest short stories in world literature. There were some other American stories of the 1820's read with genuine pleasure today— William Austin's "Peter Rugg, the Missing Man" (1824), for example—but most of the decade was given over to melodrama, to sentimental romance, or to didacticism. The popular reputations of the literary lions of the day have biodegraded quite as thoroughly as most of the paper on which they imposed their writings. Even the best among them—James Kirke Paulding (1778-1860), Catharine Sedgwick (1789-1867), Nathaniel Parker Willis (1806-1867), John Neal (1793-1876), Timothy Flint (1780-1840), James Hall (1793-1868)—are now little more than historical footnotes.

Point of view may be as important in literary history as in literature. In America the decade of the 1820's represented a tremendous falling off if the standard of comparison is the best of Irving's *The Sketch Book of Geoffrey Crayon, Gent.* On the other hand, if the standard is all other short narrative of the immediately preceding decades, then the 1820's represented a period of regular, if unhurried, advances in the skill and sophistication with which writers approached short fiction in general and this new form, the modern short story, in particular.

The true decade of advance for the genre—in America and, as shall be seen, in Europe—was the 1830's, which saw three different kinds of revolutions, one authored by Nathaniel Hawthorne, one by Edgar Allan Poe, and one by Augustus Baldwin Longstreet.

Nathaniel Hawthorne

Hawthorne's career began in a kind of imitation of the development of the modern short story. His earliest works were rather old-fashioned tales—"The Hollow of the Three Hills" (1830) and "Sir William Phipps" (1830)—and he also produced an early sketch, "Sights from a Steeple" (1831), which was much vaunted in his day; but these early works are finally insignificant. Hawthorne created the kind of artistic success destined to stand time's most stringent tests only when he combined the best of these two antecedent traditions in "My Kinsman, Major Molineux" (1832). Here, on the one hand, is a form close to the local New England legends he so loved to read and to compose—he opens with a paragraph of history referring to a real historian, sets the scene in historical Boston, gives a rough time for the event, builds his climax around the kind of episode (tarring and feathering a minor Tory official) which might have earned a brief footnote or inspired some oral tale. To this frame, however, Hawthorne adds the sort of rich imagery, the close psychological analysis, and the compelling specific detail which characterized his many experiments in the essay-sketch tradition. The result is neither essay, sketch, nor tale, but one of the finest modern short stories anyone ever wrote.

Similar patterns dominate "Young Goodman Brown" (1835). Many mistakenly try to read the story as a kind of simplistic parable, but Henry James, among others, emphatically disagreed: "this, it seems to me, is just what it is not. It is not a parable, but a picture, which is a very different thing." As in "My Kinsman, Major Molineux," Hawthorne here relies on intensive imagery and detailed psychological analysis to move well beyond the traditional tale and to create a truly modern short story. Here, as in many other short pieces, he borrows much from the tale tradition—striking incident, dramatic situation, Gothic motifs, and so on. In his best work he does not, however, borrow plot in the strict sense of the term—that is, plot in the sense of a causal sequence of events leading to a climax. J. Donald Crowley and many other critics have described a "processional mode" which Hawthorne tends to substitute for plot. In these two stories, as in many others, Hawthorne develops the central experience through a series of tableaux or vivid scenes which occur in front of the character's eyes. The mode, which tends to be much more passive than active, seems to have been instinctive with Hawthorne, but a case could be made that he borrowed the technique from the contemporary descriptive sketch. Certainly the pattern dominated his own sketches; and, oddly enough, until he published *The Scarlet Letter* in 1850, it was these works firmly in the essay-sketch tradition rather than the short stories (or "tales" as his contemporaries would have called them) for which Hawthorne was principally recognized. In various personal comments, such as the 1851 Preface to *Twice-Told Tales* (1837), Hawthorne alluded to the public conception of himself as "a mild, shy, gentle, melancholic, exceedingly sensitive, and not very forcible man," generally, that is, as the author of such popular pieces as "Little Annie's Ramble," "A Rill from the Town Pump," and "The Toll-Gatherer's Day." What R. H. Fogle called "a general nineteenth-century mistrust of plot" helped cause many of those works least read in our own day to be among the most popular in his own. A contemporary, Henry T. Tuckerman, noted a "melodramatic" and a "meditative" strain in Hawthorne's fiction, and, like a great many contemporary readers and critics, revealed a decided preference for the latter, those more akin to the essay-sketch tradition.

Edgar Allan Poe

One tends to think of the early nineteenth century as the heyday of the "traditional" short story—that is, the short story dominated by plot—but in fact experimental or innovative or unplotted short fiction was' at least as popular in the time of Hawthorne and Poe as it is in our own. Perhaps the most important reason for our myopia is that in May, 1842, Edgar Allan Poe's highly laudatory and immensely influential review of Hawthorne's *Twice-Told Tales* was published; Poe's essay is almost universally recognized as the very first attempt to develop a cogent formal theory of the modern short story. Most critics today recognize that Poe's theory applies much more closely to his own work than to that of Hawthorne, who himself wrote Poe in June, 1846, that he admired Poe more "as a writer of tales than as a critic upon them. I might often—and often do—dissent from your opinions in the latter capacity, but would never fail to recognize your force and originality in the former." In an 1847 review for *Godey's Magazine*, five years after his first attempt, Poe was still refining his theory, but in essence he still held that a story must be judged wholly on the basis of the effect it creates; he further insisted that only the most finely adapted and consciously applied technical skill could ensure the desired effect. The technical skill itself should focus tightly on incident and arrangement of incident (in 1847 he added "tone" to his blueprint).

Many scholars credit Poe's theory with an immense influence on the subsequent development of the short story. Certainly Poe's disciple Fitz-James O'Brien (c. 1828-1862) and many others would seem to have constructed their houses of fiction brick by brick according to Poe's blueprint; but how well does the blueprint describe antecedent fiction, such as Hawthorne's? According to Hawthorne and according to the best critics among his contemporaries and among our own, not very well. How well does the blueprint fit Poe's own fiction? Again, not very well. Poe does often have a climactic scene at the conclusion of his stories, but he most often and most successfully prepares for that conclusion not by developing a strong plot, a strong series of tightly integrated actions, but by intensely, powerfully, mercilessly overwhelming his readers with a dizzying atmosphere of sensually overwhelming imagery. As countless critics have commented, even in his most dramatic stories, in "The Fall of the House of Usher" (1839), in "Ligeia" (1838), and in "The Masque of the Red Death" (1842), Poe relies on a minimum of incident and on a maximum of imagery to prepare for his final effect.

Poe seems to have intuitively realized the fact and to have acknowledged its truth in the text of his most popular, and perhaps his finest, short story, "The Fall of the House of Usher." The story's epigraph keys us to the significance of an intensely sensitive awareness, and the story's first paragraph depicts a narrator powerfully affected not by any incident or arrangement of incident, but by imagery—the aspect of the house he describes so powerfully. Poe as book reviewer focuses on effect created by consciously manipulated patterns of incident; Poe's narrative protagonist focuses on effects created by the subconscious powers of imagery: "there *are* combinations of very simple natural objects which have the power of thus affecting us, still the analysis of this power lies among considerations beyond our depth." The reader who falls under Poe's spell in the story can only agree. Poe does have some stories more dependent on incident—"The Black Cat" (1843), for example, and "The Pit and the Pendulum" (1843)—but strangely enough he has other works which he called "tales" that have practically no incident whatever and which even today most readers would be much more inclined to consider sketches than true stories—"The Elk" (1844) is an example.

What conclusions should one draw? Poe's description of the intensively plotted story of effect described Hawthorne's best fiction and Poe's own best relatively poorly. Much more was going on than reasoned analysis could master. On the other hand, Poe might be said to have outlined his analysis as more an ideal to be sought (various desirable but unattainable ideals form the constant focus of his poems and stories) than as a reality already achieved. In this sense—that is, as a call to greater artistry in a genre too often considered a subcategory of journalism rather than as a nascent art form—Poe's theory seems to have been much more successful. Earlier writers treated structure, form, and technique with a rather cavalier disregard; N. P. Willis, for example, had a habit of writing a loose introductory descriptive sketch and following it with an only marginally related incident. Poe's insistence on applying the kind of unremitting attention to technique which conventional wisdom associated only with lyric poetry demanded for the short story a respect as literature which it had never before achieved.

Augustus Baldwin Longstreet and Frontier Humor

Irving created the modern short story by combining the inherent narrative interest of incident and plot (which already existed in the tale) with a tendency toward fully developed character, realism, specific detail and vivid imagery, and close psychological analysis (which characterized work in the essay-sketch tradition). Hawthorne brought to the form an intellectual commitment and a profound moral depth which raised the short story above mere entertainment and endowed it with the high worth associated with the finest poems, novels, and plays. In his criticism, Poe demanded on the one hand that readers acknowledge the new form's right to be considered as true literature, and, on the other, insisted that writers must bring the sorts of technical, artistic resources that alone could justify such a claim. In his own fiction, Poe demonstrated the power and subtlety possible when a writer marshaled the vast array of resources at hand.

Had these pioneering giants left anything out? Evidently many of their contemporaries believed so, for, quite independently of the short-story tradition which these men conspired to create, a quite different mode of short fiction was inventing itself.

Irving, Poe, Hawthorne, and their associates considered themselves among the cultured elite. Each took many of his most fundamental literary values from the Eastern establishment which borrowed its own from Europe, particularly from England. Meanwhile, below and beyond the Appalachians, in the barbarous regions of the "Southwestern frontier," in Tennessee, Georgia, Alabama, Mississippi, Arkansas, and other relatively unsettled areas of what then constituted the United States, relatively primitive living conditions had reduced the cultural level of the pioneering settlers below that of the established section of the Eastern seaboard. Down there, literature consisted not of delicate sensibilities written in Latinate phrasings, but in a vigorous telling of exaggerated oral tales. Scholars such as Constance Rourke and Bernard De Voto consider this oral tradition of outrageous storytelling to be the true original American art form and feel that it is as old as America. Scholars usually identify as the first appearance of this mode in written literature Augustus Baldwin Longstreet's *Georgia Scenes, Characters, Incidents, Etc. in the First Half Century of the Republic* (1835), but three years earlier Longstreet had begun publishing these treatments of the barbarous Georgians native to the Augusta area. A year before that, in 1831, William T. Porter had begun publishing the *Spirit of the Times*, a national magazine that soon began publishing narrative letters and other contributions from its widely distributed readership. The popularity which Longstreet and Porter achieved inspired a number of later frontier humorists, among them George Washington Harris (1814-1869), Joseph Glover Baldwin (1815-1864), Johnson J. Hooper (1815-1862), and Harden Taliaferro (1818-1875). In the opinion of many, the two great individual masterpieces of the genre are "The Big Bear of Arkansas" (1842) by Thomas Bangs Thorpe (1815-1878) and "The Celebrated Jumping Frog of Calaveras County" (1865) by Mark Twain.

Longstreet and his peers tended to isolate the more literary and sophisticated elements of the essay-sketch tradition in a gentleman (or a dude) who dominated frame material bracketed at the beginning and at the end. Within this frame, as Walter Blair long ago explained, we have a "mock-oral tale," a story designed as nearly as possible to capitalize on the virtues of the orally rendered stories any traveler could hear on the frontiers of the polite establishment.

One important element was humor, a feature with which Irving succeeded but with which Poe, Hawthorne, and most of their polite contemporaries seem to have failed miserably. These writers from the frontier based much of their humor on violence, physical grotesqueness, and cruelty, however, and a considerable amount of their material is offensive to modern sensibility. Another element important to the genre was an almost exaggerated realism. Except for his two great stories, Irving's fiction tended to drift toward the same Romantic environments that so often seduced Hawthorne and Poe. The frontier humorists wrote of immediate life, full of spavined horses, ripped trousers, spilled liquor, and hostile husbands; they wrote of their farms, shops, quiltings, revivals, militia meetings: of all that was most vivid, vital, and real to them.

In many ways the most significant element of Southwestern humor, and perhaps its greatest gift to Mark Twain and his finest gift to subsequent American literature, was the sense of a genuine speaking voice. The writing style of the established writers to the Northeast was emphatically artificial and valued highly for that very quality. No one ever really spoke as Poe and Hawthorne wrote, and their artificiality was central to their art. The frontier humorists delighted in introducing gifted folk storytellers and, so far as possible, allowing them to exploit on the page the priceless virtues of a concrete, unaffected, vital, and vivid oral narrative. Nothing quite like it had ever been seen before. In its finest form, *The Adventures of Huckleberry Finn*, it would never be bettered by anything in American literature.

England and the Beginnings of the Modern Short Story

By 1840, then, in the modern short story, American literature could boast the triumphs of Southwestern literature as well as masterpieces by Irving, Hawthorne, and Poe, even though as an independent country America could measure its existence only in decades. What was being produced in the great European literatures, especially in English literature? Curiously enough, the country with the greatest literary heritage on earth, although it could boast much excellent short fiction, had not yet produced creditable modern short stories. Many of England's finest writers experimented, often unsuccessfully, with shorter forms: Sir Walter Scott (1771-1832), who had helped give Irving's career a great boost, produced some fine ghost stories and an interesting tale, "The Two Drovers" (1827), which develops from an essay framework. Beginning in 1820, Charles Lamb (1775-1834) published his *Essays of Elia* in the *London Magazine*; these were a series of brilliant familiar essays with everything required of a short story—psychologically rich character, sharply imaged setting, at least a minimal narrative flow—everything but a focus on a unique, particular experience meaningful for its own sake (the only likely exception might be "Dream Children," published in 1822, which is sometimes anthologized as a short story). Hannah More (1745-1833) published an enormously popular series of moral tales much too didactic to be considered true fiction. Maria Edgeworth (1767-1849) and Mary Russell Mitford (1787-1855) produced work marred by sentimentality and superficiality, but some pieces verge close to the modern short story.

Again and again, however, as T. O. Beachcroft points out, the best English writers seemed inclined to treat the kind of material most appropriate to a short story only as an episode in a novel or as a brief narrative poem. Countless examples of short stories *manqué* from the early nineteenth century might be drawn from Jane Austen's novels or from certain narrative poems of such poets as William Wordsworth or George Gordon, Lord Byron. William Makepeace Thackeray (1811-1863) published a series of condensed novels, summary parodies of popular contemporary genres, and a handful of other short fictions, mostly old-fashioned series of incidents unified chiefly by the life of a central character.

England's great popular and artistic success in short fiction during this period was unquestionably *Sketches by Boz*, which Charles Dickens (1812-1870) published in 1836; yet the fact that the greatest book of British short fiction from 1800 to 1840 hardly stands comparison with the least of that writer's novels gives us some sense of the way the British imagination scaled its proprieties. The *Sketches by Boz*, Dickens' first great success, owes much more to the essay-sketch tradition than to the tale. The young journalist who authored these sketches devoted his time, considerable energies, amazing powers of observation, and incomparable imagination to representing in brief prose pieces some of the multifarious scenes, characters, and activities he encountered in his endless jaunts through the London streets. In these pieces his sentimentality and melodrama are at (for him) a minimum, and his comic appreciation of color, contrast, and human oddity under no perceptible restraint. The book is absolutely delightful, but contains no real short stories. Some of these narratives have something of a plot, but in none does the author focus on creating a tightly focused, genuinely meaningful human experience of the sort we expect in the modern short story. It is senseless to try to fault Dickens for failing to achieve something he never attempted, but many writers much inferior to Dickens in all but a sense of form have produced much finer short fiction.

Why is it that, working from essentially the same literary traditions, the Americans produced so many very fine modern short stories by 1840 when the English had produced none? There have been many half-baked theories to explain British predominance in the novel and American precedence in the short story during the period in question (and in fact it was well into the 1880's before a writer born and bred in England produced a respectable—not outstanding—volume of short stories, Thomas Hardy's *Wessex Tales* in 1888). Some suggest that the rushed pace of American economic life and its business morality equating time and money forced American writers to generate works which might be read in short snatches of time, the physically slower pace of British life promoting longer narratives. This is nonsense. For one thing, during the period in question the rush-quotient did not differ appreciably from one side of the ocean to the other. For another, a great many British magazines flourished because of serialized novels, each monthly segment approximating a short story in length. Thus the consideration of physical length or of reading time seems finally an irrelevant consideration.

Much more important, and more commonly accepted as a reason for the national tendencies toward novels or toward stories, were the contemporary copyright laws, or the lack of them. In essence writers' works were protected by copyright only in their country. As a result American publishers could reprint any British novels they chose without paying a penny in royalties. The relatively higher status of British writers, and the fact that their works were freely available, made American publishers reluctant to publish novels by Americans. Economic conditions thus forced, or at least strongly encouraged, American writers to focus on publishing short fiction in magazines and giftbooks (books usually of prose, poetry, and artwork which were published annually and intended largely as Christmas gifts), where payments to authors were minimal. Even the copyright theory should be taken with a grain of salt. For one thing, it does not explain the fact that the English, novelists of brilliance, failed to produce higher quality short fiction for their own magazines (which published discrete fictions as well as serialized novels). For another, it ignores the triumphs of James Fenimore Cooper (1789-1851) and others who, long before the copyright laws were altered at the turn of the century, demonstrated that American novels could reward American publishers (and readers) quite handsomely. The contemporary copyright laws were a factor but should not be overrated.

Another factor, as Hawthorne, James, and other American writers have lamented, is that the novel as a form seems best adapted to a complex social environment, one in which manners, classes, and traditions carry enormous weight. The short story as a form has traditionally had a focus more psychological than sociological, more individual than social. Those cultures, or those individual minds, which pay relatively more imaginative attention to society than to the individual would seem naturally to have more affinity for the novel than for the short story.

Of more importance seems to have been a quite distinct factor, one which helps explain not only why the British turned to novels during the period and the Americans to stories but also why so many individual writers who have attempted both forms are able to achieve real success only in one or in the other. Although many individual exceptions exist, in general the novel as a form tends to emphasize evolutionary changes which take place over a long period of time; the short story as a form tends to focus on a sharp change which occurs in a brief period of time, sometimes no more than a moment. Americans as a people are notorious for a mentality which demands immediate results and which focuses on the short term; Britons as a people are famous for their historical sense which emphasizes the part each smaller unit plays in some much longer evolutionary change. It was a Briton who first proposed the biological theory of natural selection occurring over eons, an American who first measured the speed of light. In some way the British mind seems predisposed to the kind of gestalt a novel represents; the Americans seem more predisposed to that of the short story. For whatever reason, the best short stories in English in the nineteenth century were not written by the English.

Germany and the Beginnings of the Modern Short Story

Previous discussion has shown how the early nineteenth century American short story developed essentially from a synthesis of the best which two divergent traditions offered. The Americans' model for the essay-sketch tradition came primarily from England; for contemporary Americans and Englishmen, however, the dominant written model for the other strain, that of the tale tradition, consisted chiefly of the literary *Märchen* (folktales) and *Novellen* (longer and relatively more realistic stories) of then fashionable German writers. As was earlier noted, for example, the vast and immediate popularity the brothers Grimm, Jacob (1785-1863) and Wilhelm (1786-1859), achieved by publishing short narratives based on their researches into Germanic folklore. Irving based "Rip Van Winkle" on a tale in a similar collection by Otmar. Such stories we call "fairy tales" in English, although often they contain no fairies at all, but witches, trolls, giants, or ogres. What they all *do* contain is emphasis on a striking incident or series of incidents which take precedence over character, setting, and all other elements. In addition, if true folktales, they share a common origin in folk traditions; each, in this sense, is (despite the inevitable variations incorporated by each individual narrator) a very old story.

In contrast to these traditional folktales there developed in Germany a tradition of *Novellen*. The term *Novellen* derives from the Italian term *novella*, which signifies "a small new thing." The sense of the word "new" in *Novellen* and "novella" (and in the French term *nouvelle*) might be taken to mean "unusual or surprising," but in fact it seems most probably to have developed to distinguish a basically or at least largely original story from an essentially traditional story. The *Novellen* do tend to have a relatively more complex and realistic social background, but otherwise any artificial distinction between *Märchen* and *Novellen* becomes quite problematic when there is in both genres of German tale a fondness for particular settings (often isolated and grotesque), a frequent use of type characters (young lovers, bellicose aristocrats, sinister intellectuals), a focus on dramatic incident (some define the *Novellen* in terms of a requisite surprising "turning-point" or *Wendepunkt*), and so on.

Historically, the German form itself, like its name, owes an imposing debt to the largely Latin tradition of short tales involving—to mention only a few of the very best among many other works—Giovanni Boccaccio's *Decameron* (1349-1351; *The Decameron*, 1620), Marguerite de Navarre's *Heptameron* (1558), and Miguel de Cervantes' *Novelas ejemplares* (1613; *The Exemplary Novels*, 1640). Apparently the first German author to use the term *Novelle* was Christopher Martin Wieland (1733-1813), a particular favorite of Poe, who in 1772 offered the following brief description:

> The term "Novelle" is applied especially to a kind of narrative [tale] that differs from long novels by the simplicity of [its] plot [plan] and the small bulk of [its] fable, or, the relationship between them [the *Novellen* and novels] is like that of a small play to a great tragedy or comedy.

A. G. Meissner, who published a German translation of Boccaccio's *The Decameron* in 1782, published a volume of original stories, *Novellen des Rittmeisters Schuster*, four years later. The first genuine artistic climax in the German form, however, came in 1795 with Johann Wolfgang von Goethe's *Unterhaltungen deutscher Ausgewanderten* (*Conversations of German Emigrants*, 1854), a series of frame tales told within a contemporary setting which reflects the troubled political situation of the times. The relatively more rational social and moral emphases in Goethe's *Unterhaltungen deutscher Ausgewanderten* in the later history of the *Novelle* altered in the direction of irrationality and exploration of personal and more specifically imaginative concerns.

Among the more important and more widely influential early nineteenth century writers of the *Novelle* were E. T. A. Hoffmann (1776-1822), Ludwig Tieck (1773-1853), Heinrich von Kleist (1777-1811), and Friedrich La Motte-Fouqué (1777-1843), and among the form's prominent critics (whose influences on Poe's theories are problematic) were Friedrich von Schlegel (1772-1829) and his brother August Wilhelm von Schlegel (1767-1845). The Schlegels' intensive emphasis on the artistic importance of unity of effect seems to have captured Poe's critical imagination much as the German fiction writers' dramatic, surprising, emotional, mysterious, often fantastic, and at times quite grotesque stories popularized the mode Anglo-American writers called Gothic, a mode which dominated much of the best short fiction in English until the 1850's, and some even beyond that. Yet various theorists of their time and of today would remind us that despite a heavy emphasis on fantasy, on the irrational, and on the supernatural, there was also a contrary impulse toward realism, one which entered the form in embryo when the *Novelle* initially divorced itself from the *Märchen* and which gradually grew throughout the nineteenth century until in the later decades, up to about 1890, the form's dominant mode was "Poetic Realism." This impulse to acknowledge the actualities of coherent environment and at the same time to emphasize irrationality and chaos; the antithetical impulses toward amoral narcissistic self-analysis on the one hand and toward moral imperative on the other; the vacillation between the asocial individual and the socially dominated individual; and the loyalties divided between the comic and the tragic—these and other tendencies of the early nineteenth century *Novelle* have been variously exploited in myriad patterns into the twentieth century.

Russia and the Beginnings of the Modern Short Story

The origins of the Russian short story, like those of Russian literature itself, most scholars trace to Alexander Pushkin (1799-1837). Before Pushkin, in prose as in verse, there were two predominant "literary" strains in Russia: on the one hand, a vigorous tradition of oral folklore and, on the other, a written tradition dominated by foreign models, especially by the French. In fact, during Pushkin's time, French was the language affected by the elite; Pushkin's education was essentially French, his early reading emphasized French literature, and, startling though the fact may be, the father of Russian literature began his career as a writer in the French language.

As with the great American and European short-story writers, however, although his formal education emphasized polite written literature, Pushkin was informally introduced to a rich folkloric tradition of oral tales bursting with sharply defined characters, improbable incidents, and marvelous settings—the Russian *narodnye skazki* (folktales) and *volsebnye skazki* (fairy tales).

Pushkin began as a poet, and a long-verse narrative, *Ruslan i Lyudmila* (1820; *Ruslan and Liudmila*, 1974), was his first great success. He went on, however, to produce masterpieces in all the major genres—the play *Boris Godunov* (1831), the brilliant verse novel *Eugene Onegin* (1825-1832, 1833), and, most important for our purposes, in 1831 *Povesti Belkina* (the tales of the late Ivan Petrovitch Belkin), a framed group of five dramatic and romantic short stories—but his masterpiece of short fiction is "The Queen of Spades" (1834). By Poe's standards the piece is long (about ten thousand words, it is divided into chapters) and rambling, with a need for tighter focus, but it may be considered the first great short story in Russian literature.

Normally considered the second great Russian writer, although actually much more of a contemporary, Nikolai Gogol (1809-1852) brought to the form emphases that magnificently complemented those which dominated Pushkin's work. Pushkin was drawn relatively more to the Byronic mode of Romanticism, to European models, and to aristocratic characters and backgrounds. The much earthier Gogol began his career with a group of stories strongly based on Ukranian folklore, *Vechera na Khutore bliz Dikanki* (1831-1832; *Evenings on a Farm Near Dikanka*, 1926). Here the folk models and backgrounds are as important to Gogol as the aristocratic and European are to Pushkin. The following years saw Gogol's great innovative fantasies "Diary of a Madman" (1835), *The Nose* (1836; English translation, 1915), and finally the masterpiece on which he worked for a number of years, *The Overcoat* (1842; English translation, 1915). The latter work brilliantly combines three distinctive elements of Gogol's work—first, a humor quite alien to the short story as Pushkin imagined it; second, a marvelous strain of fantasy akin to but finally quite distinct from that of the folklore he so loved; and third, a marvelous sense of realism. Fyodor Mikhailovich Dostoevski and Ivan Turgenev, and various other Russian Realists, have had attributed to them the quip, "We all came out from under Gogol's overcoat." Paradoxical as it may seem, this humorous tale of an insignificant clerk who wreaks revenge as a ghost did contain the seeds of precisely observed detail, of a specific social group's mores and behavior, and of a fidelity to life as the mass of his readers would recognize it that led directly to the fictions, short and long, of the giants of Russian literature, Turgenev, Dostoevski, Count Leo Tolstoy, and even beyond to Anton Chekhov and to various others, to the social criticism in Yevgeni Ivanovich Zamyatin's fantasies, Mikhail Mikhailovich Zoshchenko's mild satires, and to much of the very best of modern Russian fiction.

France and the Beginnings of the Modern Short Story

Anomalies and paradoxes abound in the short story. One is that the French, celebrated for their emphasis on logic and rationality (or alternately reviled for their penchant for contentious rationalization), have spent much less energy defining their basic critical terms for short fiction, *conte* and *nouvelle*, than people such as the Germans and the Americans have expended analyzing their own. Yet the French have among the world's very richest traditions in short fiction generally and in the short story in particular.

Conte, apparently the older French term, seems quite close to the word "tale"— on the one hand connoting emphasis on a dramatic (often supernatural or fantastic) central incident or incidents, and on the other hand forming part of numerous compound terms: *conte de fées* (fairy tale), *conte moral* (moral tale), *conte oriental* (oriental tale), and so on. *Nouvelle*, which in one sense means "news," would seem a literary term derived from the Italian term *novella* and the Spanish *novela* to indicate works such as the short fictions of Boccaccio and Cervantes which tend to be more realistic than *contes*, more integrated with a social milieu, and which often have more narrative complications.

The French critic Ferdinand Brunetière distinguished between the forms by setting the *conte* and the *roman* (the novel) as two poles with the *nouvelle* in between. The *roman* he considered the most realistic, the *conte* the least realistic. The *nouvelle* he believed dealt with subjects which might be extraordinary, unusual, or quite rare, but between the poles represented by the other two. Alfred Engstrom recognizes the same polar arrangement, but distinguishes among the three primarily on the basis of length and of narrative complexity, with the *conte* limited to a single and tightly integrated focus, the *nouvelle* limited to a single line of development (which may involve several linked incidents, no one of which is the story's primary focus), and the *roman* with plural lines of development. The *nouvelle* Engstrom equates with the English term novelette; the *conte* he considers the true short story, and he exiles from the genre any work with unrationalized supernatural elements, that is, works that contain incidents which cannot be considered "realistic" in the common sense of the term.

One may assume, in fact should assume, that neither scheme is really definitive, for both *conte* and *nouvelle* are quite elastic and even overlapping terms. One may assert, however, that a quite new and distinct sort of *conte* or *nouvelle* developed in France in the early decades of the nineteenth century and that this new form may be identified with the modern short story. In many ways the finest candidate for the first true French short story is "Mateo Falcone," which Prosper Mérimée (1803-1870) published in the *Revue de Paris* in May, 1829. In this brilliant, powerful story and in three others published later that year, "La Vision de Charles XI," "Tamango," and "L'Enlèvement de la redoute," Mérimée showed the ability to compress his action and to focus on a single incident, to create through closely observed detail a sense of a real environment, and to develop characters who possessed genuine psychological depth.

The following year, 1830, saw the first short stories of France's great colossus of the nineteenth century novel, Honoré de Balzac (1799-1850): "El Verdugo," "Une Passion dans le désert," "Un Episode sous la terreur," and in the following years several more, many of the later ones figuring as integral elements of his vast complex of novels, *La Comédie humaine* (1829-1848; *The Comedy of Human Life*, 1885-1893, 1896). Balzac constantly favored the more dramatic, more romantic materials, compulsively highlighting violence and strong emotions and at the same time constantly exploiting the novelist's predilection for questions of social forces and of social identity.

Théophile Gautier (1811-1872), the third important French writer to figure prominently in the short story's early history, published "La Cafetière" in 1831 and a handful of others at irregular intervals in the following years. Of the three, Gautier is indubitably the most Poesque (although in fact Poe did not publish his first short story, "Metzengerstein," until 1832), favoring idealized type characters, fantastic incidents, and exotic settings; in fact, as with Poe, Gautier's powerfully suggestive imagery often carries the burden of emphasis, meaning, and power in his short stories.

Other French writers produced significant short fiction before 1840—Charles Nodier (1780-1844), Gérard de Nerval (1808-1855), and others—but it was these three early masters who provided French literature with a new kind of short fiction, a story which tended to concentrate its interest tightly on a single, focused narrative event rather than dissipating its energies in a long train of incidents, a story which valued the psychological dimension of its characters quite as much as it valued their predilection for fantastic situations, and a story which replaced summary background with a sharply observed imagery designed to create a powerful and often suggestive environment in which the characters and incidents could credibly exist.

The grounds had been laid for one of the world's greatest short-story traditions, although the form's greatest writers, among them none greater than Guy de Maupassant, were yet to arrive on the scene.

Walter Evans

SHORT FICTION: 1840-1880

Notes Toward a Theory of the Short Story

Beginning in the mid-twentieth century, American literary critics have become increasingly concerned with what Aristotle termed the art of literature in general as well as its various species. As a result of René Wellek and Austin Warren's *Theory of Literature* in 1948, the revival of the Aristotelian tradition encouraged by R. S. Crane's *Critics and Criticism* in 1952, and Northrop Frye's *Anatomy of Criticism* in 1957, as well as the American discovery of early Russian Formalism and modern European Structuralism, books on poetics and literary theory roll off commercial and university presses in growing numbers. Particularly energetic have been efforts to establish a poetics for that species of literature which seems most resistant to theory—that is, prose fiction or narrative. Studies on the nature of narrative, the rhetoric of fiction, the theory of fiction, and the poetics of prose dominate the field both in number and importance.

On making even the most casual survey of these studies, however, one soon discovers an assumption so pervasive that it is seldom announced, much less questioned. When critics use the terms "prose fiction" and "narrative," they mean that relative latecomer to the hallowed realms of art and academic concern—the novel. They seldom mention, except as an afterthought, the form of prose fiction which has developed with sophistication and vigor alongside the novel—at least since the beginnings of the nineteenth century—the short story. This attitude toward the short story, an attitude which hardly makes the form worth mentioning in the rarefied atmosphere of current criticism about "serious" literature, is not new in Anglo-American literary studies; it is, in fact, as old as criticism of the short story itself. In 1884, when Brander Matthews published the first discussion of the short-story genre since Edgar Allan Poe's famous 1842 review of Nathaniel Hawthorne's *Twice-Told Tales* (1837), he noted the "strange neglect" of the short story in histories of prose fiction.

The reasons for this neglect, which has persisted up to the present, are too complex to recount here. One of the most basic reasons, however, is the general devaluation of genre theory in Anglo-American criticism until recently; a truly critical history of a literary form is simply not possible without a generic theory of that form. Fifty years separate Fred Lewis Pattee's *The Development of the American Short Story* (1923) and Arthur Voss's *The American Short Story: A Critical Survey* (1973), but their similarities sum up histories of the American short story. Both are surveys, filled with names, titles, dates, and sketchy considerations of influence, but neither is critical or theoretical and neither is informed by a generic theory of the form. R. S. Crane, in his *Critical and Historical Principles of Literary History* (1971), insists that the inductive development of distinctions of species is an essential task before one can write a narrative history. Wellek and Warren suggest that one of the most obvious values of genre study is that it calls attention to the internal development of literature; Wellek even goes so far as to say that the "history of genres is indubitably one of the most promising areas for the study of literary history."

Most comments about the short story focus on the form's midway position between the novel and the lyric poem. Poe himself placed the short story next to the lyric as offering the opportunity for the highest practice of literary art. Most critics since have not really disagreed and have, in fact, compared the short story to the lyric in various ways. Except for the fact that the short story shares with the novel the medium of prose, there is a fundamental difference between the two forms: although the short story is committed to prose fictional representations of events, it makes use of the plurasignification of poetry—using metaphoric overdetermined language because of the basically subjective nature of the form or its *multum in parvo* necessity to use the most suggestive but economical means possible.

The Russian Formalist critic, B. M. Ejxenbaum, says that the novel and the short story are not only different in kind, but also "inherently at odds." Genetically, the novel is a syncretic form, either developed from collections of stories or complicated by the incorporation of "manners and morals" material. The short story, on the other hand, is a "fundamental, elementary (which does not mean primitive) form." The difference between the two, says Ejxenbaum, is one of essence, "a difference in principle conditioned by the fundamental distinction between big and small forms." According to Ejxenbaum, the important implication arising from difference in size has to do with the difference between the endings of short stories and novels. Because the novel is structured on the linking of disparate materials and the paralleling of intrigues, the ending usually involves a "point of let-up." The short story, however, constructed on the basis of a contradiction or incongruity, "amasses its whole weight toward the ending." This built-in necessity of the form has, of course, been the source of much of the popular appeal of the short story and also the cause of the resultant scorn by the critics. Not all short stories depend on the kind of snap ending that O. Henry mastered, yet shortness of the form does seem inevitably to necessitate some sense of intensity of structure that is lacking in the novel.

Another suggestion about the implications of the shortness of the form has been made by Georg Lukács in his pre-Marxist *The Theory of the Novel* (1916). Although Lukács has since repudiated this early attempt to formulate a general dialectic of literary genres, his comments on the short story here offer some fruitful bases for further consideration. Perceiving that the short story is a fictional form which deals with a "fragment of life," lifted out of life's totality, Lukács says that the form is thus stamped with its origin in the author's "will and knowledge." The short story is inevitably lyrical because of the author's "form-giving, structuring, delimiting act." Its lyricism lies in pure selection. Yet, regardless of this lyricism, the short story must deal with event; and the kind of event it focuses on, says Lukács, is one that "pin-points the strangeness and ambiguity of life," the event that suggests the arbitrary nature of experience whose workings are always without cause or reason. The result of the form's focus on "absurdity in all its undisguised and unadorned nakedness" is that the lyricism is concealed behind the "hard outlines of the event" and thus the view of absurdity is given the "consecration of form: meaninglessness *as* meaninglessness becomes form; it becomes eternal because it is affirmed, transcended and redeemed by form." Consequently, says Lukács, the short story is the most purely artistic literary genre.

When Lukács says that the short story is the most purely artistic form, he means that it is the least conceptual form—that it deals with experiences which refuse to be reduced to a concept or to be integrated into a larger conceptual system. Such experiences can only be selected. This is what Frank O'Connor means in *The Lonely Voice* (1963) when he says that whereas the novel makes use of the essential form of the development of character or incident as we see it in life, for the short-story writer there is no such thing as essential form. "Because his frame of reference can never be the totality of a human life, he must forever be selecting the point at which he can approach it, and each selection he makes contains the possibility of a new form as well as the possibility of a complete fiasco." Thus the basic difference between the two forms is the difference between pure and applied storytelling, and the pure storytelling that is found in the short story is more artistic than the applied storytelling that is found in the novel. Lukács says that the short story expresses the "very sense and content of the creative process." The result is that the short story is a highly self-conscious, even a self-reflexive, form that often tends to be about the nature of story itself.

The fact that the short story pinpoints the strangeness of life is due precisely to the fact that the short story focuses on fragments that are not only detached from the conceptual framework we call the totality of life but also that reveal the absurdity of that conceptual framework, even, as Albert Camus would put it, the absurdity of hoping for a meaningful conceptual framework. Because the individual experience thus detached is always meaningless, it can have nothing but form; the only possible integration for it is the integration within itself. He who focuses on the fragment of experience must necessarily sense absurdity or meaninglessness, or else its polar extreme, meaningfulness that transcends the "normal," the conceptual, the everyday. It is a clear indication of the modern temperament that a contemporary short-story writer such as Donald Barthelme can say, "Fragments are the only forms I trust."

The revelation in the short story is, as Robert Langbaum describes the revelation of nineteenth century poetry in his *The Poetry of Experience* (1957), not a formulated idea that dispels mystery but a perception that advances in intensity to a deeper and wider, a more inclusive mystery. When Mark Schorer said that the short story is an art of "moral revelation" and the novel an art of "moral evolution," he was assuming the nonconceptual character of the experience depicted in short stories and the conceptual nature of experience in the novel. Evolution is a linear process manifested as cause and effect—the essence of the conceptual experience. Revelation is, by its very nature and definition, without cause. Something shows forth that was not there before. Evolution implies a teleology, an evolving toward some end; revelation has no such end.

The short story's method, however, is to present a glimpse through external meaninglessness to essential and immanent meaning. At least since James Joyce, it has been recognized that the short story's way of meaning is by means of the epiphany. Moreover, the "whatness" of the object that Joyce describes in aesthetic terms is equivalent to the "thouness" Martin Buber describes in moral terms. As Langbaum suggests, the epiphany is a way of knowing or apprehending value when value is no longer objective. This simply means that the epiphany mode is a radical return to the primitive mythic mode when there was no such thing as objective value, when all value by its very nature was subjective. The modern return to this mode begins with the early nineteenth century when external values are discredited and the short fictional form and the short lyric form become the most appropriate genres for the new milieu. The short story has always been an antisocial form, either in its adherence to mythic relationships or in its adherence to secularized psychological replacements of the lost mythic relationship. The short story as a modern artistic form seeks to replace the lost mythic perception with intense subjectivity and a revival of archetypes.

Short stories thus present synchronic invariants of human action, not the diachronic variants of social interaction. Since the short story does deal with such universals regardless of social surroundings, there was a need to hear stories long before there was a need to read the mimetic depictions of everyday reality. It is the liminal nature of human existence, even the religious nature of human existence as Philip Wheelwright and William James have described it, that gives rise to the short story. The English short-story writer Christina Stead says: "The belief that life is a dream and we the dreamers only dreams, which comes to us at strange, romantic, and tragic moments, what is it but a desire for the great legend, the powerful story rooted in all things which will explain life to us and, understanding which, the meaning of things can be threaded through all that happens." Human beings need to hear stories for the same reason they need to experience religion, says Canadian writer Hugh Hood. "Story is very close to liturgy, which is why one's children like to have the story repeated exactly as they heard it the night before. The scribe ought not to deviate from the prescribed form. That is because the myths at the core of story are always going on."

This notion of the story as liturgy is also suggested by Indries Shah in his discussion of the Sufi teaching story. Such stories do not teach by concept but rather by some more intuitive method of communication, by rhythm, or, as the structuralists would say, by a deep structure that lies beneath the conscious level of concept. We must go back to an early stage to prepare ourselves for story, says Shah, a stage in which we regard story as the "consistent and productive parallel or allegory of certain states of mind. Its symbols are the characters in the story. The way in which they move conveys to the mind the way in which the human mind can work.

The fact that the short story does not deal with social reality means that it tends to thrive best in societies where there is a diversity or fragmentation of values and people. This diversity has often been cited as one reason why the short story became quickly popular in the nineteenth century in America. In 1924, Katherine Fullerton Gerould said that American short-story writers have dealt with peculiar atmospheres and special moods, for America has no centralized society. "The short story does not need a complex and traditional background so badly as the novel does." Ruth Suckow also suggested in 1927 that the chaos and unevenness of American life made the short story a natural expression. The life in America was so multitudinous that "its meaning could be caught only in fragments, perceived only by will-of-the-wisp gleams, preserved only in tiny pieces of perfection." The more firmly organized a country is, says Seán O'Faoláin, "the less room there is for the short story—for the intimate close-up, the odd slant, or the unique comment." Frank O'Connor also notes that in those countries in which society does not seem adequate or sufficient for the repository of acceptable values we find the short story to be the most pertinent form. "The novel," says O'Connor, "can still adhere to the classical concept of civilized society, of man as an animal who lives in a community . . . ; but the short story remains by its very nature remote from the community—romantic, individualistic, and intransigent."

These considerations lead O'Connor to formulate his famous theory that the short story always presents a sense of

> outlawed figures wandering about the fringes of society. . . . As a result there is in the short story at its most characteristic something we do not often find in the novel—an intense awareness of human loneliness. Indeed, it might be truer to say that while we often read the novel again for companionship, we approach the short story in a very different mood. It is more akin to the mood of Pascal's saying: *Le silence éternel de ces espaces infinis m'effraie.*

The antisocial nature of the short story is one of its most predominant features. To understand this aspect of the short story, we might use, *mutatis mutandis*, a description T. S. Eliot once made of Henry James's fiction:

> The general scheme of James's fiction is not one character, nor a group of characters in a plot or merely in a crowd. The focus is a situation, a relation, an atmosphere to which the characters pay tribute. The real hero in any of James's stories is a social entity of which the men and women are constituents.

The focus of short fiction is also an atmosphere or situation to which the characters pay tribute and of which they are constituents. Because the short-story situation, however, is like that of dream or myth, indeed, because the short story is always more atmosphere than event, its meaning is difficult to apprehend. As Joseph Conrad's Marlow understands when he attempts to tell the story of Mr. Kurtz and the journey into the heart of darkness, the meaning of an episode is not within like a kernel, "but outside, enveloping the tale which brought it out only as a glow brings out a haze." Marlow impatiently asks, "Do you see the story? Do you see anything? It seems to me I am trying to tell you a dream—making a vain attempt. No relation of a dream can convey that notion of being captured by the incredible which is the very essence of dreams."

The atmosphere that plays about the short story is not the social atmosphere or social entity of James's fiction, or by extension, of the novel generally; rather, it is an antisocial entity. If it is religious or numinous, we must remember that Herbert Otto in his study of the Holy has pointed out that the numinous can have a violent and frightening Dionysian aspect as well as a Christlike one. Regardless of which aspect it takes, the short story, like the mythic aura of Christ and Dionysus, represents both the human and the divine; for both Christ and Dionysus are gods of showing-forth, of revelation, of epiphany. Both demand of their followers strange and paradoxical requirements: that we lose ourselves to find ourselves, that we plunge into the irrational, the incredible, into all that is against social law and human order in the everyday world.

Historical and Formal Background to the Short Story Before Poe

There is no such phenomenon as a totally new genre. Genres that appear to be new, such as the American short story in the 1840's, are the results of reactions against and integration of preexisting literary forms. The short story drew primarily from five such forms: the folktale, the medieval romance, the eighteenth century essay or sketch, the eighteenth century novel, and the romantic lyric. From the folktale, the short story takes its focus on a single event, usually an event that cannot be explained in terms of everyday reality. From the eighteenth century essay or sketch, it takes its focus on a personalized point of view—a definite teller whose attitude toward the story he is telling is as important as the story itself. Washington Irving's famous tales are perfect examples of this combination of folktale and point of view. Although Irving borrowed his plots from German folklore, he borrowed his teller's tone from Joseph Addison and Richard Steele. Irving himself drew attention to his concern with tone and point of view in a letter:

> For my part, I consider a story merely as a frame on which to stretch my materials. It is the play of thought, and sentiment, and language; the weaving in of characters, lightly, yet expressively delineated; the familiar and faithful exhibition of scenes in common life; and the half-concealed vein of humor that is often playing through the whole—these are among what I am at, and upon which I felicitate myself in proportion as I think I succeed.

From the medieval romance and the eighteenth century novel, the short story gets its focus on a symbolic or projective fiction, but one in which real people are involved. This experiment in fiction began in the late eighteenth century, of course, with Horace Walpole's *The Castle of Otranto* (1764). Walpole said that *The Castle of Otranto* was an attempt to "blend the two kinds of romance, the ancient and the modern." That is, he wished to retain the imagination and improbability of the medieval romance but make use of the convention of character verisimilitude of the novel. As Walpole says in his Preface,

> Desirous of leaving the powers of fancy at liberty to expatiate through the boundless realms of invention, and thence of creating more interesting situations, he wished to conduct the mortal agents in his drama according to the rules of probability; in short, to make them think, speak, and act as it might be supposed mere men and women would do in extraordinary positions.

The result in the Gothic story is essentially a projective fiction embodying emotional states, yet a fiction in which characters with their own thoughts, fears, and anxieties—in short, psychologies—are enmeshed. The effect, to use Mary Shelley's *raison d'être* of another famous Gothic fiction, *Frankenstein* (1818), is a fiction that, however impossible as a physical fact, "affords a point of view to the imagination for the delineating of human passions more comprehensive and commanding than any which the ordinary relations of existing events can yield."

This is a basic romantic view, of course, which also infused the epoch-making *Lyrical Ballads* (1798) and which underlies an important distinction between the romantic lyric and the eighteenth century poetry that went before it. The basic romantic fascination with medievalism and folk material springs from their realization of the basic religious or spiritual source of both the old romance and the folk ballad. The romantics' fascination with the old ballads and tales was part of their effort to recapture the primal religious experience, to demythologize it of the dogma that had reified the religious experience and to remythologize it by internalization and projection. In order to preserve the old religious values without the old mythological trappings, they secularized the religious encounter by perceiving it as a basic psychic process, by taking it back from the priests who had solidified it and experiencing it in stark uniqueness and singleness. This is indeed the focus in the Preface to the *Lyrical Ballads* and in Samuel Taylor Coleridge's discussion of his and William Wordsworth's dual tasks in *Biographia Literaria* (1817). The uniting of the old ballad material with the lyric voice of a single individual perceiver in a concrete situation gave rise to the romantic lyric. Robert Langbaum has discussed this creation of a subjective point of view in a concrete dramatic situation in his *The Poetry of Experience*. The positioning of a real speaker in a concrete situation encountering a particular phenomenon which his own subjectivity transforms from the profane into the sacred is the key to the romantic breakthrough.

The ballad story previous to Wordsworth and Coleridge existed detached from a teller, a projective fiction independent of an individual teller and tone. In the nineteenth century it became infused with the subjectivity of the poet and projected on the world as the basis for a new mythos. The thrust was dual. As Coleridge says, his own task was to focus on the supernatural, "yet so as to transfer from our inward nature a human interest and a semblance of truth sufficient to produce for these shadows of imagination that willing suspension of disbelief for the moment, which constitutes poetic faith." Wordsworth was to choose subjects from ordinary life and "excite a feeling analogous to the supernatural by awakening the mind's attention from the lethargy of custom and directing it to the loveliness and the wonders of the world before us." Clear examples of this dual project are Coleridge's lyrical story "The Rime of the Ancient Mariner" and Wordsworth's lyrical story "Resolution and Independence." The poems are representative of two primary modes of fiction—what Carl Jung calls the "visionary" and the "psychological" respectively. In Northrop Frye's terminology, they correspond to the basic difference between the romance mode and the novel mode, and therefore the basic difference between the tale and the short story. In the first, the characters are psychic archetypes; in the second they are primarily social personae.

The moral values in these poems are those of sympathy, identification, and love—the primary values of romantic axiology, most explicitly delineated in Percy Bysshe Shelley's *A Defence of Poetry* (1840). They later become the primary values of Nathaniel Hawthorne's stories in America. In the *Lyrical Ballads*, the ballad or "story" element, the hard outlines of the event, are subsumed by the lyrical element, which is foregrounded. For Hawthorne and Poe, however, in America it is the story element that is foregrounded. The lyrical element exists as the personal voice of the teller, a teller who responds personally to the event, but whose tone is somewhat delyricized by the influence of the "talk-of-the-town" tone of the eighteenth century essay and sketch.

Both Fred Lewis Pattee and Edward J. O'Brien in their 1923 histories of the American short story place the birth of the form with Washington Irving's combination of the style of Addison and Steele with the subject matter of German Romanticism. Pattee says about Irving's *The Sketch Book of Geoffrey Crayon, Gent.* (1819-1820): "It is at this point where in him the Addisonian Arctic current was cut across by the Gulf Stream of romanticism that there was born the American short story, a new genre, something distinctly our own in the world of letters." O'Brien, focusing more on the classical Arctic than the Gulf Stream romanticism, says that the short story began when Irving detached the story from the essay, especially the personal essay of the "talk-of-the-town." It is obvious that Irving's Diedrich Knickerbocker is more like the eighteenth century Roger de Coverley than he is the anonymous folk storyteller of the ancient ballad.

H. S. Canby has also noted Addison's influence on Irving which resulted in a classical restraint and a gentle humor in his stories, but it is with Hawthorne's and Poe's mutations and development of the romantic impulse that the short story more properly begins. Poe's contribution, says Canby, was to do for the short story what Coleridge and John Keats were doing for poetry: to excite the emotions and to apply an impressionistic technique to his materials to hold his stories together. Hawthorne, however, uses a moral situation as the nucleus to hold his stories together. Hawthorne was, in fact, the first American story writer to build a story on a situation, an "active relationship between characters and circumstances." Pattee agrees that Hawthorne was the first to touch "the new romanticism with morals" and that both Hawthorne and Poe differ from E. T. A. Hoffmann's and Ludwig Tieck's "lawless creative genius" and "wild abandon" by exercising deliberate control and art. Pattee also suggests that Poe's important contribution was his realization that the tale is akin to the ballad form, but that like the lyric, it was dependent on an emotional, rather than a conceptual unity. For Poe, says Pattee, the story was a "lyrical unit, a single stroke of impressionism, the record of a moment of tension." Alfred C. Ward, in his 1924 study of the modern American and English short story, is quite right in noting that what links Hawthorne's stories with those of writers of the twentieth century is that they both "meet in the region of half-lights, where there is commerce between this world and 'the other-world.'" The difference between short-story writers before Hawthorne and those after him, however, is that while this region of half-lights for the preromantic existed in the external world of myth and the religious externals of allegory, for writers after the romantic shift the realm exists within what James has termed Hawthorne's "deeper psychology." Many critics since Ward have agreed with him that the brief prose form "affords a more suitable medium than the novel for excursions into the dim territory of the subconscious." In the first "theory" of the short story after Poe, Brander Matthews makes a brief suggestion that the short story has always been popular in America because the Americans take more thought of things unseen than the English. Matthews was also the first to notice, although he does not develop the point, that although Poe depicts things realistically or objectively, a shadow of mystery always broods over them. The subtle movement from Hoffmann's and Tieck's fairy-tale-like unrealities and supernatural events to Poe's psychological stories which push psychic responses to such extremes that they *seem* supernatural marks the beginnings of the short story.

Bliss Perry, in an unusual departure from usual histories of prose fiction at the turn of the century, devotes a chapter to the short story in his 1902 study entitled *A Study of Prose Fiction*. He notes that because of the shortness of the form, if the story is concerned with character, the character must be "unique, original enough to catch the eye at once." The result of this necessity for choosing the exceptional rather than the normal character is that the short story is thrown upon the side of romanticism rather than realism. Perry also notes another point about the short story that has remained constant since its inception:

> Sanity, balance, naturalness; the novel stands or falls, in the long run, by these tests. But your short story writer may be fit for a madhouse and yet compose tales that shall be immortal. . . . The novelist has his theory of the general scheme of things which enfolds us all, and he cannot write his novel without betraying his theory. . . . But the short story writer, with all respects to him, need be nothing of the sort.

Both Alberto Moravia and Richard Kostelanetz have recently noted this characteristic of the short story in opposition to the novel.

This insistence on the basic romantic nature of the short story, both in its focus on unusual events and on the subjectivity of the form, was strongly voiced in the late nineteenth century when Ambrose Bierce entered the argument then raging between William Dean Howells and Henry James over the romance versus the novel form. In his attack on the Howells school of fiction, Bierce says, "To them nothing is probable outside the narrow domain of the commonplace man's commonplace experience." The true artist, says Bierce, is one who sees that life is "crowded with figures of heroic stature, with spirits of dream, with demons of the pit. . . . The truest eye is that which discerns the shadow and the portent, the dead hands reaching, the light that is the heart of darkness." Even James says that he rejoices in the anecdote which he defines as something that "oddly happened" to someone. More recently, Flannery O'Connor has placed the short story within the modern romance tradition, a form in which the writer makes alive "some experience which we are not accustomed to observe everyday, or which ordinary man may never experience in his ordinary life."

The only extended critical discussion of this romantic element in the short story is Mary Rohrberger's *Hawthorne and the Modern Short Story: A Study in Genre* (1966). Comparing Hawthorne's comments in his prefaces with comments by modern short-story writers, Rohrberger notes that both share the romantic notion that reality lies beyond the extensional, everyday world with which the novel has always been traditionally concerned. "The short story derives from the romantic tradition," says Rohrberger:

> The metaphysical view that there is more to the world than that which can be apprehended through the senses provides the rationale for the short story which is a vehicle for the author's probing for the nature of the real. As in the metaphysical view, reality lies beyond the ordinary world of appearances, so in the short story, meaning lies beneath the surface of the narrative.

Poe, Hawthorne, and Gogol:
The Beginnings of the Short Story

Poe's romantic allegiance to poetry and his debt to Wordsworth and especially Coleridge for his theories about the nature of poetry and the imagination is made clear in his many reviews and critical essays. For Poe, the highest genius can be best employed in the creation of the short rhymed poem; it is poetry that elicits the poetic sentiment—"the sense of the beautiful, of the sublime, and of the mystical." If one wishes to write in prose, however, Poe says, "the fairest field for the exercise of the loftiest talent" is the tale; for the tale is the closest one can get to poetry when writing mere prose. The basic difference between poetry and the tale form for Poe is that while the tale is concerned with truth, the poem is concerned with beauty and pleasure; and truth, Poe makes quite clear in his discussion of Hawthorne's *Twice-Told Tales*, means the presentation of a theme by means of the author's ability to use a "vast variety of modes or inflections of thought and expression." Furthermore, what Poe admires in Hawthorne in addition to the central attribute of the short story— "Every word *tells* and there is not a word that does *not* tell"—is that Hawthorne not only displays a novelty of theme but a novelty of tone as well.

The most troublesome element of Poe's theory of the short story, however, lies in his remarks on the tale's "single effect," for these comments led in the early twentieth century to a misplaced concern with the tricks a writer may use to construct a story for effect rather than with how a story complexly affects the reader. For a further consequence of misreading Poe has been that many critics have taken the phrase "single effect" to mean "simple effect." Part of the problem is the critical bias against the very "shortness" of prose narrative that Poe most insisted on. The usual assumption is that narrative by its very nature is concerned with movement and therefore character development and change. Since change is a complex phenomenon influenced by a multitude of forces, it follows that the novel can more plausibly present change than the short story. As Thomas Gullason has recently pointed out (*Studies in Short Fiction*, 1973), Mark Schorer's famous distinction between the short story as the "art of moral revelation" and the novel as the "art of moral revolution" does seem to contribute to various stereotypes which have deadened the response of readers to short fiction. The distinction is damaging to the short story, however, only if we accept the prevailing bias that the nature of narrative is to present change plausibly and that the novel is thus the narrative norm. Unfortunately, Gullason does accept this, asserting that "it is mainly in terms of 'moral evolution' or growth that a fiction becomes organic—lifelike, plausible, multidimensional, and long-lived. Moral revelation alone usually leaves a fiction artificial, unrealistic, one-dimensional, and short-lived." In short, Gullason attempts to defend the short story by suggesting that it is really more like the novel than previous stereotypes have led us to believe—that it is realistic and has an "everyday quality" applicable to general reality. The best way to redeem the short story from previous critical neglect is not to ignore its unique characteristics but rather to focus on how the very shortness of the story compels it to deal with a different mode of reality and knowledge from that of the novel and therefore how it has a different effect on the reader. One way to achieve this and better understand what Poe meant by "single effect" is to make use of approaches developed by philosophy and anthropology to the nature of myth. The most helpful are those of Ernst Cassirer. What is being suggested is that the short story, although separate stories may indeed structure myths as different constitutive units, is primarily a literary mode that embodies and recapitulates mythic perception itself.

Once we hypothesize this as a central characteristic of the short story, we can better defend Poe's insistence on the unique or single effect of the form; we can better combat the bias against it which, confusing novel with story and history with myth, insists that the short story have a plausible, everyday quality; and we can better justify the comments already made that the short story is centered around emotion, intuition, and fleeting perceptions that consequently give it its mysterious, dreamlike quality. In short, we can begin to see that the bias for the novel as narrative norm and the consequent neglect of the short story is the same bias that Cassirer describes as modern man's preference for theoretical thinking over mythical thinking.

Not only is mythic perception impregnated with emotional qualities and surrounded by a specific atmosphere, but it is also characterized by a focus on the immediate present. Cassirer says, thought is "captivated and enthralled by the intuition which suddenly confronts it. It comes to rest in the immediate experience, the sensible present is so great that everything else dwindles before it." From this point of view, Poe's stress on the "immense force" of the short story "derivable from *totality*" and the great importance of "unity of impression" to make possible the "deepest effects" becomes more significant. The short story, more than other modes of narrative, requires complete absorption. Moreover, it is the only form of narrative with which the reader can be completely absorbed for the *totality* of the narrative experience. As Poe says, "During the hour of perusal the soul of the reader is at the writer's control. There are no external or extrinsic influences—resulting from weariness or interruption." Similarly, Cassirer says, when one is under the spell of mythic thinking, "it is as though the whole world were simply annihilated; the immediate content so fills his consciousness that nothing else can exist beside and apart from it." Cassirer says the characteristic of such an experience is not expansion, but an impulse toward concentration; "instead of extensive distribution, intensive compression. This focussing of all forces on a single point is the prerequisite for all mythical thinking and mythical formulation."

The short-story form manifests this impulse toward compression and demands this intense focusing for the totality of the narrative experience primarily because it takes for its essential subject the mysterious and dreamlike manifestations of what Cassirer calls the "momentary deity." The production of these deities, the first phase of the developent of theological concepts, does not involve investing them with mythico-religious images. Rather, Cassirer says:

> It is something purely instantaneous, a fleeting, emerging and vanishing mental content. . . . Just let spontaneous feeling invest the object before him, or his own personal condition, or some display of power that surprises him, with an air of holiness, and the momentary god has been experienced and created. In stark uniqueness and singleness it confronts us . . . as something that exists only here and now, in one indivisible moment of experience, and for only one subject whom it overwhelms and holds in thrall.

Many, perhaps most, short stories present characters thus overwhelmed and enthralled by something within or without them which they invest with mythic rather than logical significance. Roderick Usher's obsession with the horror of the house that he can neither name nor understand, Goodman Brown's compulsion toward the witches' sabbath, Bartleby's absorption with the wall that makes him prefer to do nothing—none of these experiences can be accounted for logically; neither can they be presented in terms of everyday reality. In fact, they are characterized by their removal from everyday reality. Thus, the short story is the form best able to embody this mythic experience. As Cassirer says:

> It is as though the isolated occurrence of an impression, its separation from the totality of ordinary, commonplace experience produced not only a tremendous intensification, but also the highest degree of condensation, and as though by virtue of this condensation the objective form of the god were created so that it veritably burst forth from the experience.

Hawthorne's critical comments about art are less developed than Poe's and confine themselves primarily to prefaces in which he discusses the nature of the romance form. Hawthorne, however, no less than Poe, is concerned with the mythic and the mysterious. Hawthorne's comments about the romance can be applied equally to the short tale, for as Northrop Frye has pointed out, the romance bears the same relation to the tale form as the novel does to the more developed short story. In the former, the characters are archetypes which serve the function of the mythic plot; in the latter, the characters are wearing their social masks. The romance and the tale are visionary forms, while the novel and the short story tend more toward psychologizing and verisimilitude. Hawthorne, although he may have expressed a longing to master the techniques of realism, found such techniques impossible to reconcile with his own vision of the superiority of moral truth over physical truth. In fact, Hawthorne's technique is to spiritualize the material and thus, in true romantic fashion, discover true or "sacred" reality always immanent in the "profane" physical world. As he notes in his Preface to *The House of the Seven Gables* (1851), Hawthorne finds that the romance, while governed by its own laws, is not bound by the laws of fact and is therefore freer than the novel. Hawthorne's stories, like Poe's, follow the laws of their own conventions rather than the laws of external reality. Thus, to use Northrop Frye's term, they are less "displaced" than the novel; they do not try to conceal their conventions under the cover of verisimilitude.

Another central element of fiction for Hawthorne, one that accompanies Poe's emphasis on tone, is the importance of atmosphere. In the Preface to *The Blithedale Romance* (1852), Hawthorne laments the loss of the "old world" conventional privileges of the romance. Among American writers there is no "Faery Land" which has its own rules that govern it so that it can be placed equally alongside nature, no realm of reality that is so much like the real world in its truth and laws that in its "atmosphere of strange enchantment," the "inhabitants have a propriety of their own." Without such an atmosphere, Hawthorne says, the characters of the imagination "must show themselves in the same category as actually living mortals." It is precisely this atmosphere of fantasy in which real people dwell, however, that begins to make itself felt as central to the genius of the short story. It is that "neutral territory somewhere between the real world and fairy-land, where the Actual and the Imaginary may meet and each imbue itself with the nature of the other."

One final element in Hawthorne's fiction which further contributes to the development of the short story as a genre is a thematic view also shared by Poe—the importance of sympathy. For Hawthorne, as it was for Shelley in *A Defence of Poetry*, sympathy was the great secret of morals. Shelley says, "A man, to be greatly good, must imagine intensely and comprehensively; he must put himself in the place of another and of many others; the pains and pleasures of his species must become his own." It is obvious that in Hawthorne's fiction, isolation and alienation exist for those who, like Ethan Brand and Giovanni, lack "the key of holy sympathy." Although Poe's fiction, because it seems less obviously concerned with moral themes than that of Hawthorne, appears to lack the element of sympathy; this is not, however, the case. Poe's first-person narratives, such as "The Tell-Tale Heart," "The Black Cat," and others, demand of the reader a sympathy and participation in much the same way that Robert Langbaum says is required for the narrators of Robert Browning's monologues. Moreover, the nature of sympathy becomes a metaphysical principle for Poe in his prose poem *Eureka* (1848), in which he points to a universal brotherhood of atoms themselves. It is a cosmology which for Poe has a moral implication: "No one soul is inferior to another."

Lest one might think these combinations of elements—the fantastic and dreamlike with the real, a focus on sympathy, an emphasis on unity, and a concern with the story following its own laws—are an isolated American occurrence, it is best that we now turn to a development in Russian literature in 1842—the same year as Poe's famous review—the publication of Nikolai V. Gogol's *The Overcoat*. Frank O'Connor in his study of the short story has suggested that Ivan Turgenev's famous remark, "We all came out from under Gogol's 'Overcoat,' " is applicable not only to Russian writers, but is a general truth as well. O'Connor points to this story as marking the origin of the short-story form. For O'Connor, *The Overcoat* is like nothing in the world of literature before it.

> It uses the old rhetorical device of the mock-heroic, but it uses it to create a new form that is neither satiric nor heroic, but something that perhaps finally transcends both. So far as I know, it is the first appearance in fiction of the Little Man, which may define what I mean by the short story better than any other terms I may later use about it.

O'Connor goes even further and suggests that if one wanted an accurate key description of what is central to the short story, he could do no better than quote Akaky Akakyevitch's plaintive tacit cry to those who harass him: "I am your brother." The phrase indicates both the isolation of Akaky and his need for sympathy. In Akaky, O'Connor finds a central type of figure in the short story, because always in the short story, O'Connor says, there is a "sense of outlawed figures wandering about the fringes of society. . . . As a result there is . . . an intense awareness of human loneliness."

This cry for human sympathy, this sense of isolation and loneliness, however, is not the only thing that characterizes *The Overcoat* and makes it stand out as a unique new fictional creation. The passage from which O'Connor quotes is referred to in Russian criticism as the "humane passage." Indeed, the classical Russian view of the story in the nineteenth century is that the story is one of the first Russian works about the "little man" oppressed by the crushing regime of the czars, that the story is a realistic one with social significance; its only blot is the introduction of the fantastic at the end. In the 1920's, however, in what has now become a significant contribution to the Russian Formalist movement, the critic Boris Ejxenbaum discovered the technical and formal genius of Gogol's story. Ejxenbaum says that *The Overcoat* is a masterpiece of grotesque stylization in which Gogol takes the basic narrative technique known in Russian criticism as *skaz* (the oral narrative of a lowbrow speaker) and juxtaposes it against the sentimental rhetoric of the tone to make the reader uneasy about whether to sympathize with Akaky or laugh at him. The "humane passage" exists not simply to make us feel the oppression of the "little man" but rather to create a contrapuntal tension between comic *skaz* and sentimental rhetoric. "This pattern," says Ejxembaum, "in which the purely anecdotal narrative is interwoven with a melodramatic and solemn declaration, determines indeed the entire composition of 'The Overcoat' as a grotesque." The effect of the story is a "playing with reality"—a breaking up of the ordinary so that the unusual logical and psychological connections of reality turn out, in this constructed world of the story, to be unreal.

This is precisely the kind of play with reality, although admittedly with a different tone, in which Hawthorne was engaged; it is also similar to the tone of combined mock seriousness and sarcasm in which Poe delighted. Ejxenbaum says that the structure of a short story always depends in large part on the kind of "role which the author's personal tone plays in it."

Hawthorne's stories are obviously very close to their folklore and Gothic origins. The genius of Hawthorne that sets him apart from the anonymity of folklore and the plot focus of the Gothic, however, is not only his own personal tone but also his awareness that the conventions of folklore and the Gothic are really the embodiments of unconscious, even mythic, reality. Moreover, although many of his stories seem allegorical, they are less allegorical in the traditional sense than they are early attempts to perform in prose fiction the function that romantic poetry had served: to find the spiritual and moral meaning beneath the external physical and social reality of human life and events. The result, says Haytt H. Waggoner, is that we have no name for Hawthorne's type of story—not quite allegories, not quite symbolic, but somewhere in between. In fact, Hawthorne's type of story is the result of a merging of the representative fiction of allegory and the mimetic fiction of the novel. Thus, the stories seem to be both determined by the characters within them and at the same time determined by the story of which the characters are only functions. This focus tends to make the short story more aware of its own artifice and illusion than the novel, therefore more aware of its own process of ordering. The result is often a dreamlike story that is aware of itself as dream.

The problem of the dream nature of "Young Goodman Brown" is related to its modal situation halfway between realism and romance. If we ask whether the story is a dream told as if it were reality, or whether it is a reality told as if it were a dream, we realize that we cannot make that determination. The story begins with a concern with the oneiric as Faith tells Brown that she has been troubled with dreams; he wonders if a dream has warned her of his journey on this one night of the year. Of course at the end of the story, Hawthorne teases the reader with the question: "Had Goodman Brown fallen asleep in the forest and only dreamed a wild dream of a witch meeting?" The problem of the story is: if it is a dream, when did the dream begin and who is dreaming it? There is certainly no point in the story when Brown falls asleep, as is typical of the traditional dream-vision story. Moreover, if the forest meeting is a dream, then the whole story must be dream, for Brown knows where he is going from the beginning; and indeed from the point of view of the story as a projective fiction, both Faith and Brown are merely functions of a dreamlike folklore allegory—that is, Hawthorne's "dream."

Because Brown seems to have his own consciousness and seems at times to be uncertain about what lies before him in the forest, the story has its mimetic aspect as well. The crucial moment in the forest when Brown calls out to Faith to resist the evil one is clearly a breakthrough moment when he manifests his own will and becomes a psychological character rather than a parabolic function. This uncertainty as to the nature of reality in the story is intrinsically related to the moral-thematic impact of the story. "Young Goodman Brown" is not a simple initiation story of a youth becoming aware of evil, but rather a mimetic-symbolic story of the movement from *faith* that reality is simply its surface appearance to *knowledge* that reality is complex and hidden; it is a movement from an unquestioned sense of community to a realization that community must be constantly developed. In this sense it is a romantic story of the fall in perception from a unified sense of reality to the awareness of separation and the realization of the necessity of healing that separation. Instead of making the effort of sympathy and love to unite himself with others, however, Brown turns from them forever; having lost the absolute, he cannot live with ambiguity.

Another Hawthorne story that seems part parable and part mimetic representation is "The Minister's Black Veil." Although the minister has his own psychology and thus much of the story depicts his personal suffering, Hawthorne transforms the veil (rather the minister himself makes this transformation) into a symbolic object and the story into a parable—not a parable in the usual sense of a simple story to illustrate a moral, but rather a parable in the basic root sense of the word; that is, a story that probes basic mystery. The minister does not hide his face to conceal some secret personal sin (as he might in a realistic story) but rather to objectify his metaphysical awareness that the meaning of sin is separation. The thematic thrust of the story is similar to that in "Young Goodman Brown"; the minister, made aware of basic human separation, now tries to perform his ministerial function by teaching others that same awareness through the emblem of the veil. The moral implication of this awareness, as it often is for Hawthorne, is that life must be lived with the realization of separation so that the individual will see the need to have sympathy for the other—the need to project the self into the other, penetrate behind the social veil that we all wear. The story is also similar to Herman Melville's *Bartleby the Scrivener* (1856) in that the minister's black veil is like Bartleby's wall: an emblem of all that stands in the way of human communication. What makes Hawthorne's story more than a simple allegory is not only the complex meaning of the veil but also the fact that the minister is consciously aware of the meaning of the veil. His "madness" in the mimetic world of the story, which makes him treat a simple object as if it were its metaphysical meaning, is a function of his symbolic role in the parabolic world of the story.

The loss of the absolute and the entrance into ambiguity is also depicted in "My Kinsman, Major Molineux," a story which combines actuality (this time a historical transition that takes place in America) with myth and dreamlike reaiity. Young Robin, the rustic youth on his first visit to town just after his eighteenth birthday, has all the characteristics of the conventional folktale initiate setting out to seek his fortune in the world. His evening of ambiguity as he searches for his kinsman from whom he seeks preferment is a symbolic journey in which he encounters figures of human ambiguity: sexuality in the form of the young girl with the scarlet petticoat, death in the elder man with his "sepulchral hems" which evoke the "thought of the cold grave," authority in the nightwatchman who warns Robin he will be in the stocks by daylight, and ultimate duality in the Janus-faced man who suggests both a fiend of fire and a fiend of darkness.

Each time Robin is rebuffed in his quest for his kinsman, he tries to rationalize an explanation; finally reason is rebuffed so often that he begins to doubt not only reason but also the state of his present reality. He recalls his father and home and asks: "Am I here or there" and his mind vibrates between fancy and reality. When a stranger comes by, he cries, "I've been searching half the night, for one Major Molineux; now, sir, is there really such a person in these parts, or am I dreaming?" Indeed, at this point in the story the reader may well feel that Robin's encounters have been so grotesque and mysterious that the story *is* the embodiment of a dream or a myth. Also at this point, however, the mystery is explained by reality itself as Robin sees the crowd coming down the street with the tarred-and-feathered kinsman; the historical framework—of the colonists rejecting governors appointed by the king—supplies the realistic motivation to account for all the seemingly mythical events of the night. Hawthorne, however, never completely "naturalizes" his fictions; the realistic explanation does not dislodge the mythic aura of the events. Furthermore, the stranger with Robin at the end is not realistically explained; he is solely a function of the parabolic story—a mythic elder companion to Robin's new awareness, a denizen of the fable element of the story.

The same kind of fantasy and reality integration constitutes the nature of Hawthorne's most difficult story, "Rappaccini's Daughter," probably Hawthorne's most complex treatment of reality, fantasy, fairy tale, myth, legend, and symbol. In the preface to the story (which Hawthorne attributes to M. de l'Aubépine), Hawthorne recognizes his own ambiguous situation between the transcendentalists, who are concerned with spiritual and the metaphysical, and the great body of writers who address the "intellect and sympathies of the multitude," that is, the realists. Aubépine, says Hawthorne, "generally contents himself with a very slight embroidery of outward manners—the faintest possible counterfeit of real life—and endeavors to create an interest by some less obvious peculiarity of the subject."

Giovanni, like Goodman Brown and Robin, is primarily an inhabitant of the real world (that is, the mimetic aspect of the fiction) who is confronted with a dreamlike or fablelike fantasy. This encounter is complicated by the fact that the story is a maze of inversions of our usual expectations of good and evil, spirit and body, innocence and experience. Beatrice, like Dante's guide, is a spiritual figure of allegory; but she is also, like Mary Shelley's Frankenstein monster, a creation of nineteenth century science. When Giovanni first sees Rappaccini in the garden walking through the flowers as if they are malignant influences, his imagination connects the garden with the mythic story of the Garden of Eden. "Was this garden, then, the Eden of the present world?" Giovanni thus both creates and walks innocently into the stuff of myth itself; however, it is the Eden story turned upside down. Rappaccini is both god figure who created the garden and serpent figure who sets up the downfall of Giovanni, who is indeed the new Adam. Beatrice is Eve, brought up without contact with the fallen world. Giovanni is fallen man who must be seduced back into paradise again. The result of the story is that Giovanni, like Goodman Brown, cannot live with the mysterious mixture of spirit and body that Beatrice seems to represent: "Am I awake?" he cries. "Have I my senses? What is this being? Beautiful shall I call her, or inexpressibly terrible?"

Thus, instead of a story of the fall from grace into reality, we have instead a story of how fallen Adam tempts Eve into reality, even as she tries to tempt him into the fall back into grace again through faith and love. Giovanni's efforts to bring Beatrice into the "limits of ordinary experience" is evidence of his lack of acceptance and love; it means the death of the denizen of the romance world of fiction and thus the end of the story. "Rappaccini's Daughter" is about the conflict between reality and fantasy, materiality and spirit, empiricism and faith; and thus it is about the very conflict between characters like Giovanni, with psychological verisimilitude, and characters like Beatrice, who exist for the sake of the story as parable. The conflict is an inevitable one for the short story, taking as it does elements both from the old parable and romance form and from the conventions of the realistic eighteenth century novel. The classic example of a Poe story which involves this same kind of interaction is "The Fall of the House of Usher," in which the realistic narrator confronts Roderick, who by his very obsession has been turned into a purely symbolic figure. Melville exploits the mixture of the two fictional conventions even further in *Bartleby the Scrivener* as the short story moves more within the realistic tradition of the late nineteenth century.

The European mind has always been more hospitable to Poe than the American mind. Charles Baudelaire led the French in a discovery of Poe while he was still being scorned as a hack and a misfit in America. Recently, the French Structuralists have resurrected Poe from many years of critical condescension by considering his stories from a point of view of both new theories in psychoanalysis and new theories of narrative. American empiricism has simply been unconcerned with the basically phenomenological point of view of Poe's works. One of the most basic criticisms of Poe's stories, and an influential one because it is by W. H. Auden, is that Poe's stories have one damaging negative characteristic: "There is no place in any of them for the human individual as he actually exists in space and time." Poe's characters, says Auden, are "unitary states" who cannot exist except operatically. Yvor Winters' famous criticism of Poe as a classic case of obscurantism is based on a similar assumption—that Poe is not concerned with human experience, only emotion, and that he exhibits a "willful dislocation of feeling from understanding." In fact, says Winters, Poe is interested in the creation of an emotion for its own sake, not in the understanding of experience." These views of Poe are common in American and English criticism. They result from a common genre error when a critic approaches a short story and scorns it because it does not follow the mimetic conventions of the novel. One can certainly admit that many of Poe's characters are unitary states without at the same time admitting that Poe is unconcerned with human understanding. As has already been shown, the short story from its beginnings is more closely aligned to projectionist fiction and a lyrical point of view than to the realistic fiction and rational point of view of the novel.

The best place to begin a consideration of the nature of Poe's stories is with a relatively unassuming story depicted in a basically realistic technique: the simple revenge story of "The Cask of Amontillado." The key to understanding the story is to perceive it as a monologue with a listener within the story. The narrator at the beginning addresses a definite "you" who he says "well know the nature of my soul." At the end of the story we discover that the present telling-time of the story takes place fifty years after the told event. The final line of the story—"*In pace requiescat*"—thus refers both to Fortunato, whose bones have never been discovered, and to Montresor, who is making the present confession, we assume, to a priest. The entire story is a complex tissue of irony; just as Montresor has made sure that none of his servants will be home by ordering them not to leave, so does he lure Fortunato into the catacombs by urging him to go home. Moreover, the irony takes on a structure of mocking and grotesque echo-action. As Fortunato begs Montresor to release him and screams in despair, Montresor echoes his words and screams. The central irony of the mock action in the story, however, turns on a reversal of Montresor's dual requirements for the perfect revenge and an ironic inversion of the symbolic meaning of Montresor's family coat of arms. Montresor says: "A wrong is unredressed when retribution overtakes its redresser. It is equally unredressed when the avenger fails to make himself known as such to him who has done the wrong." When we realize, however, that the mocking screams of Montresor border on hysteria, when we realize that he is not making confession of his crime, when we note that his heart grew sick after walling up Fortunato, and when we remember that Montresor does not let Fortunato know that his murderous act is indeed an act of revenge—then it becomes clear that Fortunato has more closely fulfilled the revenge criteria than has Montresor. The coat of arms—a human foot which crushes a serpent, but whose fangs remain embedded in the heel—is equally ironic. If the Montresor family is represented by the foot which crushes the serpent Fortunato, then we note that the serpent still clings to the heel. The family motto—No one harms me with impunity—thus applies to Fortunato as well as it does to Montresor. Every element in the story contributes to this single, but certainly not simple, ironic effect. Tone is the key to the story's meaning. There is, however, one more ironic turn of the screw in the story; although Montresor is now confessing, and thus, presumably, repentant for his crime, the very fact that the reader enjoys the clever ironic ways he tricked Fortunato indicates that by his very tone of telling, Montresor is enjoying it again also and is thus not repentant. Even though he is on his deathbed, he relives with glee the experience; and although he confesses, his tone damns him completely.

Although Poe disliked allegory, calling it the lowest form of art, his "The Pit and the Pendulum" and "The Masque of the Red Death" are both forms of allegory; however, they are more complex than the traditional conceptual allegorical fiction because of their dreamlike nature and because their elements symbolize complex metaphysical and psychological reality. "The Pit and the Pendulum" is very close to a self-contained dream story, but, like Franz Kafka's stories, it has enough of verisimilitude to give it the feeling of reality experienced as if it were nightmare. The entire story is dream and Poe is the dreamer; it is pure projective fiction from the beginning when the narrator says "I was sick—sick unto death" until the end when the loud blast of the trumpets marks his rescue from the dream by awakening him. The story is marked by many considerations of dream phenomenon in the beginning, as if the dreamer could consciously consider the curious epistemological and ontological status of dream itself. "Arousing from the most profound slumber," he says, "we break the gossamer web of *some* dream. Yet in a second afterward (so frail may that web have been) we remember not that we have dreamed." Moreover, the story is marked by a struggle to control the actions of the dream instead of being controlled by them; throughout the story the narrator undergoes a constant struggle to escape the machinations of the dream mechanism that controls him, but each time a danger is thwarted, a new danger is thrown in his way; for there is no way to escape the dangers that threaten one in dream except to awaken from the dream itself. The events that threaten the narrator—the pit, the pendulum, the walls that close in on him, the rats—are thus all of his own making; yet they are outside his control at the same time, for they are products of his own unconscious. The dilemma of the narrator is an objectification of the dilemma of all characters in this kind of self-conscious fiction—the dilemma of making one's story and being trapped by the story at the same time. The thematic content of the dream, however, is universal rather than personal; for it is a dream of being trapped by time (the pendulum), being prey to the nausea of body itself (the rats), and being threatened by the unknown and un-namable (the pit). As Harry Levin says of this story, it is an existential allegory that transcends the conceptual nature of allegory and becomes oneiric symbolism.

"The Masque of the Red Death" is allegorical fiction also, but again it is more complex than we usually assume allegory to be, both because it is tempered by Poe's characteristic irony and because it is infused with his concern to symbolize the nature of art itself. Prince Prospero is, like William Shakespeare's master magician in *The Tempest* (1611), a representation of the desire not simply to escape from death but to escape from life into a replacement world of fantasy and art. The story is an objectification of the attempt to escape from dynamic life (which inevitably results in death) into the static life of the art work (which means eternity). The first key to this understanding of the story lies in the title. The avatar of the pestilence death in the story is red, the color of blood, and blood is the symbol of life; however, it is Poe's view that life itself is the curse because it leads inevitably to death. Thus, Prospero shuts himself up within the castle and surrounds himself with clowns, improvisatori, dancers, musicians, actors; in short, figures who mimic life rather than participate in it. What Prospero in effect does is to enclose himself within the hermetically sealed art work itself, which says, as all romantic art works do: "the external world could take care of itself." The masked figure dabbled with blood is Poe's image of death masquerading as life, for it suggests that the sign of blood is always a masque for the death that lies beneath life or is inherent within it. When the revelers try to seize the figure, they find that it has no tangible form; for death that is inherent in life is a nothingness that can be neither grasped nor escaped.

Poe deals with the problem of trying to escape death in another story that is not so much allegory as it is surrealistic and symbolic psychological fiction. "The Tell-Tale Heart" presents a narrator who is mysteriously obsessed with the eye of the old man with whom he lives. The key to this unexplained obsession lies in the double meaning of the title of the story and in the pun Poe plays on the word "eye" itself. Although the title seems to refer to the end of the story, when the narrator thinks that the old man's beating heart has "told on him," that is, exposed his crime to the police, more generally the title refers to the only tale the heart can tell: the tale of time, as each heartbeat echoes the tick of the clock bringing one closer and closer to death. This is the tale that the narrator wishes to escape, and his obsessive concern to slow down and stop time altogether in his spying on the old man indicates this. The narrator's obsession with the eye is related to his identification with the old man. As he spies on him, the narrator delights that the old man is "listening just as I have done." He comments on the old man's groan of fear, "I knew the sound well." He then chuckles, "I knew what he felt and pitied him." The madness of the narrator is a metaphysical madness, for he hates the eye because it has come to mean "I" to him. The irony of the story is that the narrator wishes to escape death by destroying the "I"; that is, his own ego. He wishes to escape the tale the heart tells by destroying the self he has projected on the old man. The narrator's attempts to destroy the "I" by destroying the "eye" are ironically fulfilled at the end when he hears the beating of his own heart and thinks it is the old man's. The story consistently mixes up external and psychological reality to reveal a metaphysical meaning. Its refusal to separate the inner reality from the outer one is a typical device of Poe, and it is an influential one that characterizes the short story as a genre.

Poe's "The Fall of the House of Usher" presents a character configuration and a plot development that is typical of the short story from its beginnings up to the present day. It is the story of an actual or mimetic character, the narrator, who encounters a character who has been transformed into a parabolic figure by his own obsession with metaphysical mysteries. The story begins with the narrator's entrance into a world of ambiguity and myth; it is an entrance into the realm of story itself. It looks backward to Rip Van Winkle's entrance into the world of legend even as it looks forward to the encounter the narrator has with the ambiguous Bartleby in Melville's famous story. That the narrator enters the world of the art work itself is emphasized by his unsuccessful attempts to account for the feeling of gloom the house creates in him. He notes that while "there *are* combinations of very simple natural objects which have the power of thus affecting us, still the analysis of this power lies among considerations beyond our depth." What he is considering here is the romantic notion of the mystery of the imaginatively constructed art work—that it is not the elements but their combination that constitutes the mysterious unexplainable effect the art work has on us.

Usher himself is best known as one who is fascinated by art, especially the intricacies of music—that art form which Poe thinks to be the highest, because the most mysterious, source of the poetic sentiment. The effect of "The Fall of the House of Usher," however, is that of the poetic sentiment carried to its disastrous logical extreme—the poetic sentiment that has distanced itself so completely from material reality that it no longer has contact with the actual. Roderick Usher lives completely within the house of art, so detached from physicality that his senses cannot tolerate anything but the most insipid food, can stand only certain kinds of clothing, cannot bear odors, can bear only the faintest light. His music is wild and abstract; his paintings are not of things but ideas. When the narrator tries to determine what Usher fears, Usher can only suggest that it is fear itself. Indeed, Usher is afraid of nothing, but it is a nothing similar to that experienced by the old waiter in Ernest Hemingway's "A Clean, Well-Lighted Place"—a felt nothing that he knows too well. It is the *nada* that waits for the artist who so pursues his quest of pure art that he cuts himself off from any external reality and thus can only feed on his own subjectivity. Roderick's twin sister Madeline functions to embody (as the old man's eye does in "The Tell-Tale Heart") a projection of Roderick's gradual withdrawal. His attempt to bury his own obsession returns to destroy him. Roderick's dilemma of being caught between the world of the art work and the real world—in which the art work gradually displaces the real world—is objectified in the scene in which the narrator reads to Usher from a Gothic romance; the actions of the fiction are echoed by the actions of Madeline as she breaks out of her entombment. At the end of the story when Madeline enters the room and collapses onto Roderick, she symbolically collapses back into him. Then in a compressed symbolic climax, Roderick collapses back into the house and the house collapses back into the nothingness that is the tarn. The ultimate end of the artist who cuts himself off from actuality to live in the realm of the art work is the nothingness that results from devouring the self.

This is the Poe in whom Baudelaire saw the genius, and this is the Poe who contributes so much to the genius of the short story as a form—a form that combines mimesis and romance, myth and actuality, and that is supremely conscious of its own processes of doing so. The narrator of "The Fall of the House of Usher" is left with the memory of the encounter and thus with an obsessive tale to tell. The end of the events of the story is the beginning of the endless telling of it. As Randall Jarrell says about stories, "we take pleasure . . . in repeating over and over, until we can bear it, all that we found unbearable."

Before moving on to Melville's *The Piazza Tales* (1856), which mark a transition, especially in *Bartleby the Scrivener*, toward a more realistic emphasis in the short story, the romantic stories of the 1840's and 1850's in France and England, as well as the beginnings of poetic realism in Russia, will be briefly examined.

Romantic Short Fiction in Europe and England

Albert George, in his book *Short Fiction in France: 1800-1850* (1964), notes that the history of short fiction has been mostly ignored in France because of its oral origins and plebeian associations. In the 1820's and 1830's, however, the short story began to be popular in France in the magazines even though the romantics continued the long tradition of the short tale in the folktale and the oral anecdote. Almost all critics agree that the formal short story, as Poe defines it, came into being in France in 1829 with the publication of Prosper Mérimée's "Mateo Falcone." Honoré de Balzac's "Passion in the Desert" and "La Grande Bretèche" appeared in 1830 and 1832 respectively. Yet regardless of this introduction of a new formal control in short fiction, the short story, or *conte*, during the romantic period of the 1840's and 1850's in France is a combination of romantic fantasy, the supernatural, and a whimsical or satiric tone.

Typical of romantic whimsy and the supernatural is Théophile Gautier's "The Mummy's Foot," published in 1840. It is a story which derives from the earlier Gothic fiction of E. T. A. Hoffmann, but is presented in a new lightness of tone by a first-person narrator whom the reader cannot take seriously. The narrator buys the foot of an Egyptian princess in a bric-a-brac shop and then later dreams of returning the foot and traveling with the princess to a mummy afterlife; he awakes to find the foot gone. The plot is, as the narrator says of the foot itself, "charming, bizarre, and romantic," but it is ultimately silly; however, the plot is the least of the story. Tone, in fact, is everything here, as the romantic dilettantish narrator confronts in mock seriousness the absurdity of a one-footed princess and later is introduced to "the mummies of her acquaintance." What the story represents in the development of short fiction is a movement toward the sophistication of the supernatural and a satire of the dream-vision convention itself; it both develops the romantic dream vision and ironically undercuts that vision at the same time; it signals a trivializing of a convention and a self-parody which is the first step toward the establishing of a new convention, in this case the convention of realistic verisimilitude.

Gérard de Nerval's story "Pandora," although presented in more brittle satiric tones, is similarly a sign of the naturalizing of romanticism. Published in 1854, it integrates mythical and dream reality into the sophisticated social setting of the realistic convention of Balzac. If Gautier's inspiration is Hoffmann, Nerval's is Johann Wolfgang von Goethe; and his story, embodying the tension between the sensuous and the supernatural, has a more significant metaphysical thematic base than does Gautier's. The central character, in his adoration of Pandora, elevates her to a symbolic status even as he transforms himself into the tormented Prometheus. The dream of hallucinatory vision embodied here is more believable than in "The Mummy's Foot," because it is inextricably intertwined in the story rather than set apart from it. In this way, Nerval anticipates the style of Kafka by confusing reality and dream so purposefully that dream takes on an ontological status equal to that of phenomenal reality. Moreover, the narrator in "Pandora," a writer self-consciously aware of his own work, notes in the story that "Pandora" is a continuation of an earlier work and also inserts a confidential letter into the narrative addressed to Gautier himself in which the narrator and the writer of the letter are the same man. This self-reflexive technique confuses the point of view quite purposely to entangle elements of fiction and reality within the fiction itself. Again, when a work of fiction becomes self-consciously aware of itself as fiction and thus parodies the very conventions upon which it depends, we know we are on the brink of a shift to another generic convention.

It has often been noted that Prosper Mérimée's later stories do not match in impact and artistic control his earlier ones such as "Mateo Falcone." One of his best-known stories, however, published in the 1840's, "The Abbé Aubain," marks a complete break from the romantic supernaturalism and self-parody of Gautier and Nerval and establishes the short story as a realistic and radically ironic form. On the one hand, the story is reminiscent of the early Italian novellas of Giovanni Boccaccio in its satire on human vanity; on the other hand, because of its ironic reversal at the end, it points toward the kind of trick story that Guy de Maupassant made so popular in the latter part of the century in France. The story is told almost entirely in the form of letters from a wealthy, sophisticated society woman (who has moved to the country) to a friend in the city. As is typical of such a radically first-person form (which is actually transcribed monologue), much of the pleasure of the story lies in the reader's opportunity to mock the lady for her superficiality, which she reveals unawares. Her condescension toward the parish priest throughout the story allows the reader to laugh at her foolishness at the end. For although she fancies that the priest is in love with her (an infatuation that she finds amusing and which she uses to entertain herself), we discover in the last letter (which the priest writes to his old professor) that he has instead been using her to gain preferment and thus escape the country to a higher position in the Church. The concealment of this information, which is the only thing that makes this a story at all, is possible, of course, by the use of the letter convention. At the end of the piece, we are left with two unappealing characters who have not only underestimated each other, but who also remain self-deceived. The story contributes nothing to the short story except to move it toward the kind of ironic plot reversal that Maupassant perfected in "The Necklace."

The fact that the short story did not fare well in England in the nineteenth century seems partial support for Frank O'Connor's thesis that the short story deals with the individual detached from society. Lionel Stevenson has drawn attention to the Victorian assumption that any serious work of literature should offer a well-integrated view of society—an assumption which made English authors ignore the short-story form as trivial. Not until the 1880's, when the "fragmentation of sensibility" set in in England, did the short story begin to be seen as the most appropriate form for representing such a sensibility. As has already been noted, the romantic impulse in England found its form primarily in poetry, especially the romantic lyric moving toward the dramatic monologue. The short story is a fictional parallel to such forms because they, like the short story, depend on a particular point of view, usually of a single event. In certain ways, Coleridge's "The Rime of the Ancient Mariner" is a model short story, as is Browning's "Andrea del Sarto" and "Fra Lippo Lippi." The fictional embodiment of romanticism in nineteenth century England was only an undercurrent to the development of the Victorian novel, taking its direction from the Gothic fiction of Horace Walpole, Ann Radcliffe, William Beckford, and Matthew Gregory Lewis. That short fiction in England during this period often dealt with strange and unexplainable (or at least seemingly unexplainable) events springs partially from the old folktale tradition of dealing with such events and partially from the influence of the darker side of German Romanticism. The English way to deal with the supernatural, however, is to explain it away naturalistically or play it for its simple shock effect, rather than, as in America, to exploit its metaphysical and psychological implications.

A typical example is Wilkie Collins' "The Traveler's Story of a Terribly Strange Bed." The story is about a single narrator who begins winning at gambling prodigiously and is encouraged on and seemingly protected by a dirty and wrinkled old man with vulture eyes. After breaking the bank at the gambling house, the narrator is almost killed in a four-poster bed when the top is lowered down to crush him. The story has the kind of plot and character potential of which Dostoevski could have made metaphysical capital, or that Poe could have developed into a psychological nightmare. For Collins, however, the story is a simple one of a thwarted murder attempt, in which the mysterious old man turns out to be the owner of the gambling house and the perpetrator of the plot to kill the narrator. The story is not without its suspense and not without its elements of mysterious hallucination. The bed, however, turns out to be not very "terribly strange" at all—only a smooth-running mechanism for murder. The story is indeed short and self-contained, but it is told more in a novelistic manner that focuses on realistic motivation and verisimilitude than in the true short-story manner which focuses on psychological and metaphysical mysteries.

Edward Bulwer-Lytton's story "The Haunted and the Haunters: Or, The House and the Brain" (1859) is a ghost story with a ratiocinative twist. The narrator of the story is a dilettantish ghost hunter who spends a night in a mysterious house in order to disprove, or at least to explain, the strange phenomena that have been reported there. Indeed, mysterious manifestations do take place during his night in the house: a child's footprints are seen, ghastly exhalations are felt, and ghostly voices are heard. The narrator discovers clues that the previous residents of the house had been involved in mysterious events of love and death—events that somehow had given rise to the phenomena. The narrator, however, is little interested in the lives that seem perpetuated in the house; his only concern is to explain the events and to prove his theory that the supernatural is only a natural law of which we have been previously ignorant. The final solution involves not the elaborate ratiocinative devices of Poe's detective figures, nor does the haunting of the house suggest the sort of psychological hallucination and dream reality of Poe's horror stories. In fact, the discovery of a powerful lodestone, some amber and rock crystal lumps, and a magic symbol in a secret chamber do little to explain anything. The final discovery is that a famous charlatan who once lived in the house has left behind a mechanism which preserves his own powerful will and affects the occupants of the house. The motivation for his action, however, is left vague and unexplored. A more typical short story would have involved the narrator in the story in some crucial way; but here, he only exists to explain, in pseudoscientific ways, the mystery of the phenomenon. How the events take place is all that is important, not why they happen or what they mean.

A more pertinent example of the failure to exploit the particular characteristics of the short-story genre in England can be seen in a tale by Charles Dickens. One would think that Dickens, with his focus on the outcast figure on the fringe of society and his mastery of the grotesque and extreme situation, would have found the short story a most viable vehicle. In "The Signalman" (1866), however, Dickens has all the plot and character elements of a successful short story but fails to use them in an intense and revealing way. The narrator of the story, who identifies himself as a "man who had been shut up within narrow limits all his life, and who being at last set free, had a newly awakened interest" in the world around him, encounters a railway signalman. The narrator descends through an extremely deep cutting of clammy stone, that becomes oozier and wetter as he goes down, to the signalman's post; it is solitary and dismal and has an earthy, deadly smell and so much cold wind rushing through it that the narrator feels as if he had "left the natural world." The signalman himself has the potentially symbolic task of watchfulness and exactness; in fact, he seems to exist only for this purpose and has learned a language of telegraphic communication that sets him apart from the phenomenal world.

The story, however, is a structure of potential elements that are never realized. The signalman's function and his cavernous location down the ravine, which the narrator finds "easier to mount than to descend," seem the materials of symbolic fiction; the narrator himself, who has been confined within narrow limits, seems the stuff of psychological drama; the central events of the story—the signalman's perception of a specter with the left arm across the face and the right one waving violently as if to say, "For God's sake, clear the way"—has all the elements of the *Doppelgänger* motif; and the final event in the story, when the signalman has been killed and the narrator sees an actual embodiment of the specter make the waving gesture, has the potential of involving the narrator in the story. All these elements could have come together in a story about the nature of isolation, concretely realized and vividly symbolized. Instead, what we have is a simple demonstration of the psychic phenomenon of precognition. The potential of the story, either psychologically or morally, that a Poe or a Hawthorne could have developed is never fulfilled or even suggested in a unified way. For Dickens, these elements are interesting in themselves, but they do not come together in the single and unified complex effect that marks the mastery of the short-story genre.

For whatever reason, because of individual poetic genius or because of the difference in social milieu, Ivan Turgenev could have transformed the Dickens material into a unified, lyric, and symbolic story. There is no question that *A Sportsman's Sketches* (1852) is one of the great collections of short fiction in the nineteenth century. Frank O'Connor says it may well be the greatest book of short stories ever written. Turgenev is a distinctly romantic writer, but a romantic writer moving toward realism. Strongly influenced by the German Romantics—Hoffmann, Tieck, Novalis—Turgenev had a strong sense of the irrational and an adherence to the mysterious saving power of love. Marina Ledovsky, in her 1973 study entitled *The*

Other Turgenev, describes the characteristics of Turgenev's tales in a way that could be a description of the short-story form itself: "The peculiarity of the structure of the mysterious tales consists in the alternating and at times fusing of extremely realistic, prosaic events with fantastic episodes. . . . Thus the irrational and alogical are woven into banal reality to create a grotesque setting on two planes." As is true for the short story generally, Turgenev's realism is not an indication of a philosophic acceptance of the primary reality of the physical and phenomenal world; rather, it is simply a technique for involving everyday reality with the immanently mysterious world of the irrational. This is why the short story often involves the grotesque, and why the form, as exemplified in Turgenev, suggests the entanglement of the physical world with the dreamlike world of story itself. Turgenev's two best-known stories— "The Country Doctor" and "Bezhin Meadow"—are exemplars of the short story as a form; so completely do they represent the short story that their subject matter is the world of story itself.

"The Country Doctor" is a framed story in which the sportsman narrator, taken by a fever, calls in a district doctor who tells him a "remarkable story" which the sportsman then relates to the reader in the doctor's own words. The story is one about the doctor's trip to tend a beautiful sick young girl in the home of her poor but cultivated mother. The girl's slow death over a period of days is ironically the doctor's one moment of life—life elevated from his everyday routine. The tale the doctor tells of his falling in love with the girl and her falling in love with him reaches its climax and crux when the doctor realizes that she loves him only because she is going to die. The doctor says he understands that "if she had not believed herself on the point of death, she would never have given me a thought; but say what you like, there must be something appalling about dying at twenty-five without ever having loved; that was the thought that tormented her, and that was why, in despair, she seized on me." What adds another excruciating turn of the screw is that the girl, having proclaimed her love for the doctor, is desperate to die. When she begs the doctor that she must die, that he promised her that she would die, he says, "It was a bitter moment for me, for many reasons."

The conception of the story is a stroke of genius, for it combines for the doctor a moment of the highest fulfillment, yet at the same time a moment of the deepest despair precisely because of the fulfillment itself. Yet the real genius of the story lies in the telling itself, as the doctor in his hurried yet halting way tries both to justify the experience and to understand it. It is a typical Turgenev device, as it was later to be for Anton Chekhov, to have the story end in understatement. After the story is told and the narrator takes the doctor's hand in unspoken sympathy, the doctor suggests a game of Preference and offhandedly says he has since married a woman as common as he is, "a spiteful hag, I must say, but luckily she sleeps all day." The last paragraph of the story is: "We got down to Preference for copeck stakes. Trifon Ivanich won two and a half roubles from me—and went home late, very pleased with his victory." Such an ending is not to suggest that we have been tricked into a sympathy for the doctor which he does not deserve. On the contrary, it is an indication of the depth of his significant loss that he is content with the trivial win. For the central irony of the story is that if he had won, that is, if the girl had lived, he would have lost. His only win is the memory, the story itself, and that is a constant source of both joy and torture for him. There is no sentimentality in the story, nor is there cynicism. It is simply the recounting of a moment in time when the evanescent possibility to be elevated from the everyday occurred—a recounting which indeed suggests that the only possibilities for such transcendence are, by their very nature, evanescent. Transcendence is a strange and lyrical moment surrounded by the mundane and the ordinary; it is one of the functions of the short-story form to depict such moments in all their bittersweetness.

"Bezhin Meadow" is an even more complex story about the transition from the ordinary phenomenal world into the extraordinary world of dream, wish, and thus story itself. The tale begins with the sportsman getting lost; as he experiences a sense of disorientation, he cries, "Where on earth am I?" and we realize, as we do with Rip Van Winkle's strange trek up the mountain, with Young Goodman Brown's journey into the forest, and with the narrator in "The Fall of the House of Usher" as he approaches the ominous house that the sportsman is nowhere on earth, that he has moved from the terrestrial into a realm of folktale and dream. The landscape he travels through is a familiar one in romantic poetry and the short-story genre:

> The hollow was like an almost symmetrical cauldron with sloping sides. At the bottom of it rose, bolt upright, several large white stones, which seemed to have crept down there for a secret conclave, and the whole place had such a deaf-and-dumb feeling the sky hung so flatly and gloomily above it, that my heart shrank. Some little creature was squeaking faintly and plaintively among the stones.

Floundering through this mythic landscape, the sportsman comes upon a group of peasant boys tending horses. As he pretends to sleep, he hears the five boys tell the following stories. Fedya tells the first story of a ghost in a papermill which frightened him and some of his friends and then made a sound of choking and coughing like a sheep. Kostya tells the story of a carpenter who confronts a water sprite in the forest and crosses himself in fear that it is the devil; at this act she begins to cry and tells him that if he had not crossed himself he could have lived with her merrily forever; since that time the carpenter goes about grieving. Ilyusha tells a story of the kennelman Ermil, who, seeing a lamb on the grave of a drowned man, strokes it and says "Baa-lamb, baa-lamb," to which the lamb bares its teeth and answers him back. Pavel tells a story of the coming of Trishka, the antichrist, who turns out to be only the barrelmaker who had bought himself a new jug and had put the empty jug over his head. Finally, Kostya tells of a little boy who drowned in the river near where the boys are and whose mother has not been right in the head since. At the end of this story, Pavel, who has told the only "supernatural" story with a naturalistic explanation, comes back from the river and says that he has heard the drowned boy call to him from under the water.

The story has no plot, is not *about* a single event except for the narrator's encounter with the realm of story itself. "Bezhin Meadow" projects a basic romantic image of man; like Shelley's poet who is a nightingale singing in the darkness, the boys tell their stories and light up a small place. The stories themselves are kernels of short stories—folk legends of mysterious encounters with hope, wish, pathos, madness. Pavel is central in the narrator's consciousness because of his attempts to find some rational explanation for the supernatural events; but he too is drawn into the dream world of story until the virtual world itself is transformed and he hears the voice of the drowned child. The irony of the story is the irony of all the stories we tell of those things that frighten us, for we tell them as a way of dealing with our fears. It is a story of the storytelling impulse as an example of Freud's repetition compulsion, a basic urge to control the uncontrollable by managing it in the form of story itself. For Turgenev, as for all great storytellers, the nature of reality lies not in hard events, but rather in human emotions that construct those events and make them meaningful. Story is a primal form of expressing the emotion-made nature of reality—a primal form of expressing the reality of wish, of dream, of feeling, of the ultimately unexplainable, that yet must be integrated and coped with.

Although Dostoevski is often praised as a prophetic voice of the twentieth century existential sensibility, and his novels are often cited as exemplars of the philosophical novel, little has been said of his use of, and contribution to, the short-story form. Indeed, in his short fictions, the focus is less on the formal perfection of a lyrical form to penetrate psychological and metaphysical mysteries than it is on the presentation of a conceptual philosophic position. Among his stories, "The Crocodile" is a satire of civil service bureaucracy and "The Dream of a Ridiculous Man" is a parable which sets forth his own Christian existentialism. Even the two stories singled out for discussion—*Notes from the Underground* (1864) and "The Peasant Marey"—have been analyzed mainly for their conceptual or parabolic content. What is to be suggested is that, both formally and thematically, the stories fall within the tradition of short fiction in the nineteenth century.

First of all, the Underground Man is a clear example of that isolated individual which Frank O'Connor suggests is central to the short-story form. He is a "characterless creature" who has cut himself off from the social world and feeds instead on his own subjectivity. Like Melville's Bartleby, he has confronted a wall before which he is impotent. In his story "Apropos of the Wet Snow," he recounts the experiences which have led him to the underground and thus to his philosophic monologue. Basically, "Apropos of the Wet Snow" recounts his attempts to involve himself in real life, attempts to love and be loved; but they are attempts which fail because of his morbid self-consciousness and his bookish posturing and artificiality. The Underground Man's relationship with the characters in the story are basically the same as his relationship with the readers in the monologue: he tries to win them over even as he mocks them. The Russian critic Konstantin Mochulsky sums up this dilemma and the theme of the story in a way that marks its similarity to the theme of many of the stories of Hawthorne: "A strongly developed person recoils from the world, desperately defends his own autonomy, and, at the same time, is attracted to others and understands his dependence on them." The tragedy of "Apropos of the Wet Snow" is, Mochulsky says, the tragedy of human communication. Mochulsky notes that this tension also dominates the monologue section of the story, for it is a monologue which is in the nature of a dialogue. Although the Underground Man insists that he needs no reader, each statement is intended to make an impression on the reader.

Although the monologue has received the most critical attention, it is the story "Apropos of the Wet Snow" which constitutes the center of the work. The monologue is, as Ralph Matlaw has suggested, a false start, leading the reader away from the real subject of the work. Before he can recall and reveal, the narrator evades and attempts to build up an image of the self through philosophic speculaton. It is the story that depicts his encounters with "the real thing" and his failures both because of his confusion between real life and art life and his own self-consciousness. His situation in the two parts of the stories are echoed in the monologue of J. Alfred Prufrock and in James's story of John Marcher in "The Beast in the Jungle" a generation later.

"The Peasant Marey" is a story within a story which depicts the relationship of a memoried or storied past event to an intolerable present situation. The present time of the story is Easter week and the narrator is in prison. Disgusted by the violence and disorder of his surroundings, and affected by a hissed whisper to him by a political prisoner—"I hate these scum"—the narrator loses himself in memories of when he was nine years old and heard a shout of "wolf," but was comforted by one of his father's peasants, Marey, who told him that the shout was in his fancy only. After the narrator resurrects this incident (which he says must have lain hidden in his soul for twenty years), he looks on his fellow prisoners with more sympathetic eyes; for now he feels that the very criminal he had found so disgusting may be the very Marey who had comforted him as a child.

The parabolic nature of the story is simple enough: that one must recognize the basic humanity of all people regardless of their external appearances. The mode of the story—in which a memory is revived and relived as a key to a present situation—is more complex. For the story of Marey and the boy who heard "wolf" is a play with the folktale of the boy who cried "wolf." Whereas the folktale is about a boy who so often presents a fantasy as if it were a reality that when he confronts the reality no one believes him and he is devoured by it, Dostoevski's story is about a fantasy (or memory or story) which reminds the narrator that the external reality he perceives around him is appearance only—that the significant reality resides in the story—the very story that he remembers and constructs. Thus, as often in the short-story form, the fiction becomes more real than the external reality.

The Well-Made Story and the Movement Toward Realism

After the era of Hawthorne and Poe in America, the short story ceased to be a distinctive form until Henry James revived it as a serious art form in the 1880's. This does not mean, however, that important changes in the form did not take place in the

1850's, 1860's, and 1870's—changes that have affected the development of the form up to the present day. The primary movement in this period was, of course, the shift toward realism; and realism is neither a philosophic assumption nor a literary convention that is conducive to the basically romantic and psychological/metaphysical nature of the short-story form. Herman Melville's *Bartleby the Scrivener* is an exception, because even as it points forward to the highly polished psychological tales of Henry James, it points backward to Poe's psychological hallucinations and Hawthorne's moral parables. Beyond Melville's distinctive contribution to the short story in the 1850's, the other two movements in the development of the form that dominate the period up to the 1880's are the stories of local color and the so-called "well-made" stories. Of the many examples of local-color stories that dominate the period, the short stories of Bret Harte and Mark Twain have been chosen to comment on. Of the well-made story, the best-known stories of Fitz-James O'Brien, Thomas Aldrich, and Edward Everett Hale have been selected for commentary.

Frederick Lewis Pattee, in his 1923 study of the short story, has noted the avalanche of female authors that followed Hawthorne and Poe in the 1850's and filled the magazines with sentimental stories. Hawthorne himself said in 1855, "America is now wholly given over to a d——d mob of scribbling women. I should have no chance of success while the public taste is occupied with their trash—and should be ashamed of myself if I did succeed." Besides Melville, the only other figure in the 1850's to contribute (for better or worse) to the future of the short story was Fitz-James O'Brien. His 1859 story, "What Was It?," makes use of the fantasy and supernatural elements that Poe perfected, but it also points ahead to the journalistic style of O. Henry. "What Was It?" is a well-made, formally constructed story far superior to similar stories by Wilkie Collins and Edward Bulwer-Lytton but very much inferior to the intricate blendings of fantasy and reality that Poe achieved.

Character development in the story is slight; Harry, the narrator, serves primarily to tell the story of his capture of an invisible ghoulish figure. He is a writer and a smoker of opium and somewhat of an amateur expert on supernaturalism. The central event takes place in a boarding house, reputed to be haunted, on a night after he and a friend, Dr. Hammond, have been smoking opium and talking. On this particular night, instead of talking about the light or Ariel side of life, as was their custom, they discuss the darker or Caliban side. Hammond brings up the philosophic question to Harry: "What do you consider to be the greatest element of terror?" Dr. Hammond thinks of various effects in the works of Brockden Brown and Bulwer-Lytton and thinks that if only he were master of a literary style he could write a story like Hoffmann on this particular night.

After retiring, the narrator of "What Was It?" tries to get the horrible thoughts of the discussion out of his mind; he feels something drop from the ceiling onto his chest and try to strangle him with bony hands. After a struggle, he subdues the thing and turns on the light, only to find nothing. In contrast to the usual such dream-vision awakenings, however, the thing is still there; it is invisible, but it is still a concrete "thereness." Later when they call in a doctor to chloroform the thing and make a cast of it, what is revealed is a four-footed, manlike creature with muscular limbs; the narrator describes it only as something that surpasses figures from Doré or Callot. Now the creature becomes a burden—something they can neither release, nor keep, nor kill. Finally the creature dies, seemingly having starved to death, and is buried. What the story is, given O'Brien's fascination with *The Tempest*, is an objectification of fantasy—the intrusion into virtual reality of an abstract, yet emotionally created, object of terror that the narrator and doctor have been discussing. In fact, the entire house of boarders has been infected psychologically with dark fantasies, for they have been reading a book entitled *The Night Side of Nature* before the creature appears. Thus within the fantasy entitled "What Was It?" we have an actual objectification of the fantasies of the fictional characters. Such a self-reflexive motif, while not as expert as similar motifs in Poe, is more polished than stories of other supernatural writers in the 1850's and 1860's.

Herman Melville's short fiction has been little appreciated until recently. Pattee only briefly mentions him in his 1923 study of the short story. Of the mass of criticism that has been published on Melville's short stories in the last twenty years, the story that has received the most attention (and rightfully so) is *Bartleby the Scrivener*. In nothing else that Melville wrote, says Newton Arvin, "did he achieve by the accumulation of details themselves commonplace, prosaic, and humdrum, a total effect of such strangeness and even madness as this." The story has been discussed by numerous critics as an autobiographical parable of Melville's feeling of artistic failure, as a case study in schizophrenia, and as a social allegory of how the system crushes the little man. The one discussion that approaches the story as a short story is an article by Robert Marler (*American Literature*, May, 1974), which argues that *Bartleby the Scrivener* marks a transition from the "tale" form, in which characters are unitary figures or archetypes, to the true "short story," in which characters have their own psychologies and are wearing their social personae. Marler says that *Bartleby the Scrivener* is a fully developed short story because it is embedded in a social context and is a reflection of the narrator's mind. It is not Bartleby's story, says Marler, but a story of the narrator's movement from a state of ignorance to a state of knowledge.

There is not sufficient space here to argue with all of Marler's points which indicate that the story is the first true short story and therefore radically different from the "tale" form that preceded it; it is not a point worth belaboring. The difference between *Bartleby the Scrivener* and the stories of Hawthorne and Poe is indeed a result of a step toward realism. Even though Melville focuses on the prosaic and the commonplace in the story, however, the effect is as psychologically mysterious as a story by Poe and as morally complex as a story by Hawthorne; for the prosaic and the commonplace are transformed here into symbol. Although the story takes place in an actual setting—an office in New York's Wall Street—as the story develops, we gradually discover that Wall Street serves less as a social situation than as a symbolic backdrop to Bartleby's story. Indeed, it is a story filled with walls—both blank walls which Bartleby faces and dividing walls that separate him from others. The story is symbolic in the sense that Bartleby himself, for no discernible reasons, has transformed the physical walls around him into metaphors for all the psychological and metaphysical walls that stand between man and understanding of the world. If Bartleby is mad, his madness is that of one who, like Dostoevski's Underground Man or Hawthorne's minister with the black veil, has understood too clearly that nothing can be understood at all. By his transformation of a real object—the wall—into a symbolic object and his consequent reaction to the object as if it were the significance he has projected on it, Bartleby himself is transformed into a symbolic figure. Bartleby then becomes a "wall" for the narrator, something opaque and mysterious, something that cannot be explained rationally. Indeed, the story *is* the narrator's story; it is his effort to "replay" the experience with Bartleby both as a means of justifying his actions and of understanding what the experience meant.

The basic conflict between Bartleby and the narrator is, as pointed out by Norman Springer (*PMLA*, 1965), that while the narrator is a man of assumptions, Bartleby is an embodiment of preferences. Thus, Bartleby exists to demonstrate the inadequacy of all assumptions. The narrator perceives, as does the narrator of "The Fall of the House of Usher," that the mysterious figure before him has "nothing ordinarily human about him." When the narrator asks Bartleby during one of his "dead-wall reveries" why he will do no more copying, Bartleby replies, "Do you not see the reason for yourself?" His reference is to the wall he stares at. Even if the narrator could see in the metaphysical, yet mad, way that Bartleby sees and were to ask him why the wall makes him withdraw from life, Bartleby could answer only that the wall means "nothing." It would be a nothing that is a tangible, felt reality in the way Hemingway's old waiter understands it in "A Clean, Well-Lighted Place," a *nada* that butts all heads at last. The frustration that the narrator feels at not being able either to understand Bartleby or to help him is a result not only of the narrator's safe and secure position, which Bartleby comes to challenge, but also of the impossibility of what Bartleby tacitly demands. For what Bartleby presents is the radical challenge to charity and love that Christ requires. Bartleby tacitly asks to be understood although he refuses to aid in that understanding; he asks to be loved although he infuriatingly rebuffs all efforts the narrator makes to help him. Bartleby is indeed a particularly painful case of the inability of one to penetrate to the core of the other and say "I-Thou," for he is the "other *par excellence*" who comes soley to challenge the narrator's easy assumptions.

The relationship between Bartleby and the narrator is different from the relationship between Roderick Usher and his narrator only in that the focus shifts. In "The Fall of the House of Usher," the symbolic figure Usher is foregrounded, and we know little of the narrator's mind except his puzzlement and inability to understand. In *Bartleby the Scrivener*, it is indeed the narrator's inability to understand, and by extension the basic human inability to understand, which is foregrounded into the subject matter of the story. Although there are no immediate heirs to this shift of emphasis in the short story in America, it does dominate the form from Henry James and Joseph Conrad on up through the twentieth century. We now see in Flannery O'Connor, Eudora Welty, Bernard Malamud, and other contemporary writers short-story situations in which an ordinary person in the phenomenal world confronts some mysterious character or figure who throws him or her out of an often uneasy placidity into the mystery of human communication and love (or the impossibility of either), and we see the loneliness that inevitably results.

Fred Lewis Pattee points out that the gradual rise of realism and the magazine *Atlantic Monthly* dominated the short-story form in America in the 1860's. Of the many stories published in *Atlantic Monthly* during this period, commentary will be kept to the most famous, Edward Everett Hale's "The Man Without a Country," a tremendously popular story at the time, which remains worthy of note because of its so-called realism. The story is told by a first-person narrator, and the tone is that of a cautionary tale for young military men. Philip Nolan, the man without a country, is presented as a "real" man involved in an actual event (Aaron Burr's attempted overthrow of the country), but the historical framework serves only the purpose of establishing the event as having really happened and of motivating Nolan's unique sentence—the carrying out of which is the main material of the story. Nolan's character is not explored, and his personal motivation is not developed. The traitorous act itself is described rather in terms of some sort of a satanic temptation. Burr is described simply as a "gay deceiver" who "seduces" Nolan "body and soul."

When Nolan damns the United States at his trial and vows, "I wish I may never hear of the United States again," the court sentences him to fulfill his wish. He is transferred back and forth on Navy vessels for fifty years, never closer than one hundred miles to United States soil. All officers and crewmen on the ships are forbidden to make any reference to the United States; his reading material is carefully censored, even to the deletion of references to the United States in foreign books and newspapers. The story is primarily narrative, with only a few scenes that indicate Nolan's growing loneliness and awareness of the extremity of his situation. The actual thematic thrust of the story, for all its realistic plot detail, is of a man tempted into a traitorous act by a figure who has become legendary in American history. The result of Nolan's act is that he is not only forced to have his wish fulfilled—a wish he discovers to be a curse—but also he himself is turned into a legendary figure in a cautionary tale. Just as the early short story concerns a mythic figure presented as a man, Hale's story presents a man being transformed into a mythic figure—the stuff of continuing story. Regardless of whatever surface verisimilitude a short story may manifest, its so-called "realism" is always mixed with the mythic and the storylike.

Bret Harte is not a realist in any sense except for the fact that he situates his stories in a specific locality for which he establishes a Western atmosphere and a set of social customs. His characters are types who serve the ironic function of his stories. Moreover, Harte's "local color" is primarily romantic, for he creates his own self-contained little world in which he stylizes the customs, caricatures the characters, and romanticizes the surroundings. Although his effect was strongly felt at the time his first stories appeared in *Overland Monthly* in 1868, his reputation has not fared well since. In his best story, "Tennessee's Partner," his humorous and ironic point of view and his carefully controlled technique make a definite contribution to the short-story genre; for here he creates a story that, as all good stories do, seduces the reader into a response quite contrary to what the actual events of the story suggest on the surface.

Arthur Hobson Quinn has said that Harte taught nearly every American writer of short stories some of the essentials of his art. Quinn suggests that Harte's sense of humor "preserved in him that sense of proportion which was one of his great gifts to the development of the short story." Harte would have been happy to accept this as his major contribution, for in his *Cornhill* article of 1899, he singles out humor as the factor which finally diminished the influence of English models on the short story in America and helped create a distinctly American form:

> It was *Humour*—of a quality as distinct and original as the country and civilization in which it was developed. It was first noticeable in the anecdote or "story," and after the fashion of such beginnings, was orally transmitted. It was common in the barrooms, the gatherings in the "country store," and finally at public meetings in the mouths of "stump orators."

According to Harte, it is the storyteller's tone and point of view that determine the meaning of a short story, for it is his moral perspective which should direct the reader's response to the story. "Tennessee's Partner" has a dramatically defined narrator with a voice and purpose of his own. After relating how Tennessee's partner went to San Francisco for a wife and was stopped in Stockton by a young waitress who broke at least two plates of toast over his head, the narrator says that he is well aware that "something more might be made of this episode, but I prefer to tell it as it was current at Sandy Bar—in the gulches and barrooms—where all sentiment was modified by a strong sense of humor." It is this barroom point of view, in fact, which dominates the whole story; and once we are willing to accept this tone, the story takes on a new and not so pathetic dimension. The narrator fully intends for this story to be, not the occasion for tears, but for sardonic laughter.

When Tennessee's partner invites the men to Tennessee's funeral, the narrator says, "Perhaps it was from a sense of humor, which I have already intimated was a feature of Sandy Bar—perhaps it was from something even better than that, but two thirds of the loungers accepted the invitation at once." That "something better," which sentimental readers have always been willing to accept as an indication of sympathy and perhaps regret on the part of the men for their condemnation of Tennessee, might be seen instead as the final necessary act in the ritual of complicity between the partner and the town in their vigilante justice on Tennessee. The "popular feeling" which had grown up against Tennessee in Sandy Bar could end no other way. At the trial, the narrator makes it abundantly clear that Tennessee's fate was sealed, that the trial is only to justify "the previous irregularities of arrest and indictment." The men have no doubt about his fate; they are "secure in the hypothesis that he ought to be hanged on general principles." It is this very knowledge that they are going to hang Tennessee not so much for a concrete wrong as on general principles that makes them begin to waver, until the partner, who *has* suffered a concrete wrong by Tennessee, enters the game with his attempted bribe of the judge. As a result of his taking a hand, the town helps Tennessee's partner avenge himself on Tennessee for stealing his wife, and the partner helps the town get rid of a bothersome blight on the body politic. The economical use of detail in the story, as well as its combination of sardonic humor and moral complexity, is similar to Poe's masterpiece, "The Cask of Amontillado." In its use of a narrator who quietly and cleverly controls his satiric intent, it is surely as well done as Ring Lardner's "Haircut" or Mark Twain's "The Celebrated Jumping Frog of Calaveras County."

In contrast to Harte's humorous story, about which little has been said, Mark Twain's jumping frog story has come in for much critical commentary. The story has been called a multilevel satire pitting the simplicity of the West against the cunning of the East in which, although the Westerner Jim Smily is bested in the contest by the Easterner, the West gets its revenge on the East by imposing Simon Wheeler's long-winded story on the Easterner, Mark Twain. The story itself is a clear example of Twain's own definition of the humorous in his 1895 piece, "How to Tell a Story." The humorous is told gravely, says Twain; "the teller does his best to conceal the fact that he even dimly suspects that there is anything funny about it." The humorous story always depends on the manner of the telling rather than on the matter, says Twain; and Simon Wheeler tells his story with such earnestness that "so far from imagining that there was anything ridiculous or funny about his story, he regarded it as a really important matter, and admired its two heroes as men of transcendent genius in finesse." The irony of the story is that although an Easterner beats the inveterate gambler Jim Smily, the Western story itself is the champion. The genius in finesse is Simon Wheeler (or rather his creator Mark Twain—not his auditor Mark Twain), and the framed story triumphs over the frame itself. Truly, as Bret Harte has said, the genius of the American Western story is the tone of the telling; the tone in Twain's tale is one that hovers uneasily between seriousness and triviality and between reality and parable.

The beginnings of the well-made story in America have already been noted in the stories of Edward Everett Hale and Fitz-James O'Brien. The form did not become overwhelmingly popular and influential, however, until Thomas Bailey Aldrich's "Marjorie Daw" appeared in 1873 in *Atlantic Monthly.* Its impact was similar to that created by Harte's "The Luck of Roaring Camp," Frank R. Stockton's "The Lady or the Tiger?," or more recently Shirley Jackson's "The Lottery." Like these stories, "Marjorie Daw" has come to stand as an exemplar of the short-story form in the popular imagination. As Fred Lewis Pattee has noted, "Marjorie Daw" became a type "standing for controlled artistry, a whimsical wit, and a totally unexpected denouement that sends the reader back over the story again." Although it is often suggested that Aldrich's surprise ending is the key to the story's success, the basic thematic impulse of the story is as characteristic of the short-story form as is the characteristic turn at the end. As we have been discussing it, the short story often presents a realm in which fantasy and reality are blurred or one in which fantasy becomes more real than the phenomenal world. "Marjorie Daw" is a story that takes this central characteristic as its primary theme. The epistolary form of the story, in which Edward Delaney writes letters to the laid-up John Fleming describing a beautiful young girl who lives across from him and Fleming writes back describing his growing love for the girl, is the point-of-view device that makes possible keeping the secret that there is no such girl.

The story is about the power of the writer's ability to create an "as if" reality that is more real than a real person. Delaney wishes he were a novelist with the skill of Turgenev as he begins to weave his tale of the young girl in the hammock across the way. As the letters progress, Fleming seems to feel he has known her in some previous state of existence or has dreamed her. Indeed, she is an embodiment of dream, a shadow or chimera; and Delaney marvels that Fleming could fall in love with her, even as he writes Fleming that the chimera is falling in love with him. Thus both Marjorie Daw and Fleming are transformed into fictional figures by Delaney, "a couple of ethereal beings moving in finer air than I can breathe with my commonplace lungs"; and Delaney, caught up in his own fictional creation, begins to "accept things as persons do in dreams." The end of the story is told in Delaney's last letter to Fleming, which Fleming reads when he has finally come to see Marjorie for himself, and it catches the reader with what Mark Twain would call a "snapper": "For oh, dear Jack, there isn't any colonial mansion on the other side of the road, there isn't any piazza, there isn't any hammock—there isn't any Marjorie Daw!" The reader's surprise at this ending and his subsequent going back over the story for clues to the trick is an objectification of what every reader feels when he or she has taken a fictional character to be real. "Marjorie Daw" is a story of the storytelling function itself—a discovery that characters are made of letters only.

The final figures in the development of the short story in the period from 1840 to 1880 are the self-conscious masters of fictional technique in the nineteenth century: Gustave Flaubert and Henry James. Poe's discussion of the importance of form and the artistic nature of the short story in 1842 is echoed by James in his discussion of the art of the novel in 1884. Poe's insistence that "In the whole composition there should be no word written, of which the tendency, direct or indirect, is not to the one preestablished design" is repeated by James's insistence that the novel is a "living thing, all one and continuous, like any other organism, and in porportion as it lives will it be found, I think, that in each of the parts there is something of each of the other parts." This is indeed a new criterion for the novel, one that redeems it from the realm of the popular and includes it within the realm of the artist. Furthermore, Poe's insistence on the importance of the point of view of the teller and its predominance over a simple mimetic presentation of events is also echoed by James's assertion that experience in fiction is an "immense sensibility, a kind of spider-web of the finest silken threads suspended in the chamber of consciousness . . . the very atmosphere of the mind." It is a curiosity of literary criticism that while James's essay is hailed as marking a new direction for the novel at the end of the century, Poe's similar insistence for the short story forty years earlier has been scorned as simplistic. In spite of the similarity of the two essays, many critics seem to believe that James's discussion is the first effort to justify fiction itself as an art form.

What James and Flaubert contribute to the novel form at the end of the nineteenth century is possible because of the development of the short story from the beginnings of the century. The importance of both point of view and form and their intrinsic relation to content, which seems a new departure for fiction at the end of the century, seems so only because the short story has always taken a back seat to the novel. The so-called modern novel may begin with the twentieth century, but for fiction generally "modernism" begins with the nineteenth century short story. Albert George in his study *Short Fiction in France: 1800-1850* says that Flaubert's *Three Stories* (1877) are an indication that Flaubert was the first to profit from romantic attempts to understand short fiction; they are "the superb refinement of the accumulated knowledge of a half-century." The same might be said of Henry James's *Daisy Miller*, published in 1878. Flaubert's "A Simple Heart" and James's *Daisy Miller* constitute a new beginning for the short story, a definite movement away from the romantic tale form that had dominated the century toward a new focus on realism, but a realism controlled by an ironic tone and a continuing focus on sympathy and an undercurrent of symbolism that has been unique to the short story since Gogol and Hawthorne. Flaubert's Félicité and James's Daisy are similar to Gogol's Akaky and Melville's Bartleby. They differ in that instead of being primarily functions of the story, they move to the forefront of the story and are presented as characters that can be identified with, even as they are symbolic. The kind of case that Robert Marler makes for *Bartleby the Scrivener* as marking the beginning of the true short story can be made also for "A Simple Heart" and *Daisy Miller*. In fact, Ray B. West, Jr., in his *The Short Story in America* (1952), notes that James's collection *Daisy Miller: A Study; and Other Stories* (1883) may be the first use of the term "story" in the title of a work in English. "Story" rather than "tale" has been used almost exclusively ever since.

The key to the power of "A Simple Heart," a story that Flaubert himself thought so much of that he sent it to a friend as an illustration of what he thought a story should be, lies in the complex mixture of irony and sympathy in the point of view of the teller, as well as in the use of realistic details that even in their ordinariness seem resonant with suggestive symbolism. It is the kind of technique that James Joyce brings to perfection in *Dubliners* (1914) and the kind of tone that Chekhov masters in his short stories. The interesting aspect of characterization in the story is that the only character of importance is Félicité, and she herself is characterless; she is the servant *par excellence* in that she gives herself completely to others. For all the particular detail of Félicité's life, she is finally not so much an individual character as she is representative of simplicity itself. In reading the story, one takes it incident by incident as a character study of the concrete universal, Félicité/Simplicity. It is not until the final pages of the story when she gets Loulou the parrot that we begin to suspect the symbolic nature of the story. For the parrot is a grotesque image of the kind of iconic figure that Félicité herself becomes. Flaubert says that by the age of fifty she was like a "woman made of wood," although she herself is hurt when people compare Loulou to a log of wood. Just as Félicité becomes deaf and her circle of ideas grows narrower, transforming her into a static iconic figure, so does the parrot become an iconic figure to Félicité after it is stuffed. While alive, the parrot is like a son and a lover to her; when dead he becomes an image of the Holy Ghost.

> They were linked in her thoughts; and the parrot was consecrated by his association with the Holy Ghost, which became more vivid to her eye and more intelligible. The Father could not have chosen to express himself through a dove, for such creatures cannot speak; it must have been one of Loulou's ancestors, surely.

Félicité begins to kneel to the parrot to say her prayers, and as she deteriorates, so does the bird. On her deathbed, he is brought to her with a broken wing, the tow coming out of his stomach, and the worms having devoured him; but Félicité is blind now as well as deaf and she kisses him. Although Félicité's devotion to the parrot throughout the last part of the story has something of the absurd about it, her simplicity and deteriorating condition prevent the reader from laughing at her. Although the tone of the story never drops from a kind of sympathetic distance, the conclusion runs the risk of dropping into bathos. In the moment of most poignancy, we are also confronted with the moment of most absurdity: "The beats of her heart lessened one by one, vaguer each time and softer, as a fountain sinks, an echo disappears; and when she sighed her last breath she thought she saw an opening in the heavens, and a gigantic parrot hovering above her head." The story of Félicité's treatment of the parrot is a symbolic echo of Flaubert's treatment of Félicité herself. Little more than a shadow throughout her life, Félicité can do little more than parrot others. She acts by instinct rather than rationality; she is, in the early part of the story, a representative of simplicity itself, but by her very simplicity she is transformed. In the later part of the story as the parrot becomes an iconic figure to her, so does she become an iconic figure to the reader; and that the Holy Ghost is perceived as a parrot by a peasant girl is no more absurd than that a peasant girl is perceived by the reader as a Christ figure. What Flaubert has done is what Frank O'Connor says that Gogol did so boldly and brilliantly. He has taken a mock-heroic character and imposed her image over that of the crucified Jesus, "so that even while we laugh we are filled with horror at the resemblance."

Henry James also creates a figure of simplicity in *Daisy Miller*. In a work that James himself called "the purest poetry," he creates a character that becomes a type. "Poor little Daisy Miller was, as I understand her," says James, "above all things innocent. . . . She was too ignorant, too irreflective, too little versed in the proportions of things." The whole idea of the story, James concludes, "is the little tragedy of a light, thin, natural, unsuspecting creature being sacrificed as it were to a social rumpus that went on quite above her head and to which she stood in no measurable relation." When considering why he called the story a "study," James said the reasons had escaped him, unless "they may have taken account simply of a certain flatness in my poor little heroine's literal denomination. Flatness indeed, one must have felt, was the very sum of her story." The sum of Daisy's story, however, is no more flat than that of Félicité, and for the same reasons—point of view and a symbolic undercurrent. James makes use of a *ficelle* in the story, a foil and a figure on which Daisy makes her impression. Giles Winterbourne, as his cold name implies, has an attachment to Geneva, the little metropolis of Calvinism, and has thus lost his instinct in the matter of innocence; his reason cannot help him in regard to Daisy. He can only apply a formula to her, that she is unsophisticated, even as he knows that is not the answer. The story deals with the inextricable nature of innocence and guilt. Moreover, it is a story of form versus formlessness.

Daisy Miller is very similar to Hawthorne's "Rappaccini's Daughter" in its placing a creature from another world into contact with the real world. The difference, of course, is in the mode of the telling. Instead of creating symbolic settings and using supernatural events to convey such a conflict, as Hawthorne did, James uses the realistic conflict between American innocence and European social order and sophistication. The terms of innocence and guilt, vulgarity and sophistication, formlessness and form seem natural elements of this realistic situation. Winterbourne becomes more and more angry at himself for being "reduced to chopping logic about this young lady; he was vexed at his want of instinctive certitude as to how far her eccentricities were generic, national, personal." Finally, with horror and relief, the ambiguity and the riddle of Daisy's behavior flash upon him in an ironic illumination of his own simplicity; that she was "a lady whom a gentleman need no longer be at pains to respect." Like Hawthorne's Giovanni, Winterbourne has made the mistake of judging when he should have loved; and Daisy, like Félicité, has been transformed from realistic character into icon, "a living embodiment," says Leslie Fiedler, "of the American faith that evil is appearance only." Like Bartleby, Daisy is the victim of the tragedy of being misunderstood; and like many short stories, Daisy's story is the drama of the need for the irrationality of love to transcend reason.

Conclusion

In the modern world since the beginning of the nineteenth century, when religious sanctions no longer apply; not only morality but also reality itself has become problematical, even arbitrary. Anyone who is secure in his or her own absolutist view of reality is likely to be challenged in fiction by the romantic perception of the irrational. The encounter with this mysterious deeper reality immanent in external categorical perceptions of reality can so challenge one and unsettle one's comfortable and familiar framework that he or she is unable to readjust, or at least must see that readjustment requires a radical reorientation or perspective. This is surely the significance of Goodman Brown's journey into the forest, Giovanni's encounter with Rappaccini's daughter, the narrator's encounter with Bartleby, or the guest's sojourn in the house of Usher; and in the twentieth century the irrational is confronted by Eudora Welty's traveling salesman, Flannery O'Connor's unfortunate family who meets the inevitable misfit, and Bernard Malamud's reluctant rabbi in "The Magic Barrel."

Often in the short story we are presented with characters who are *too* comfortable, too settled in their illusion that their lives are controlled and regular; they must be made aware of the problematic and arbitrary nature of their perceptions and the limitations of their awareness. Their unauthentic lives must be challenged. The short story does not reassure the reader that the world is as he or she usually sees it, nor does it assure him or her that leaps of faith can be made with anything but fear and trembling. It only presents one with the realization that "I-Thou" encounters are ambiguous, mysterious, and problematical. The reality the short story presents us with is the reality of those subuniverses of the supernatural and the fable. It presents us with the reality of the *mysterium tremendum* that suddenly erupts in the midst of the profane everyday. It presents us with those magical episodes in which we are torn away to what Martin Buber calls "dangerous extremes," in which security is shattered. It presents us with moments that make us aware that life is a becoming, a possibility of not-yet existence. As Flannery O'Connor says, it appeals to the kind of person who is willing to have his or her "sense of mystery deepened by contact with reality and sense of reality deepened by contact with mystery." It is both "canny and uncanny" at once.

The short story represents both desire and the frustration of desire, our deepest wishes censored and distorted by the external reality we must affirm to ourselves every day in order to survive. It says to us, however, that surviving is not enough, that we must make superhuman efforts in a superhuman world that always lies immanent in the world of the everyday. The short story is the most paradoxical of all fictional forms, for it gives us reality and unreality at once—gives us both the familiar and the unfamiliar, the universal and the particular. It reminds us of our separation and our possibility for unity—a unity that is not given to us, but that we must constantly make.

Charles E. May

SHORT FICTION: 1880-1920

Up until the early nineteenth century, short prose fiction was primarily a vehicle for didactic messages, often religious in nature. Romantic writers, wishing to preserve the old values without the religious dogma and mythological trappings, secularized the old stories by presenting them as basic psychic processes. The ballad tale that had previously existed as received story now became infused with the subjectivity of the teller. The famous collaboration of William Wordsworth and Samuel Taylor Coleridge in *Lyrical Ballads* (1798) marked the beginnings of this shift.

Wordsworth's task was to choose situations and scenes from everyday life and by a process of defamiliarization suggest the spiritual value latent within them. Coleridge, on the other hand, was to take supernatural stories or situations and give them the semblance of reality by making them projections of the artist's psyche. Often in these "lyrical ballads," the story element was subsumed by the lyrical element because of their emphasis on the poet's subjective impression. The German Romantics, from whom Coleridge gained many of his critical assumptions, however, were more committed to stories with the lyrical element concealed behind the hard outlines of the event. American writers, also strongly influenced by the Germans, similarly turned from Romantic poetry to Romantic tale. The short story as developed by Washington Irving, Edgar Allan Poe, and Nathaniel Hawthorne was the narrative side of what Coleridge and Wordsworth were doing with the lyric poem in England.

The United States

New literary movements often begin as a reaction against whatever literary movement is predominant at the time, especially when the conventions of the existing movement become stereotyped. Realism, which dominated the writing of fiction during the latter part of the nineteenth century in Europe and the United States, was a reaction against the stereotyped sentimentalizing of the Romantic movement that prevailed during the early part of the century. The basic difference between Romantics and realists is a philosophic disagreement about what constitutes significant "reality." For the Romantics, what was meaningfully real was the ideal or the spiritual, a transcendent objectification of human desire. For the realists, what mattered was the stuff of the physical world.

One of the first results of this focus on the everyday real rather than the transcendent ideal in American fiction was the so-called "local color" movement; for the more a writer focused on the external world, the more he or she emphasized particular places and people, complete with their habits, customs, language, and idiosyncrasies. Whereas it seldom mattered where in the physical world the stories of Hawthorne and Poe took place (for they always seemed to take place in the mind of the characters or in some fabulist world between fantasy and everyday reality), the stories of Bret Harte were grounded in the American West, just as the stories of Sarah Orne Jewett were tied to New England. The realists wished to localize characters in a physical world and ground their lives in a social reality.

Although the realist assumption, however, began to predominate in the latter part of the century, Romanticism remained; the result was two branches of the local color movement: the earthy Western folktale and the Eastern sentimental story. Sometimes these two types merged, as they did in the stories of Harte, who managed to combine the sentimental idealism of the East with the humorous realism of the West. Sometimes the conflict between the two types was satirized, as it was in Mark Twain's famous story "The Celebrated Jumping Frog of Calaveras County," in which a Western tall-tale artist gets the better of a genteel easterner. Other well-known stories of the period, such as William Dean Howells' "Editha" and Mary E. Wilkins Freeman's "A New England Nun," expose the sterility of genteel idealism when it is cut off from the facts of everyday reality and physical life.

One of the first of the so-called genteel local colorists was the New England writer Jewett, who began purposely to record the customs of her region in the 1880's. Although her best-known work, *The Country of the Pointed Firs*, published in 1896, marked a beginning of the realist technique of local color, her thematic emphasis was still Romantic. Her best-known story, "A White Heron" (1886), focuses on the conflict between flesh and spirit and the quest for a transcendent reality beyond the ordinary. Although this is a central Romantic theme, Jewett's work differed from that of earlier Romantics by focusing more on character than on plot. The most frequent criticism of Jewett is that she ignores the coarse actualities of life and that her depictions of locale are romantic and idealized.

Also part of the so-called genteel tradition of local color writers was Freeman. The title story of her best-known collection, *A New England Nun and Other Stories* (1891), focuses on a central character who is shut away from the flow of everyday life. The emphasis in the story is on the character's sense of an almost "artistic" control over the order and neatness of her solitary home and her rejection of the masculine disorder threatened by her impending marriage.

This sort of genteel withdrawal from life into an artistic and idealistic pattern receives harsh criticism from Howells, the so-called "father" of American realists, in his most famous story, "Editha" (1905). Editha extols the Romantic ideal of war so much that her fiancé, George, joins the army to please her. When he is killed and Editha goes to see his mother, the older woman chastises her severely for her foolish romanticism. As the story ends, however, Editha, while having her portrait done, is confirmed in her own view when she tells the artist about it and the woman says "how vulgar!" Although the content of the story rejects the idealistic, "artistic" view typical of romanticism for a more everyday human reality, its own form, like most Romantic short stories, is a tightly organized aesthetic pattern.

In addition to the emphasis on local color, another result of the shift from Romanticism to realism in the latter part of the century was a shift from the focus on form to the focus on content. For the Romantics, pattern was more important than plausibility; thus, their stories were apt to be more formal and "literary" than the stories of the realists. By insisting on a faithful adherence to the stuff of the external world, the realists had to allow content—which was often apt to be ragged and random—to dictate form. Because of this shift, the novel, which can expand to create better an illusion of everyday reality, became the favored form of the realists, while the short story, basically a Romantic form that requires more artifice and patterning, assumed a secondary role.

Poe and Hawthorne knew this difference between the two forms well and consequently, by means of a tightly controlled form, created a self-sustained moral and aesthetic universe in their stories. Those writers of the latter part of the nineteenth century who were committed to the short-story form instead of the novel were also well aware of this fact. For example, when Ambrose Bierce entered into the argument then raging between the Romantics and the realists, he attacked the Howells school of realist fiction by arguing, "to them nothing is probable outside the narrow domain of the commonplace man's most commonplace experience." Bierce was interested in those extreme rather than ordinary moments of human experience when reality became transmuted into hallucination. His best-known story, "An Occurrence at Owl Creek Bridge" (1891), ironically focuses on a real world that seems sterile and lifeless and a fantasy world (in the split second before death) that seems dynamic and real. Tight ironic patterning is what creates the similitude of reality in this story, not a slavish fidelity to the ordinary events of the world.

Those late nineteenth century writers who have had the most influence on the short story in the twentieth century were the ones who not only wished to present so-called "realistic" content but also were aware of the importance of technique, pattern, and form. For example, Henry James argued (as Poe did before him) in his influential essay "The Art of Fiction" (1884) that a fictional work is a "living thing, all one and continuous, like any other organism, and in proportion as it lives will it be found . . . that in each of the parts there is something of each of the other parts."

An important fictional treatment of the tension between the "real" and artistic technique is James's famous story "The Real Thing" (1893). The artist in the story pays so much attention to the social stereotype that his models represent that he is unable to penetrate to the human reality beneath the surface. As James makes clear, however, in his preface to the story, as an artist, what he is interested in is the pattern or form of the work—its ability to transcend mere narrative and communicate something illustrative, something conceptual: "I must be very clear as to what is in this idea and what I wish to get out of it. . . . It must be an idea—it can't be a 'story' in the vulgar sense of the word. It must be a picture; it must illustrate something . . . something of the real essence of the subject."

Although James's artist in the story insists that he cherishes "human accidents" and that what he hates most is being ridden by a type, the irony of which James himself is aware is that the only way an artist can communicate character is to create a patterned picture that illustrates something; there is no such thing as a "human accident" in a story. As he argues in "The Art of Fiction," a work of art is not a copy of life, but far different, "a personal, a direct impression of life." James says that the supreme virtue of a work of fiction is "the success with which the author has produced the illusion of life." The emphasis for James is on "impression" and "illusion"—both of which create and derive from artistic form and pattern.

James's focus on "impression" indicates an inevitable shift from realism as merely a kind of mirror held up to external reality to what was called either naturalism or verism during the period, in which the focus was on the writer's reaction to that external reality. As critic Mark Schorer has pointed out, Hamlin Garland's "veritism" (or verism) differs from Howells' realism chiefly in its emphasis on impressionism and its insistence that fiction develop a form based on the moment of experience. Although the artist attempts to be perfectly true to life, there is always a tone or a color that comes unconsciously into his or her work, argues Garland. Garland's reputation rests particularly on his collection of short stories, *Main-Travelled Roads* (1891), of which the best-known stories are "The Return of the Private," "Mrs. Ripley's Trip," and "Under the Lion's Paw." Garland differs from many other local-color writers of the period in his avoidance of sentimentalism and his outrage at social injustices. Most critics suggest that the impressionism in his stories moves readers closer to the more powerful impressionism of Stephen Crane.

Many critics have claimed that Crane marks the true beginnings of the modern short story in the United States. It is Crane's impressionism—the combination of the subjectivity of Romanticism with the so-called objectivity of realism—that does most to effect this transition. The result is not an emphasis on reality communicated by the mere description and narration of events one after the other in a temporal fashion but rather reality suggested by moments of time frozen into a kind of spatial stasis by the impression of the perceiver. For the impressionist, reality cannot be separated from the superimposition of attitudes, emotions, and feelings of the perceiver.

One of Crane's best-known impressionistic stories is "The Blue Hotel" (1898), in which complex image patterns convey the formal and mechanical unreality of the events. The real issue, however, of unreality versus reality here centers on the character of the Swede. The irony of the story turns on the precipitating fact that the Swede, as a result of reading dime Western fiction, enters the hotel feeling that he will be killed there. This obsession that he has entered into a fictional world that has become real prevails until the hotel keeper, Scully, takes him upstairs and convinces him that the town is civilized and real, not barbaric and fictional. When the Swede returns, he is transformed; instead of being a stranger to the conventions that he thought existed in the hotel, he becomes familiar and at home with them, too much at home.

Perhaps the best way to understand the Swede's situation is to see the story as being about the blurring of the lines between the fictional world and the real world. Scully has convinced the Swede that what he thought was reality—the childlike world of the dime Western—was a game after all. Thus, the Swede decides to "play" the game. Indeed the card game forms the center of the story and leads to its violent climax, when the Swede, following the conventions of the Western novel, accuses Johnny of cheating, even though the game is "only for fun." The fight that follows is a conventional device of the dime Western.

The Swede wins because of the superiority of his new point of view: he can now self-consciously play the fictional game that Johnny and the others take seriously; while they rage with impotent anger, he only laughs. The final irony takes place when the Swede, still within the conventions of the game, leaves the hotel and enters a bar. When he tries to bully the gambler into drinking with him, the gambler, being a professional who does not play for fun, stabs the Swede, who falls with a "cry of supreme astonishment." Thus the Swede's premonition at the beginning of the story is fulfilled: his initial "error" about the place is not an error at all; it is a violent and barbaric world.

Willa Cather's "Paul's Case" (1905) also derives from the naturalist/impressionist approach favored by Crane. Like "The Blue Hotel," it is a story in which the world of the everyday and the world of the art work become tragically blurred. Paul has a "bad case" because he wishes to be a character in the world of art, but he is trapped in the everyday world of ordinary reality. The theme of "Paul's Case" is the realistic one of the squashing of the artist by middle-class, bourgeois environment.

During the local color movement, there was also a "return to Poe" by such critics as Brander Matthews and such writers as Frank R. Stockton and Ambrose Bierce. With these writers, the focus, as in Poe, was not on the ragged reality of the everyday but on the patterned reality or ironic story. The title of Brander Matthews' book *The Philosophy of the Short Story* (1901), however, indicates that he was as much influenced by Poe's "The Philosophy of Composition" as he was by his *Twice Told Tales* review. Perhaps Matthews believed that Poe was completely serious in his famous description of how he wrote "The Raven." Most Poe critics agree that while the raven in Poe's poem is brought to life by the creative imagination, in his after-the-fact justification of the poem, it is a stuffed and lifeless affair indeed. Matthews seemed to prefer the philosophy to the creation. As a result of his misreading of Poe, the short story in the early twentieth century came to be considered merely a question of taxidermy after all.

Even then, however, Matthews' formal rules for the genre might not have had such a disastrous effect if O. Henry had not had such great popular success with his formula stories at about the same time. The writers rushed to imitate O. Henry and the critics rushed to imitate Matthews, both with the same purpose in mind: popular financial success. Anyone could write short stories if he or she only knew the rules. J. Berg Esenwein's *Writing the Short Story* (1909), Carl H. Grabo's *The Art of the Short Story* (1913), and Blanche Colton Williams' *A Handbook on Story Writing* (1917) are only three of the countless such books published in the first twenty years of the twentieth century. Finally, the serious readers and critics called for an end to it, filling the quality periodicals with articles on the "decline," the "decay," and the "senility" of the short story. One critic, Gilbert Seldes, summed up the reaction at its most extreme in *The Dial* in 1922: "The American short story is by all odds the weakest, most trivial, most stupid, most insignificant art work produced in this country and perhaps in any country."

According to many critics, the most famous source of this formalization of the American short story was, of course, O. Henry—a local colorist writer focusing on the city of New York who so emphasized the ironic pattern of his stories that his name has become associated with the formulaic short story. O Henry's popularity and his output were unprecedented. By 1920, nearly five million copies of his books were sold in the United States. Ironically, while he was being soundly scolded by the serious critics in the United States, who preferred the more serious slice-of-life stories of the Russian writer Anton Chekhov, in Russia, others were praising O. Henry for his mastery of the complex conventions of storytelling.

Stories during the latter part of the nineteenth century that succeed in sustaining the tradition of the Romantic short story and signify the transition to modernism of the new century are those that are concerned with the inner complex jungle of the psyche, such as the stories of Henry James, or the impressionistic symbolic world of violence and sensations such as the stories of Stephen Crane—not the stories by realist writers who focused on the social world.

In order to understand the shift that takes place between the end of the nineteenth century and the beginning of the 1920's—a period that marked a rebirth of the short-story form—one must look at the loss of confidence in the social codes during the period. Literary critics of the time suggested that the short stories of the nineteenth century, mainly action stories, depended on two basic faiths: that one can know right from wrong because a basic social code of values was taken for granted, and that people were what they seemed to be.

In the twentieth century, argued critic Bonaro Overstreet, perhaps as a result of World War I, people have lost these faiths and consequently are "thrown back upon a study of human nature—human motives, fears, wants, prejudices." The drama of the twentieth century is "the drama of what goes on in the mind," and the short story is an "expert medium for the expression of our deep concern about human moods and motives." In his study of this transition to the modern short story, Austin Wright says that while the world of the nineteenth century was relatively stable with substantial agreement on the worth of society and social principles as moral guidance, the world of the 1920's was "fragmented both socially and morally," with each person obliged to find the appropriate principles for guidance. It is this distinctly modern world that the modern short story, ushered in by the publication of Sherwood Anderson's *Winesburg, Ohio* (1919), reflects.

France

Many critics argue that realism began in Europe with the publication of the first installment of Gustave Flaubert's *Madame Bovary* (1857; English translation, 1886). Later, in his best-known short fiction, "La Légende de Saint Julien l'Hospitalier" ("The Legend of St. Julian, Hospitaler"), Flaubert returned to the medieval saint's legend or folktale to find a model for both its character and its form. Flaubert's moral fable, however, differs from its medieval source by representing the static and frozen nature of the medieval story itself. The subject matter of Flaubert's story, although it has a moral issue at its center, is the method by which the medieval tale is made moral and illustrative. The events of the story are frozen into timelessness even as the storyteller relates them as if they were occurring in time. The story poses an answer to the primal question "What is the true self?" by structuring the two basic means by which one tries to find the self—that is, by assertion or by denial.

The transition from Flaubert to Guy de Maupassant is relatively easy to chart, for Flaubert was an important influence on Maupassant, reading his early work and encouraging him. In the decade between 1880 and 1890, Maupassant published more than three hundred short stories in a variety of modes, including the supernatural legend, the surprise-ending tale, and the realistic story. Although he is best known for such surprise-ending tales as "La Parure" ("The Necklace") and is most respected for such affecting realistic stories as "Boule de Suif" (ball of fat), Maupassant also contributed to the sophistication of the traditional horror story by pushing it even further than Poe into the modern mode of psychological obsession and madness. Maupassant got his start as a writer in much the same way that Chekhov in Russia and O. Henry in the United States did—by publishing anecdotal and ironic sketches or stories in that most ephemeral of media: the newspapers.

Maupassant's first full volume of short fiction appeared in 1881 under the title of his second important story, "La Maison Tellier" ("Madame Tellier's Establishment"), a comic piece about a group of prostitutes who attend a first Communion. After the success of this book, Maupassant published numerous stories in newspapers and periodicals, which were then reprinted in the volumes of his stories that began to appear at the rate of approximately two a year. Many of his stories created much controversy among the French critics of the time because he dared to focus on the experiences of so-called "lowlife" characters.

In addition to the realistic stories of the lower class, however, Maupassant experimented with mystery tales, many of which are reminiscent of the stories of Poe. Instead of depending on the supernatural, these stories focus on some mysterious dimension of reality, which is justified rationally by the central character. As a result, the reader is never quite sure whether this realm exists in actuality or whether it is a product of the obsessed mind of the narrator.

In 1884, Maupassant published his most famous short story, "The Necklace," which has become one of the most famous short stories in any language. Indeed, it has become so famous that it is the story that most commonly comes to mind when Maupassant's name is mentioned, in spite of the fact that most critics agree that Maupassant's creation of tone and character in such stories as "Boule de Suif" and "Madame Tellier's Establishment" is much more representative of his genius than this ironically plotted, brief trick story about the woman who wasted her entire life to pay back a lost necklace, only to discover that it was fake.

"Le Horla" ("The Horla"), a story almost as famous as "The Necklace," focuses on the central character's intuition of a reality that surrounds human life but remains imperceptible to the senses. What makes the story distinctive is the increasing need of the narrator to account for his madness as caused by something external to himself. "The Horla" is a masterpiece of horror because it focuses so strongly on the mistaking of inner reality for outer reality, which is the very basis of hallucination.

Maupassant belongs with such innovators of the short-story form as Chekhov, Ivan Turgenev, Bierce, and O. Henry. On the one hand, like O. Henry, he mastered the ability to create the tight little ironic story that depends, as all short stories do, on the impact of the ending, but on the other hand he also had the ability, like Chekhov, to focus keenly on a limited number of characters in a luminous situation. Because of his ability to transform the short mystery tale from a primitive oral form based on legend into a sophisticated modern form in which mystery originates within the complex human mind, Maupassant is an important figure in the transition between the nineteenth century tale of the supernatural and the twentieth century short story of psychological obsession.

Germany

Although the French bias was that prose fiction is committed to deal with the actual world rather than the transcendental or the immanent, just the opposite assumption was growing in the nineteenth century in Germany. Many German critics argued that short fiction was the ideal form for the movement called "poetic realism," a phrase coined by Otto Ludwig to characterize that period between Romanticism and the beginning of naturalism in Germany—the 1830's through the 1880's. Poetic realism dealt with the realm midway between objective truth and the patterned nature of reality; thus, it united naturalism's focus on the multiplicity of things and idealism's focus on abstract unity underlying the multiplicity. Poetic realism in Germany is simply another name for what was being called impressionism in France and the United States. What must be communicated by the art work is not simply the subject, as in Romanticism, or the object, as in realism, but rather the tone or atmosphere that creates the communication between the subject and the object.

Although Thomas Mann, the most important German fiction writer of this period, is best known for his novels, he began his career writing short fiction. His greatest work in this genre, "Der Tod in Venedig" ("Death in Venice"), is particularly modern in its transformation of the temporal events of story into spatial reality by the device of the leitmotif, which Mann claims to have used in a directly musical way and which determines the whole mode of presentation of the work. The basic motifs of the story—mock action, significant encounter, transience of time, presence of death, nature of love—are repeated throughout in various guises. Moreover, the story is a classic example of short fiction's midway point between realism and myth, between external reality and subjective reality, as embodied in Aschenbach's yearning to escape the cold and rigid artwork into the passion and the impulsive life of experience itself. The story suggests that the experience that overtakes Aschenbach is one that is necessary to transform him from his inauthentic abstract self into the concrete but "messy" life of existential reality. Throughout the complex imagistic action that propels the story, Aschenbach begins to emerge as his own creation, one who has become transformed into a character in one of his own fictions; art, not an active life, has taken over the modeling of his features.

This basic conflict between the Romantic inclination toward fantasy and dream and the realist tendency toward the external world receives one of its most successful treatments in modern short fiction in Franz Kafka's "The Metamorphosis." The extreme step that Kafka takes is to make the transformation of the psychic into the physical the precipitating premise from which the entire story follows. The only suspension of disbelief required in the story is that the reader accept the premise that Gregor Samsa awakes one morning from uneasy dreams to find himself transformed into a giant dung beetle. Once one accepts this event, the rest of the story is quite prosaic, quite detailed, and (with the exception of leaving the description of Gregor purposely vague) fully externalized. "The Metamorphosis" is an exemplar of the typical short-fiction effort to present an inner state of reality as a fantastic but real outer event. Thematically, the story also is exemplary, for it presents the little man who, by his very grotesqueness, challenges the other to love him. In his transformation of the details of everyday life into hallucination and nightmare, Kafka is the prototype of the modern tendency in short fiction to challenge the realist assumption of what reality is by pushing it to grotesque extremes.

Russia

Although modern short fiction in Russia begins with Fyodor Dostoevski and Leo Tolstoy, it reaches its complete maturity with Anton Chekhov. Dostoevski's most influential short fiction, *Zapiski iz podpolya* (1864; *Notes from the Underground*, 1918), reflects the modern transition to an existential philosophy and an impressionistic technique by being structured in two parts to represent the two basic means by which one tries to know the self: introspection and narrative. It reverses the Socratic injunction that the unexamined life is not worth living to suggest the Hamlet theme—that the intensely examined life is unlivable. The basic theme of Tolstoy's "The Death of Ivan Ilych" is made clear in the classic syllogism: "Ivan Ilych is a man. All men are mortal. Therefore, Ivan Ilych is mortal." In its transformation of this abstract syllogism into a concrete reality, however, the story also reflects the modern short fiction combination of the conceptual and the concrete. Indeed, it is about the transformation of Ivan himself from abstract man into concrete man.

The most influential figure in the development of modern short fiction in Russia, and in many ways in the world at large, is Chekhov. Chekhov's short stories were first welcomed in England and the United States just after the turn of the century as examples of late nineteenth century realism, but since they did not embody the social commitment or political convictions of the realistic novel, they were termed "realistic" primarily because they seemed to focus on fragments of everyday reality. Consequently, they were characterized as "sketches," "slices of life," "cross-sections of Russian life," and were often said to be lacking those elements that constitute a really good short story. At the same time, however, other critics saw that Chekhov's ability to dispense with a striking incident, his impressionism, and his freedom from the literary conventions of the highly plotted and formalized story marked the beginnings of a new or "modern" kind of short fiction that combined the specific detail of realism with the poetic lyricism of Romanticism.

The Chekhovian shift to the "modern" short story is marked by a transition from the Romantic focus on a projective fiction, in which characters are functions in an essentially code-bound parabolic or ironic structure, to an apparently realistic episode in which plot is subordinate to "as-if-real" character. Chekhov's fictional figures, however, are not realistic in the way that characters in the novel usually are. The short story is too short to allow for character to be created by the multiplicity of detail and social interaction typical of the novel.

Once it is seen that the short story, by its very shortness, cannot deal with the denseness of detail and the duration of time typical of the novel but rather focuses on a revelatory breakup of the rhythm of everyday reality, one can see how the form, striving to accommodate "realism" at the end of the nineteenth century, focused on an experience under the influence of a particular mood and therefore depended more on tone than on plot as a principle of unity—all of which led to the significant impressionistic influence.

Although Chekhov's conception of the short story as a lyrically charged fragment in which characters are less fully rounded realistic figures than embodiments of mood has influenced all twentieth century practitioners of the form, his most immediate impact has been on the three writers of the early 1920's who have received the most critical attention for fully developing the so-called "modern" short story: James Joyce, Katherine Mansfield, and Sherwood Anderson.

The most obvious similarity between the stories of Chekhov and those of Joyce, Anderson, and Mansfield is their minimal dependence on the traditional notion of plot and their focus instead on a single situation in which everyday reality is broken up by a crisis. Typical of Chekhov's minimalist stories is the often-anthologized "Misery," in which the rhythm of the old cabdriver's everyday reality is suggested by his two different fares, a rhythm that Iona himself tries to break up with the news that his son is dead. The story would indeed be only a sketch if Iona did not tell his story to his uncomprehending little mare at the end, for what the story communicates is the comic and pathetic sense of the incommunicable nature of grief itself. Iona "thirsts for speech," wants to talk of the death of his son "properly, with deliberation." He is caught by the primal desire to tell a story of the breakup of his everyday reality that will express the irony he senses and that, by being deliberate and detailed, will both express his grief and control it. In this sense, "Misery" is a lament—a controlled objectification of grief and its incommunicable nature by the presentation of deliberate details.

The story therefore illustrates one of the primary contributions that Chekhov made to the modern short story—the expression of a complex inner state by the presentation of selected concrete details rather than either by a parabolic form or by the depiction of the mind of the character. Significant reality for Chekhov is inner rather than outer reality, but the problem he tried to solve is how to create an illusion of inner reality by focusing only on external details. The answer for Chekhov, and thus for the modern short story generally, was to find an event that, if expressed "properly"—that is, by the judicious choice of relevant details—embodied the complexity of the inner state. T. S. Eliot later termed such a technique an "objective correlative"—a detailed event, description, or characterization that served as a sort of objectification or formula for the emotion sought. Modern short-story writers after Chekhov made the objective correlative the central device in their development of the form.

Such Chekhov stories as "Sleepy" and "The Bishop" make use of another significant modern short-story technique: focusing on reality as an ambiguous mixture of the psychic and the external. "Sleepy" marks a sort of realistic halfway point between the symbolic use of the hypnagogic state by Poe and its being pushed to surrealistic extremes by Kafka. Chekhov presents a basically realistic situation of the young Varka being literally caught in a hypnagogic state between desirable sleep and undesirable reality. The two realms blend indistinguishably in her mind until the hallucination takes over completely and she strangles the baby so she can sleep as "soundly as the dead." Although the irony of the ending is obvious, it is the hypnotic rhythm of the events and the hallucinatory images that blend dream and reality that make the story a significant treatment of the short-story device of dissolving the rhythm of everyday reality into the purely psychic.

Chekhov's adoption of such an impressionistic point of view is what makes him both a master of the short story and an innovator of its modernity. Critic Peter Stowell has made a strong case for understanding Chekhov's modernism as a result of his impressionistic point of view. The ambiguous and tenuous nature of experience perceived by the impressionist, says Stowell, "drives the author to render perceptually blurred bewilderment, rather than either the subject or the object." What is rendered, says Stowell, is the mood and atmosphere that exists between perceiver and perceived, subject and object. In this way, impressionism and modernism become synonymous terms.

Like Chekhov, both Anderson and Joyce focus on the central themes of isolation and the need for human sympathy and the moral failure of inaction that dominate the modernist movement in the early twentieth century; both abjure highly plotted stories in favor of seemingly static episodes and "slices" of reality; both depend on unity of feeling to create a sense of "storyness"; and both establish a sense of the seemingly casual out of that which is deliberately patterned, creating significance out of the trivial by judicious selection of detail and meaningful ordering of the parts. The result is an objective-ironic style that has characterized the modern short story up to the present day. It is a style that, even as it seems realistic on its surface, in fact emphasizes the radical difference between the routine of everyday reality and the incisive nature of story itself as the only means to know true reality. Contemporary short-story writers push this Chekhovian realization to even more aesthetic extremes.

It is with Chekhov that the short story was liberated from its adherence to the parabolic exemplum and fiction generally was liberated from the tedium of the realistic novel. With Chekhov, the short story took on a new respectability and began to be seen as the most appropriate narrative form to reflect the modern temperament. There can be no understanding of the short story as a genre without an understanding of Chekhov's contribution to the form. Conrad Aiken's assessment of him in 1921 has yet to be challenged: "possibly the greatest writer of the short story who has ever lived." '

England/Ireland

The English, with the exception of modern Irish writers, have never excelled in the short-story form. The reason may have something to do with the English attitude toward a cohesive society. Critic and literary historian Lionel Stevenson has suggested that as soon as a culture becomes more complex, brief narratives expand or "agglomerate" and thus cause the short story to lose its identity. The fragmentation of sensibility necessary for the development of the short story did not set in in England until about 1880, at which time the form came to the fore as the best medium for presenting it. As another critic, Wendell Harris, has noted, with the fragmentation of sensibility, perspective (or "angle of vision") becomes most important in fiction, especially in the short story, in which instead of a world to enter, as in the novel, the form presents a vignette to contemplate. The essence of the short story, says Harris, "is to isolate, to portray the individual person, or moment, or scene in isolation—detached from the great continuum—at once social and historical. . . . The short story is a natural form for the presentation of a moment whose intensity makes it seem outside the ordinary stream of time . . . or outside the ordinary range of experience."

It is an interesting irony that the 1890's, the period which H. G. Wells called "The Golden Age" of the short story in England, derived, although in an indirect way, from Poe; for it was Poe who inspired Charles Baudelaire, who in turn inspired the Symbolist movement, which ultimately gave impetus to the development of the short story during this period. For Poe, and later for Baudelaire and the aesthetes, the "art" of the story itself was what was important in life, and life was important because of art's ability to make matter and events meaningful.

Increasingly, the view that art should deemphasize the social and emphasize the formal dominated what critics have called the "state of mind" that was the 1890's in English literature. Short fiction of the so-called *fin de siècle* exemplifies this view in various ways, from the allegory of George Gissing's "House of Cobwebs" (1900) to the parable form of Arthur Symons' "Christian Trevalga" (1905), and from the aesthetic embodiment of Ernest Dowson's "The Dying of Francis Donne" (1896) to the satiric shaft of Max Beerbohm's "A. V. Laider" (1916).

Gissing's best-known story, "House of Cobwebs," is primarily an allegory of the artist. Through the symbol of the house of decay and cobwebs, with its choking artichokes, Gissing suggests that the artist cannot survive the middle-class world of the realists. Symons' "Christian Trevalga" is a parable of the artist who carries the theories of Stéphane Mallarmé to their ultimate conclusions, for Christian reaches a state of music without sound just as Mallarmé desired to reach a state of literature without words.

Dowson's "The Dying of Francis Donne" and Beerbohm's "A. V. Laider" represent two opposite extremes of the short fiction of the *fin de siècle*. Dowson suggests the period's morbid self-consciousness, and Beerbohm reflects its final ability to mock itself satirically. The famous story to which "The Dying of Francis Donne" is likely to be compared is Tolstoy's "The Death of Ivan Ilych." Unlike the middle-class Ivan, however, for whom the process is ironically the only "living" he has ever experienced, Francis Donne is a doctor, a "student" of life and death. Moreover, as opposed to Ivan, for whom awareness of death begins with the absurd act of bumping his side while hanging drapes, Donne's awareness begins with his diagnostic and reasoning ability. Beerbohm's "A. V. Laider" is a clever and well-constructed manipulation of the conventions of storytelling. The story is similar in its use of storytelling as the basis of a trick played on the reader to Twain's "The Celebrated Jumping Frog of Calaveras County" and Saki's "The Open Window." Such stories lay bare by means of parody one of the form's essential characteristics: the projection of an imaginative reality that can only temporarily be taken to be real.

Another short-fiction form popular in England at the beginning of the twentieth century is the ghost story or mystery story. However, as Algernon Blackwood, one of the most influential of the mystery story writers, has made clear, the primary interest of these writers was not the ghost story as such but rather stories of extended consciousness. "My fundamental interest," said Blackwood, "is signs and proofs of other powers that lie hidden in us all; the extension, in other words, of human faculty." Fiction writers who hold to such a vision are more often likely to be short-story writers than novelists and not merely writers of the so-called supernatural story. Whereas novelists are most likely to build on the assumption that everyday reality is primary reality, true reality for the short-story writer is more often a function of the imagination.

H. P. Lovecraft has called "The Willows" the foremost Blackwood tale, an opinion with which many critics of the supernatural story agree, seeing it as typical of Blackwood's thematic structure of having an average man, through a "flash of terror or beauty," experience something beyond the sensory reality of the everyday. The ambiguity, as is usually the case in nineteenth century short fiction, is between whether one understands the experience to be external or internal—that is, whether it actually occurs in the world of the story or the events are hallucinated by the character.

The best-known story of Lord Dunsany (Edward John Moreton Drax Plunkett), "The Ghosts" is a self-conscious parody of the ghost story, for it makes explicit the conventions and rules of the genre. As is typical of such parodies, the story depends on the conventions of their generic models even as they mock them. For example, "The Ghosts" begins with a traditional description of the conventional ghost-story setting—an old house surrounded by whispering cedars and encrusted with antiquity. The problem here is to determine what ontological status the ghosts maintain:

are they real and thus manifestations of the place, or are they manifestations of the hallucinatory state of the protagonist?

To move from the stories of Dunsany to those of Saki (H. H. Munro) is to move from the world of story as a means to parody story to a world in which story is presented as joke, sometimes a bitter joke, but a joke nevertheless. Saki may very well mark a decided shift in Edwardian short fiction to the trick-ending story that dominates popular short stories both in England and in the United States at the turn of the century. Saki's most anthologized story, "The Open Window," is a particularly clear and simple example of foregrounding the process of story itself, for what makes "The Open Window" work is the uncertainty, felt both by the protagonist and by the reader, about the nature of the story that they are listening to or reading. The dramatized storyteller is the typical Saki artist who manipulates the reader into various possibilities about the genre of the story, only to reveal that the story is about the process of turning fantasy into supposed fact and only to reveal it as fantasy after all.

In his study of the short story, Walter Allen calls Walter de la Mare the most distinguished of the writers who made the Edwardian age a "haunted period" in English literature. Part of the reason for this is the "dignity" of the poetry of de la Mare as opposed to what is often called the "crude gothicism" of his contemporaries. Lord David Cecil calls de la Mare a Symbolist for whom the outer world is only an "incarnation of an internal drama." He says that de la Mare is concerned with the most profound human issues, particularly the central issue of whether the world has any objective existence or is a reflection of the mind, which alters, depending on the mood and character of the observer. For de la Mare, only the imagination makes reality significant, and what is called external reality itself is like a dream. All these characteristics, which are actually characteristics of the short-story genre itself, can be seen most readily in de la Mare's best-known and most anthologized story, "The Riddle," a delicate fable about the passing of youth.

It is no coincidence that the first British writer to be recognized as a specialist in the short story is also the champion of the romance form in the latter part of the nineteenth century. Nor is it coincidence that this short-story specialist was one of the first British short-fiction writers to focus, as did Henry James, on technique and form rather than on content alone. The writer is Robert Louis Stevenson, and many critics suggest that it is with his work that the true modern short story began in England. Both Lionel Stevenson and Walter Allen say that the watershed for the modern short story began in 1878 with the publication of "A Lodging for the Night," with Allen going so far as to say that the change to the specifically modern short story can be precisely dated at that point.

Like his fellow romance writer in the United States, Ambrose Bierce, Stevenson urges that literature, when it is in its most typical mode of narrative, flees from external reality and pursues "an independent and creative aim." For Stevenson, the work of art exists not by its resemblance to life, "but by its immeasurable difference from life." Such an awareness was indeed essential before what critics call the "modern short story" could become possible in the nineteenth century.

"A Lodging for the Night" is a strange candidate for a landmark story that marks the shift to modern short fiction. Although it is highly detailed and focuses on a specific time-limited situation, it poses more questions about its status than clear answers. The secret of the story's ambiguous mixture of horror and amusement depends solely on the nature of the poet Villon, who alternates between attending to the immediate concerns of life to assure his own preservation and taking an amused and distant view of reality to indicate his own broad view of life. Villon survives not only because of his concern with immediate things but also because he can take such an ironic view of life and death. What Stevenson has done here is to create a story about the artist who transforms reality into art stuff; the story is an exercise in this seeming paradox, indicating that reality must be dealt with both in terms of practical existence and in terms of the ambiguous mixture of amusement and horror, for life and death must be mocked in order to transform them into art at all.

Although Stevenson is the first British writer to build his career on the short-story form, Rudyard Kipling is the first to stimulate a considerable amount of criticism, much of it adverse, because of his short fiction. Much of the negative criticism that Kipling has received, however, is precisely the same kind of criticism that has often been lodged against the short-story form in general—for example, that it focuses only on episodes, that it is too concerned with technique, that it is too dependent on tricks, and that it often lacks a moral force. Lionel Trilling notes that the words "craft" and "craftily" are Kipling's favorites, and Edmund Wilson says that it is the paradox of his career that he "should have extended the conquests of his craftsmanship in proportion to the shrinking of the range of his dramatic imagination. As his responses to human beings became duller, his sensitivity to his medium increased."

Kipling's best-known stories—"The Man Who Would Be King," "Without Benefit of Clergy," "Mary Postgate," and "The Gardener"—are perfect representations of the transition point between the old-fashioned tale of the nineteenth century and the modern short story—a transition, however, that Joseph Conrad, because of the profundity of his vision, perhaps was better able to make than Kipling. Many critics have suggested that "The Man Who Would Be King" is one of Kipling's most Conrad-like stories but lament that Kipling evades the metaphysical issues implicit in the story and refuses to venture on the great generalizations forced upon Conrad in "Heart of Darkness." Although "The Man Who Would Be King" does not contain the philosophic generalizations of Conrad's tale, nor perhaps is it as subtle a piece of Symbolist fiction, nevertheless, it is a coherent piece of fabular fiction carefully constructed and thematically significant.

The story focuses primarily on the crucial difference between a tale told by a narrator who merely reports a story and a narrator who lives a story. The frame narrator is a journalist whose job it is to report the doings of "real kings," whereas Peachey, the inner narrator, has as his task the reporting of the events of a "fictional king," telling a story of two characters who project themselves out of the "as-if" real world of the frame tale into the purely projected and fictional world of their adventure. The fact that Peachey and Davrot are really only overdetermined double figures is indicated not only by Peachey's reference to himself as suffering Davrot's fate but also by the fact that if Davrot is the ambiguous god-man, then it is Peachey who must be crucified. Kipling finds it necessary of course to make this split, for not only must he have his god-man die, but he must have him resurrected as well. Peachey is the resurrected figure who brings back the head of Davrot, still with its crown, and tells the tale to the narrator. Peachey's final madness and death and the mysterious disappearance of the crowned head climax a story that embodies a complex symbolic pattern.

Most critics agree, however, that it is Joseph Conrad who creates the true modern Symbolist tale. Conrad argued that fiction must aspire to the magic suggestiveness of music, that explicitness was fatal to art, for it robs it of all suggestiveness. This is the basis of Conrad's impressionism, an impressionism that begins with Crane in the United States and is later extended by Anderson, Mansfield, and Joyce. Conrad has said that his best stories resulted from his attempt to give a story a "sinister romance, a tonality of its own, a continued vibration that . . . would hang on the air and dwell on the ear after the last note had been struck." One of Conrad's most famous impressionistic and symbolist stories is "The Secret Sharer" (1912).

Making the psychological theme of the double plausible is the central problem in Conrad's "The Secret Sharer," for the double is not only projected outside the protagonist but also dramatized in the story as an external self who has been involved in a crime apart from the protagonist and whose crime is at the core of the moral issue facing him. The story itself is split between the plot, which focuses on the stranger and the captain's efforts to protect and conceal him, and the mind of the captain, who obsessively persists in perceiving and describing the stranger Leggatt as his other self, his double. The story also depends on metaphorical details, which suggest that Leggatt has been summoned forth from the captain's unconscious as an aspect of the self with which he must deal. Although it can be said that Leggatt represents some aspect of the captain's personality that he must integrate—instinctive behavior rather than the Hamlet-like uncertainty he experiences on his first command—it is more probable that he is brought on board to make explicit and dramatically concrete the dual workings of the captain's mind, which distract him and tear him apart. This creation of an "as-if" real character to embody what are essentially psychic processes marks the impressionistic extension of the trend that began the short-story form during the Romantic period.

Like Chekhov, whom she greatly admired, Katherine Mansfield was often accused of writing sketches instead of stories, because her works did not manifest the plotted action of nineteenth century short fiction. The best-known Mansfield story similar in technique and theme to the typical Chekhov story is "The Fly." The external action of the story is extremely slight. The unnamed "boss" is visited by a retired friend whose casual mention of the boss's dead son makes him aware of his inability to grieve. The story ends with the boss idly dropping ink on a fly until it dies, whereupon he flings it away. Like Chekhov's "Misery," the story is about the nature of grief, and like Chekhov's story, "The Fly" maintains a strictly objective point of view, allowing the details of the story to communicate the latent significance of the boss's emotional state.

Mansfield, however, differs from her mentor Chekhov by placing more dependence on the fly itself, as a symbol of the death of the boss's grief, his own manipulated son, or the trivia of life that distracts one from feeling. Moreover, instead of focusing on the inarticulate nature of grief that goes deeper than words, "The Fly" seems to emphasize the transitory nature of grief; regardless of how much the boss would like to hold on to his grief for his son, he finds it increasingly difficult to maintain such feelings. Such an inevitable loss of grief does not necessarily suggest that the boss's feelings for his son are negligible; rather, it suggests a subtle aspect of grief—that it either flows naturally or else must be self-consciously and artificially sought after. The subtle way that Mansfield communicates the complexity of the boss's emotional situation by the seemingly irrelevant conversation between the boss and his old acquaintance and by his apparently idle toying with the fly is typical of the Chekhovian device of allowing objective detail to communicate complex states of feeling.

Critics of the short story such as H. E. Bates and Frank O'Connor have suggested that the modern Irish short story began with George Moore's publication of *The Untilled Field* in 1903. Others have concurred with Moore's own typically immodest assessment that the collection was a "frontier book, between the new and the old style" of fiction. One can certainly agree with critics that the stories seem unique for their time in combining the content of French naturalism with the concern for style of the *fin de siècle* aesthetics. Moore's view is that reality itself must be understood via story. This need to understand reality by means of story can be clearly seen in Moore's best-known and most anthologized work from *The Untilled Field*, "Julia Cahill's Curse," for it is a fairly clear example of Moore's effort to use the folktale mode as a means to understand social reality.

The basic situation of the tale is that of a story being told by a driver to the first-person narrator, who, on hearing the name Julia Cahill, urges the driver to tell him her story. The story, which indeed constitutes the bulk of "Julia Cahill's Curse," is of an event that took place twenty years earlier, when the priest Father Madden had Julia put out of the parish, and consequently Julia put a curse on the parish that every year a roof would fall in and a family would go to America. The basic conflict in the tale is between Julia, who in her dancing and courting represents free pagan values, and the priest, who, in his desire to restrain Julia, represents church control of such freedom.

The conflict between Julia and the priest is clear enough, but it is the relationship between the teller and the listener that constitutes the structural interest of the story, for what the tale is really about is the nature of story used to understand social reality. The story is an actual event of social reality that has been mythicized by the teller and thus by the village folk both to explain and to justify the breakdown of Irish parish life in the late nineteenth century. The teller of the tale believes that the desertion of the parish is a consequence of Julia's curse. The listener of the tale does not believe in the curse in this literal way but, as he says, for the moment he too believes it, at least in some way that is not made explicit. It is the nature of the belief that constitutes the difference and thus the significance of the story. What Moore does here is to present a story that is responded to within the story itself in both the old way and the new way—that is, as a literal story of magic and as a symbolic story to account for the breakdown of the parish life, the tension between pagan freedom and Church control.

The typically modern theme of presenting the predominance of the inner life of imagination over that of the everyday can be seen in almost a paradigmatic form in "The Clerk's Quest." Although in the "old" romance story, everyday reality is broken up by the intrusion of the supernatural, in the modern story, it is often accident, and trivial accident at that, which creates the disruption of the rhythm of everyday reality. In a self-consciously economical prose style, Moore makes it clear that it is the "slight accident" of a perfumed cheque that destroys Dempsey's "well-ordered and closely-guarded life."

Indeed, the story is a self-conscious modern version of the chivalric romance story as the clerk gives up everything to go on his sacred quest, wandering through the countryside with presents of diamonds for the ideal stimulated by a cheque smelling of heliotrope. The mood of romantic fantasy and the ironic tone of parody of chivalric romance are completely sustained and self conscious. At the conclusion of the story, the reader is torn between humor and pathos at the absurdity of the little clerk's quest as well as at its chivalric romanticism. The tragicomic result is not unlike that achieved by Chekhov, Anderson, Joyce, and Mansfield, who similarly present insignificant characters caught in a breakup of the routine of reality. The difference, here, however, is that Moore more obviously parodies the old romantic story, creating a "new" realistic version of the "old" romance form. As a result, he prepares the way for the modern technique of Joyce, who pushes the trivial and seemingly inconsequential realistic story to more subtle epiphanic extremes in the collection of short stories in Anglo-Irish literature that marks the end of the nineteenth century short-fiction tradition, *Dubliners* (1914).

Joyce's most famous contribution to the theory and technique of modern narrative is his notion of the "epiphany," which he explicitly defined in his novel *Stephen Hero* (1944): "By an epiphany he meant a sudden spiritual manifestation, whether in the vulgarity of speech or of gesture or in a memorable phrase of the mind itself. He believed that it was for the man of letters to record these epiphanies with extreme care, seeing that they themselves are the most delicate and evanescent of moments." In a Joyce story, and in many stories by other writers since Joyce, an epiphany is a formulation through metaphor or symbol of some revelatory aspect of human experience, some highly significant aspect of personal reality; it is usually communicated by a pattern of what otherwise would be seen as meaningless details and events.

Although any story in *Dubliners* would serve as an illustration of this epiphanic technique, Joyce's most famous story, "The Dead," makes it quite clear. The primary movement is from the objective world in part 1 to the lyrical quality created after Gabriel and his wife leave the party. This is paralleled by a movement in Gabriel himself from self-assertion to self-effacement. Concrete details predominate through the first two-thirds of the story, as everyday life seems to be fully embodied in the Christmas party. It is only in the last third, when Gabriel's life is transformed, first by his romantic and sexual fantasy about his wife and then by his confrontation with love and death, that the reader reflects on the story and perceives that the concrete life in the earlier sections repeatedly revealed hints of death. Only after Gabriel's epiphany, his true vision of his former self as death in life, does the reader perceive the concrete details and trivial remarks of the earlier portion as symbolically meaningful. The lyrical and symbol-laden language of the final section of the story casts a new light on the trivial details and comments of the earlier part. The story illustrates how in short fiction only the end makes what went before meaningful. Since the ultimate end is death, Gabriel's awareness and acceptance of it is the ultimate epiphany, the sacred realization that transforms the trivial into the meaningful.

Conclusion

The first one hundred years of the short story divides into two almost equal periods: the movement from Romanticism to realism between 1820 and 1880 and the movement from realism to impressionism between 1880 and 1920. It is less a straight line of development from Washington Irving's *The Sketch Book of Geoffrey Crayon, Gent.* (1819-1820) to Sherwood Anderson's *Winesburg, Ohio* than it is a one-hundred-year cycle, for it is a movement from the Romantic subjectifying of the old story form in the early part of the century to the realistic emphasis on objective reality in the latter part, and finally a return to the subjectifying of the objective world at the turn of the century. It is this return to Romanticism that marks the beginning of what is now known as modernism.

Charles E. May

SHORT FICTION: 1920-1960

Because storytelling is inherent in human nature, stories have existed throughout history. For a long time, short fiction was considered the poor relation of the novel. In the nineteenth century, however, the short story and its longer relative, the novelette or novella, were shaped as distinct art forms by Heinrich von Kleist, E. T. A. Hoffmann, Edgar Allan Poe, Nathaniel Hawthorne, Nikolai Gogol, and Guy de Maupassant. A break with the traditional stress on plotting came in the late nineteenth and early twentieth centuries, particularly with the stories of Anton Chekhov and Joseph Conrad, James Joyce and D. H. Lawrence, Franz Kafka and Ernest Hemingway.

Chekhov and Joyce can properly be called the progenitors of most twentieth century short fiction. Chekhov renders experience obliquely, by an apparently aimless arrangement of casual incidents, suggesting and implying rather than climaxing and commenting. His endings are no longer the inevitable locus of surprise or value judgment. He breaks the heroic mold with many of his characters, often dealing with lonely recluses, shy fantasists, ridiculous yet tenderhearted weaklings. Joyce sometimes has his climaxes in the middle rather than the end of his stories, during sudden moments of revelation that he calls "epiphanies." His style is highly pictorial, presenting the reader with a series of vivid images in an incantatory, lyrical prose, sometimes hypnotically repetitive, subtly and suitably modulated. The prevailing tone of his tales is one of poetic naturalness that can transmute the drabness of common life into moments of haunting beauty and poignant compassion.

After World War I, most distinguished writers of short fiction have minimized plotting, believing that a careful arrangement of events toward conflict and resolution would work against the faithfulness and expressiveness of their rendering of life. They have preferred the creation of memorable characters (William Faulkner's "A Rose for Emily," Eudora Welty's "Why I Live at the P.O."), the evocation of mood and atmosphere (Hemingway's "Hills Like White Elephants," Lawrence's "The Horse Dealer's Daughter"), the uncharted recesses of the internal landscape (Katherine Anne Porter's "Old Mortality," Colette's "Chéri"), myth and fantasy (Faulkner's "The Bear," John Cheever's "The Enormous Radio," Isak Dinesen's "The Sailor-Boy's Tale," Isaac Bashevis Singer's "The Gentleman from Cracow"), the dramatization of deep emotions (Saul Bellow's "Seize the Day," Isaac Babel's "Smert' Dolgushova" ["The Death of Dolgushov"], Yukio Mishima's "Patriotism"). Metaphor and symbol, point of view, and the reliability or dubiety of narrators grow in importance as writers seek to create fiction of complexity and sophistication.

A note about the form of short fiction called the novelette or novella or simply the short novel: it is a prose narrative longer than even long short stories yet considerably briefer than a full-length novel, consisting of fifteen thousand to fifty thousand words. As a rule, the novella moves along a single line of action, whereas a novel develops an extended series of actions that often include subplots. The novella has room for only a few characters and confines itself to a short span of time, while the rhythm of its narration is tight and exclusive, concentrating on an arc of behavior that has symbolic significance. The form encourages, as in Faulkner's "The Bear," Thomas Mann's "Mario and the Magician," and Bellow's "Seize the Day," treatment of profound philosophic or ethical issues.

The United States

Many critics consider William Faulkner (1897-1962) to be the greatest American fiction writer of the twentieth century. His range of effects, philosophical weight, originality of style, mythic grandeur, variety of characterization, and tragic intensity are without equal among modern authors in the United States. As a short-fiction writer, he is, however, uneven. Since his novels did not sell well until the late 1940's, he had to grind out many short stories for periodical publication to keep bread and meat on the table, and some of them are potboilers; others are, however, superb.

No land in fiction lives more vividly on the printed page than Faulkner's mythical Yoknapatawpha County, whose twenty-four hundred square miles are located in his native Mississippi and whose population spills in and out of his works, intimately known and traced through complex interrelations. This territory is not only realistically rendered but also mythically interpreted, with Faulkner considering the white settlers of the land as self-doomed by the curse of chattel slavery.

Faulkner's most celebrated story, "The Bear," is a novella that was published as the centerpiece of a collection, *Go Down, Moses* (1942). He insisted on regarding the collection as a novel, even though the book's organic unity is debatable. The narrative opens with Isaac ("Ike") McCaslin, a sixteen-year-old youth, guided by part-Indian, part-black Sam Fathers and accepted into a party of expert hunters. The tale maneuvers back and forth in Ike's life to develop and emphasize his maturation, as he measures himself against an immense, apparently immortal bear of the same age. The annual hunt of the bear, Old Ben, is a ritual, since none of the pursuers believes that he can actually kill the great animal, which embodies the wilderness. A great mongrel dog, Lion, is tamed by Sam Fathers and is taught to hunt; he manages to hold Old Ben at bay for a few moments. A year later, Lion traps the bear long enough for one of the hunters to kill him. When Ike is twenty-one, he inherits a prosperous plantation but renounces it, insisting that no man should own what is nature's. Moreover, he is horrified to discover that his grandfather has not only sired a child by one of his slaves but also thereafter committed incest with his black daughter. Ike now interprets the South's loss of the Civil War as God's punishment of a slaveholding society. Through his renunciation of ancestral property, he hopes to free himself from his family's sins.

In the final part of the tale, Faulkner takes the reader back three years, with Ike now eighteen, and Old Ben hunted down two years ago. Ike locates the graves of Lion and Sam Fathers and has a vision of nature's immortality. Yet in an ambiguous ending, the forces of exploitive greed seem to doom the wilderness. Still, Ike's resolute acts of conscience and forbearance make him one of Faulkner's most admirable protagonists.

Three of Faulkner's finest stories are "Barn Burning," "That Evening Sun," and "A Rose for Emily." The first is a miniature tale of maturation focusing on ten-year-old "Sarty" Snopes, son of a hard-bitten sharecropper, Ab Snopes, who specializes in burning the barns of landowners with whom he has quarreled. Little Sarty Snopes finds himself torn between loyalty to his criminal father and his own sense of honor. In a melodramatic ending, the boy believes—mistakenly—that his father has been killed and runs away from home.

"That Evening Sun" features the Compson family, who would become the principal characters in Faulkner's great novel *The Sound and the Fury* (1929). The heroine is Nancy, the Compson family's part-time cook, who is terrified of being killed by her husband, Jesus, for having prostituted herself to white men. The story stresses the helpless terror of a young black woman in a deeply racist, white-dominated community. It is the town's indifference to her fate that shows it to be the essential villain.

"A Rose for Emily" is a shockingly macabre story in which Miss Emily Grierson, a Southern lady of high repute, is discovered to have poisoned her lover, a Northern construction boss who betrayed her, and to have kept his body in an upstairs bedroom until her own death, forty years later. As an aristocrat, Miss Emily is admired by the townspeople; as a pathological recluse, she is laughed at; as a person of pride and independence, she cows the community. Her refusal to submit to conventional standards of conduct earns for her a victory over everyday respectability.

The style and tone of Ernest Hemingway (1899-1961) revolutionized modern prose fiction. He sought direct pictorial contact between eye and object, object and reader. To obtain it, he trimmed off authorial explanation or comment, making every effort to keep himself out of view as he pruned descriptions and kept his dialogue sparse, abrupt, apparently casual, powerfully compressed.

A classic example of this method at its most successful is "Hills Like White Elephants," in which the author refuses to relate himself to the characters yet puts before his readers a highly charged conflict of considerable consequence. The story takes place in Spain, during a forty-minute wait between trains. A young, unmarried couple discusses whether the woman should bear to term the fetus she is carrying. The man wants her to abort it, fearing that a child would be a "white elephant" for them. The woman wants to have the child, because she is tired of their brittle, rootless existence and is ready for a fuller life. The man's refusal to accept the responsibilities of parenthood dooms the couple to sterility and emptiness, as they lose their chance to change directions. The tone of the characters' dialogue changes subtly as they converse with barely restrained irritation, mockery, and bitterness.

In "The Killers," Nick Adams, the young protagonist of many early Hemingway tales, encounters the face of evil as an unavoidable and unalterable aspect of humanity. The style is succinct and flat, the sentence structure is simple, the clauses lack subordination, the characters lack complexity—all implying a dislocated, fragmented world. Two gangsters visit a diner, bind the help, and wait for the arrival of Ole Andreson, whom they intend to kill. Gloved and faceless, the gangsters follow a code: they are weary, bored hired guns come to do their job. When Ole does not arrive and they leave, Nick walks to the intended victim's rooming house and warns Ole, a retired heavyweight fighter, who lies on his bed inert and resigned. Nick entreats with Ole to seek police help or flee the town; Ole will do neither. "Couldn't you fix it up some way?" Nick asks. Replies Ole: "No. I got in wrong. There ain't anything to do." Living by his code, the hunted man accepts his victimization. Nick is severely shocked by his discovery of annihilating wickedness. He will leave town.

"The Snows of Kilimanjaro," Hemingway's favorite story, takes up enough material for several novels. Hemingway uses two levels of action: a writer, Harry Street, is dying of gangrene caused by an untreated thorn scratch; he alternately talks with his wife and others around him and reflects on his life. It has been a struggle between his creative and destructive urges, and Harry, in interior monologues, admits that he has traded his talent for the luxury and sloth of his marriage to a rich woman. Toward the story's end, Harry is flown over the snow-covered peaks of Mount Kilimanjaro, a symbol of both death and absolute beauty. The author, however, has failed to integrate the three levels of the story: Harry's relationship with his wife, his communings with his soul, and the surrounding African continent. Harry's potential as a fine writer is never dramatized—only his self-pity and running quarrel with most of the world.

Some of the best modern American writers of short fiction have been Southerners, with their writing distinguished for its concrete mastery of the sensory world and insistence on the elemental truths of life and death. In addition to Faulkner, the most brilliant Southern authors of tales have been Katherine Anne Porter (1890-1980), Eudora Welty (1909-   ), and Flannery O'Connor (1925-1964).

Porter's "Old Mortality" is a three-part novella featuring Miranda, her favorite character, who appears in half a dozen of her stories. In the first section, she is eight, listening to accounts of her beautiful, vivacious Aunt Amy, especially her long courtship and brief marriage to the handsome, dashing Uncle Gabriel before Amy died of an incurable illness. Part 2 consists almost wholly of shocks dispelling many of Miranda's illusions. Now ten and in a convent school, she is taken by her father to a racetrack where she meets Uncle Gabriel for the first time. To her dismay, he turns out to be coarse, alcoholic, shabby, fat, cruel. Part 3 shows Miranda, at eighteen, reconciling her illusions and disappointments in a union that transcends cynicism. On a train, returning from Uncle Gabriel's funeral, she encounters an older, feminist cousin, Eva, who provides her with a disenchanting view of Aunt Amy as a sexually hungry, wild, shallow woman. Miranda resolves to free herself from the past's legends and to begin her own life, her own legend. She has come to understand that human involvements tend to be ambiguous and that no secondhand version of anyone's life will serve her. Porter's irony is marked yet gentle, aware of both the human capacity for self-deception and the need for familial ties.

Welty's dominant mode is comic, with the range of her effects wide: exultant celebrations of folk vitality, both delicate and astringent irony, occasionally corrosive satire, high-spirited farce, and always a probing tenderness toward her people, which is Chekhovian in its lightness and clarity. While her spectrum of characters is broad, she is particularly adept at delineating the manner and idioms of proletarian rural Southerners.

One of her finest tales in this vein is "Why I Live at the P.O." Its dramatic monologuist, postmistress of the hamlet of China Grove, is cantankerous, at incessant odds with her family, and obsessively envious of her younger sister, whose marriage has shattered and who has come home to her mother. Like a Chaucerian personality, she can recall, in an unceasing flow of elliptical and baroque talk, every single slight allegedly inflicted on her. She is one of Welty's many isolated people, paranoid, vindictive and self-pitying yet possessed of irresistible gusto and a resourcefulness that prevents the reader from pitying her. In recording her protagonist's talk, Welty demonstrates eyes and ears as sharp and true as a tuning fork.

O'Connor's literary reputation has risen steeply since her death; in 1989, her collected works were published in the prestigious Library of America series—virtually formal canonization as a major writer. Her artistic virtues include subtle wit, an economical style, an eye for the maliciously revealing detail, piercingly apt imagery, a knack for sliding seamlessly between the ordinary and the sinister, an infallible sense of pace, mastery of understatement, and superlative skill in springing ironic reversals. Her few defects are a narrowness of emphasis and predictability of both technique and theme, for O'Connor prided herself on informing her tales and novels with the central teachings of Roman Catholicism. Her overriding concern with redemption impelled her, in much of her work, to impart last-moment visions of Christian belief to her main characters. Like Welty, O'Connor is a comic writer, with a Dickensian fondness for eccentric personalities as well as a gothic penchant for eruptions of disorder and violence.

Her most celebrated story, "A Good Man Is Hard to Find," presents the reader with sardonically treated, shocking events. On the surface, a homicidal maniac, called the Misfit, slaughters a family of innocent people whom he happens to encounter on the road. Read carefully, the tale becomes a commentary on general human values. The family begins a banal vacation trip on a chord of dissonance: the grandmother is self-centered and sly; her son, Bailey, is weak and surly; his wife is a dull frump; the children are snotty. Their first stop is at Red Sammy's barbecue tower, where the proprietor informs them that a good man is hard to find. Then the grandmother persuades her son to turn the car in the direction of an old plantation she had known in her childhood. He takes a dirt road to it, and she, by causing her cat to terrify the driver, is responsible for the resulting accident and the consequent confrontation with the Misfit and his henchmen. Professing goodness, the grandmother nevertheless seals the family's fate. In calling the mass murderer "one of my own children," is she surmounting her earlier vanity and expressing a Christlike grace, or is she simply selfishly pleading for her life? Is the Misfit, unmoved by his victims' appeals, a Grand Inquisitor, a psychotic, a lost pilgrim, a demon, the Devil himself? Such indeterminacy is built into this densely ambiguous, powerful text.

John Cheever (1912-1982), in brilliant stories beginning in the late 1930's, established a recognizable landscape that can be called "Cheever Country." In it, people hang together, or often fall apart, in Manhattan apartments, vainly awaiting their fortunes ("The Pot of Gold"), or they live in the Waspy, alcoholic suburbs of Westchester or Fairfield County. In "The Swimmer," during his summer-afternoon plunge homeward, the swimmer finds the air turning chill, flowers blooming out of season, his body weakening with age, and his home, once he reaches it, closed up. The reader is no longer in a recognizable community but in the realm of legend, with the protagonist discovering his life in ruins. In "Torch Song," a New Yorker encounters a mistreated woman over a period of years; he comes to realize that the men who insult and injure her are vainly defending themselves against the Angel of Death. Cheever's characters' sleep is troubled by nightmares as they stumble through wastelands of greed, lust, furtive frustration and coldness of heart despite their well-mannered, privileged upper-middle-class status. Cheever is essentially a mythic writer, drawing a fine tone of fable through his fiction in a lyrical prose unmatched in complexity, melody, and precision by his contemporaries.

In "The Enormous Radio," the marriage of a Manhattan couple, the Westcotts, is realistically treated. Their apartment, manners, tastes, speech, and behavior all seem typical and blandly complacent. Then, Cheever introduces the fantasy of an enormous, expensive radio that shreds the veil that not only the Westcotts but also their neighbors in the building have drawn over their secret lives: adulteries, wife-beatings, thefts, insults, obscenities, stinginess, and quarrels, quarrels, quarrels. Irene Westcott protests to her husband that *their* marriage is not sordid and hateful like the marriages of the others. She proves to be mistaken, as her husband bitterly attacks her for her extravagance, duplicity, mendacity, and hypocrisy. Is the Westcotts' marriage better after this bout of truth telling? The radio's voice is "suave and noncommittal."

Of the many Jewish writers who rose to prominence after World War II, only a few excel in short fiction: Bernard Malamud (1914-1986), Saul Bellow (1915-   ), and Philip Roth (1933-   ). The patron saint of these authors is Fyodor Dostoevski, whose characters must always search for meaning, who cannot permit life to flow without anxious examination. Jews came to the United States with a rich tradition of devotion to learning, and when that drive detached itself from Talmudic faith, it often became passionately involved in secular ideas and moral challenges. Moreover, the horror of the Holocaust stands behind all postwar Jewish American fiction, even when not explicitly acknowledged as a patrimony. The protagonist in many texts by Jewish writers is the victim, the dangling man, the schlemiel or bungler, with both his impulse toward decency and his proneness to failure, bereft, wandering, fooled and bewildered.

Alone among American authors, Malamud has focused on the Jew as representative man—and on the schlemiel as representative Jew: isolated, displaced, misunderstood, an apostate from society's gospel of material success. In Malamud's stories, the protagonist has frequent opportunities for suffering, submitting to loss, pain, humiliation, deception, sometimes ignominy. His characters usually triumph as human beings only by virtue of their failures in the world at large. Unashamedly romantic and moralistic, Malamud's fiction delineates the broken dreams and private griefs of the spirit, the anguish of the heart, the ungovernable course of compassion. Far from the mainstream of American culture, his work often stands guard against the temptations toward assimilation, rendering New York City as a pale or shtetl, a somber and often joyless world where dread and punishment are daily staples.

In his best-known tale, "The Magic Barrel," Malamud's tone shuttles from the promise of a fairy tale to the sadness of a sardonic parable. Its protagonist, Leo Finkle, is a rabbinical student nearing graduation who decides to marry so he can have a good chance of winning a congregation. Finkle is scholarly and ascetic but essentially godless, and he is fearful of his inability to love anyone. He calls in a marriage broker, Pinye Salzman, half con man and half spiritual exemplar. Most of Salzman's candidates, however, bear the marks of defeat. Then Leo falls in love with a snapshot accidentally included in a packet of pictures left him by the wily Salzman. The matchmaker is horrified when Leo insists on meeting *this* woman—it is Salzman's daughter, Stella, whose sorrowful father describes her as "wild, without shame. . . . Like an animal." Leo insists on a meeting. His rapture, on seeing Stella, is both exotic and religious: "He pictured, in her, his own redemption. Violins and lit candles revolved in the sky. Leo ran forward with flowers outthrust." Malamud's ending is ambiguous and paradoxical. Will the unworldly Leo discover his salvation through loving the sinful, whorish Stella? In the story's last sentence, Salzman chants prayers for the dead. Because his daughter is lost to him? Because of his role in bringing Leo and Stella together? Because he mourns Leo's loss of innocence? Malamud leaves the reader with problems and possibilities.

Bellow, born in Canada but living in the United States since he was nine, is generally recognized as the dominant prose writer of the generation following Faulkner's and Hemingway's. His fiction has a European flavor in its fondness for philosophical, historical, and political debate and its stress on his characters' intense, gloomy mental lives, which often cast them adrift in seas of hallucination and guilt. One of the crucial themes of Bellow's work is the anguished attempt of his protagonists to get a grip on existence in a lonely and dehumanizing world, to try to understand an infinitely elusive, sometimes senseless, universe.

Perhaps his most accomplished text is the novella *Seize the Day* (1956), which exhibits his concentrated power at its best and curbs his natural tendency to lecture the reader. The effect is one of extreme compression along the lines of classical tragedy, with a single day of the hero's—or the antihero's—life summing up and invoking a judgment upon his entire history. Tommy Wilhelm is a middle-aged Manhattan salesman, out of a job, fat, divorced, behind in his alimony payments, scorned by his ex-wife, rejected by his father. He is a buffeted buffoon, humiliated before others, adrift, stumbling through the routines of life. The reader meets Tommy on a day of panic, when his world seems to be collapsing as he discovers that he has lost his remaining savings by having foolishly played the stock market under the influence of a fast-talking sharper, the psychiatrist Dr. Tamkin. The *carpe diem* injunction of the title is ironic, for Tommy has never had the courage or the drive to turn an opportunity to his advantage. At the end of the tale, the scheming Tamkin has fled, Dr. Adler coldly refuses to aid his son, Tommy's wife has hounded him for money, and he is broke and desperate. He knows that only love can make his life bearable, but his vanity and self-pity thwart his emotions. Then Bellow concludes with a splendid catharsis: Tommy wanders along Broadway into a Jewish funeral service and there releases his grief in a great surge at the coffin of the unknown corpse. He finds himself sharing and universalizing his suffering. In the story's last sentence, Tommy "sank deeper than sorrow, through torn sobs and cries toward the consummation of his heart's ultimate need."

Roth was to create his unmistakable schlemiel in the protagonist of his most popular novel, *Portnoy's Complaint* (1969). In *Goodbye, Columbus* (1959), the short-story collection that launched Roth's career to critical acclaim, he investigates Jewish middle-class rather than lower-class life, dealing with the tensions between assimilation into the larger American culture and ethnic identity, public image and private passion, material success and spiritual failure. While influenced by Malamud and Bellow, Roth owes a larger debt to F. Scott Fitzgerald. In the long, sharply satiric title story, he relates the defeat in love of a poor, Jewish young man by a brutally materialistic, wealthy Jewish family. In "Eli, the Fanatic," the conflict is between Hasidic and secularized Jews. In "The Conversion of the Jews," the motif suggests the validity of diverse religious beliefs, with tolerance of pluralism triumphing over closed-minded faith.

Roth's best story is "Defender of the Faith," in which Sergeant Nathan Marx, assigned to a Missouri training company after European combat, encounters over and over again the wiles of trainee Sheldon Grossbart, who cunningly uses their shared roots in the New York Jewish community to abuse Marx's humaneness, generosity, and scrupulosity. Marx's dilemma is thorny: how to be a good person, a good soldier, and a good Jew in a conniving and insensitive world. He decides that the best way to be a defender of his faith is to reject Grossbart's advantage mongering, yet he finds that he can restore the balance of Justice's scales only by descending to Grossbart's level of lying and trickery. The tough-minded Roth affirms that a worthy end does justify unworthy means. This is a complex, powerfully imagined tale, sharply observed in its command of dialogue and characteristic gestures. Even though Roth proceeded to use the novel rather than the tale as his preferred medium, his fictive debut shows him to be a masterful storyteller.

Great Britain and Ireland

The short stories and novellas of D. H. Lawrence (1885-1930) are usually not the forum for exploring a new set of ideas in his visionary career. While not the product of his most fertile imagination, however, the best of them are often superior in structure and more artistically realized than his novels, keeping to a minimum his tendency to exhort the reader or to repeat himself. Their recurring themes are the distortion of love by possessiveness, materialism, or false romanticism, the pressure of class feelings upon male/female relationships, and the interplay of antagonism and tenderness that marks the sexual battlefield.

In "Tickets, Please," one of the young inspectors of a train line, John Thomas, charming but promiscuous, begins to date Annie, one of the girl conductors, but he drops her when she begins to take him seriously. Annie then organizes a group revenge on him, joined by a number of the other women equally picked up and then rejected by "Coddy" Thomas. They trap him, rough him up, humiliate him, then find themselves nonplussed by their bright, maenadlike frenzy; the story thus ends on a note of uneasy irresolution, with the young women unable to understand fully their paradoxical impulses of aggressiveness and surrender. They are financially independent yet wish to fulfill themselves in marriage. "Coddy's" masculine pride and arrogance both infuriate and attract them. As soon as they have redressed the balance between the sexes, they feel lost and miserable, appalled by their victory over the macho male.

"The Horse Dealer's Daughter" opens at a moment of family crisis: three brothers have failed in the business passed to them from their father. Their sister, Mabel, especially mourns the death of her mother as she keeps house. Lonely, sullen, isolated among her egotistical brothers, she attempts suicide as a desperate fulfillment. A young doctor rescues her from drowning in a stagnant pond, carries her back to the house, strips off her clothes, and wraps her in warming blankets. When she awakens, she asks him, directly, "Do you love me, then?" The shock of the exposure has transcended her inhibitions. He finds himself unable to withdraw from her, able only to yield and declare a reciprocal love. He and the woman have undergone a deathly baptism and have been reborn, contrary to their previous intentions. Their delivery of each other is also a crucial self-discovery. This is a totally unsentimental, compelling dramatization of the triumph of love and life.

In *The Fox*, a novella, Lawrence achieves a wonderfully naturalistic narrative in which, as often in his work, an outsider liberates people from convention, isolation, and repression. Two women, March and Banford, nearing thirty, are struggling to manage an isolated, small farm. March is ruddy, physically effective, dominant; Banford is frail, oversensitive, passionless. The fox who preys on the chickens represents wild nature endangering their way of life. Enter a young Canadian soldier, Henry, whose prominent cheekbones and bright eyes remind March of the fox. He, too, represents the danger and discord of an intruder. Henry kills the fox, then encounters Banford's resentment of his presence, and realizes that he has no hope of successfully wooing March while she is still on the farm. He proposes to the older March, she half-consents, then relapses into indecision when with the needy Banford. In a willed accident, Henry axes a tree in such a way that one of its boughs kills Banford. Relieved and released, March agrees to marry Henry and start a new life with him in Canada. Lawrence's command of atmosphere, setting, and dialogue is classically perfect without overworking the symbolism of the fox.

Graham Greene (1904-1991) is a master of the politics of disenchantment and sadness, dealing usually with characters who are seedy, melancholy, disloyal, fallen, and despairing. He invests his narratives with a probing moral concern, often colored by his conversion to Roman Catholicism, and dramatizes his themes in patterns of intrigue, flight, pursuit, and sometimes annihilation. While some of his tales are trivial digressions from his longer fiction, others are splendidly crafted. He came to appreciate the opportunities offered by short fiction for unified tone and precision of language and declared that he had never written anything better than the stories "The Destructors," "A Chance for Mr. Lever," "Under the Garden," and "Cheap in August."

"The Basement Room" is generally considered Greene's finest story. It is narrated by the dying, sixty-seven-year-old Philip Lane, still living with the traumatic effects of a day in his life when he was seven and entrusted, in his parents' absence, to the care of two household servants, Mr. and Mrs. Baines. Young Philip loves and admires the butler Baines while fearing his malevolent, nagging, housekeeping wife. The story focuses on Philip's meeting a young woman, Emily, whom Baines presents to him as his niece but who is clearly his mistress. Philip is now thrust into an adult world of duplicity and malice as the boy becomes a pawn in the match between the hostile couple. When Mrs. Baines returns unexpectedly and discovers her husband's infidelity, it is Philip who unwillingly betrays him. Then, after the wife falls over the banister to her death, it is again Philip who, exhausted by the pressure of events, incriminates Baines. Sixty years later, Philip still suffers from death of the heart, having led a wasteful, loveless, empty life, unable to be more than a dilettante. The story guides the reader to many of Greene's major concerns: the innocence of childhood, to be contaminated by the adult world, the victory of betrayal over trust, and the relative impotence of good when it encounters evil.

"The Destructors," Greene's most chilling story, focuses on a brilliant but sociopathic teenager, Trevor, son of an architect who has "come down in the world" to a clerkship after World War II. Trevor gains leadership of a gang when he enthralls its members with his proposal to pull down the grand and stately house of "Old Misery," a kind old man whose home was built by the great Sir Christopher Wren. Trevor achieves the status of a demonic destructive artist as he orchestrates the ruination of the house in virtuoso fashion. The tale is a parable of England's confused and impoverished society during the immediate postwar period. The elegant house, symbolizing aristocratic values, is brought to rubble by a cruelly insensitive new generation. Creativity is harnessed to destruction in a Manichean fashion. On a political level, "The Destructors" can be understood as an allegory on the seductive appeal of power which, once unleashed, gains totalitarian momentum. The story's nightmarish implications are alarming.

The Irish writer Frank O'Connor (1903-1966), born Michael Francis O'Donovan, was a younger member of the distinguished Irish Literary Renaissance headed by William Butler Yeats. Most of his writing consisted of short stories dealing with the soul of the Irish people. More entertaining, witty, and charming than his great compatriot James Joyce, O'Connor is also a more uneven craftsman, some of whose work is slight and poorly resolved. At his best, however, O'Connor has produced some of the finest short fiction of the twentieth century.

"Guests of the Nation" may be his most powerful story. Two British soldiers, Hawkins and Belcher, are held hostage by Irish guards who play cards with them, engage them in spirited arguments, and become their friends, even though their two nations are at war with each other in the early 1920's. When news arrives that four Irish prisoners have been killed by their captors, the Irish soldier in charge insists on shooting the two hostages in reprisal. The perky little Hawkins protests that they are all "chums" and declares his readiness to join his Irish friends' side—to no avail. The sweet-tempered, generous Belcher reveals his desertion by an adulterous wife, then accepts his deadly fate stoically. The narrator, revolted by the barbarity of warfare, is desolated by the loss of two warm human beings: "And anything that ever happened to me after I never felt the same about again."

"The Drunkard" shows to superb effect O'Connor's talent for mixing humor and irony with shrewd psychology. An alcoholic father looks forward to honoring the life and death of a friend, Mr. Dooley, by indulging himself at the postburial celebration. His young son, Larry (who narrates the tale), however, downs his dad's porter, gets sick, and has to be rushed home by his embarrassed father. Forced into sobriety by the circumstances, the father is unjustly scolded by his wife for corrupting their child. The next morning, however, the wife-mother expresses her gratitude to Larry for having served as his father's guardian angel, preventing him from—at least, this time—disgracing and impoverishing the household. Role reversal dominates this hilarious story, with little Larry monitoring his childlike, improvident father, and imitating him on a noisy, tipsy promenade from pub to home. Instead of composing a temperance tract, O'Connor has written an enchanting tale about human vanities and frailties.

Europe

Thomas Mann (1875-1955) is the most representative German author of the twentieth century, ranking with the era's greatest prose masters. His work is filled with polarities and ironies: a conservative style yet boldly experimental subject matter, barbaric vitalism arrayed against decadent civilization, nationalism opposed to cosmopolitanism, and varying conceptions of the artist as hero, priest, and charlatan. Mann wrote some of the century's most distinguished short fiction. Some of the tales, such as "Der Tod in Venedig" ("Death in Venice") and "Tonio Kröger," were published prior to 1920; others, such as "Unordnung und frühes Leid" ("Disorder and Early Sorrow") and "Mario und der Zauberer" ("Mario and the Magician"), came thereafter.

"Disorder and Early Sorrow," composed shortly after Mann had finished his titanic novel *Der Zauberberg* (1924; *The Magic Mountain*, 1927) is one of his subtlest, deftest, and most understated texts. The "disorder" is German society's ills after World War I, with prices astronomically inflated, commodities scarce, and traditional ideas and modes as deflated as the currency. The "early sorrow" is felt by five-year-old Ellie, the youngest and favorite daughter of a historian, Professor Cornelius. The girl becomes infatuated with a handsome but dull student who has jocularly danced with her at a house party. The sorrow is most painfully felt by Ellie's father, for Dr. Cornelius knows both that she is previewing the inevitable withdrawal of her affections from him to a lover and that he can in no significant way prevent the pains of life's disappointments from befalling her. Allegorically, the values of German middle-class culture are threatened by incoherent, undisciplined currents of revolutionary change. Professor Cornelius realizes that his preference for the past has become outdated.

In "Mario and the Magician," written in 1929, Mann gives high aesthetic form to an indictment of Fascism in a novella that he termed "a tale with moral and political implications." The work falls into two parts: in the first, a German family visiting an Italian beach town encounters a series of increasingly unpleasant incidents, redolent of intolerance and overheated nationalism. The second division stars the hypnotist Cipolla, ill-humored, hunchbacked, chauvinistic, sadistic, sinister, driven by his inferiority complex. He is a malevolent and demonic artist, using his talent to degrade his public. Cipolla is finally shot by Mario, a modest and ordinary waiter, whom the illusionist has mocked beyond endurance. Allegorically, Mann implies that the hypnotic spell of totalitarianism can be lifted by the forces of decency and dignity. History has usually proved him wrong.

The Baroness Karen Blixen-Finecke (1885-1962), who took the pen name Isak Dinesen, is Denmark's greatest modern writer. Her tales, which she did not begin publishing until she was forty-nine, are consciously anachronistic, depending on often improbable fantasies, constant metamorphoses, enigmatic signs, elemental magic, highly mannered characterization, and mazelike patterns of stories set within stories. She likened herself to Scheherazade, making up narratives to save her life and provide her public with new visions that would change hearts and minds.

In "Sorrow-Acre," Dinesen pits against each other archaic and modern modes of feeling and thinking. The plot, derived from a Jutland folktale, deals with a peasant woman who, to save her son from execution, is required by the local lord to reap between sunrise and sunset a field of rye, which ordinarily would require four men to reap in a day. The woman fulfills the bargain but then drops dead; the superhuman feat is memorialized by the name "Sorrow-Acre," thereafter attached to the field. The action is viewed through the eyes of the lord's nephew, Adam, who has encountered new humanitarian ideas while visiting England. He threatens to leave the estate forever, unless his uncle releases the woman from the cruel compact. The uncle will not yield, replying that to do so would be to lighten the woman's exploit, to deprive it of tragic significance. Two worldviews are opposed: humanitarianism set against a manorial culture that values the law above individual suffering. The nephew is reconciled to the presence of evil in the world and decides to stay with his uncle.

"Skibsdrængens Fortælling" ("The Sailor-Boy's Tale") uses marvelous elements to dramatize a young man's initiation into adulthood. A nineteen-year-old deckhand, Simon, sees a peregrine falcon entangled in tackle yarn. He rescues her but not without being hacked on the thumb. On shore, he becomes infatuated with a teenage girl and, in his anxiety to keep a tryst with her, accidentally kills a Russian sailor. Pursued by the Russian's shipmates, Simon is rescued by an old Lapp woman who shelters him, mingles her blood with his, and reveals herself as a witch who had metamorphosed herself into the falcon that he had freed. The next morning, she pushes him on his way and prophesizes that he will be faithful to the sea his life long. The charm of Dinesen's fable lies in its use of fairy-tale elements to dramatize the transformation that entry into maturation constitutes.

Isaac Bashevis Singer (1904-1991) was born in Poland of a Hasidic rabbinical family. In 1935, anticipating the German invasion of Poland, he emigrated to the United States but continued to write in Yiddish. Dipping his pen in an inkwell of demonology, he excels in dramatizing a varied, forceful, and frequently fantastic vision of Eastern Europe's vanished Jewry, finding his imagination most at home in the culture of the shtetl—the small Jewish ghetto village of nineteenth century Poland. The short story is Singer's natural medium, affording an appropriate vehicle for his compact, coiled, and clipped style, which reflects the Yiddish oral tradition: ironic, nervous, staccato, and proverbial. His greatest stories breathe an enigmatic moral tone, of life as a dance on the grave with both evil and death imminent. No loving God smiles His benefactions upon His chosen people. The reader catches none of the sentimental idealism of such Yiddish writers as Sholom Aleichem, none of the soft dreaminess of Marc Chagall's tailors and fiddlers floating lyrically over rooftops. Instead, Satan's forces often hold sway, with the world a moral Armageddon and people staring into the shattered ruins of their lives as if into a bottomless pit. Despite his traditional techniques, Singer has a modern sensibility, caustic, unsettling, absurdist, regarding the world as incoherent, arbitrary, and mysterious.

"Gimpel Tam" ("Gimpel the Fool"), his most famous story, is narrated by the title character who is, of course, a schlemiel as well as a holy simpleton. He is wholly gullible, eager to believe all he is told and to trust everyone, particularly his sluttish wife, Elka, none of whose six children are his. Yet Singer's characterization of Gimpel is enigmatic: like a Shakespearean character, he may choose to play the fool so as to retain his moral sanity in an exploitive, mendacious world. When people become relativists in Singer's writings, they become tortured by doubts. Gimpel prefers an absolute faith, finding the value of his life in a total openness to suffering and ridicule. He is certain he is doing God's will; the reader may have doubts.

"The Gentleman from Cracow" has a poor, tiny village tempted by unaccustomed luxury when, miraculously, a wealthy, widowed doctor arrives bearing many alms. He organizes a splendid ball, providing appropriate clothes for all, spreading gold everywhere, and announcing that he will choose his new wife at the festival. At the ball, the doctor dances with the whorish Hodle, promises a dowry of ten thousand ducats to every woman who will wed, but, when denounced by a true believer, he sets the town on fire and reveals his identity as the Chief of Devils, with an eye in his chest and a tail of serpents. Hodle is discovered to be the witch Lilith, while evil spirits celebrate their unholy union. Purged of their greed and lust, the villagers, poor again, resign themselves to their small existence.

Sidonie-Gabrielle Colette (1873-1954) is of the same generation as André Gide (1869-1951) and Marcel Proust (1871-1922), and she greatly admired the latter, sharing with him a remarkable talent for acutely rendering vibrating, sensual recollections of childhood experiences. In the 1920's Colette produced a series of novellas that were masterpieces: *La Maison de Claudine* (1922; *My Mother's House*, 1953), *La Naissance du jour* (1928; *A Lesson in Love*, 1932), *Sido* (1929; English translation, 1953), and, by far the most famous: *Chéri* (1920; English translation, 1929) and *La Fin de Chéri* (1926; *The Last of Chéri*, 1932).

Even though the last two were published six years apart, they form one continuous love story. They relate the liaison between Léa, an aging courtesan, and the extremely handsome but also extremely dependent Frédéric Peloux, nicknamed Chéri; the lovers' ages differ by twenty-four years. The scene is Paris, the setting, the demimonde, the period, 1906-1919. In the first novella Léa is the gracefully protective mistress, Chéri the moody, narcissistic taker of her tenderness. He will soon be married to Edmée, a beautiful, wealthy young woman. Chéri returns from his honeymoon tense and irritable, bursts into Léa's bedroom and insists that they resume their relationship. Heroically, Léa decides not to do so, instead sending him back to his wife.

The Last of Chéri continues in the postwar Paris of 1919. Chéri, now thirty-two, is unable to cope with what he regards as the frenetic busyness of his wife in a military hospital. He feels empty and apathetic, unable to take hold of life. Once more returning to Léa, Chéri discovers her to be a corpulent, gray-haired woman who has put eroticism behind her. Chéri clings to his memory of Léa as a mother-mistress, refusing to recognize the inevitability of natural changes. Disgusted with life, listless, depressed, he ends up shooting himself in the temple.

Léa is a splendidly drawn character, one of the strongest and most memorable in modern fiction. Colette uses sensory imagery with superb skill, creating potently erotic scenes without any explicit rendering of intercourse. She relies instead on oblique observations, color symbolism, and incisive notation of the intricate network of vital details and habits surrounding a relationship. She explores and accepts life's joys and pains as inevitable and fascinating aspects of existence, with no metaphysical anguish, no ideological premises, no social commitment, no estrangement and much wonder, delight, and tact.

Jean-Paul Sartre (1905-1980) constituted himself a prodigiously creative one-man band of modern thought and literature, doing important work in philosophy, psychology, drama, biography, literary criticism, journalism, political pamphleteering, and film writing, as well as fiction. In 1939, he published five short stories under the title of *Le Mur* (*The Wall and Other Stories*, 1948), later to appear in England and the United States as the more provocative *Intimacy*. Each tale focuses on a particular physical or emotional experience in order to dramatize a particular philosophical concept. The body of Sartre's ideas is, of course, his version of existentialism, according to which human beings are cast into a godless world without any preordained or privileged position or "essence." Every individual must therefore invent the values by which he or she lives by doing just that—living them. Human beings' freedom can lead to exhilaration but also to anguish, since they must continually define their nature by their behavior in an irrational, absurd world. As one character says in the play *Huis-clos* (1944; *No Exit*, 1947), "You are—your life, and nothing else."

The title story of the collection seeks to refute the contention of the German philosopher Martin Heidegger (1889-1976) that individuals can live meaningfully toward their own death and thus humanize, even heroize it, as Kyo Gisors does in André Malraux's novel *La Condition humaine* (1933; *Man's Fate*, 1934). The protagonist, Pablo Ibbieta, is a Spanish Republican who has been taken prisoner by Franco's Falangists in the Civil War. Together with Tom, an Irishman from the International Brigade, and Juan, a teenage Spaniard who took no part in politics, he is condemned to death. Sartre concentrates on the feelings that Pablo has as he contemplates his impending nothingness. While young Juan goes into sobbing hysterics and Tom urinates in his pants through sheer terror, Pablo, though sweating heavily in his cold cell, does his best to confront death with Hemingwayesque stoicism, seeking to remain "terribly hard."

In the face of death, Pablo decides that nothing matters to him anymore—his mistress, his comrades, his political cause. The wall of his prison becomes a symbol of his coming annihilation, with death nullifying all meaning. In the morning, given fifteen minutes to decide whether he would be willing to save his life by revealing the whereabouts of his friend and leader, Juan Gris, Pablo decides to play a trick on his captors. He tells them that Gris is hiding in the cemetery, knowing that Gris is at his cousins' home. It turns out that Gris, however, having quarreled with his cousins, did flee to the gravediggers' shack; when the Falangists find him there, they kill him. Hearing of this absurd coincidence, Pablo can only collapse in delirious laughter.

When Albert Camus (1913-1960) received the Nobel Prize in December, 1957, he pledged himself to distill a literature of dignity and courage from a century often at war, beset by self-doubts, and threatened by disintegration. In the collection of six stories he issued earlier that year, *L'Exil et le royaume* (1957; *Exile and the Kingdom*, 1958), he largely fulfilled that promise. All the tales are studies in exile, all deal with people trying to find a country where they will be fully at home. Four are set in Camus' native Algeria, one in Brazil, one in France. Each work is subtly written and builds to an inevitable climax, in the manner of Maupassant or Lawrence.

In "L'Hôte" ("The Guest"), Camus admirably dramatizes his absurdist philosophy that life is difficult and lacks ultimate meaning but that nevertheless a man defines himself by the quality of his moral decisions and his courage in acting on them. The protagonist is a French Algerian schoolteacher, Daru, who has charge of a one-room school for Arab children in the middle of a bleak Algerian plateau, which he nevertheless loves as his birthplace. He is given the unwelcome duty of transporting an Arab prisoner to police headquarters at a village about four hours away. This is not part of Daru's job, but police shorthandedness in the face of an incipient Arabian revolt has thrust it upon him. A sensitive, humane, and compassionate person, Daru treats his prisoner as a guest rather than as a member of an inferior culture. He rebels against the notion of handing the Arab, who had killed in a tribal dispute, over to French authorities for a trial.

The story centers on Daru's dilemma. Should he obey a gendarme's orders and deliver the Arab to the French? Should he take the Arab to his nomadic tribe? Should he give the Arab his freedom? Daru solves his dilemma by taking his guest to a high plateau from which he gives the Arab the choice of walking either to a French prison or to his freedom. The Arab chooses prison, and Daru returns sadly to his classroom, only to find, chalked on the blackboard, the threat: "You have handed over our brother. You will pay for this." This text poignantly illustrates both the necessity and the burdensome nature of individual moral choice. In Camus's world, human beings live, choose, suffer, and die essentially alone. At the story's end, Daru finds himself isolated in every sense, perilously misunderstood, a martyr to Camus' sorrowful humanism.

The Russian author Isaac Babel (1894-1941) remains a haunting anomaly in modern literature. This Jewish writer, who once called himself a "past master of the art of silence," left behind him, besides a few scenarios and plays, fewer than four hundred pages of published short fiction. Whatever else he might have written but was not ready to publish was lost to the world when Babel was arrested by Joseph Stalin's police in 1939, to die soon after—whether by bullet or illness—in a Soviet concentration camp. Yet his slim literary legacy has sufficed to establish his reputation as one of the twentieth century's important European writers.

As an artist, Babel is full of ambivalences and paradoxes: He is a Soviet writer who welcomes the revolution yet dramatizes its terror through the mindless, ruthless savagery of the cossacks. He is a self-consciously Jewish intellectual, a "chap with specs," who is nevertheless driven to strike blows against his cultural heritage by celebrating guiltless violence, primitive energy, and even aimless destruction. He is a traditional Russian writer, with debts to Leo Tolstoy and Chekhov, who identifies strongest with Maupassant and Gustave Flaubert, secondarily with Stephen Crane and Hemingway. The example of Flaubert seems the most compelling in Babel's monklike devotion to his art and untiring struggle with language to find exactly the right phrase or word for each nuance of statement. "No iron can stab the heart" (he writes in the story "Guy de Maupassant") "with such force as a period put just at the right place."

The crucial experience of Babel's life was his service with a regiment of cossacks in 1920, during the civil war that followed the Russian Revolution. In the superb tales that he derived from this event, collected in *Konarmiia* (1926; *Red Cavalry*, 1929), he contrasts, in story after story, the glamorous but cruel grace of the cossacks with the humaneness, physical inadequacy and pacifism of the Jews. In "Moi pervyi gus" ("My First Goose"), the Jewish newcomer to the cossack brigade is snubbed for his intellectualism, until he ingratiates himself by killing, in particularly grotesque fashion, a goose belonging to an old woman. Now admitted to the fellowship of the group, the narrator's "heart, stained with bloodshed, grated and brimmed over," in a last sentence loaded with enigmas.

The primary impact of the *Red Cavalry* collection is one of shock. The stories are lean, hard, terse, intense, gorgeously colored, kinesthetic. Babel is ready to wrench language to gain nervous immediacy, even to inflict psychic wounds on the reader. He specializes in interweaving extremes of behavior. In "The Death of Dolgushov," a badly wounded cossack by that name has his entrails hanging over his knees and begs the Jewish narrator for a mercy killing; the narrator refuses, being soft and scrupulous. A comrade of Dolgushov then does the job and turns furiously on the Jew: "You guys in specs have about as much pity for chaps like us as a cat has for a mouse." He cocks his rifle to shoot the narrator, who has the courage to ride away slowly, "feeling the chill of death in my back." Another cossack diverts the executioner from double murder, catches up with the narrator, and offers him a shriveled apple. The Jew is hardly ever accepted on terms of egalitarian fellowship with the bloodthirsty cossack. Babel strains for a union of passion and tenderness but usually fails to achieve it, being honest enough to discover them tragically dissociated in modern life.

Even though Vladimir Nabokov (1899-1977) spent nineteen years in the United States, his Russian roots and the three-fourths of his life in Europe strongly stamp him as a continental author. In his productive career, he composed about forty stories as well as novels, poetry, memoirs, and literary criticism. His early stories are set in the post-World War I era, with Germany the usual location, and sensitive, exiled Russian men the usual protagonists. Nabokov displays in these tales his abiding fascination with the interplay between reality and fantasy as well as his devotion to style, commanding a remarkable precision of language and nuanced tones ranging from grandeur to irony to parody.

In "Signs and Symbols," Nabokov wrote his most sorrowful and possibly finest story. An elderly, poor Russian émigré couple go to visit their son on his birthday; he is in a sanatorium, diagnosed as afflicted with "referential mania," whereby the patient considers all events occurring anywhere near him as veiled references to his own life. On their trip to the sanatorium, the machinery of existence seems to malfunction in a variety of frustrating ways. Once there, they are told that their son has again attempted suicide and should not be disturbed. Back home, in the story's last section, the couple decides to bring the son back to their apartment; each parent will spend part of the night with him. A telephone call, however, indicates that this time the troubled son has succeeded in escaping this world. Artistically, this story is virtually flawless: it is intricately patterned, densely textured, intense in tone and feeling. Nabokov, the literary jeweler, has here cut more deeply than his usual surfaces, has abandoned gamesmanship and mirror play to face the grimmest horrors of a sometimes hopeless world.

Alberto Moravia (1907-1990), born as Alberto Pincherle, was Italy's leading writer of fiction for at least five decades. His novels and stories are grounds for battles of the sexes that sometimes seem as grueling as a fight to the finish, with sex a sickness and love a torment. Eroticism for Moravia, however, is only a metaphor for dealing with even deeper problems of human existence. For his protagonists, sex is never an end in itself; instead, it is an expression of will, a means to power. Moravia is fundamentally a romantic moralist who indicts egotism, greed, the bourgeois mentality that frustrates natural instincts, the social decadence that leads to fascism. The problem that most preoccupies him is the moral consequences of acts of will—or failure to act as a result of hypersensitive passivity. His prose, hard and urgent, is reminiscent of Stendhal, as is his union of cool observation with lyrical fervor.

Perhaps Moravia's most successful novelette is *Agostino* (1944; English translation, 1947). It explores the agonies, bewilderments, and frustrations of adolescence with infernal accuracy. As a sensitive boy of thirteen, Agostino finds himself powerfully attracted to his beautiful, stately mother who has recently been widowed. When she strikes up a friendship with a handsome, womanizing swimmer at the beach, Agostino attaches himself to a gang of tough, cruel working-class lads who mock him for his middle-class status and sexual innocence. In the center of this vulgar group is a six-fingered, grotesque beach attendant, Saro, whose inclinations are manifestly homosexual and whose cruises on a sailboat constitute parodies of a Homeric epic. Agostino's previous Eden of unconditional bonding with his mother is transformed into a disheartening world of anguish, aggression, and amorality. The proletarian gang unjustly accuses him of pederasty, brutalizes and exploits him. His tenderness for his mother changes into pained awareness of her erotic drives. Agostino ends up being misunderstood as well as mistreated, aware that "a long, unhappy time would have to pass" before he will reach adulthood. The story is a masterfully accurate study of the suffering that coming of age can entail.

Asia

In his forty-five years, the Japanese author Yukio Mishima (1925-1970), often compared by critics to either Gide or Hemingway, produced a staggering amount of literary works: forty novels, twenty plays, eighty stories, and uncounted essays. He became the most internationally celebrated talent among his nation's twentieth century authors, eclipsing the Nobel Prize-winning Yasunari Kawabata (1899-1972) and the distinguished Jun'ichirō Tanizaki (1886-1965). Writing with a fluid Western flair, sometimes slick but often subtle, sardonic, sex-obsessed, Mishima dredges up the explosive passions and capricious violence buried in the Japanese subconscious, commenting with sharp irony and grisly humor on their modern manifestations, relating his country's feudal past to its materialistic present.

Mishima's most notorious story is "Yūkoku" ("Patriotism"). It was inspired by the Army Rebellion of 1936, which he would invest with increasing symbolic significance as his own special brand of reactionary patriotism evolved. On February 26, 1936, twenty-one officers in Japan's Imperial Army attempted to overthrow what they considered an insufficiently militant government and succeeded in assassinating three cabinet ministers. When an angry Emperor Hirohito insisted on severe punishment for these mutineers, several of them committed ritual suicide—seppuku. In Mishima's tale, the hero is a young lieutenant whose comrades have kept him ignorant of the attempted coup out of consideration for his recent marriage. The following day, he is ordered to march against his rebellious friends. Unable to resolve his dilemma of conflicting loyalties, the officer purifies himself in a bath, makes love to his wife, then performs the act of seppuku. His bride thereupon thrusts a dagger into her throat.

So intrigued was Mishima by the dramatic dynamics of this story that he made a powerful, twenty-four-minute film of it in which he starred in the officer's role. Ten years later, life was made to imitate art. On November 25, 1970, accompanied by four cadets whom he had trained, Mishima visited the commandant of Japan's Self-Defense Force in Tokyo. The commandant was forced, at sword point, to assemble his regiment in the courtyard. Mishima exhorted this captive audience to rise up with him against a spineless postwar democracy that no longer revered the country's imperial tradition. Jeered and hissed by the young men, Mishima broke off his harangue and committed seppuku. Honor satisfied, one of his cadets beheaded him with a long sword, completing the ritual. His macabre death served to endow many of his works with an eerie aroma of art anticipating the extinction of the artist.

Latin America

Prior to World War II, Latin American writers relied on traditional realism in their representations. Since then, this regionalist writing has undergone a series of drastic changes to become one of contemporary literature's most imaginative and avant-garde art forms. The progenitor of this revolution is the brilliant, intricate Argentine author Jorge Luis Borges (1899-1986), intellectually as well as structurally one of the most sophisticated and complex of twentieth century authors. His fictive world stems from his encyclopedic and often esoteric readings in not only literature but also philosophy and theology, with his tales exuding an aura of fantastic elaboration. He loves to play out abstract intellectual games by pushing an initial situation or concept to its logical extreme, regardless of realistic plausibility or psychological consistency.

Like Sartre and Camus, Borges is a philosophical absurdist—but with a difference. He does not share their commitment to social justice or to individual responsibility and freedom of choice. He subordinates his characters to the control of his plots, content to draw them as archetypal figures created solely to illustrate ideas. Borges' protagonists are usually engaged in a vain quest for knowledge, power, or salvation, since he considers all pursuits of truth as vain endeavors. His stories can often be read as parables of an ambiguous universe, rich in metaphysical implications, filled with mazes of hearsay and confusion, with dreams, mirrors, and labyrinths that destroy any assumption of stability, harmony, or progress.

In "La biblioteca de Babel" ("The Library of Babel"), Borges sketches a cosmic library with an infinite array of bookcases, lamps, hallways, and staircases, which represent the cosmos. The narrator, a tired old librarian, has spent his life vainly searching for a certain book, among countless billions of books, which will be the cipher and compendium of all the others. Unable to find it, he is yet unwilling to accept the thesis of recent skeptics who think of the library—that is, the world—as indecipherable and meaningless. The library conveys Borges' notion of modern man alienated in a mysterious world. Yet the librarian tries to seek solace in the belief that, while the human species will eventually become extinct, the universe—that is, the Library—will endure forever because it is "limitless and periodic." If an eternal traveler were to traverse its vastness in any direction, he would find it cyclical, with the same volumes repeated in the same disorder—which would amount to a kind of order. This story amounts to a virtuoso performance brooding symbolically over human beings' intellectual exertions as they pathetically try to disentangle and understand an inexplicable universe or to console themselves with dreamy speculations.

"Tlön, Uqbar, Orbis Tertius," Borges' longest and most demanding tale, expresses nearly all of his central ideas, preoccupations, and mannerisms. It opens with the narrator Borges hearing his friend, Adolfo Bioy Casares, alluding to Uqbar, an exotic land he has read about in his *Anglo-American Cyclopaedia*. Bioy's encyclopedia contains a long article on this country in Asia Minor, but other copies of this work lack the entry. Uqbar's literature is invariably fantastic in mode and set on the imaginary planet of Tlön. Two years later, the narrator comes across one volume of an encyclopedia about Tlön. The imaginary inhabitants of fancied Tlön are all idealists of the Berkeleian type, believing that the universe is a subjective projection of the mind and lacks material existence. Consequently, Tlön's language has no nouns, (which presuppose a world of objects), things tend to efface themselves when they are forgotten, and materialism is inconceivable as a philosophy.

In a "Postscript, 1947" (even though Borges composed this text in 1940), a letter brought to the narrator's attention discloses that a secret society of scholars, including Bishop Berkeley, was founded in seventeenth century England to invent an idealistic country, and that, in the nineteenth century United States, an eccentric American atheistic tycoon financed the Tlön project, which resulted in a forty-volume encyclopedia regarding this planet, whose projected title was *Orbis Tertius*. In the 1940's, Tlön's fantastic world intruded upon the real world, with the widespread distribution of the Tlön encyclopedia. People were fascinated by descriptions of this ordered, logical region, and Tlön's history and languages are now taking control of school curricula, displacing English, French, and Spanish. "Now, in all memories, a fictitious past occupies the place of any other. . . . The world will be Tlön."

Borges' partiality for philosophical idealism animates this superb story. He shows how reality depends on one's perceptions, how the mind can create, modify, or destroy both past and present. The tale's conclusion underscores Borges' skepticism: the narrator ignores Tlön's incursions to concentrate on translating into Spanish the major work of the seventeenth century English baroque writer, Sir Thomas Browne: *Urn Burial*. Eventually, Borges implies, the vogue of idealism will yield to another, and that to another, ad infinitum.

Conclusion

Like all art forms, short fiction between 1920 and 1960 both reflects and shapes the culture of the period, which is dominated by modernism and postmodernism. To be sure, some of the authors discussed (Welty, Frank O'Connor, Singer, Dinesen, Colette) use traditional fictive techniques and themes to link their vision of humanity to nineteenth century perspectives. Most writers of note, however, imbue their tales with the sense of loss, alienation, and despair that characterizes their age. Short fiction is natural to modern culture's nervousness, impatience, skepticism, intensity, and preference for quickness and compression.

Most writers, from Faulkner and Hemingway to Sartre to Mishima to Borges, question the existence of a coherent and stable social order as they revolt against traditional literary forms. They elevate individual existence over society (Roth, Camus, Babel, Nabokov), unconscious feeling over conscious reasoning (Faulkner, Flannery O'Connor, Malamud, Lawrence), passion and will over intellection and systematic morals (Porter, Cheever, Moravia), dense actuality over practical reality (Greene, Bellow, Mann). They exhibit personal urgency as well as experimental verve. In sum, theirs is a disturbing imagination of disaster, subverting previously accepted modes of existence and revealing the abyss of nothingness over which human lives are precariously poised.

Gerhard Brand

SHORT FICTION SINCE 1960

The one thing that can be said with certainty about the short story since 1960, particularly in the United States, is that the form has been alive and thriving. During this period, more short fiction has been written and published than ever before. One means of gauging this vitality is with a survey of the dozens upon dozens of reviews and journals publishing short fiction: *The New England Review, Georgia Review, Grand Street, Fiction, The Paris Review, Short Story, Mademoiselle, The Kenyon Review, The New Yorker, Cimarron Review, The Missouri Review, Ploughshares,* and *Antæus,* to name only a handful. Another means of gauging the health of the genre would be to take note of how many truly fine contemporary writers have seriously devoted themselves to the art and craft of writing stories. That list would include writers whose talents have been widely recognized (John Cheever, Joyce Carol Oates, Robert Coover, John Updike, Donald Barthelme, Peter Taylor, Raymond Carver, Alice Walker, Louise Erdrich, Mary Robison, and dozens of others) as well as those whose work is only beginning to be recognized (Lynne Sharon Schwartz, François Camoin, W. D. Wetherell, Gladys Swan, Barry Targan, Kazuo Ishiguro, Alberto Alvaro Rios and many others). Between June, 1989, and June, 1990, *The New York Times Book Review* included reviews of about eighty-five American and Canadian short-story collections. Each year, *The Best American Short Stories,* an increasingly popular volume introduced by an essay by that year's guest editor, collects some of the best work produced in the United States, as do *Prize Stories: The O. Henry Awards* and *Pushcart Prize.*

Perhaps the central point to be made is that the short story is one of the leading genres—if not, in fact, *the* leading genre—in the last half of the twentieth century. There is something about the formal dictates of the short story that neatly aligns itself with the historical and psychological temperament of today's society. In other periods, too, various literary forms have, for a variety of reasons, been ascendant or dominant. For the Elizabethans, it was drama; for the Romantics, it was poetry; for the moderns, the novel. In today's "postmodern" world, the short story attracts because the reader can comfortably consume it in one sitting; it can be conveniently read within the little spare time that modern lives afford. This age, furthermore, is an age of narrative indulgence; readers in modern times have little time or patience for laboring over the arcane constructions and erudite symbolic resonances of poetry. Finally, there might be something distinctively postmodern in the very nature of the story—its concentration on the moment, its inevitable fragmentary condition, its predisposition toward irony, its reluctance to come to hard and lasting conclusions—which oddly appeals to, and speaks to, the cultural condition of humankind in the latter part of the twentieth century. All one can ever really get a glimpse of is a fragile shard of human experience; in like manner, the world of the short story is heterogeneous and truncated.

It is easier to make sweeping statements and offer tentative explanations for the phenomenon than to characterize accurately the developments in the short story since 1960, taking into consideration the diversity and number of voices represented. A logical means of proceeding, at least to begin with, is chronologically, beginning with the 1960's and noting important movements and landmarks along the way.

The 1960's: The Avant-Garde and the Old Guard

Though historical periods can never be tidily demarcated, sometime in the early 1960's literary fashion and style began to undergo radical change. The deaths of Richard Wright in 1960, Ernest Hemingway in 1961, William Faulkner in 1962, and Flannery O'Connor in 1964 signaled the end of an era. These changes not so surprisingly coincide with a series of events that rocked the political stage, reverberating in the individual consciousness: the Bay of Pigs Invasion, the assassination of John F. Kennedy, the Vietnam War, the assassinations of Robert F. Kennedy and Martin Luther King, Jr., the 1968 Democratic National Convention in Chicago, and the Cold War.

The literary experimentation of the 1960's must be seen in this context. The likes of Barthelme, Coover, William Gass, Ronald Sukenick, Grace Paley, and John Barth are often (perhaps unfairly) lumped together in discussions of what has been called variously metafiction, irrealism, fabulism, and postmodernism. Consciously departing from conventional realism, these writers focused, in the words of Thomas E. Kennedy, on "the absurd, surreal, nonsequiturs of our everyday lives which consist largely of a series of repetitions which rarely seem to 'progress' at all."

Barth's acknowledged influences include Laurence Sterne, Henry Fielding, Cervantes, and *The Thousand and One Nights*. The writer seeking innovation must, Barth contended, look no longer to Henry James, Leo Tolstoy, Gustave Flaubert, Anton Chekhov, Hemingway, or any other great masters in the realist tradition for models. Thus it is that the Father in Paley's "A Conversation with My Father," pleads with his daughter, a writer, to "write a simple story just once more . . . the kind de Maupassant wrote, or Chekhov, the kind you used to write. Just recognizable people and then write down what happened to them next." Barth's announced interest was not in conventional realistic narrative plots but, rather, in the nature of artifice itself and in extending the limits of what language could in fact do. In Barth's landmark *Lost in the Funhouse* (1968) can be seen many of these innovations. The first piece in the volume, "Frame-Tale," the author describes, in the preface, as a kind of Möbius strip. Vertically, along the outer edge of the page, apparently meant to be cut out, twisted, and taped end-to-end, is the phrase: "ONCE UPON A TIME THERE/ WAS A STORY THAT BEGAN." This is only the beginning of the fun and games, which consistently subvert traditional expectations of what a story is "supposed" to do, frustrating or amusing readers as they lose themselves in the artifice. Continually interrupting a supposed narrative course of "Lost in the Funhouse," for example, are self-reflexive comments, which call attention to the story's fictive quality: "What is the story's theme?" "How long is this going to take?" "Is there really such a person as Ambrose, or is he a figment of the author's imagination?"

Another fine collection to come out of this period is Coover's *Pricksongs and*

Descants (1969), which like *Lost in the Funhouse*, might be thought of as a series of études on the nature of fiction making. Clearly in debt to the Argentine writer Jorge Luis Borges, whose *Labyrinths* (1962, 1964) had considerable influence on American writers during the 1960's and 1970's, Coover's stories call attention to their fictive, invented nature. In "The Babysitter," for example, so many different versions of "events" are given that the reader simply cannot decide which version is "true." That, of course, is the point. No version is true. Stories are just that—stories, imaginary constructions with little or no ontological basis in ordinary reality.

In the preface to his collection *In the Heart of the Heart of the Country and Other Stories* (1968), William H. Gass reflects on the making of the stories in the volume and articulates his views on the form. "The material that makes up a story must be placed under terrible compression, but it cannot simply release its meaning like a joke does. It must be epiphanous, yet remain an enigma. Its shortness must have a formal function: the deepening of the understanding, the darkening of the design." The stories in the volume live up to the author's aesthetic credo. Each story is tight. Gass uses language with a rare sense of economy and precision; works, in fact, seem as much objects in themselves, luminous and tactile, as signifying parts of speech. Stories such as "The Pedersen Kid" and "Icicles" magnificently evoke the cold sweep of the midwestern landscape, with all of its Scandinavian influence. Most experimental formally is the title story, which is broken down into sections with titles such as "A Place," "My House," "A Person," "The Church," "Politics," "Education," and "Business." Like Coover and Barth, Gass has extended the reach of how stories can be constructed.

Longer lasting and more influential than other experimental work has been that of Barthelme. One reason, no doubt, is that Barthelme's teaching has had an impact on a younger generation of writers. Another is that throughout the 1960's and 1970's Barthelme's production of stories never flagged. In 1964 came *Come Back, Dr. Caligari*, in 1968 *Unspeakable Practices, Unnatural Acts*, in 1970 *City Life*, in 1972 *Sadness*, in 1974 *Guilty Pleasures*, in 1976 *Amateurs*, and in 1979 *Great Days*. The collection *Sixty Stories*, which came out in 1981, brought together many works from earlier volumes and cinched Barthelme's reputation.

Barthelme's work is difficult to characterize. Often it has been branded obscure, and much of it certainly is. Frequently, elements in stories are incongruous and narrative logic is derailed. Something of Barthelme's absurdist vision of the modern world bears a likeness to that of Samuel Beckett. The nameless characters in "The Leap," for example, decide to act sometime soon but not today. Miss Arbor, in "A Shower of Gold," tells another character, "*You* may not be interested in absurdity . . . but absurdity is interested in *you*." Stories such as "A Shower of Gold" seem to offer crisp parodies or spoofs of prevailing conventions and practices, while stories such as "The President," "The Indian Uprising," and "Robert Kennedy Saved from Drowning"—by their titles if nothing else—invite readers to speculate regarding some unspecified connection between the story and their own political and historical context. Regardless of how much readers understand, they are always left wondering what Barthelme is doing, and, whatever it is, admiring the effort.

It is important to realize, in constructing any literary history, that many things are going on at the same time. The natural tendency of the historian is to accent the "new" while downplaying or even ignoring concurrent happenings. While experimentalism may be what is ultimately selected as being "representative" or "distinctive" in the 1960's, much else was taking place in the period.

To begin with, significant contributions were made by black writers whose voices, perhaps empowered by the Civil Rights movement of the 1960's, forcefully, energetically, and colorfully portrayed lives too often sadly ignored by mainstream, white America. Two important collections of short fiction produced during this period were James Baldwin's *Going to Meet the Man* (1965) and Ernest J. Gaines's *Bloodline* (1968). No doubt, Baldwin was dramatically struck by the extent of bigotry and racism in the United States upon his return there after a long sojourn in Europe, mainly France. "This Morning, This Evening, So Soon," included in *Best American Short Stories, 1961*, somewhat autobiographical, tells the story of a black American singer coming back to the United States with his son and Swedish wife, Harriet. The return becomes a return to prejudice and psychological bondage. In the title story, Baldwin takes the reader into the psyche of a warped and hate-ridden Southern sheriff. The much-anthologized "Sonny's Blues" symbolically enacts the conciliatory power of art to overcome ingrained suspicions and resentment.

Gaines has been driven by what he often has termed "that Louisiana thing." The stories in *Bloodlines*, such as "A Long Day in November," "Just Like a Tree," and "The Sky Is Gray," draw upon Gaines's intimate connection to his Louisiana roots. Gaines has a marvelous ear for dialogue, and his first concern is to tell a good story. The stories that he tells, however, inevitably raise questions involving racial identity, the effect of heritage on characters, generational differences, moral values, and the place of religion and education in personal lives. Like Langston Hughes and Richard Wright before them, and many younger writers since, Gaines and Baldwin each struggled to achieve a sense of artistic integrity while remaining aware of social responsibilities.

Most prolific indeed during this period, from the 1960's through the 1990's, has been Joyce Carol Oates. Oates, as critic and fiction writer, is ubiquitous, and no survey of American short fiction during this period would be complete without mention of her work. If any theme unites Oates's work, which is experimental at times and realistic at others, it might be that she tends to portray characters vulnerable or at risk, as in "Gay" or "Where Are You Going, Where Have You Been?" or her revision of Chekhov's "Lady with a Pet Dog." Very often, the tension in an Oates work involves the specter of violence, that all-American pastime. Very often, too, her focus is on young women and their unique struggles, usually involving men.

While, again, we recall the more radical literary experimentation of the 1960's, the dominant vein of short fiction produced during the 1960's and 1970's might actually be those plentiful realistic fictional representations of white, middle-class, Anglo-

Saxon, suburban life. The names of John Cheever and John Updike loom almost larger than life.

The publication of *The Stories of John Cheever* (1978) not only solidified the writer's personal reputation, already firmly established by his longtime association with *The New Yorker*, but also demonstrated that a collection of short fiction, at least by a writer of great stature, could be a commercial success. Cheever, reared in Quincy, Massachusetts, has much in common with his New England predecessors Nathaniel Hawthorne and Henry James. Cheever brilliantly captures both a sense of New England, as place, and the psychological character of the white, middle-class individuals who have run it for so many years. Cheever's work is preoccupied with the struggles of individuals to reconcile their deeper, sometimes darker, natures with the social stage upon which they are forced to act, although reluctantly. As Cheever put it in the preface to his collected stories, "The constants that I look for in this somewhat dated paraphernalia are a love of light and a determination to trace some moral chain of being. Calvin played no part at all in my religious education, but his presence seemed to abide in the barns of my childhood and to have left me with some undue bitterness." Beneath respectable surfaces lie loneliness, alcoholism, deep and powerful lusts, and a profound emptiness. As realistic as Cheever's stories often are, he frequently pushes experience in the direction of the surreal, such as in "The Swimmer," where the very action of the story seems all at once preposterous and understandable, and time is fractured in personal, mythical, and societal planes.

Updike, born in Pennsylvania and educated at Harvard University, has drawn on similar raw materials as those upon which Cheever relied. In an early story, "A Dogwood Tree," Updike described tentatively what might be taken as his artistic modus operandi: "To transcribe middleness with all its grits, bumps, and anonymities, in its fullness of satisfaction and mystery: is it possible or, in view of the suffering that violently colors the periphery and that at all moments threatens to move into the center, worth doing?" During the 1960's, Updike produced three collections of short fiction: *Pigeon Feathers and Other Stories* (1962), *Olinger Stories: A Selection* (1964), and *The Music School* (1966). Many of these stories depend on memory, reaching back, nostalgically, toward the characters' youth, to find solace and wholeness. Others center on the uncomfortable realities of maturity: the problems surrounding fidelity and marriage, the maintenance of hope, the elusiveness of happiness and love. Schweigen, the writer in "The Music School," is just such a character, propelled by a hard-edged, almost naturalistic vision of the world. Updike is without question one of the contemporary masters of the genre in its realistic mode, defining and portraying a central vein of American middle-class experience.

The Resurgence of Realism: Toward the 1990's

Though some proponents of experimentalism, such as Barthelme, continued working the vein through the 1970's, this literary fashion had, for all intents and purposes, lost its steam by the mid-1970's. Writing in the space reserved for the guest editor of *The Best American Short Stories*, Oates in 1979 wrote, "It seems to me that metafiction's ironies have begun to run out, or to repeat themselves with dismaying frequency." This conclusion Oates reached after observing:

A gap of sorts has widened between what might be called traditional fiction, with its emphasis on psychologically "realistic" characters in recognizable settings who are moved, usually with some direction, through time and space, and what might be called meta-fiction: prose that aspires to the bodiless condition of poetry, or pure sound, the "new music" of Barthelme's story, which is no longer entirely new, though its dissonances and relentless non sequiturs make claims of newness.

No particular style dominated in the 1970's. In characterizing the stories forming the 1976 *Best American Short Stories*, editor Martha Foley noted, "Their variety is astonishing. They can be innovative or traditional, realistic or romantic, light-hearted or tragic, concise as a fable or long as a novella." For this period, it is much easier to identify certain productive practitioners of the art of the short story than it is to characterize trends. Notable voices emerging or carrying on during this period include those of Andre Dubus, Russell Banks, Leslie Marmon Silko, Barry Targan, Frederick Busch, Oates, Paul Bowles, Ann Beattie, Wright Morris, Alice Walker, Peter Taylor, Stanley Elkin, Sharon Sheehe Stark, Gladys Swan, Charles Baxter, Ron Hansen, Guy Davenport, and Lynne Sharon Schwartz. This list in itself is suggestive of the diversity to be found among the stories of the 1970's.

The style that gradually gained ascendance in the latter part of the 1970's and 1980's has been called "neo-realism," "minimalism," or "K-Mart Fiction." Its prime proponents have been Beattie, Carver, Tobias Wolff, Bobbie Ann Mason, Alice Adams, Mary Robison, and Frederick Barthelme (Donald's younger brother).

As unfair as it might be to lump such divergent writers together in a group and put a label on them, they do all seem to share certain thematic and stylistic concerns. Above all, they all signal a deliberate return to "realism," almost with a vengeance. Of course, realism has never died. It has always existed as a popular mode of fiction writing. It had—and no doubt will have again, in time—merely lost its edge in trend-setting literary circles. The realism seen in the short fiction of the 1980's, however, must be distinguished from that, for example, of the contemporary realist Updike. The stories of this new generation of writers have sought not so much to supply readers with a full and accurate picture of the world as to insert certain poignant facts and tell a story as economically and efficiently as possible. The assumption of many of these writers seems to be that contemporary readers would immediately recognize this world as their own and fill out the picture themselves.

Carver's philosophy can be summed up in the following statement: "It's possible to write about commonplace things and objects using commonplace but precise language, and to endow these things—a chair, a window curtain, a fork, a stone, a woman's earring—with immense, even startling power. It is possible to write a line of seemingly innocuous dialogue and have it send a chill along the reader's spine." Elsewhere, in a 1987 interview with the Paris-based American literary journal *Frank*, Carver, distinguishing himself from the more experimental tradition that had preceded him, claimed: "The work of many of the writers who came into prominence in the Sixties is not going to last. . . . Literature is coming back to the things that count. . . . Readers have gotten tired of fiction that's gotten too far away from the real concerns." Readers might bear in mind that while Carver's stories reached the height of their popularity, they began to appear as early as the mid-1960's, at the same time that Coover, Barth, and Barthelme were enjoying their widest following.

Immensely popular have been the stories of Carver that deal with "the things that count" and "the real concerns." They have been so popular, in fact, that Carver clones began to spring up in droves in literary magazines across the United States. Chief among the volumes of stories published before Carver's death in 1988 are *Will You Please Be Quiet, Please?* (1976), *What We Talk About When We Talk About Love* (1981), and *Cathedral* (1984). Carver's characters, typified in stories such as "Boxes" and "What We Talk About When We Talk About Love," generally feel hemmed in by their work and relationships and seem able to communicate only within the frames of their first-person tales.

Mason's Kentucky bears more likeness to Carver's and Wolff's Northwest than one might originally think, rather like the dull uniformity of the nationwide franchises, which their characters frequent. Mason's characters, like Carver's, are generally lower-middle-class, are concerned with their jobs, shop at discount stores at malls, watch Phil Donahue and Johnny Carson on television, listen to Hank Williams, drive trucks, eat fried chicken, and bemoan a vacancy in their lives. Mason herself has described her own work as "southern Gothic going to the supermarket." This blend can be seen in "Shiloh," one of Mason's best-known stories. The two main characters are Norma Jean Moffitt, who works at Rexall Drugs, where she has "acquired an amazing amount of information about cosmetics," and her husband Leroy, who is laid up from a trucking accident and makes model log cabins out of Popsicle sticks. The story unrolls, like television, in the present tense, in a series of connected narrative units. All scenes point to the final one in which the young couple finally fulfill Norma Jean's mother's plea for them to visit the old Civil War battlefield at Shiloh, shrouded for her in a mist of romantic memories. Norma Jean transforms the meaning of the site by using it as a place to inform her husband of her intention to leave him.

It is no accident that the kind of neorealism popular in the 1980's coincided with the Reagan-Bush decade, an era marked by growing personal and national indebtedness, a turning away from social responsibilities, and the unabated pursuit of personal wealth. The characters in Carver's and Mason's stories seem to have benefited little, if at all, from the reputed era of national prosperity and economic growth. Their lives are impoverished and dull, as they hang on from paycheck to paycheck, thinking only of their cars, their jobs, and their apartments—living cynically with little drama or hope for improvement in their condition.

Ethnic Voices

The identification of various stylistic trends in the short story goes only so far in accounting for recent activity in the genre. Fresh categories need to be made that recognize contributions of writers rooted either in a regional allegiance or ethnic heritage.

Black writers have perhaps found the novel a form better suited than the short story for the wider sweeps of cultural critique. Alice Walker, John Edgar Wideman, Charles Johnson, and Toni Morrison have notably devoted their talent to the novel, with great success. Among those who have gained recognition for their stories are Walker, Toni Cade Bambara (whose "The Lesson" is a commonly anthologized work), and James Alan McPherson. Chronicling the contemporary Native American experience have been Leslie Marmon Silko, Louise Erdrich, and James Ferry. Similarly, Sandra Cisneros has written compellingly of the experience of Mexican Americans (*Woman Hollering Creek and Other Stories*, 1991), as has David Wong Louey of the Asian American.

Particularly significant and powerful have been the contributions to the short story made by Jewish American writers. Though the short story oeuvre of Nobel laureate Saul Bellow is not large, those stories he has written are absolutely first-rate. Like the work of his contemporary Bernard Malamud, Bellow's fiction explores the meaning of Jewishness within the context of the American experience. Malamud, speaking of his role as a Jewish writer, has said, "I handle the Jew as a symbol of the tragic experience of man existentially. I try to see the Jew as universal man. Every man is a Jew though he may not know it." The rich heritage and distinctive linguistic texture these writers bring to bear on their art can be seen for example, in stories such as Malamud's "The First Seven Years" and "The Mourners," Bellow's "Mosby's Memoirs" and "The Silver Dish," Paley's "Goodbye and Good Luck," Roth's "The Conversion of the Jews," and Elkin's "Criers and Kibbitzers, Kibbitzers and Criers."

Cynthia Ozick is another Jewish writer who has devoted serious attention to the relation between the present and the past, notably the Holocaust, and between the Jewish experience in Central and Eastern Europe and in the United States. Ozick's craftsmanship, tough language, and philosophical depth are virtually peerless. The writer in her story "Yiddish in America," Ostrover, who still writes in Yiddish after his immigration to the United States, bears an uncanny resemblance to Isaac Bashevis Singer, yet another Jewish writer who has added color to the American literary scene after immigrating from Poland in 1935. Something of an anomaly in American letters, Singer continued to write in Yiddish. The majority of Singer's stories are set in a temporally indistinct past of towns and cities of his native Poland: Rampol, Chełm, Lublin, and Warsaw. They are filled with imaginative storytelling, magical transformations, grotesque and supernatural human beings, unlikely events, dwarfs, devils, and angels. They are, in other words, rather as if the paintings of Marc Chagall had come to life, and become imbued with narrative content. Even Singer's contemporary Jewish Americans, traveling from New York to Miami, share much of the reality that shapes and informs the lives of Gimpel, Zlateh, or the Spinoza of Market Street. Singer's world, like the twentieth century, is one in which cruelty coexists with kindness, horror with happiness, and love with violence and hatred.

God's plan is humanly incomprehensible, and the only course for human beings is to register the absurdities and endure the suffering along with the miraculous.

Among a younger generation of Jewish American short-story writers, Mark Helprin and Sharon Lynne Schwartz deserve mention. Helprin's stories, metaphysically gripping and linguistically masterful, have been collected in two fine volumes: *A Dove of the East and Other Stories* (1975) and *Ellis Island and Other Stories* (1981). In the title story of the latter volume, Helprin re-creates in remarkable detail the experiences of early Jewish immigrants at Ellis Island; "North Light—A Recollection in the Present Tense" retrieves and inscribes the memories of an Israeli soldier in the Six-Day War. The title story of Schwartz's *The Melting Pot and Other Subversive Stories* (1987) portrays the predicament of a young Jewish woman and her relationship with Sanjay, an Indian American. Both seek ways to deal with their ethnic heritages and at the same time fit into mainstream American culture.

Writers of the New South

No other region of the United States has in the past half century or more produced such a rich and distinctive fiction than has the South, with its unique culture, flavor, and historical experience. The profoundly powerful wave of literary production in the South, which began in the 1920's and was carried on by the likes of William Faulkner, Katherine Anne Porter, Eudora Welty, and Robert Penn Warren, has been followed by second and third waves. The work of many of these writers can be found in *The New Writers of the South: A Fiction Anthology* (1987), edited by Charles East. While Southern writers of the first half of the twentieth century chronicled intense struggles with history (the legacy of the Civil War) and its presence in personal memory, contemporary Southern writers write about the unique problems posed by the evolving shape and identity of the New South. It has been said of Southern writing that its impulse has always been to try desperately to hang on to what has already slipped away by preserving that waning order in fictional form. That certainly has been the case in contemporary Southern writing, which reaches back toward rural landscapes and seeks to clarify a connection to the past. Jan Nordby Gretlund has written that "the general tendency in Southern fiction today is a concern with loneliness and the disintegration of minds, lives, marriages, families, relationships, community, and tradition."

One of the foremost practitioners of the short story in the South, consistently producing over the past several decades, is Peter Taylor. Like most Southern writers, Taylor depicts a world in which characters strive to hold on to old ways and live by old loyalties in the face of an increasingly powerful, inexorable newer order, one more racially integrated, more urban, and propelled by Snopesian values. Indicative of this vision is that found in the title story of his volume *In the Miro District and Other Stories* (1977). The conflict in the story, set in Nashville, centers on a generational rift between a grandson and his grandfather, an old Civil War veteran.

While writers such as Taylor have insisted that "the past is still real and present somehow and is demanding something of all men . . . who pass that way" (*A*

Summons to Memphis), others, such as Barry Hannah, have often tried to shirk the burden of the past. "All the generations of wonderful dead guys behind us," writes Hannah in *Boomerang*. "All the Confederate dead and the Union dead planted in the soil near us. All of Faulkner the great. Christ, there's barely room for the living down here." Hannah's fiction, here and elsewhere, has an irreverent tone that is, ironically, distinctly characteristic of the Southern rebel character against which he sets himself.

In surveying the contemporary Southern literary scene one cannot help noticing how much of the fiction is being written by women. Virtually every state of the Old Confederacy is represented: Shirley Ann Grau (Louisiana), Mary Hood (Georgia), Rebecca Hill (Tennessee), Beverly Lowry (Texas), Jill McCorkle (North Carolina), Ann Beattie (Virginia), Mary Ward Brown (Alabama), Josephine Humphreys (South Carolina), Ellen Gilchrist (Mississippi), and Bobbie Ann Mason (Kentucky). These writers are particularly sensitive to the struggles of women in the changing world around them, a world that remains, at heart, extremely conventional and male-dominated. These changes in gender roles may, in part, account for the great amount of marital distress in contemporary Southern fiction, indeed all contemporary American fiction. In Mason's "Shiloh," for example, readers see Norma Jean wielding barbells while her husband's ego shrivels in his unemployment. Much ambivalence, even among women writers, surrounds the women's liberation movement. A woman in Hood's ironically titled "Inexorable Progress" hands out pamphlets against the ERA, saying that it threatens traditional family values. Her reception is little different than it would have been had she been campaigning on the other side. Things in the South sometimes do not seem to want to move in any direction.

In a story such as Ruth Moose's "King of the Comics," the struggle between old and new values is seen in the relationship between a mother and a daughter. The daughter complains to her mother that a young man has tried to pull off her clothes. It soon becomes apparent that the mother, rather than placing the blame on the boy, becomes angry at her daughter. "If you had been wearing a bra," she finally announces, "this would not have happened." The struggle, however, is not merely against the patriarchy, but, as it is with many of Faulkner's characters, against an increasingly mechanized, scientific, and industrial order. In the tradition of the Southern agrarians of the 1930's remains an effort to uphold aesthetic, humanistic, and agrarian values.

Thematic Concerns of Contemporary Short Fiction

This discussion, particularly the last section, has been laced with observations concerning the thematic preoccupations of contemporary short-story writers. Yet in the interests of trying to define more precisely the relation between the story and contemporary American society, the discussion might more explicitly focus on the thematic content of these stories. Just what are the issues with which contemporary writers are grappling? Leslie Fiedler once asserted that, historically, there have been only two subjects for the short story—terror and isolation. On a most fundamental level, this may hold true, though these concerns have manifested themselves in quite specific configurations in modern times. Certainly, at the core of most stories are human relationships, the pressures and strains that interactions place on characters. Central, then, are family relationships—between brothers, fathers and sons, spouses, sisters, mothers and daughters, and so forth. In the contemporary story, the reader frequently encounters narratives that, in some fashion, center on the breakup of the family. Updike's "Separating," Rick DeMarinis's "Gent," and Dubus's "Rose," come to mind as particular examples of this theme's enactment.

Victimization, of various racial groups, children, and women, has been yet another significant thematic concern, as a survey of published stories reveals. Anya Achtenberg's "Cold Ground" addresses the problem of homelessness. T. Coraghessan Boyle's "Carnal Knowledge" is woven around concerns for animal rights, particularly mass-produced turkeys. Alice Schell's "Slamming on Pig's Misery," Madison S. Bell's "Dragon's Seed," and Mona Simpson's "I Am Here to Tell You It Can Be Done" all deal daringly and boldly with child abuse. Ewing Campbell's "Sen-Sen," E. S. Goldman's "Good Works," and (again) Simpson's "I Am Here to Tell You It Can Be Done" lay bare the ugliness of religious charlatanism and hypocrisy, the kind brought to public attention through the misdeeds and transgressions of Jim and Tammy Faye Bakker and Jimmy Swaggart.

Contemporary writers have also sought ways in fiction of coming to terms with unpleasant chapters of the past. While during the Vietnam War remarkably little fiction was written about that experience, it has subsequently been a subject for a good many writers, first among whom is Tim O'Brien, whose novel *Going After Cacciato* (1987) is doubtless one of the best pieces of American literature to come out of the Vietnam experience. In "How to Tell a True War Story," O'Brien wrestles with the problems of writing "realistic" fiction about a war so surreal and far-removed from the experiences of the ordinary reader. In another successful story, "Field Trip," O'Brien's narrator makes a pilgrimage back to the rice paddies of Vietnam with his ten-year-old daughter, seeking to locate the site of a buddy's death. W. D. Wetherell's "Hundred Year War" develops the Vietnam theme from a different angle. Back in Washington, D.C., a Vietnamese cab driver, Ngo Quang, suffers the abuses of anti-Asian sentiments and in his own way tries tangibly to seek connection with his homeland and the United States, symbolically, by snaking his way to the Vietnam War Memorial, the wall, as if protecting himself from the threat of machine-gun fire.

Not only in this story but also in others (such as the fine volumes *The Man Who Loved Levittown*, 1985, and *Hyannis Boat and Other Stories*, 1989), Wetherell has created stories that attempt somehow to define just what the American experience in the second half of the twentieth century means. Nowhere can this be better seen, perhaps, than in "The Mall: A History" and "The Next Sound You Hear." In the former, which begins with the arresting line, "It's hard to go shopping without thinking of the end of the world," the narrator measures his own development against that of a particular Long Island mall, which had at various intervals figured in his life's meandering narrative. The view that emerges is one of a transitory life-style, where one store or fashion or friendship gives way, overnight, to another.

A clash of values again figures in "The Next Sound You Hear," a story of Silva, a disc jockey who has sought refuge from barbarism in northern New Hampshire only to find himself tormented by another disc jockey, Dr. Weird, proponent of heavy metal and idol of teenagers. Dr. Weird systematically and perversely destroys and defaces Silva's classical record and tape library, including the likes of Giacomo Puccini, Claude Debussy, and Gustav Mahler. Dramatically, Wetherell represents the cult of intimidation posed by the mechanisms of popular culture and the sense of despair growing over those who might hope to escape its clutches or hold on to the more classical, canonized artifacts of Western culture. At one point, Silva complains to his wife, with sorrow if not bitterness:

> It's not even different up here anymore. Before we could pretend it was, but it isn't, not in a real
> sense. Everywhere is the same now. We've been here fifteen years and we still live like strangers.
> Before we could console ourselves with the forest and the lake and all, but now they've been
> spoiled, too. If we have to endure ugliness, I want to endure it in a place I belong.

Doubtless this is the sentiment of more than one American.

Not all contemporary stories dwell wholly in the realm of the serious. In fact, it would be a great oversight not to acknowledge the great quantity of wit found in contemporary stories. The clever conceits, for example, of stories such as Gordon Weaver's "The Interpreter," Barry Targan's "Harry Belten and the Mendelssohn Violin Concerto," Bellow's "The Silver Dish," T. Coraghessan Boyle's "Carnal Knowledge," and Lynne Sharon Schwartz's "The Last Frontier" make them linger pleasantly in the reader's memory.

Taken collectively, considered as a tapestry or quilt made of small pieces, the contemporary short story can be thought of as a manifestation of that great American Whitmanesque vision of the United States. All walks of life are represented, all classes, all ethnic groups, side by side. Together they might be taken as that great American poem which is the United States itself.

Widening the Compass

Theorists such as Jacques Derrida, Michel Foucault, Edward Said, and Michel de Certeau have devoted considerable attention to the relation between the center and the periphery, and the consequences of these relations of power on various forms of cultural production, including literature. This survey of short fiction since 1960 has quite consciously centered on developments in the United States. The predicament of the Third World writer has elsewhere been described at length. Certainly one of the reasons readers in the United States do not know more about literature of other cultures (let alone their own) is that they have limited access to it. When translations are made, there is always a lag time between the work's first appearance and its appearance in translation. Most works are simply not translated into English because there is neither the will nor the prospect of profit.

When scope of inquiry is expanded, however, one can readily ascertain that the short story has enjoyed considerable good health in other cultures, too. The best that can be done, perhaps, in the limited space available here, is to identify a number of works available to English readers and worthy of their attention.

For starters, one of the finest writers of short stories is William Trevor, who hails from Ireland. Prodigious indeed has been Trevor's output over the past several decades, including titles such as *The Day We Got Drunk on Cake and Other Stories* (1967), *The Ballroom of Romance and Other Stories* (1972), *Angels at the Ritz and Other Stories* (1975), *Lovers of Their Time and Other Stories* (1978), *Beyond the Pale and Other Stories* (1981), *The News from Ireland and Other Stories* (1986), and *Family Sins and Other Stories* (1990). Across the Irish Sea, one of the foremost English writers registering the pulse of English life for a good many decades is V. S. Pritchett.

Since "El Boom," the dramatic explosion of Latin America in the 1960's, the public has become aware of the large body of fine work being produced in that region. A good collection of stories to begin with is *The Eye of the Heart* (1973). Marjorie Agosin has put together an anthology of fiction by contemporary women writers in Latin America, *Landscapes of a New Land* (1989).

The short story has long been a popular genre in the Middle East. In Egypt, besides the well-known writings of Yusuf Idris and Naguib Mahfouz, the stories of Yahyia Taher Abdullah (*The Mountain of Green Tea*, 1983) and Alifa Rifaat (*Distant View of a Minaret*, 1983), both translated by Denys Johnson-Davis, are exciting. William Hutchins has also edited a collection of contemporary Egyptian stories, brought out by The American University in Cairo Press. A. B. Yehoshua's stories, collected in *The Continuing Silence of a Poet* (1991), depict realities and contradictions of life in contemporary Israel.

For stories from Africa, one can turn to *African Short Stories*, selected and edited by Chinua Achebe and C. L. Innes (1985) or *African Short Stories* (1985). K. Natwar-Singh has edited and introduced *Stories from India* (1972).

Interest in fiction coming out of Eastern Europe and the Soviet Union will likely grow as a result of the radical political changes that have swept across that region. It will, of course, take some time for events to take aesthetic form and then to be translated. A number of collections of later Russian/Soviet fiction are, however, available: *Bad Company and Other Stories* (1986); *Balancing Acts: Contemporary Stories by Russian Women* (1989); *The New Soviet Fiction* (1989), sixteen short stories compiled by Sergei Zalygin; and *New Voices: A Collection of Soviet Short Stories* (1985), compiled by Yuri Lupusov.

Furrows, Peasants, Intellectuals, and the State (1990), compiled by Helen F. Siu, pulls together stories from contemporary China, as have *Best Chinese Stories, 1949-1989* (1989) and *Contemporary Chinese Short Stories* (1983). Several anthologies contain contemporary Japanese short fiction, among them *The Showa Anthology*, vol. 2 (1985); *Stories by Contemporary Japanese Women Writers* (1982); *Contemporary Japanese Literature* (1977), edited by Howard Hibbett; Kenzaburō Ōe's *Five from the Ashes: Stories on Hiroshima and Nagasaki* (1985); and *This Kind of Woman: Ten Stories by Japanese Women Writers, 1960-1976* (1982).

Even the cursory survey of short fiction from around the world shows astonishing diversity and richness. For registering the individual's relations to things, circumstances, desires, dreams, personal tragedy, and trauma, the form of the short story continues to be extraordinarily versatile, full of yet unrealized potential.

Allen Hibbard

SHORT STORY CRITICISM:
AN ANNOTATED BIBLIOGRAPHY

Allen, Walter. *The Short Story in English.* Oxford, England: Clarendon Press, 1981. A historical study of the development of the form in England and America. Primarily a series of biographical discussions of authors and summary discussions of stories. Good for providing a framework for the development of the form.

Averill, Deborah. *The Irish Short Story from George Moore to Frank O'Connor.* Washington, D.C.: University Press of America, 1982. An introductory study of the Irish short story intended primarily for teachers and students. Surveys historical conditions in the nineteenth and early twentieth centuries that contributed to the development of the Irish short story and discusses the major stories of George Moore, James Joyce, Seumas O'Kelly, Daniel Corkery, Liam O'Flaherty, Seán O'Faoláin, and Frank O'Connor. Discusses each writer's basic style or concept of form and recurrent themes.

Aycock, Wendell M., ed. *The Teller and the Tale: Aspects of the Short Story.* Lubbock: Texas Tech Press, 1982. A collection of papers presented at a scholarly conference focusing on various aspects of short fiction, including its oral roots, the use of silences in the text, and realism versus antirealism.

Bader, A. L. "The Structure of the Modern Short Story." *College English* 7 (1945): 86-92. Counters the charge that the short story lacks narrative structure by contrasting the traditional "plotted" story with the modern story, which is more suggestive, indirect, and technically patterned.

Baldeshwiler, Eileen. "The Lyric Short Story: The Sketch of a History." *Studies in Short Fiction* 6 (1969): 443-453. A brief survey of the lyrical (as opposed to the epical) story from Ivan Turgenev to John Updike. The lyric story focuses on internal changes, moods, and feelings, utilizing a variety of structural patterns depending on the "shape of the emotion itself."

Baldwin, Dean. "The English Short Story in the Fifties." In *The English Short Story, 1945-1980,* edited by Dennis Vanatta. Boston: Twayne, 1985. Argues that after World War II, Great Britain experienced a bureaucratization of everyday life. Focuses on stories of social protest, especially those of Alan Sillitoe; the supernatural stories of Sylvia Townsend Warner and Muriel Spark; the mainstream writers H. E. Bates, V. S. Pritchett, Spark, and Rhys Davies; and the major writers Doris Lessing, Sillitoe, Roald Dahl, Angus Wilson, William Sansom, and Elizabeth Taylor.

Bates, H. E. *The Modern Short Story: A Critical Survey.* Boston: The Writer, 1941, 1972. A history of the major short-story writers and their work since Edgar Allan Poe and Nikolai Gogol. More focus on English and European short-story writers than most histories.

Bayley, John. *The Short Story: Henry James to Elizabeth Bowen.* New York: St. Martin's Press, 1988. A discussion of some of what Bayley calls the "special effects" of the short-story form, particularly its relationship to poetic techniques and devices. Much of the book consists of analyses of significant stories by Henry James, Ernest Hemingway, Rudyard Kipling, Anton Chekhov, D. H. Lawrence, James Joyce, and Elizabeth Bowen.

Beachcroft, T. O. *The Modest Art: A Survey of the Short Story in English.* London: Oxford University Press, 1968. A historical survey of the major figures of the English short story from Geoffrey Chaucer to Doris Lessing. The result of the basic difference between antique stories (listening) and modern stories (reading) is that modern short-story writers attempt to portray rather than expound. They remove their own personality from the story and present the flash of insight through poetic needs.

Benjamin, Walter. "The Storyteller: Reflections on the Words of Nikolai Leskov." Reprinted in *Modern Literary Criticism: 1900-1970,* edited by Lawrence Lipking and A. Walton Litz. New York: Atheneum, 1972. Benjamin claims that the art of storytelling is coming to an end because of the widespread dissemination of information and explanation. The compactness of a story precludes analysis and appeals to readers by the rhythm of the work itself. For the storyteller, the old religious chronicle is secularized into an ambiguous network in which the worldly and the eschatological are interwoven.

Black, John, and Colleen M. Seifert. "The Psychological Study of Story Understanding." In *Researching Response to Literature and the Teaching of Literature,* edited by Charles R. Cooper. Norwood, N.J.: Ablex, 1985. Argues that when people read stories, they use the same psychological processes to comprehend the events in the story that they use to comprehend life. By studying how people respond to stories, psychologists can discover how people understand and remember. Cognitive research has shown that the knowledge of the world that readers bring to a story determines their understanding, whereas their memory of it is organized around schemata.

Bone, Robert. *Down Home: A History of Afro-American Short Fiction from Its Beginnings to the End of the Harlem Renaissance.* New York: Capricorn Books, 1975. Provides a background for the African-American folktale, the Brer Rabbit Tales, and the local-color writers; devotes a chapter each to Paul Laurence Dunbar, Charles Waddell Chesnutt, Jean Toomer, Langston Hughes, and Arna Bontemps. Also contains a chapter on the Harlem Renaissance, with mention of Zora Neale Hurston and others. Shows how the African-American short story is the child of a mixed heritage.

Bonheim, Helmut. *The Narrative Modes: Techniques of the Short Story.* Cambridge, England: D. S. Brewer, 1982. A systematic and statistical study of the short-story form, focusing on basic short-story techniques, especially short-story beginnings and endings. Argues that a limited set of techniques is used in story endings again and again. Discusses open and closed endings and argues that dynamic modes are more apt to be open, while static ones are more apt to be closed.

Boulanger, Daniel. "On the Short Story." *Michigan Quarterly Review* 26 (Summer, 1987): 510-514. A highly metaphoric and impressionistic study of the form that focuses primarily on the detached nature of the short story. Claims that there is a bit of Pontius Pilate in the short-story writer, for he or she is always removed from the tragic outcome. Points out how there are no class distinctions in the short story, no hierarchy.

Bowen, Elizabeth, ed. *The Faber Book of Modern Short Stories.* London: Faber & Faber, 1936. Bowen suggests that the short story, because it is exempt from the novel's often forced conclusiveness, more often approaches aesthetic and moral truth. She also suggests that the short story, more than the novel, is able to place the individual alone on that "stage which, inwardly, every man is conscious of occupying alone."

Boyce, Benjamin. "English Short Fiction in the Eighteenth Century: A Preliminary View." *Studies in Short Fiction* 5 (1968): 95-112. Discusses the types of short fiction found in periodicals and inserted in novels: character sketch, Oriental tale, stories of passion. Usually the purpose was didactic and the mode was either "hovering pathos" or "hovering irony." The most distinctive characteristic is the formal, even elegant language.

Brown, Suzanne Hunter. "Discourse Analysis and the Short Story." In *Short Story Theory at a Crossroads*, edited by Susan Lohafer and Jo Ellyn Clarey. Baton Rouge: Louisiana State University Press, 1989. A helpful analytical survey of the research being carried on by psychologists into the nature of discourse, storyness, and cognitive response to narrative.

Brushwood, John S. "The Spanish American Short Story from Quiroga to Borges." In *The Latin American Short Story: A Critical History*, edited by Margaret Sayers Peden. Boston: Twayne, 1983. Horacio Quiroga was the first Spanish American writer to pay close attention to how a story is created. The late 1920's and early 1930's were characterized by innovative narration, a movement to regionalism took place in the mid-1930's, and a return to innovation and cosmopolitanism characterized the early 1940's.

Burgess, Anthony. "Anthony Burgess on the Short Story." *Journal of the Short Story in English*, no. 2 (1984): pp. 31-47. Burgess admits that he disdains the short story because he cannot write it. He says that the novel presents an epoch, while the short story presents a revelation. Discusses different types of stories, distinguishing between the literary short story, which is patterned, and the commercial form, which is anecdotal.

Carens, James F. "In Quest of a New Impulse: George Moore's *The Untilled Field* and James Joyce's *Dubliners*." In *The Irish Short Story: A Critical History*, edited by James F. Kilroy. Boston: Twayne, 1984. Carens provides analyses of the major stories in these two most influential collections of Irish short fiction. Discusses the major contributions of the stories of Moore and Joyce responsible for creating the modern Anglo-Irish short story. Explains Moore's influence on Joyce, analyzing Joyce's "Counterparts" as a reworking of Moore's "The Clerk's Quest."

Chatman, Seymour. "New Ways of Analyzing Narrative Structure, with an Example from Joyce's *Dubliners*." *Language and Style* 2 (1969): 3-36. A "test" of the narrative theories of Roland Barthes and Tzvetan Todorov, with a detailed analysis of James Joyce's "Eveline." The story is considered both in terms of the internal relations of the narrative and the external relations between narrator and reader.

Clarke, John H. "Transition in the American Negro Short Story." *Phylon* 21 (1960): 360-366. A shorter version of this article appears as the introduction to *American Negro Short Stories*, edited by John Henrik Clarke (1966). A brief historical survey of the African-American short story from Paul Laurence Dunbar and Charles Waddell Chesnutt at the beginning of the twentieth century, through the Harlem Renaissance of the 1920's, to the emergence of Richard Wright, who marked the end of the double standard for black writers.

Connolly, Julian. "The Russian Short Story, 1880-1917." In *The Russian Short Story: A Critical History*, edited by Charles A. Moser. Boston: Twayne, 1986. Most of this essay focuses on Nikolai Leskov, Anton Chekhov, Maxim Gorky, Ivan Bunin, and Leonid Andreyev. Briefly discusses the Symbolist movement's influence on Russian literature at the end of the nineteenth century.

Cortázar, Julio. "Some Aspects of the Short Story." *Arizona Quarterly*, Spring, 1982, 5-17. A discussion of the invariable elements that give a good short story its particular atmosphere. Says that the novel and the short story can be compared to the film and the photograph. The short story's most significant element is its subject, the act of choosing a real or imaginary happening that has the mysterious property of illuminating something beyond itself.

Current-Garcia, Eugene. *The American Short Story, Before 1850*. Boston: Twayne, 1985. Focuses on the types of magazine fiction before 1820. Devotes individual chapters to Washington Irving, Nathaniel Hawthorne, and Edgar Allan Poe. Also includes a chapter on William Gilmore Simms and the frontier humorists, such as George Washington Harris. The shift toward realism in the last chapter is largely a result of the fiction of Herman Melville.

Current-Garcia, Eugene, and Walter R. Patrick. Introduction to *American Short Stories*. Rev. ed. Chicago: Scott, Foresman, 1964. A historical survey of the American short story through four periods: Romanticism, realism, naturalism, and the modern period of both traditionalists (those who have carried on the Poe/de Maupassant/James tradition) and experimentalists (those who have focused more on the fragmented inner world of the mind).

_____, eds. *What Is the Short Story?* Rev. ed. New York: Scott, Foresman, 1974. Although this volume is primarily a short-story anthology, it contains a generous selection of mostly American criticism on the short story, arranged in chronological order. Contains a four-page general bibliography on the short story.

Dollerup, Cay. "The Concepts of 'Tension,' 'Intensity,' and 'Suspense' in Short-Story Theory." *Orbis Litterarum* 25 (1970): 314-337. A heavily documented survey of critical theory in German, Danish, and English on the concepts of intensity or tension in the short story and how these terms have been applied to linguistic rhythm, contrast, character, structure, and reader suspense in the form.

Duncan, Edgar Hill. "Short Fiction in Medieval English: A Survey." *Studies in Short*

Fiction 9 (1972): 1-28. A survey of short pieces in the Old English period, primarily in verse, that have in common the characteristic of "artfully telling a story in a relatively brief compass" and that focus on "singleness of character, of action, and/or impression." The fall of the angels and the fall of man in the *Genesis B*, the St. Guthlac poems, and *The Dream of the Rood* are analyzed.

_____. "Short Fiction in Medieval English: II. The Middle English Period." *Studies in Short Fiction* 11 (1974): 227-241. A brief sampling of short fiction elements in the "shorter romance" form, the exemplary narrative, the beast tale, and the fabliau introduced to Middle English by the French. Also noted are paraphrases of biblical stories, saints' lives, and the dream visions of *The Pearl* and Geoffrey Chaucer's "The Book of the Duchess" and the "Prologue to the Legend of Good Women."

Dunleavy, Janet Egleson. "Mary Lavin, Elizabeth Bowen, and a New Generation: The Irish Short Story at MidCentury." In *The Irish Short Story: A Critical History*, edited by James F. Kilroy. Boston: Twayne, 1984. Discusses Mary Lavin's art as economic, disciplined, and compressed; argues that she neither romanticizes nor trivializes Irish experience. Discusses the basic characteristics of the fiction of Elizabeth Bowen, Benedict Kiely, Michael McLaverty, and Bryan MacMahon.

Eichenbaum, Boris. *O. Henry and the Theory of the Short Story.* Translated by I. R. Titunik. Michigan Slavic Contributions. Ann Arbor: University of Michigan, 1968. Originally published in 1925, this essay is a good example of the early Russian Formalist approach to fiction through a consideration of genre. Eichenbaum poses a generic distinction between the novel and the short story, suggesting that the former is a syncretic form while the latter is fundamental, elementary. Short stories are constructed on the basis of a contradiction, incongruity, error, or contrast, and, like the anecdote, build their weight toward the ending.

Engstrom, Alfred G. "The Formal Short Story in France and Its Development Before 1850." *Studies in Philology* 42 (1945): 627-639. After making distinctions between the *nouvelle* and the conte (a complex line of action versus a compressed one), Engstrom points out the lack of any significant examples of conte until Prosper Mérimée's "Mateo Falcone" (1829), the first formal short story in French literature. The only other significant contributors to the form before 1850 are Honoré de Balzac and Théophile Gautier.

Evans, Walter. "The English Short Story in the Seventies." In *The English Short Story, 1945-1980*, edited by Dennis Vanatta. Boston: Twayne, 1985. Focuses on new writers of the period, such as Susan Hill, Angela Carter, Gabriel Josipovici, and Christine Brooke-Rose. The emphasis here is on different themes: personal crises, the individual in conflict in society; briefly discusses the avant-garde, especially Josipovici and Brooke-Rose; claims the decade's finest collection of stories is *The Ebony Tower* (1974) by John Fowles.

Ferguson, Suzanne C. "Defining the Short Story: Impressionism and Form." *Modern Fiction Studies* 28 (Spring, 1982): 13-24. Argues that there is no single characteristic or cluster of characteristics that distinguish the short story from the novel;

suggests that what is called the modern short story is a manifestation of impressionism rather than a discrete genre.

_____. "The Rise of the Short Story in the Hierarchy of Genres." In *Short Story Theory at a Crossroads*, edited by Susan Lohafer and Jo Ellyn Clarey. Baton Rouge: Louisiana State University Press, 1989. A historical/critical survey of the development of the English short story, showing how social factors influence the rise and fall of the prestige of the form.

FitzGerald, Gregory. "The Satiric Short Story: A Definition." *Studies in Short Fiction* 5 (1968): 349-354. Defines the satiric short story as a subgenre that sustains a reductive attack upon its objects and conveys to its readers a significance different from its apparent surface meaning.

Flora, Joseph M., ed. *The English Short Story, 1880-1945*. Boston: Twayne, 1985. A collection of essays on a number of British short-story writers during the period, including Rudyard Kipling, D. H. Lawrence, Virginia Woolf, Saki, A. E. Coppard, P. G. Wodehouse, and V. S. Pritchett.

Fonlon, Bernard, "The Philosophy, the Science, and the Art of the Short Story, Part II." *Abbia* 34 (1979): 429-438. A discussion of the basic element of story, including character, conflict. Lists elements of intensity, detachment, skill, unity of effect. This essay presents primarily a set of rules aimed at inexperienced writers.

Friedman, Norman. "Recent Short Story Theories: Problems in Definition." In *Short Story Theory at a Crossroads*, edited by Susan Lohafer and Jo Ellyn Clarey. Baton Rouge: Louisiana State University Press, 1989. A critical review of major short-story critics, including Mary Rohrberger, Charles May, Susan Lohafer, John Gerlach, and others. Argues against those critics who support a deductive, single-term, mixed category approach to definition of the form. Urges that what is needed is a more inductive approach that follows the principle of suiting the definition to the facts rather than trying to suit the facts to the definition.

_____. "What Makes a Short Story Short?" *Modern Fiction Studies* 4 (1958): 103-117. Makes use of Neo-Aristotelian literary theory to determine the issue of the short story's shortness. To deal with the problem, Friedman says, one must ask the following questions: What is the size of the action? Is it composed of a speech, a scene, an episode, or a plot? Does the action involve a change? If so, is the change a major one or a minor one?

Gerlach, John. "The Margins of Narrative: The Very Short Story, the Prose Poem, and the Lyric." In *Short Story Theory at a Crossroads*, edited by Susan Lohafer and Jo Ellyn Clarey. Baton Rouge: Louisiana State University Press, 1989. Explores the basic requirements of a story, focusing particularly on two minimalist stories by Enrique Anderson Imbert and Scott Sanders, as well as a short prose poem by W. S. Merwin. Argues that neither mere length nor fictionality are the constituents of story, but rather point.

_____. *Toward the End: Closure and Structure in the American Short Story*. Tuscaloosa: University of Alabama Press, 1985. A detailed theoretical study of the American short story, focusing particularly on the importance of closure, or the ending of the form; examines a number of stories in some detail in terms of the concept of closure.

Gordimer, Nadine. "South Africa." *The Kenyon Review* 30 (1968): 457-461. The strongest convention of the novel, its prolonged coherence of tone, is false to the nature of what can be grasped as reality in the modern world. Short-story writers deal with the only thing one can be sure of—the present moment.

Gullason, Thomas A. "The 'Lesser' Renaissance: The American Short Story in the 1920s." In *The American Short Story: 1900-1945*, edited by Philip Stevick. Boston: Twayne, 1984. A historical survey of some of the major short-story writers of the 1920's in the United States. The essay analyzes briefly some of the best known stories of Sherwood Anderson, F. Scott Fitzgerald, Ring Lardner, Ernest Hemingway, Dorothy Parker, Katherine Anne Porter, and William Faulkner.

_____. "Revelation and Evolution: A Neglected Dimension of the Short Story." *Studies in Short Fiction* 10 (1973): 347-356. Challenges Mark Schorer's distinction between the short story as an "art of moral revelation" and the novel as an "art of moral evolution." Analyzes D. H. Lawrence's "The Horse Dealer's Daughter" and John Steinbeck's "The Chrysanthemums" to show that the short story embodies both revelation and evolution.

_____. "The Short Story: An Underrated Art." *Studies in Short Fiction* 2 (1964): 13-31. Points out the lack of serious criticism on the short story, suggests some of the reasons for this neglect, and concludes with an analysis of Anton Chekhov's "Gooseberries" and Nadine Gordimer's "The Train from Rhodesia" to disprove the charges that the short story is formulaic and lacks life.

Hanson, Clare, ed. Introduction to *Re-reading the Short Story*. New York: St. Martin's Press, 1989. Claims that the short story is a vehicle for different *kinds* of knowledge, knowledge that may be in some way at odds with the "story" of dominant culture. The formal properties of the short story—disjunction, inconclusiveness, obliquity—connect with its ideological marginality and with the fact that the form may be used to express something suppressed/repressed in mainstream literature.

_____. *Short Stories and Short Fictions, 1880-1980*. New York: St. Martin's Press, 1985. Argues that during this period, the authority of the teller, usually a first-person "framing" narrator who guaranteed the authenticity of the tale, was questioned by many modernist writers; argues that the movements from "teller" to indirect free narration, and from "tale" to "text" were part of a more general movement from "discourse" to "image" in the art and literature of the period. Chapters on Rudyard Kipling, Saki, W. Somerset Maugham, James Joyce, Virginia Woolf, Katherine Mansfield, Samuel Beckett.

_____. "Things out of Words: Towards a Poetics of Short Fiction." In *Rereading the Short Story*, edited by Clare Hanson. New York: St. Martin's Press, 1989. Argues that the short story is a more literary form than the novel; also claims that short stories are framed, an aesthetic device that gives the sense of completeness, which allows gaps and absences to remain in the story; thus readers accept a degree of mystery or elision in the short story that they would not accept in the novel.

Harris, Wendell V. "Beginnings of and for the True Short Story in England." *English Literature in Transition* 15 (1972): 296-276. The true short story did not begin in England until Rudyard Kipling discovered the means to control the reader's angle of vision and establish a self-contained world within the story that keeps the reader at a distance. The externality of the reader to the story's participants is a basic characteristic of the short story.

——————————. "English Short Fiction in the Nineteenth Century." *Studies in Short Fiction* 6 (1968): 1-93. After distinguishing between "short fiction" appearing before 1880 and "short story" after 1880, Harris surveys examples from both periods. The turning point was the definition posed by Brander Matthews, which first appeared in the *Saturday Review* in 1884.

——————————. "Vision and Form: The English Novel and the Emergence of the Short Story." *Victorian Newsletter*, no. 47 (1975): 8-12. The short story did not begin in England until the 1880's because the presentation of isolated individuals, moments, or scenes was not considered a serious intellectual task for fiction to undertake. Only at the end of the century was reality perceived as congeries of fragments; the primary vehicle of this perception is the short story.

Hedberg, Johannes. "What Is a 'Short Story?' And What Is an 'Essay'?" *Moderna Sprak* 74 (1980): 113-120. Reminds readers of the distinction between the Chekhovian story (lack of plot) and the Maupassant story (anecdotal and therefore commercial). Discusses basic characteristics of the essay and the story; claims they are similar in that they are both a whole picture in miniature, not merely a detail of a larger picture—a complete work, not an extract.

Hendricks, William O. "Methodology of Narrative Structural Analysis." In *Essays in Semiolinguistics and Verbal Art*. The Hague: Mouton, 1973. Structuralists, in the tradition of Vladimir Propp and Claude Levi-Strauss, usually bypass the actual sentences of a narrative and analyze a synopsis. This essay is a fairly detailed discussion of the methodology of synopsizing (using Faulkner's "A Rose for Emily" as an example), followed by a brief discussion of the methodology of structural analysis of the resultant synopsis.

Hesse, Douglas. "A Boundary Zone: First-Person Short Stories and Narrative Essays." In *Short Story Theory at a Crossroads*, edited by Susan Lohafer and Jo Ellyn Clarey. Baton Rouge: Louisiana State University Press, 1989. Argues that the precise boundary point between essays and short stories does not exist. Analyzes George Orwell's essay "A Hanging" as a short story and William Carlos Williams' short story "Use of Force" as an essay. Also discusses essays and stories that fall in a boundary zone between essay and story.

Hogan, Robert. "Old Boys, Young Bucks, and New Women: The Contemporary Irish Short Story." In *The Irish Short Story: A Critical History*, edited by James F. Kilroy. Boston: Twayne, 1984. A general survey of contemporary Irish short-story writers such as old-guards Anthony C. West, James Plunkett, William Trevor, and

Patrick Boyle; young buck writers Eugene McCabe, John Morrow, Bernard Mac Laverty, Desmond Hogan, and Gillman Noonan; and women writers such as Edna O'Brien, Maeve Kelly, Emma Cooke, Kate Cruise O'Brien, and Juanita Casey.

Holloway, John. "Identity, Inversion, and Density Elements in Narrative: Three Tales by Chekhov, James, and Lawrence." In *Narrative and Structure: Exploratory Essays*. Cambridge, England. Cambridge University Press, 1979. Holloway is concerned with looking at stories in which almost nothing happens. He says there is a distinctive kind of narrative episode introduced by an item that is then followed by another item in inverse relationship to the first, which cancels it out and brings the reader back to where he or she started.

Ingram, Forrest L. "The Dynamics of Short Story Cycles." *New Orleans Review* 2 (1979): 7-12. A historical and critical survey and analysis of short stories that form a single unit, such as James Joyce's *Dubliners* (1914), Ernest Hemingway's *In Our Time* (1924, 1925), and Sherwood Anderson's *Winesburg, Ohio* (1919). Suggests some of the basic devices used in such cycles.

Jarrell, Randall. "Stories." In *The Anchor Book of Stories*. New York: Doubleday, 1958. Jarrell's introduction to this collection focuses on stories as being closer to dream reality than the waking world of everyday. There are two kinds of stories: stories-in-which-everything-is-a-happening (in which each event is so charged that the narrative threatens to disintegrate into energy) and stories-in-which-nothing-happens (in which even the climax may lose its charge and become one more portion of a lyric continuum).

Joselyn, Sister Mary. "Edward Joseph O'Brien and the American Short Story." *Studies in Short Fiction* 3 (1965): 1-15. Attempts a synthesis of O'Brien's philosophic and aesthetic attitudes, which may have determined his choices of "best stories." Discusses O'Brien's contribution to the history, theory, and growth of the American short story.

Jouve, Nicole Ward. "Too Short for a Book." In *Re-reading the Short Story*, edited by Clare Hanson. New York: St. Martin's Press, 1989. An impressionistic, noncritical essay about story length. Discusses *The Thousand and One Nights* as an archetypal model standing behind all stories, collections of stories, and storytelling. Makes a case for collections of stories that stand together as organic wholes rather than single individual stories that stand alone.

Kagan-Kans, Eva. "The Russian Short Story, 1850-1880." In *The Russian Short Story: A Critical History*, edited by Charles A. Moser. Boston: Twayne, 1986. Focuses primarily on Ivan Turgenev, Leo Tolstoy, Fyodor Dostoevski, and the radical, populist, and feminist writers of the period. Representative stories of the writers are discussed and analyzed in terms of their contributions to the form and their relationship to, or reflection of, Russian social life at the time.

The Kenyon Review International Symposium on the Short Story. Contributions from short-story writers from all over the world on the nature of the form, its current economic status, its history, and its significance. Part 1, volume 30, issue 4, 1969, pp. 443-490: Christina Stead (England), Herbert Gold (United States), Erih Koš

(Yugoslavia), Nadine Gordimer (South Africa), Benedict Kiely (Ireland), Hugh Hood (Canada), Henrietta Drake-Brockman (Australia). Part 2, volume 31, issue 1, 1969, pp. 58-94: William Saroyan (United States), Jun Eto (Japan), Maurice Shadbolt (New Zealand), Chanakya Sen (India), John Wain (England), Hans Bender (West Germany), and "An Agent's View" by James Oliver Brown. Part 3, volume 31, issue 4, 1969, pp. 450-502: Ana María Matute (Spain), Torborg Nedreaas (Norway), George Garrett (United States), Elizabeth Taylor (England), Ezekiel Mphahlele (South Africa), Elizabeth Harrower (Australia), Mario Picchi (Italy), Junzo Shono (Japan), Khushwant Singh (India). Part 4, volume 32, issue 1, 1969, pp. 78-108: Jack Cope (South Africa), James T. Farrell (United States), Edward Hyams (England), Luigi Barzini (Italy), David Ballantyne (New Zealand), H. E. Bates (England).

Kilroy, James F. Introduction to *The Irish Short Story: A Critical History*. Boston: Twayne, 1984. An abbreviated survey of the Irish short story, beginning with Maria Edgeworth's *Castle Rackrent* (1800). The focus is on the relationship between historical and social events in Ireland and the development of fiction in Ireland, including political conflicts and upheavals and the rise of periodical publication.

——————. "Setting the Standards: Writers of the 1920's and 1930's." In *The Irish Short Story: A Critical History*, edited by James F. Kilroy. Boston: Twayne, 1984. The major Irish writers who set the standards for short fiction in the 1920's and 1930's were Liam O'Flaherty, Frank O'Connor, and Seán O'Faoláin. Kilroy compares and contrasts the three writers by analyzing some of their best-known stories. The essay also includes brief discussions of Daniel Corkery and Seamus O'Kelley.

Kimbel, Ellen. "The American Short Story: 1900-1920." In *The American Short Story, 1900-1945*, edited by Philip Stevick. Boston: Twayne, 1984. A historical survey of the development of the short story in the first two decades of the twentieth century. Begins with Henry James and writers such as Edith Wharton and Willa Cather who were strongly influenced by his work. Discusses the innovations of Sherwood Anderson and points out how he differs from earlier writers in developing the modern short story.

Kostelanetz, Richard. "Notes on the American Short Story Today." *The Minnesota Review* 5 (1966): 214-221. Contemporary short-story writers focus on extreme rather than typical experiences and tend to emphasize the medium of language itself more than ever before. In a shift that pulls the genre farther away from narrative and pushes it closer to nonlinear forms of poetry, the contemporary short-story writer attempts to depict the workings of the mad mind, to simulate the feel of madness itself.

Leitch, Thomas M. "The Debunking Rhythm of the American Short Story." In *Short Story Theory at a Crossroads*, edited by Susan Lohafer and Jo Ellyn Clarey. Baton Rouge: Louisiana State University Press, 1989. Argues that a particular kind of closure is typical of the American short story. Uses the phrase "debunking rhythm" to characterize the kind of story in which a character realizes the falseness of one kind of knowledge but achieves no new kind of knowledge to take its place.

Lewis, C. S. "On Stories." In *Essays Presented to Charles Williams.* Grand Rapids, Mich.: Wm. B. Eerdmans, 1966. Although stories are series of events, this series, or what is called plot, is only a necessary means to capture something that has no sequence, something more like a state or quality. Thus, the means of "story" is always at war with its "end." This very tension, however, constitutes the story's chief resemblance to life. "We grasp at a state and find only a succession of events in which the state is never quite embodied."

Lindstrom, Naomi. "The Spanish American Short Story from Echeverria to Quiroga." In *The Latin American Short Story: A Critical History*, edited by Margaret Sayers Peden. Boston: Twayne, 1983. Discusses the first Latin American short story, Estaban Echeverría's 1838 "The Slaughtering Grounds." Discusses the movement from Romanticism to realism and naturalism and then to modernism; notes that whereas Edgar Allan Poe and Guy de Maupassant were not taken so seriously elsewhere, they were taken more seriously in Latin America. Latin American readers see them as providing channels to alternate realms of experience.

Lohafer, Susan. "A Cognitive Approach to Storyness." *Short Story*, Spring, 1990, 60-71. A study of what Lohafer calls "preclosure," those points in a story where it could end but does not. Studies the characters of such preclosure sentences— where they appear, what they signal—as part of a more general effort to clarify what constitutes storyness.

_____. *Coming to Terms with the Short Story.* Baton Rouge: Louisiana State University Press, 1983. A highly suggestive theoretical study of the short story that focuses on the sentence unit of the form as a way of showing how it differs from the novel.

_____. "Preclosure and Story Processing." In *Short Story Theory at a Crossroads*, edited by Susan Lohafer and Jo Ellyn Clarey. Baton Rouge: Louisiana State University Press, 1989. Analysis of the responses to a story by Kate Chopin in terms of identifying those sentences that "could" end the story but do not. This essay is a continuation of Lohafer's study of what she has defined as preclosure in short fiction.

Luscher, Robert M. "The Short Story Sequence: An Open Book." In *Short Story Theory at a Crossroads*, edited by Susan Lohafer and Jo Ellyn Clarey. Baton Rouge: Louisiana State University Press, 1989. Discusses the need for readers of story cycles such as *Winesburg, Ohio* (1919) to extend their drive to find pattern to cover a number of individual sequences. Compares story cycles with mere aggregates of stories as well as with novelistic sequences.

McMurray, George R. "The Spanish American Short Story from Borges to the Present." In *The Latin American Short Story: A Critical History*, edited by Margaret Sayers Peden. Boston: Twayne, 1983. Discusses Jorge Luis Borges as a writer who ushers in a new literary era in South America and the shift during the 1950's to political and social problems. Argues that the most talented Spanish American writer since Borges is Julio Cortázar from Argentina. Also discusses José Donoso and Carlos Fuentes.

Marcus, Mordecai. "What Is an Initiation Story?" *The Journal of Aesthetics and Art Criticism* 14 (1960): 221-227. Distinguishes three types of initiation stories: those that lead protagonists only to the threshold of maturity, those that take the protagonists across the threshold of maturity but leave them in a struggle for certainty, and decisive initiation stories that carry protagonists firmly into maturity.

Marler, Robert F. "From Tale to Short Story: The Emergence of a New Genre in the 1850's." *American Literature: A Journal of Literary History, Criticism, and Bibliography* 46 (1974): 153-169. Using Northrop Frye's distinction between the tale (embodies "stylized figures which expand into psychological archetypes") and the short story (deals with characters who wear their "*personae* or social masks"), Marler surveys the critical condemnation of the tale form and the increasing emphasis on realism in the 1850's. The broad shift is from Edgar Allan Poe's overt romance to Herman Melville's mimetic portrayals, especially in "Bartleby the Scrivener."

Matthews, Brander. *The Philosophy of the Short-Story.* New York: Longmans, Green, 1901. An expansion of an 1882 article in which Matthews sets himself forth as the first critic (since Edgar Allan Poe) to discuss the short story (Matthews contributed the hyphen) as a genre. By asserting that the short story must have a vigorous compression, must be original, must be ingenious, must have a touch of fantasy, and so on, Matthews set the stage for a host of textbook writers on the short story that followed.

Maugham, W. Somerset. "The Short Story." In *Points of View: Five Essays.* Garden City, N.Y.: Doubleday, 1958. As might be expected, Maugham's preference is for the well-made story exemplified by Guy de Maupassant's "The Necklace." Most of the essay, however, deals with Chekhov and Mansfield biographical material.

May, Charles E. "Artifice and Artificiality in the Short Story." *Story* 1 (Spring, 1990): 72-82. Discusses the artificial and formalized nature of the endings of short stories, arguing that the short story is the most aesthetic narrative form; discusses the ending of several representative stories.

_____. "Chekhov and the Modern Short Story." In *A Chekhov Companion,* edited by Toby Clyman. Westport, Conn.: Greenwood Press, 1985. A detailed analysis of Anton Chekhov's influence on the development of the modern short story; isolates Chekhov's most important innovations in the form and then shows how these elements have been further used and developed by such modern writers as Katherine Mansfield, Ernest Hemingway, Bernard Malamud, Raymond Carver, and others.

_____. "Metaphoric Motivation in Short Fiction: 'In the Beginning Was the Story.'" In *Short Story Theory at a Crossroads,* edited by Susan Lohafer and Jo Ellyn Clarey. Baton Rouge: Louisiana State University Press, 1989. A discussion of how short fiction moves from the "tale" form to the "short story" form through motivation by metaphor in "Fall of the House of Usher," "Bartleby the

Scrivener," "The Legend of Sleepy Hollow," and "Young Goodman Brown."
_____. "The Nature of Knowledge in Short Fiction." *Studies in Short Fiction* 21 (Fall, 1984): 227-238. A theoretical study of the epistemological bases of short fiction. Argues that the short story originates as a primal mythic mode that develops into a metaphoric mode.
_____. *Short Story Theories*. Athens: Ohio University Press, 1976. A collection of twenty previously published essays on the short story as a genre in its own right.
_____. "A Survey of Short Story Criticism in America." *The Minnesota Review*, Spring, 1973, 163-169. An analytical survey of criticism beginning with Edgar Allan Poe and focusing on the short story's underlying vision and characteristic mode of understanding and confronting reality.
_____. "The Unique Effect of the Short Story: A Reconsideration and an Example." *Studies in Short Fiction* 13 (1976): 289-297. An attempt to redefine Edgar Allan Poe's "unique effect" in the short story in terms of mythic perception. The short story demands intense compression and focusing because its essential subject is a manifestation of what philosopher Ernst Cassirer calls the "momentary deity." A detailed discussion of Stephen Crane's story "An Episode of War" illustrates the concept.

Menikoff, Barry. "The Problematics of Form: History and the Short Story." *Journal of the Short Story in English*, no. 2 (1984): 129-146. After a brief introduction on how the short story has been neglected, Menikoff comments briefly on the importance of Charles May's *Short Story Theories* (1976) and then discusses essays on the short story that appeared in *Critical Survey of Short Fiction* (1981) and a special issue of *Modern Fiction Studies* (1982). A sketchy and crotchety survey that adds little to an understanding of the short-story form.

Miall, David. "Text and Affect: A Model for Story Understanding." In *Re-reading the Short Story*, edited by Clare Hanson. New York: St. Martin's Press, 1989. A discussion of what readers are doing in emotional terms when they read, using the defamiliarization model of the Russian formalists. Focuses on three aspects of emotion: self-reference, domain crossing, and anticipation. Basically determines that whereas literary texts constrain response by means of their shared frames and conventions, their affective response is highly divergent.

Mish, Charles C. "English Short Fiction in the Seventeenth Century." *Studies in Short Fiction* 6 (1969): 223-330. Mish divides the period into two parts: 1600-1660, in which short fiction declined into sterile imitation and preciousness, and 1660-1700, in which it was revitalized by the French influence of such works as Madame de la Fayette's *La Princesse de Clèves* (1678; *The Princess of Clèves*, 1679). The French direction toward interiorization, psychological analysis and verisimilitude in action and setting, combined with the English style of the self-conscious narrator, moves fiction toward the novel of the eighteenth century.

Moffett, James. "Telling Stories: Methods of Abstraction in Fiction." *ETC.* 21 (1964): 425-50. Charts a sequence covering an "entire range" of ways in which stories can be told, from the most subjective and personal (interior monologue and dramatic monologue) to the most objective and impersonal (anonymous narration). Includes examples of each type.

Moravia, Alberto. "The Short Story and the Novel." In *Man as End: A Defense of Humanism.* Translated by Bernard Wall. New York: Farrar, Straus & Giroux, 1969. The basic difference between the novel and the short story is that the novel has a bone structure of ideological themes whereas the short story is made up of intuitions of feelings.

Moser, Charles A., ed. "Pushkin and the Russian Short Story." In *The Russian Short Story: A Critical History.* Boston: Twayne, 1986. Says that Pushkin reworked older tales, gave old plots a new twist, and "toyed with literary conventions." Argues that the short story might have developed as a genre that combined prose and verse. Discusses the brevity and surprise endings of the stories. Focuses on Pushkin's contribution to the short story as a genre: brevity, surprise endings, and self-consciousness of narrative technique. Discusses the innovations of Pushkin's stories as well as their influence on subsequent Russian writers.

Neuhauser, Rudolf. "The Russian Short Story, 1917-1980." In *The Russian Short Story: A Critical History,* edited by Charles A. Moser. Boston: Twayne, 1986. Discussion of postrevolution writers in Russia such as Yevgeny Zamyatin, as well as the influence of Russian formalist critics and writers such as Viktor Shklovsky and Boris Eikhenbaum. A brief discussion of Isaac Babel is included here, although his influence on the short story as a form should probably make him loom higher than this. Separate sections are devoted to Russian literature and World War II, the thaw after the death of Joseph Stalin, the woman question, and science prose and village prose.

Oates, Joyce Carol. "The Short Story." *Southern Humanities Review* 5 (1971): 213-214. The short story is a "dream verbalized," a manifestation of desire. Its most interesting aspect is its "mystery."

O'Brien, Edward J. *The Advance of the American Short Story.* Rev. ed. New York: Dodd, Mead, 1931. A survery of the development of the American short story from Washington Irving to Sherwood Anderson. The focus is on contributions to the form by various authors: Irving's development of the story from the eighteenth century essay, Nathaniel Hawthorne's discovery of the subjective method for psychological fiction, Edgar Allan Poe's formalizing, Bret Harte's caricaturing, Henry James's development of the "central intelligence," and Anderson's freeing the story from O. Henry formalism.

——————. *The Dance of the Machines: The American Short Story and the Industrial Age.* New York: Macaulay, 1929. Chapter 4 of this rambling polemic against machinelike standardization of the industrial age describes thirty characteristics that the short story ("the most typical American form") shares with the machine: for example, it is patterned, impersonal, standardized, speeded-up, and cheap.

O'Connor, Flannery. "Writing Short Stories." In *Mystery and Manners,* edited by

Sally and Robert Fitzgerald. New York: Farrar, Straus & Giroux, 1969. In this lecture at a Southern writers conference, O'Connor discusses the two qualities necessary for the short story: "sense of manners," which writers get from the texture of their immediate surroundings, and "sense of mystery," which is always the mystery of personality—"showing how some specific folks *will* do, in spite of everything."

O'Connor, Frank. *The Lonely Voice: A Study of the Short Story.* Cleveland: World Publishing, 1963. The introductory chapter contains extremely valuable "intuitive" criticism by an accomplished master of the short story. The basic difference between the novel and the short story is that in the latter one always finds an intense awareness of human loneliness. O'Connor believes that the protagonist of the short story is less an individual with whom the reader can identify than a "submerged population group"—that is, someone outside the social mainstream. The remaining chapters of the book treat this theme in the works of Ivan Turgenev, Anton Chekhov, Guy de Maupassant, Rudyard Kipling, James Joyce, Katherine Mansfield, D. H. Lawrence, A. E. Coppard, Isaac Babel, and Mary Lavin.

O'Faoláin, Seán. *The Short Story.* New York: Devin-Adair, 1951. This book on the technique of the short story claims that technique is the "least part of the business." O'Faoláin illustrates his thesis that personality is the most important element by describing the personal struggles of Alphonse Daudet, Anton Chekhov, and Guy de Maupasssant. He does his duty to the assigned subject of the book by also discussing the technical problems of convention, subject, construction, and language.

Orel, Harold. *The Victorian Short Story: Development and Triumph of a Literary Genre.* Cambridge, England: Cambridge University Press, 1986. Contains chapters on Joseph Sheridan Le Fanu, Charles Dickens, Anthony Trollope, Thomas Hardy, Robert Louis Stevenson, Rudyard Kipling, H. G. Wells, and Joseph Conrad. Focuses on the relevant biographical and sociocultural factors and says something about writers' relationships with editors and periodicals. Does not attempt a formal history of the evolution of the genre.

O'Rourke, William. "Morphological Metaphors for the Short Story: Matters of Production, Reproduction, and Consumption." In *Short Story Theory at a Crossroads*, edited by Susan Lohafer and Jo Ellyn Clarey. Baton Rouge: Louisiana State University Press, 1989. Explores a number of analogies drawn from the social and natural sciences to suggest ways of seeing how the short story is different from the novel: the novel has a structure like a vertebrate, whereas the short story is like an exoskeletal animal; the novel is a macro form whereas the short story is a micro form.

O'Toole, L. Michael. *Structure, Style, and Interpretation in the Russian Short Story.* New Haven, Conn.: Yale University Press, 1982. An analysis of a few major stories by Nikolai Leskov, Nikolai Gogol, Alexander Pushkin, Maxim Gorky, Ivan Turgenev, and Anton Chekhov, in terms of the formalist theories of Viktor Shklovsky, Boris Eikhenbaum, Boris Tomashevsky, Mikhail Bakhtin, and Vladimir Propp, and the structuralist theories of Roland Barthes and Tzvetan Todorov. The introduction provides a general methodological introduction to interpretation through structural analysis.

Patrick, Walton R. "Poetic Style in the Contemporary Short Story." *College Composition and Communication* 18 (1957): 77-84. The poetic style appears more consistently in the short story than in the novel because metaphorical dilations are essential to the writer who "strives to pack the utmost meaning into his restricted space."

Pattee, Fred Lewis. *The Development of the American Short Story.* New York: Harper & Row, 1923. The most detailed and historically full survey of the American short story from Washington Irving to O. Henry. Charts the changes in taste of the short-story reading public and indicates the major contributions to the form of such classic practitioners as Irving, Nathaniel Hawthorne, Edgar Allan Poe, and Bret Harte. Surveys the effect of the "Annuals," the "Ladies' Books," local color, Brander Matthews' *The Philosophy of the Short-Story* (1901), and the writing handbooks.

Peden, William. *The American Short Story: Continuity and Change, 1940-1975,* 2d ed. Boston: Houghton Mifflin, 1975. Includes chapters on publishing and the short story since 1940; the stories of suburbia by John Cheever, John Updike, and others; stories of physical illness and abnormality by James Purdy, Tennessee Williams, Flannery O'Connor, Joyce Carol Oates; stories by Jewish writers such as Bernard Malamud, Saul Bellow, J. D. Salinger, Grace Paley, Philip Roth, and Isaac Bashevis Singer; stories by black writers such as Langston Hughes, Richard Wright, Ann Petry, Toni Cade Bambera.

_____. *The American Short Story: Front Line in the National Defense of Literature.* Boston: Houghton Mifflin, 1964. A discussion of major trends in the American short story since 1940. The center of the book consists of a chapter on those writers who focus on everyday life in contemporary society (John Cheever, John O'Hara, Peter Taylor, John Updike, J. F. Powers, and J. D. Salinger) and a chapter on those who are preoccupied with the grotesque, abnormal, and bizarre (Carson McCullers, O'Connor, James Purdy, Truman Capote, and Tennessee Williams). An additional chapter surveys other short-story subjects such as the war, minorities, regions, and science fiction.

_____. "The American Short Story During the Twenties." *Studies in Short Fiction* 10 (1973): 367-371. A highly abbreviated account of the causes of the explosion of short stories during the 1920's. Some of the causes discussed are the new freedom from plotted stories, new emphasis on "now-ness," the boom of little magazines, and the influence of cinematic techniques.

Penn, W. S. "The Tale as Genre in Short Fiction." *Southern Humanities Review* 15 (Summer, 1981): 231-241. Discusses the genre from the perspective of structure. Primarily uses suggestions made by Jonathan Culler in *Structuralist Poetics* for constructing a poetic persona in the lyric poem, what Culler calls an "enunciative posture"—that is, the detectable or intuited moral relation of the implied author to both the world at large and the world he or she creates. Develops two kinds of tales: the radical oral and the exponential oral.

Pickering, Jean. "The English Short Story in the Sixties." In *The English Short Story, 1945-1980*, edited by Dennis Vanatta. Boston: Twayne, 1985. Pickering says that few of the cultural developments in England in the 1960's were reflected in the short story and claims that the short story was in decline during the period. Focuses on short-story collections by Roald Dahl, William Sansom, Doris Lessing, V. S. Pritchett, and H. E. Bates.

_____. "Time and the Short Story." In *Re-reading the Short Story*, edited by Clare Hanson. New York: St. Martin's Press, 1989. A rehash of the old distinction between the short story as an art of revelation and the novel as an art of evolution. General implications that derive from this distinction are that short-story writers do not need to know all the details of their characters' lives and that the short story is doubly symbolic. Structure, theme, characterization, language are influenced by the short story's particular relation to time as a moment of revelation.

Poe, Edgar Allan. Review of *Twice-Told Tales*. *Graham's Magazine*, May, 1842. The first critical discussion of the short story, or the tale as Poe terms it, to establish the genre as distinct from the novel. Because of its sense of totality, its single effect, and its patterned design, the short story is second only to the lyric in its demands on high genius and in its aesthetic beauty.

Pratt, Mary Louise. "The Short Story: The Long and the Short of It." *Poetics* 10 (1981): 175-194. A theoretical discussion of the form; presents eight ways that the short story is better understood if its dependence on the novel is understood.

Prince, Gerald. *A Grammar of Stories: An Introduction.* The Hague: Mouton, 1973. An attempt to establish rules to account for the structure of all the syntactical sets that we intuitively recognize as stories. The model used is Noam Chomsky's theories of generative grammar.

Pritchett, V. S. "Short Stories." *Harper's Bazaar* 87 (July, 1953): 31, 113. The short story is a hybrid, owing much to the quickness and objectivity of the cinema, much to the poet and the newspaper reporter, and everything to the "restlessness, the alert nerve, the scientific eye and the short breath of contemporary life." Makes an interesting point about the collapse of standards, conventions, and values which has so bewildered the impersonal novelist but has been the making of the story writer.

Propp, Vladimir. *Morphology of the Folktale*, edited by Svatava Pirkova-Jakovson. Translated by Laurence Scott. Bloomington: Indiana University Research Center, 1958. All formalist and structuralist studies of narrative owe a debt to this pioneering early twentieth century study. Using one hundred fairy tales, Propp defines the genre itself by analyzing the stories according to characteristic actions or functions.

Reid, Ian. *The Short Story.* London: Methuen, 1977. A brief study in the Critical Idiom series. Deals with problems of definition, historical development, and related generic forms. Good introduction to the short story as a genre.

Rhode, Robert D. *Setting in the American Short Story of Local Color: 1865-1900.* The Hague: Mouton, 1975. A study of the various functions that setting plays in the local-color story in the late nineteenth century, from setting as merely background to setting in relation to character and setting as personification.

Rohrberger, Mary. "Between Shadow and Act: Where Do We Go from Here?" In *Short Story Theory at a Crossroads,* edited by Susan Lohafer and Jo Ellyn Clarey. Baton Rouge: Louisiana State University Press, 1989. A thought-provoking review of a number of modern short-story critics and theorists, largely by way of responding to, and disagreeing with, the strictly scientific and logical approach to definition of the form suggested by Norman Friedman. Also includes a restatement of the view that Rohrberger enunciated in her earlier book on Nathaniel Hawthorne, in which she argues for the essentially romantic nature of the short-story form.

_____. *Hawthorne and the Modern Short Story: A Study in Genre.* The Hague: Mouton, 1966. Attempts a generic definition of the short story as a form that derives from the romantic metaphysical view that there is more to the world than can be apprehended through the senses. Hawthorne is the touchstone for her definition, which she then applies to twentieth century stories by Eudora Welty, Ernest Hemingway, Sherwood Anderson, William Faulkner, and others.

_____. "The Question of Regionalism: Limitation and Transcendence." In *The American Short Story, 1900-1945,* edited by Philip Stevick. Boston: Twayne, 1984. This essay's focus is on such writers as Ruth Suckow, Jesse Stuart, Langston Hughes, and Jean Toomer. Calls Toomer's *Cane* (1923) the most significant work produced by the Harlem Renaissance and compares it with Sherwood Anderson's *Winesburg, Ohio.* Also discusses Ellen Glasgow, Sinclair Lewis, James T. Farrell, Erskine Caldwell, John O'Hara, and John Steinbeck.

Ross, Danforth. *The American Short Story.* Minneapolis: University of Minnesota Press, 1961. A sketchy survey that measures American stories since Edgar Allan Poe against Aristotelian criteria of action, unity, tension, and irony. Ends with the Beat writers who rebel against the Poe-Aristotle tradition by using shock tactics.

Ruthrof, Horst. "Bracketed World and Reader Construction in the Modern Short Story." In *The Reader's Construction of Narrative.* London: Routledge & Kegan Paul, 1981. Discusses the "boundary situation" as the basis for the modern short story. In the pure boundary situation, the reader's act of bracketing transforms the presented crisis into the existential experience of the reading act.

Schirmer, Gregory A. "Tales from Big House and Cabin: The Nineteenth Century." In *The Irish Short Story: A Critical History,* edited by James F. Kilroy. Boston: Twayne, 1984. Surveys the short fiction of Maria Edgeworth, William Carleton, and Joseph Sheridan Le Fanu, among others. Schirmer emphasizes the ironic voice of Edgeworth's *Castle Rackrent* (1800), the comic realism and the sophisticated use of narrative voice of Carleton, and the use of the gothic tradition and psychological complexity of Le Fanu.

Schlauch, Margaret. "English Short Fiction in the Fifteenth and Sixteenth Centuries." *Studies in Short Fiction* 3 (1966): 393-434. A survey of types of short fiction from the romantic *lai* to the exemplum, and from the bawdy fabliau to the novella. Schlauch's conclusions are that modern short-story writers are heirs both in subject matter (for example internal psychological conflict) and in technique (such as the importance of dialogue) to a long tradition that antedates the seventeenth century, a tradition that is still worth studying.

Shaw, Valerie. *The Short Story: A Critical Introduction.* London: Longman, 1983. A desultory discussion of the form, without a theoretical approach and little sympathy for a unified approach to the form. The focus is on British story writers primarily, with one chapter on the transitional figure Robert Louis Stevenson. Other chapters deal with the patterned form to the artless tale form, with chapters on character, setting, and subject matter. Shaw says that the short story cannot be defined by unity of effect or by a history of its "favorite devices and eminent practitioners."

Smith, Horatio E. "The Development of Brief Narrative in Modern French Literature: A Statement of the Problem." *PMLA* 32 (1917): 583-597. Surveys the confusion between the conte and *nouvelle* and calls for a critical investigation of the practice and theory of the French forms similar to those published on the American short story and the German *Nouvelle*.

Steirle, Karl-Heinz. "Story as Exemplum—Exemplum as Story: On the Pragmatics and Poetics of Narrative Texts." In *New Perspectives in German Literary Criticism*, edited by Richard E. Amacher and Victor Lange. Translated by David Wilson et al. Princeton, N.J.: Princeton University Press, 1979. A generic discussion of how we move from exemplum, which is definite, to story, which is relativistic. Argues that if one wants to find the link between the short story and the exemplum, the answer must be found in Immanuel Kant's theory of discernment—that is, the ability to realize the particular as contained in the general.

Stevenson, Lionel. "The Short Story in Embryo." *English Literature in Transition* 15 (1972): 261-268. A discussion of the "agglomerative urge" in the English fiction of the eighteenth and nineteenth centuries that contributed to the undervaluing of the short story. Not until 1880, when the fragmentation of the well-integrated view of society began in England, did the short story come into its own in that country.

Stevick, Philip, ed. *Anti-Story: An Anthology of Experimental Fiction.* New York: Free Press, 1971. An influential collection of contemporary short fiction with a helpful introduction that characterizes antistory as against mimesis, reality, event, subject, the middle range of experience, analysis, and meaning.

—————, ed. Introduction to *The American Short Story: 1900-1945.* Boston: Twayne, 1984. Stevick's extensive introduction to this collection of essays by various critics is a helpful historical overview of the development of the twentieth century short story. A good introduction to many of the features of the modern short story and how they came about at the beginning of the century.

Stinson, John J. "The English Short Story, 1945-1950." In *The English Short Story,*

1945-1980, edited by Dennis Vanatta. Boston: Twayne, 1985. Discusses some of the reasons why the short story was in decline in England during this period and claims there was no new direction in the form of the time. Discusses W. Somerset Maugham, A. E. Coppard, Graham Greene, Sylvia Townsend Warner, V. S. Pritchett, and Angus Wilson.

Stroud, Theodore A. "A Critical Approach to the Short Story." *The Journal of General Education* 9 (1956): 91-100. Makes use of American "New Criticism" to determine the pattern of the work—that is, why apparently irrelevant episodes are included and why some events are expanded and others excluded.

Sullivan, Walter. "Revelation in the Short Story: A Note of Methodology." In *Vanderbilt Studies in Humanities*, edited by Richard C. Beatty, John Philip Hyatt, and Monroe K. Spears. Vol. 1. Nashville: Vanderbilt University Press, 1951. The fundamental methodological concept of the short story is a change of view from innocence to knowledge. The change can be either "logical" (coming at the end of the story) or "anticipated" (coming near the beginning); it can be either "intra-concatinate" (occurring within the main character) or "extra-concatinate (occurring within a peripheral character). Thus defined, the short story did not begin until the final years of the nineteenth century.

Summers, Hollis, ed. *Discussions of the Short Story*. Boston: D. C. Heath, 1963. The nine general pieces on the short story are the Poe and Bader essays listed above, Ray B. West's first chapter, Seán O'Faoláin's chapter on "Convention," a chapter each from Percy Lubbock's *Craft of Fiction* and Kenneth Payson Kempton's *The Short Story*, Bret Harte's "The Rise of the Short Story," and excerpts from Brander Matthews' book. Also includes seven additional essays on specific short-story writers.

Szávai, János. "Towards a Theory of the Short Story." *Acta Litteraria Academiae Scientiarum Hungariae, Tomus* 24 (1982): 203-224. Discusses the Boccaccio model as a genre that gives the illusion of reflecting reality directly and spontaneously, whereas it is actually a complex, structured entity that both retains and enriches the basic structure of the story. The enrichment resides, on the one hand, in the careful preparation of the *point* and its attachment to a key motif and, on the other, in the introduction of a new dimension in addition to the anecdote.

Terras, Victor. "The Russian Short Story: 1830-1850." In *The Russian Short Story: A Critical History*, edited by Charles A. Moser. Boston: Twayne, 1986. Points out that 1830 was a watershed in the history of Russian literature in that it marked the end of the golden age of poetry and the shift to prose fiction, particularly short fiction. Discusses the Romantic origins of short fiction in Russia with Alexander Pushkin, the transition to psychological realism with Mikhail Lermontov, the significant contributions of the stories of Nikolai Gogol, the transition to the so-called natural school, and the early works of Fyodor Dostoevski and Ivan Turgenev.

Thurston, Jarvis, O. B. Emerson, Carl Hartman, and Elizabeth Wright, eds. *Short Fiction Criticism: A Checklist of Interpretation Since 1925 of Stories and Novel-*

ettes (American, British, Continental), 1800-1958. Denver: Alan Swallow, 1960. This checklist of interpretations of individual stories was brought up to date by Elizabeth Wright in the Summer, 1969, issue of *Studies in Short Fiction* and has been supplemented by Wright, George Hendrick, and Warren Walker in each summer issue thereafter.

Todorov, Tzvetan. "The Structural Analysis of Literature." In *Structuralism: An Introduction*, edited by David Robey. London: Clarendon Press, 1973. The "figure in the carpet" in Henry James's stories is the quest for an absolute and absent cause. The cause is either a character, an event, or an object; its effect is the story readers are told. Everything in the story owes its existence to this cause, but because it is absent, the reader sets off in quest of it.

Trask, Georgianne, and Charles Burkhart, ed. *Storytellers and Their Art.* New York: Doubleday Anchor, 1963. A valuable collection of comments on the short-story form by practitioners from Anton Chekhov to Truman Capote. Noteworthy in part 1 are "Definitions of the Short Story" and "Short Story vs. Novel."

Voss, Arthur. *The American Short Story: A Critical Survey.* Norman: University of Oklahoma Press, 1973. A comprehensive but routine survey of the major short-story writers in American literature. Valuable for an overview of the stories and criticism, but contains nothing original.

Wain, John. "Remarks on the Short Story." *Journal of the Short Story in English* 2 (1984): 49-66. Wain argues that the short story is a form of its own, with its own laws and logic, and that it is a modern form, beginning with Edgar Allan Poe. Says the novel is like a painting, whereas the short story is like a drawing, which catches a moment and is satisfying on its own grounds. He says there are perfectly successful short stories and totally unsuccessful ones, and nothing in between.

Watson, James G. "The American Short Story: 1930-1945." In *The American Short Story, 1900-1945,* edited by Philip Stevick. Boston: Twayne, 1984. Claims that the period between 1930 and 1945 had the most prolific outpouring of short fiction in the history of American literature. Focuses on the importance of the little magazines and discusses the contributions of Ernest Hemingway, William Faulkner, and F. Scott Fitzgerald.

Welty, Eudora. "The Reading and Writing of Short Stories." *The Atlantic Monthly,* February, 1949, 54-58; March, 1949, 46-49. An impressionistic but suggestive essay in two installments that focuses on the mystery of the story and the fact that one cannot always see the solid outlines of the story because of the atmosphere that it generates.

West, Ray B. "The American Short Story." In *The Writer in the Room.* Detroit: Michigan State University Press, 1968. Originally appeared as West's introduction to *American Short Stories* (Thomas Y. Crowell, 1959). Contrasts the short story's "microscopic" focus on inner motives with the novel's "telescopic" view of human beings from the outside. The novel is concerned with human beings' attempt to control nature through social institutions; the short story presents the individual's confrontation with nature as an indifferent force.

_____. "The Modern Short Story and the Highest Forms of Art." *English Journal* 46 (1957): 531-539. The rise of the short story in the nineteenth century is a result of the shift in narrative view from the "telescopic" (viewing nature and society from the outside) to the "microscopic" (viewing the unseen world of inner motives and impulses).

_____. *The Short Story in America: 1900-1950.* Chicago: Henry Regnery, 1952. Probably the most familiar and most often recommended history of the American short story. Takes up where Fred Lewis Pattee's book leaves off, but it lacks the completeness or the continuity necessary for an adequate history. Chapter 1, "The American Short Story at Mid-Century," is a short survey in itself of the development of the short story since Washington Irving, Nathaniel Hawthorne, and Edgar Allan Poe. Chapter 4 is devoted completely to Ernest Hemingway and William Faulkner.

Wharton, Edith. "Telling a Short Story." In *The Writing of Fiction.* New York: Charles Scribner's Sons, 1925. The chief technical difference between the novel and the short story is that the novel focuses on character while the short story focuses on situation; "and it follows that the effect produced by the short story depends almost entirely on its form."

Williams, William Carlos. *A Beginning on the Short Story: Notes.* Yonkers, N.Y.: The Alicat Bookshop Press, 1950. In these "Notes" from a writers' workshop session, Williams makes several interesting, if fragmentary and impressionistic, remarks about the form: the short story, as contrasted with the novel, is a brush-stroke instead of a picture. Stressing virtuosity instead of story structure, it is "one single flight of the imagination, complete: up and down." It is best suited to depicting the life of "briefness, brokenness, and heterogeneity."

Wright, Austin. *The American Short Story in the Twenties.* Chicago: University of Chicago Press, 1961. Using a canon of 220 stories, one set selected from the 1920's and the other from the immediately preceding period, Wright examines differing themes and techniques to test the usual judgments of what constitutes the "modern short story." The examination ends in proving only that the short story of the 1920's is different from the short story of the earlier period, that of the naturalists.

_____. "On Defining the Short Story: The Genre Question." In *Short Story Theory at a Crossroads*, edited by Susan Lohafer and Jo Ellyn Clarey. Baton Rouge: Louisiana State University Press, 1989. Discusses some of the theoretical problems involved in defining the short story as a genre. Argues for the formalist view of a genre definition as a cluster of conventions.

_____. "Recalcitrance in the Short Story." In *Short Story Theory at a Crossroads*, edited by Susan Lohafer and Jo Ellyn Clarey. Baton Rouge: Louisiana State University Press, 1989. A discussion of stories with endings that resist the reader's efforts to assimilate them and to make sense of them as a whole. Such final recalcitrance, Wright claims, is the extreme kind of resistance that the short story has developed to thwart final closure and reduce the complexity of the story to a conceptual understanding.

Charles E. May

SHORT-FICTION CHRONOLOGY

B.C.

c. 4000	*Tales of the Magicians* (Egyptian)
c. 2000	*The Epic of Gilgamesh* (Sumerian)
c. 750	Homer flourished
c. 564	Aesop died
c. 5th century	*Jatakas* (Indian)
c. 300	Theophrastus, *Characters*
c. 270	Theocritus, idylls, mimes
c. 100	Aristides, Milesian tales
	Tale of Daniel and Susanna (from the Apocrypha)

A.D.

c. 8	Ovid, *Metamorphoses*
c. 1st century	Phaedrus, *Fabulae Aesopiae*
c. 400	*Vitae Patrum*
c. early 6th century	*Panchatantra* (Indian)
c. 6th century	Gregory the Great, *Dialogues*
c. 800	*The Thousand and One Nights* (in one form)
c. late 8th century	*Fates of the Apostles*
c. 9th century	*Romulus* (Latin)
c. 10th century	*Avian*
	Blickling Homilies (Anglo Saxon)
c. 990-997	Aelfric, *Sermones Catholici, Passiones Sanctorum*
c. 1000	*Beowulf*, manuscript written
c. 1100	*The Mabinogion* (Welsh), early tales written
	The Book of the Dun Cow (Irish)
	Chanson de Roland (*The Song of Roland*)
c. 1164-1180	Chrétien de Troyes, wrote earliest extant Arthurian romances in the vernacular
c. late 12th century	Marie de France, Breton *Lais*
c. 1200	*The Thousand and One Nights*, has substantially taken shape
	Odo of Cheriton, *Fabuale*
c. early 13th century	Snorri Sturluson, Prose Edda
	Aucassin and Nicolette
c. 1250	*Dame Siriz*
c. 1275	*"The Fox and the Wolf"*
c. 13th century	*Gesta Romanorum*
	Ancren Riwle
c. 1280-1350	South English Legendary
c. 1303	Robert Mannyng of Brunne, *The Handlyng of Synne*
c. early 1300's	*Northern Homilies*
	Northern Legendary

1313	Giovanni Boccaccio born
1349-1351	Giovanni Boccaccio, *The Decameron*
1371-1372	*The Book of the Knight of La Tour Landry*
1375	Giovanni Boccaccio dies
c. 1383-1384	John Gower, *Confessio Amantis*
1387-1400	Geoffrey Chaucer, *The Canterbury Tales*
1485	Sir Thomas Malory, *Le Morte d'Arthur*
16th century	*The Thousand and One Nights* has taken final form
1526	Beatrice, *Hundred Mery Talys*
1550-1553	Giovan Francesco Straparola, *The Pleasureful Nights*
c. 1553	*Lazarillo de Tormes*
1558	Marguerite de Navarre, *Heptameron*
1566	William Painter, *The Palace of Pleasure*
1567	Fenton, *Tragical Discourses*
1568	*Lazarillo de Tormes* translated into English
1576	George Pettie, *A Petite Pallace of Pettie His Pleasure*
1579	John Lyly, *Euphues, The Anatomy of Wit*
1580	Michel Eyquem de Montaigne, *The Essays*
1581	Barnaby Riche, *Riche His Farewell to Militarie Profession*
1591	Robert Greene, *A Notable Discovery of Coosenage*
1593	Theophrastus' *Characters* translated into English
1597	Thomas Deloney, *The Gentle Craft*
1608	Joseph Hall, *Characters of Vices and Virtues*
1609	Thomas Dekker, *The Ravens Almanacke*
1613	Miguel de Cervantes, *The Exemplary Novels*
1614	Sir Thomas Overbury, *Characters*
1620	*Westward for Smelts*
1623	Charles Sorel, *Francion*
1628	John Earle, *Microcosmographie*
1664	Jean de La Fontaine, *Tales and Short Stories in Verse*
1688	Aphra Behn, *Oroonoko*
1691-1694	*The Gentleman's Journal*, edited by P. A. Motteux
1692	William Congreve, *Incognita*
1694	Voltaire born
1697	Charles Perrault, *Histoires et contes du temps passé, avec des moralités*
1700	John Dryden, *Fables*
1704-1712	*The Thousand and One Nights*, first European translation (French) by Antoine Galland
1706	*The Thousand and One Nights*, partial translation of Galland's version into English
	Daniel Defoe, "The True Relation of the Apparition of One Mrs. Veal"

1709-1711	Sir Richard Steele and Joseph Addison, *The Tatler*
1711-1712, 1714	Joseph Addison and Sir Richard Steele, *The Spectator*
1720	Mrs. Manley, *The Power of Love: In Seven Novels*
1722	Benjamin Franklin, "Dogood Papers"
1725	Mrs. Haywood, *Secret Histories, Novels, and Poems* (2d ed.)
1732	Benjamin Franklin, "Alice Addertongue," "Celia Single," "Anthony Afterwit"
1739	Voltaire, "Voyage de monsieur le baron de Gangan"
1747	Voltaire, *Zadig*
1750-1752	Samuel Johnson, *The Rambler*
1752	Voltaire, "Micromégas"
1759	Voltaire, *Candide*
1762	Oliver Goldsmith, *The Citizen of the World*
1773	Ludwig Johann Tieck born
1776	E. T. A. Hoffmann born
1778	Voltaire dies
1795-1798	Hannah More, Tracts
1797	Ludwig Tieck, *Volksmärchen*
1799	Sir Walter Scott, *An Apology for Tales of Terror*
	Honoré de Balzac born
	Alexander Pushkin born
1801	Maria Edgeworth, *Moral Tales for Young People*
1804	Maria Edgeworth, *Popular Tales*
	Nathaniel Hawthorne born
1805	Hans Christian Andersen born
1807-1808	Washington Irving, *Salmagundi* ("Sketches from Nature" appeared in October, "The Little Man in Black" in November)
1809	Edgar Allan Poe born
	Nikolai Gogol born
1809-1812	Maria Edgeworth, *Tales of Fashionable Life*
1811	Théophile Gautier born
1812	Jacob and Wilhelm Grimm, *Grimm's Fairy Tales*
	Charles Dickens born
1812-1817	Ludwig Tieck, *Phantasus*
1814-1815	E. T. A. Hoffmann, *Fantasiestücke in Callots Manier*
1818	Ivan Turgenev born
1819	Leigh Hunt, "A Tale for a Chimney Corner"
	Herman Melville born
1819-1820	Washington Irving, *The Sketch Book of Geoffrey Crayon, Gent.* ("Rip Van Winkle," May, 1819; "The Spectre Bridegroom," November, 1819; "The Headless Horseman," March, 1820)

1819-1821	E. T. A. Hoffmann, *The Serapion Brethren*
1821	Fyodor Dostoevski born
1822	Charles Brockden Brown, *Carwin the Biloquist and Other American Tales and Pieces*
	Washington Irving, *Bracebridge Hall*
	Charles Lamb, "Dream Children"
	E. T. A. Hoffmann dies
1823	Charles Lamb, "Old China"
	Beginning of vogue in England of gift book annuals
1824	Washington Irving, *Tales of a Traveller* and letter to Henry Brevoort
	William Austin, "Peter Rugg, The Missing Man"
	Sir Walter Scott, "Wandering Willie's Tale" (in *Redgauntlet*)
1824-1832	Mary Russell Mitford, *Our Village*
1826	*The Atlantic Souvenir*, beginning of American gift book vogue
1827-1828	Sir Walter Scott, *Chronicles of the Canongate*, first series ("The Highland Widow," "The Two Drovers," "The Surgeon's Daughter")
1828	Leo Tolstoy born
1829	Sir Walter Scott, "My Aunt Margaret's Mirror," "The Tapestried Chamber"
	Prosper Mérimée, "Mateo Falcone"
1830	Nathaniel Hawthorne, "The Hollow of the Three Hills"
1831	Alexander Pushkin, *The Tales of the Late Ivan Petrovitch Belkin*
1831-1832	Nikolai Gogol, *Evenings on a Farm Near Dikanka*
1831-1861	*The Spirit of the Times*
1832	Washington Irving, *The Alhambra*
	James Hall, *Legends of the West*
	J. P. Kennedy, *Swallow Barn*
	A. B. Longstreet begins publishing his sketches
	Nathaniel Hawthorne, "My Kinsman, Major Molineux"
	Edgar Allan Poe, "Metzengerstein"
	Honoré de Balzac, "La Grande Breteche"
1834	Albert Pike, *Prose Sketches and Poems Written in the Western Country*
	Alexander Pushkin, "The Queen of Spades"
1835	A. B. Longstreet, *Georgia Scenes*
	Nikolai Gogol, "The Diary of a Madman"
	Mark Twain born
1836	Charles Dickens, *Sketches by Boz*

	Hamlin Garland born
1861	Rebecca Harding Davis, "Life in the Iron Mills"
1862	O. Henry (William Sidney Porter) born
1863-1864	Mrs. Gaskell, "Cousin Phillis"
1864	Nathaniel Hawthorne dies
1865	Mark Twain, "The Celebrated Jumping Frog of Calaveras County"
	Rudyard Kipling born
1867	Mark Twain, *The Celebrated Jumping Frog of Calaveras County, and Other Sketches*
1868	Bret Harte, "The Luck of Roaring Camp"
1869	Alphonse Daudet, *Letters from My Mill*
1870	Bret Harte, *The Luck of Roaring Camp and Other Sketches*
	Charles Dickens dies
	Ivan Bunin born
1871	Henry Kingsley, "Our Brown Passenger"
	Stephen Crane born
	William Dean Howells, *Suburban Sketches*
	Théophile Gautier dies
1873	Thomas Bailey Aldrich, *Marjorie Daw and Other People*
1875	Henry James, *A Passionate Pilgrim*
	Hans Christian Andersen dies
	Thomas Mann born
1876	Fyodor Dostoevski, "The Peasant Marey"
	Friedrich Spielhagen, *Novellen*
	Sherwood Anderson born
1877	Sarah Orne Jewett, *Deephaven*
	Gustave Flaubert, *Three Tales*
1878	Henry James, *Daisy Miller*
1879	Henry James, *The Madonna of the Future*
	George Washington Cable, *Old Creole Days*
1880	Joel Chandler Harris, *Uncle Remus: His Songs and Sayings*
	Guy de Maupassant, "Boule de Suif"
1881	George Washington Cable, *Madame Delphine*
	Guy de Maupassant, *Madame Tellier's Establishment and Short Stories*
	Fyodor Dostoevski dies
1882	Frank R. Stockton, "The Lady, or the Tiger?"
	Robert Louis Stevenson, *The New Arabian Nights*
	Charles Reade, *Readiana*
	Virginia Woolf born
	James Joyce born
	Guy de Maupassant, *Mademoiselle Fifi and Other Stories*

1883   Ivan Turgenev dies
           Franz Kafka born
1884   Charles Egbert Craddock (Mary Noailles Murfree), *In the*
           Tennessee Mountains
           Guy de Maupassant, "The Necklace"
           Anton Chekhov, *Skazki Melpomeny*
1885   Brander Matthews, "The Philosophy of the Short-Story"
           D. H. Lawrence born
1886   Sarah Orne Jewett, *A White Heron*
           Robert Louis Stevenson, *The Strange Case of Dr. Jekyll and*
           Mr. Hyde
           Leo Tolstoy, *The Death of Ivan Ilyich*
           Anton Chekhov, *Pystrye rasskazy*
1887   Mary E. Wilkins Freeman, *A Humble Romance and Other*
           Stories
           Arthur Conan Doyle, *A Study in Scarlet*
           Anton Chekhov, *V sumerkakh* and *Nevinnye rechi*
1888   Rudyard Kipling, *Plain Tales from the Hills*
           Thomas Hardy, *Wessex Tales*
           Katherine Mansfield born
1890   Sarah Orne Jewett, *Tales of New England*
           Katherine Anne Porter born
1891   Hamlin Garland, *Main-Travelled Roads*
           Ambrose Bierce, *Tales of Soldiers and Civilians*
           William Dean Howells, *Criticism and Fiction*
           Herman Melville dies
1892   T. W. Higginson, "The Local Short-Story"
1893   Ambrose Bierce, *Can Such Things Be?*
           Guy de Maupassant dies
           Henry James, *The Real Thing*
1894   Luigi Pirandello, *Amori senza amore*
           Kate Chopin, *Bayou Folk*
           Robert Louis Stevenson dies
           Isaac Babel born
1896   Sarah Orne Jewett, *The Country of the Pointed Firs*
           Stephen Crane, *The Little Regiment and Other Episodes of*
           the American Civil War
1897   William Faulkner born
1898   Henry James, *The Turn of the Screw*
           Stephen Crane, "The Blue Hotel," *The Open Boat and*
           Other Tales of Adventure
           Anton Chekhov, "Gooseberries"
           Frederick Wedmore, "The Short Story"

	Charles R. Barrett, *Short Story Writing: A Practical Treatise on the Art of the Short Story*
	Anton Chekhov, "The Lady with the Dog"
	Stephen Crane, *The Monster and Other Stories*
1899	Edith Wharton, *The Greater Inclination*
	W. Somerset Maugham, *Orientations*
	Bret Harte, "The Rise of the Short Story"
	Ernest Hemingway born
	Vladimir Nabokov born
	Jorge Luis Borges born
1900	Stephen Crane, *Wounds in the Rain* and *Whilomville Stories*
	Jack London, *The Son of the Wolf*
	Stephen Crane dies
1902	Joseph Conrad, *Heart of Darkness*
	Bret Harte dies
1903	George Moore, *The Untilled Field*
	Thomas Mann, *Tonio Kröger*
1904	James Joyce, "The Sisters," "Eveline," "After the Race"
	Saki (H. H. Munro), *Reginald*
	Anton Chekhov dies
	Isaac Bashevis Singer born
	O. Henry, *Cabbages and Kings*
1905	Willa Cather, *The Troll Garden*
	Jean-Paul Sartre born
1906	O. Henry, *The Four Million*
1907	Alberto Moravia born
1908	O. Henry, *The Voice of the City*
	Joel Chandler Harris dies
1909	Henry S. Canby, *The Short Story in English*
	Sarah Orne Jewett dies
	Eudora Welty born
1910	O. Henry, "A Municipal Report"
	Joseph Conrad, "The Secret Sharer"
	Lord Dunsany, *A Dreamer's Tales*
	Mark Twain dies
	O. Henry dies
	Leo Tolstoy dies
1911	Katherine Mansfield, *In a German Pension*
	Saki (H. H. Munro), *The Chronicles of Clovis*
	E. M. Forster, *The Celestial Omnibus and Other Stories*
1912	Thomas Mann, *Death in Venice*
1913	Albert Camus born
1914	James Joyce, *Dubliners*

	D. H. Lawrence, *The Prussian Officer and Other Stories*
	Saki (H. H. Munro), *Beasts and Super-Beasts*
1915	Edward J. O'Brien, *The Best Short Stories of 1915* (annual volumes follow)
	Saul Bellow born
	Ivan Bunin, "The Gentleman from San Francisco"
	Franz Kafka, *The Metamorphosis*
	Ring Lardner, *You Know Me, Al*
1916	Lord Dunsany, *The Last Book of Wonder* (in England, *Tales of Wonder*)
	Anton Chekhov, *The Tales of Chekhov* (English translation by Constance Garnett completed in 1922)
	Henry James dies
1918	Theodore Dreiser, *Free and Other Stories*
	Maxim Gorky, *Stories of the Steppe*
1919	Sherwood Anderson, *Winesburg, Ohio*
	Franz Kafka, "A Country Doctor" and "In the Penal Colony"
	First year of the annual O. Henry competition
1920	F. Scott Fitzgerald, *Flappers and Philosophers*
	Katherine Mansfield, *Bliss and Other Stories*
1921	Sherwood Anderson, *The Triumph of the Egg*
	Stephen Crane, *Men, Women, and Boats*
	W. Somerset Maugham, *The Trembling of a Leaf*
	A. E. Coppard, *Adam and Eve and Pinch Me*
1922	F. Scott Fitzgerald, *Tales of the Jazz Age*
	Katherine Mansfield, *The Garden Party and Other Stories*
1923	Ernest Hemingway, *Three Stories and Ten Poems*
	Sherwood Anderson, *Horses and Men*
	Katherine Mansfield, *The Doves' Nest and Other Stories*
	A. E. Coppard, *The Black Dog*
	Elizabeth Bowen, *Encounters*
	F. L. Pattee, *The Development of the American Short Story*
	Katherine Mansfield dies
1924	Ernest Hemingway, *In Our Time*
	Franz Kafka, "A Hunger Artist"
	Anton Chekhov, *Letters on the Short Story, the Drama, and Other Literary Topics* (in English)
	Joseph Conrad dies
	Franz Kafka dies
1925	Ernest Hemingway, *In Our Time* (enlarged edition)
	Flannery O'Connor born
	Yukio Mishima born

1926	F. Scott Fitzgerald, *All the Sad Young Men*
	Isaac Babel, *Red Cavalry*
1927	Ernest Hemingway, *Men Without Women*
1928	H. E. Bates, *Day's End and Other Stories*
	Thomas Hardy dies
	Gabriel García Márquez born
1930	Katherine Anne Porter, *Flowering Judas and Other Stories*
	Mary E. Wilkins Freeman dies
	D. H. Lawrence dies
1931	William Faulkner, *These Thirteen*
	Isaac Babel, *Tales of Odessa*
	Frank O'Connor, *Guests of the Nation*
1932	Conrad Aiken, "Mr. Arcularis," "Silent Snow, Secret Snow"
	Seán O'Faoláin, *Midsummer Night Madness and Other Stories*
	Marcel Aymé, *The Picture-Well*
1933	Sherwood Anderson, *Death in the Woods and Other Stories*
	Ernest Hemingway, *Winner Take Nothing*
1934	William Faulkner, *Doctor Martino and Other Stories*
	William Saroyan, *The Daring Young Man on the Flying Trapeze*
	D. H. Lawrence, *The Tales of D. H. Lawrence*
	Isak Dinesen, *Seven Gothic Tales*
	Marcel Aymé, *The Dwarf*
1935	F. Scott Fitzgerald, *Taps at Reveille*
	John O'Hara, *The Doctor's Son and Other Stories*
	Ignazio Silone, *Mr. Aristotle*
1936	Thomas Mann, *Stories of Three Decades*
	Rudyard Kipling dies
1938	Ernest Hemingway, *The Fifth Column and the First Forty-nine Stories*
	William Faulkner, *The Unvanquished*
	John Steinbeck, *The Long Valley*
	Richard Wright, *Uncle Tom's Children*
	Marcel Aymé, *Derriere Chez Martin*
1939	Katherine Anne Porter, *Pale Horse, Pale Rider*
	Jean-Paul Sartre, *The Wall and Other Stories*
1940	William Saroyan, *My Name Is Aram*
	Dylan Thomas, *Portrait of the Artist as a Young Dog*
	Hamlin Garland dies
1941	Eudora Welty, *A Curtain of Green and Other Stories*
	Jorge Luis Borges, "The Garden of Forking Paths"

	Sherwood Anderson dies
	James Joyce dies
	Virginia Woolf dies
	Isaac Babel dies
1942	William Faulkner, *Go Down, Moses*
	Mary McCarthy, *The Company She Keeps*
	Mary Lavin, *Tales from Bective Bridge*
	Isak Dinesen, *Winter's Tales*
1943	Eudora Welty, *The Wide Net and Other Stories*
	John Cheever, *The Way Some People Live*
	Virginia Woolf, *A Haunted House and Other Short Stories*
	Marcel Aymé, *The Walker Through Walls*
1944	Katherine Anne Porter, *The Leaning Tower and Other Stories*
	Frank O'Connor, *Crab Apple Jelly: Stories and Tales*
	Jorge Luis Borges, *Ficciones, 1935-1944*
1947	Vladimir Nabokov, *Nine Stories*
	J. F. Powers, *Prince of Darkness and Other Stories*
	Marcel Aymé, *Le Vin de Paris*
1948	Truman Capote, *Other Voices, Other Rooms*
1949	William Faulkner, *Knight's Gambit*
	Eudora Welty, *The Golden Apples*
	Shirley Jackson, *The Lottery*
	Truman Capote, *A Tree of Night and Other Stories*
	Angus Wilson, *The Wrong Set*
1950	William Faulkner, *Collected Short Stories of William Faulkner*
	Mary McCarthy, *Cast a Cold Eye*
	Ray Bradbury, *The Martian Chronicles*
	Marcel Aymé, *En Arriere*
1951	Carson McCullers, *The Ballad of the Sad Café and Other Works*
	W. Somerset Maugham, *The Complete Short Stories of W. Somerset Maugham*
1952	Frank O'Connor, *The Stories of Frank O'Connor*
1953	J. D. Salinger, *Nine Stories*
	Jean Stafford, *Children Are Bored on Sunday*
	Erskine Caldwell, *Complete Stories*
	John Cheever, *The Enormous Radio and Other Stories*
	Yukio Mishima, *Death in Midsummer and Other Stories*
	Ivan Bunin dies
1955	Flannery O'Connor, *A Good Man Is Hard to Find*
	Eudora Welty, *The Bride of the Innisfallen and Other Stories*

Dylan Thomas, *Adventures in the Skin Trade and Other Stories*

Thomas Mann dies

1956   J. F. Powers, *The Presence of Grace*

1957   Isaac Bashevis Singer, *Gimpel the Fool and Other Stories*

James Purdy, *Color of Darkness*

Albert Camus, *Exile and the Kingdom*

Isak Dinesen, *Last Tales*

1958   Vladimir Nabokov, *Nabokov's Dozen*

Bernard Malamud, *The Magic Barrel*

John Cheever, *The Housebreaker of Shady Hill and Other Stories*

Isak Dinesen, *Anecdotes of Destiny*

Samuel Beckett, *Stories and Texts for Nothing*

1959   Philip Roth, *Goodbye, Columbus*

John Updike, *The Same Door*

Alan Sillitoe, *The Loneliness of the Long-Distance Runner*

1960   Albert Camus dies

1961   Isaac Bashevis Singer, *The Spinoza of Market Street*

Tillie Olsen, *Tell Me a Riddle*

Richard Wright, *Eight Men*

John Cheever, *Some People, Places and Things That Will Not Appear in My Next Novel*

J. D. Salinger, *Franny and Zooey*

Ernest Hemingway dies

James Purdy, *Children Is All*

1962   John Updike, *Pigeon Feathers and Other Stories*

Jorge Luis Borges, *Labyrinths* (in English)

William Faulkner dies

1963   Bernard Malamud, *Idiots First*

J. D. Salinger, *Raise High the Roof Beam, Carpenters*, and *Seymour: An Introduction*

Joyce Carol Oates, *By the North Gate*

Doris Lessing, *A Man and Two Women*

1964   John Cheever, *The Brigadier and the Golf Widow*

Doris Lessing, *African Stories*

Jean Stafford, *Bad Characters*

Donald Barthelme, *Come Back, Dr. Caligari*

Flannery O'Connor dies

1965   Flannery O'Connor, *Everything That Rises Must Converge*

James Baldwin, *Going to Meet the Man*

1966   John Updike, *The Music School*

Joyce Carol Oates, *Upon the Sweeping Flood*

1984   Saul Bellow, *Him with His Foot in His Mouth and Other*
                    Stories
                Truman Capote dies
                Thomas Pynchon, *Slow Learner: Early Stories*
                Irwin Shaw dies
                Liam O'Flaherty dies
1985   Italo Calvino dies
                Stanley Elkin, *Early Elkin*
                Thomas M. Disch, *Torturing Mr. Amberwell*
                Shirley Ann Grau, *Nine Women*
1986   Bernard Malamud dies
                Jorge Luis Borges dies
                Truman Capote, *I Remember Grandpa: A Story*
1987   Robert Coover, *A Night at the Movies*
                James Baldwin dies
                Erskine Caldwell dies
1988   Raymond Carver, *Where I'm Calling From*
                Italo Calvino, *Under the Jaguar Sun*
                Paul Bowles, *Unwelcome Words*
                Mavis Gallant, *In Transit*
                Raymond Carver dies
1989   Alice Adams, *After You've Gone*
                Samuel Beckett dies
                Ben Okri, *Stars of the New Curfew*
                Jane Smiley, *Ordinary Love and Good Will*
                Donald Barthelme dies
1990   J. G. Ballard, *War Fever*
                Alberto Moravia dies
                Arthur C. Clarke, *Tales from the Planet Earth*
1991   Margaret Atwood, *Wilderness Tips*
                Ann Beattie, *What Was Mine and Other Stories*
                Saul Bellow, *Something to Remember Me By*
                Nadine Gordimer, *Crimes of Conscience*
                Joanne Greenberg, *With the Snow Queen and Other Stories*
                Graham Greene dies
                Isaac Bashevis Singer dies
                Seán O'Faoláin dies

Walter Evans

TERMS AND TECHNIQUES

Aestheticism: The European literary movement, with its roots in France, that was predominant in the 1890's. It denied that art needed to have any utilitarian purpose and focused on the slogan "art for art's sake." The doctrines of aestheticism were introduced to England by Walter Pater and can be found in the plays of Oscar Wilde and the short stories of Arthur Symons. In American literature, the ideas underlying the aesthetic movement can be found in the short fiction of Edgar Allan Poe.

Allegory: A literary mode in which characters in a narrative personify abstract ideas or qualities and so give a second level of meaning to the work, in addition to the surface narrative. Two famous examples of allegory are Edmund Spenser's *The Faerie Queene* (1590, 1596) and John Bunyan's *The Pilgrim's Progress* (1678). Modern examples may be found in Nathaniel Hawthorne's story "The Artist of the Beautiful" and the stories and novels of Franz Kafka.

Allusion: A reference to a person or event, either historical or from a literary work, or to a literary work itself, that gives another literary work a wider frame of reference and adds depth to its meaning. For example, Sylvia Townsend Warner's story "Winter in the Air" gains greater suggestiveness from the frequent allusions to William Shakespeare's play *The Winter's Tale* (c. 1610-1611), and her story "Swans on an Autumn River" is enriched by a number of allusions to the poetry of William Butler Yeats.

Ambiguity: Refers to the capacity of language to suggest two or more levels of meaning within a single expression, thus conveying a rich, concentrated effect. Ambiguity has been defined by William Empson in *Seven Types of Ambiguity* (1930) as "any verbal nuance, however, slight, which gives room for alternative reactions to the same piece of language." It has been suggested that because of the short story's highly compressed form, ambiguity may play a more important role in the form than it does in the novel.

Anachronism: An event, person, or thing placed outside—usually earlier than—its proper historical era. Shakespeare uses anachronism in *King John* (c. 1596-1597), *Antony and Cleopatra* (c. 1606-1607), and *Julius Caesar* (c. 1599-1600). Mark Twain employed anachronism to comic effect in *A Connecticut Yankee in King Arthur's Court* (1889).

Anecdote: The short narration of a single interesting incident or event. An anecdote differs from a short story in that it does not have a plot; it relates a single episode and does not range over different times and places.

Antagonist: A character in fiction who stands in opposition, or rivalry, to the protagonist. In Shakespeare's *Hamlet, Prince of Denmark* (c. 1600-1601), for example, King Claudius is the antagonist of Hamlet.

Anthology: A collection of prose or poetry, usually by various writers. Often serves to introduce the work of little-known authors to a wider audience.

Aphorism: A short, concise statement that states an opinion, precept, or general truth, such as Alexander Pope's "Hope springs eternal in the human breast."

Apostrophe: A direct address to a person (usually absent), inanimate entity, or abstract quality. Examples are the first line of William Wordsworth's sonnet "London, 1802," "Milton! Thou should'st be living at this hour," and King Lear's speech in Shakespeare's *King Lear* (c. 1605-1606), "Blow, winds, and crack your cheeks! rage! blow!"

Archetypal theme: Recurring thematic patterns in literature. Common archetypal themes include death and rebirth (Samuel Taylor Coleridge's *The Rime of the Ancient Mariner,* 1798), paradise-Hades (Coleridge's "Kubla Khan"), the fatal woman (Guy de Maupassant's "Doubtful Happiness"), the earth goddess ("Yanda" by Isaac Bashevis Singer), the scapegoat (D. H. Lawrence's "The Woman Who Rode Away"), the return to the womb (Flannery O'Connor's "The River").

Archetype: The term was used by psychologist Carl Jung to describe what he called "primordial images" that exist in the "collective unconscious" of humankind and are manifested in myths, religion, literature, and dreams. Now used broadly in literary criticism to refer to character types, motifs, images, symbols, and plot patterns recurring in many different literary forms and works. The embodiment of archetypes in a work of literature can make a powerful impression on the reader.

Architectonics: A term borrowed from architecture to describe the structural qualities, such as unity and balance, of a work of literature. If the architectonics are successful, the work will give the impression of organic unity and balance, like a solidly constructed building in which the total value is more than the sum of the parts.

Asides: In drama, short passages generally spoken by one dramatic character in an undertone or directed to the audience, so as not to be heard by other characters on stage.

Atmosphere: The mood or tone of a work; it is often associated with setting but can also be established by action or dialogue. The opening paragraphs of Poe's "The Fall of the House of Usher" and James Joyce's "Araby" provide good examples of atmosphere created early in the works and which pervades the remainder of the story.

Ballad: Popular ballads are songs or verse that tell dramatic, usually impersonal, tales. Supernatural events, courage, and love are frequent themes, but any experience that appeals to ordinary people is acceptable material. Literary ballads—narrative poems based on popular ballads—have frequently been in vogue in English literature, particularly during the Romantic period. One of the most famous is Samuel Taylor Coleridge's *The Rime of the Ancient Mariner* (1798).

Black humor: A general term of modern origin that refers to a form of "sick humor" that is intended to produce laughter out of the morbid and the taboo. Examples are the works of Joseph Heller, Thomas Pynchon, Günter Grass, and Kurt Vonnegut, Jr.

Broadside ballad: A ballad printed on one side of a large, single sheet of paper and sung to a popular tune. Dating from the sixteenth century in England, the subject of the broadside ballad was a topical event or issue.

Burlesque: A work that, by imitating attitudes, styles, institutions, and people, aims to amuse. Burlesque differs from satire in that it aims to ridicule simply for the sake of amusement rather than for political or social change.

Canon: The standard or authoritative list of literary works that are widely accepted as outstanding representatives of their period and genre. In recent literary criticism, however, the established canon has come under fierce assault for its alleged culture and gender bias.

Caricature: A form of writing that focuses on unique qualities of a person and then exaggerates and distorts those qualities in order to ridicule the person and what he or she represents. Contemporary writers, such as Flannery O'Connor, have used caricature for serious and satiric purposes in such stories as "Good Country People" and "A Good Man Is Hard to Find."

Character type: The term can refer to the convention of using stock characters, such as the *miles gloriosus* (braggart soldier) of Renaissance and Roman comedy, the figure of vice in medieval morality plays, or the clever servant in Elizabethan comedy. It can also describe "flat" characters (the term was coined by E. M. Forster) in fiction who do not grow or change during the course of the narrative and who can be easily classified.

Chronicle: The precursors of modern histories, chronicles were written accounts of national or world events. One of the best known is the *Anglo-Saxon Chronicle*, begun in the reign of King Alfred in the late nineteenth century. Many chronicles were written in Elizabethan times, and these were used by Shakespeare as source documents for his history plays.

Classic/Classicism: A literary stance or value system consciously based on the example of classical Greek and Roman literature. While the term is applied to an enormous diversity of artists in many different periods and in many different national literatures, it generally denotes a cluster of values including formal discipline, restrained expression, reverence of tradition, and an objective rather than subjective orientation. Often contrasted to Romanticism.

Climax: Similar to crisis, the moment in a work of fiction at which the action reaches a turning point and the plot begins to be resolved. Unlike crisis, the term is also used to refer to the moment in which the reader's emotional involvement with the work reaches its highest point of intensity.

Comic story: Encompasses a wide variety of modes and inflections, such as parody, burlesque, satire, irony, and humor. Frequently, the defining quality of comic characters is that they lack self-awareness; the reader tends not to identify with them but perceives them from a detached point of view, more as objects than persons.

Conceit: A type of metaphor that makes highly intellectualized comparisons between seemingly disparate things. It is associated with the Metaphysical poets and the Elizabethan sonneteers; examples can also be found in the poetry of Emily Dickinson and T. S. Eliot.

Conflict: The struggle that develops as a result of the opposition between the protagonist and another person, the natural world, society, or some force within the self. In short fiction, the conflict is most often between the protagonist and some strong force either within the protagonist or within the given state of the human condition.

Connotation/Denotation: Denotation is the explicit, formal definition of a word, exclusive of its emotional associations. When a word takes on an additional meaning, other than its denotative one, it achieves connotation. For example, the word "mercenary" denotes a soldier who is paid to fight in an army not of his own region, but connotatively a mercenary is an unprincipled scoundrel who kills for money.

Conte: French for tale, a conte was originally a short adventure tale. In the nineteenth century, the term was used to describe a tightly constructed short story. In England, the term is used to describe a work longer than a short story and shorter than a novel.

Crisis: A turning point in the plot, at which the opposing forces reach the point that a resolution must take place.

Criticism: The study and evaluation of works of literature. Theoretical criticism, as for example in Aristotle's *The Poetics* (fourth century B.C.) sets out general principles for interpretation. Practical criticism (Coleridge's lectures on Shakespeare, for example) offers interpretations of particular works or authors.

Dénouement: Literally, "unknotting"; the conclusion of a drama or fiction, when the plot is unraveled and the mystery solved.

Detective story: The "classic" detective story (or "mystery") is a highly formalized and logically structured mode of fiction in which the focus is on a crime solved by a detective through interpretation of evidence and clever reasoning. Many modern practitioners of the genre, however, such as Raymond Chandler, Patricia Highsmith, and Ross Macdonald, have placed less emphasis on the puzzlelike qualities of the detective story and have focused instead on characterization, theme, and other elements of mainstream fiction. The form was first developed in short fiction by Edgar Allan Poe; Jorge Luis Borges has also used the convention in short stories.

Deus ex machina: Latin, meaning "god out of the machine." In the Greek theater, it referred to the use of a god lowered out of a mechanism onto the stage to untangle the plot or save the hero. It has come to signify any artificial device for the easy resolution of dramatic difficulties.

Device: Any technique used in literature in order to gain a specific effect. The poet uses the device of figurative language, for example, while the novelist may use the devices of foreshadowing, flashback, and so on, in order to create a desired effect.

Didactic literature: Literature that seeks to instruct, give guidance, or teach a lesson. Didactic literature normally has a moral, religious, or philosophical purpose, or it will expound a branch of knowledge (as in Vergil's *Georgics*, c. 37-29 B.C., for example). It is distinguished from imaginative works, in which the aesthetic product takes precedence over any moral intent.

Doggerel: Strictly speaking, doggerel refers to rough and jerky versification, but the term is more commonly applied to worthless verse that contains monotonous rhyme and rhythm and trivial subject matter.

Doppelgänger: A double or counterpart of a person, sometimes endowed with ghostly qualities. A fictional *Doppelgänger* often reflects a suppressed side of his or her personality, as in Fyodor Dostoevski's novella *Dvoynik* (1846; *The Double*, 1917) and the short stories of E. T. A. Hoffmann. Isaac Bashevis Singer and Jorge Luis Borges, among other modern writers, have also employed the *Doppelgänger* with striking effect.

Dream vision: An allegorical form common in the Middle Ages, in which the narrator or a character falls asleep and dreams a dream that becomes the actual framed story. Subtle variations of the form have been used by Hawthorne in "Young Goodman Brown" and by Poe in "The Pit and the Pendulum."

Dualism: A theory that the universe is explicable in terms of two basic, conflicting entities, such as good and evil, mind and matter, or the physical and the spiritual.

Eclogue: In Greek, the term means literally "selection." It is now used to describe a formal pastoral poem. Classical eclogues are constructed around a variety of conventional themes: the singing match, the rustic dialogue, the lament, the love lay, and the eulogy. During the Renaissance, eclogues were employed as veiled satires.

Effect: The total, unified impression, or impact, made upon the reader by a literary work. Every aspect of the work—plot, characterization, style, and so on—is then seen to directly contribute to this overall impression.

Elegy: A long, rhymed, formal poem whose subject is meditation upon death or a lamentable theme; Alfred, Lord Tennyson's *In Memoriam* (1850) is a well-known example. The pastoral elegy, such as Percy Bysshe Shelley's *Adonais* (1821), uses a pastoral scene to express grief at the loss of a friend or important person.

Emotive meaning: The emotion that is commonly associated with a word. In other words, emotive meaning includes the connotations of a word, not merely what it denotes. Emotive meaning is contrasted with cognitive or descriptive meaning, in which neither emotions nor connotations are involved.

Epic: Although this term usually refers to a long narrative poem that presents the exploits of a central figure of high position, the term is also used to designate a long novel that has the style or structure usually associated with an epic. In this sense, for example, Herman Melville's *Moby Dick* (1851) and James Joyce's *Ulysses* (1922) may be called epics.

Episode: In Greek tragedy, the segment between two choral odes. Episode now refers to an incident presented as a continuous action. In a work of literature, many discrete episodes are woven together to form a more complex work.

Epistolary fiction: A work of fiction in which the narrative is carried forward by means of letters written by the characters. Epistolary novels were a quite popular form in the eighteenth century. Examples include Samuel Richardson's *Pamela* (1740) and *Clarissa* (1748). The form has not been much used in the twentieth century.

Essay: A brief prose work, usually on a single topic, that expresses the personal point of view of the author. The essay is usually addressed to a general audience and attempts to persuade the reader to accept the author's ideas.

Essay sketch tradition: The first sketches can be traced to the Greek philosopher Theophrastus in 300 B.C., whose character sketches influenced seventeenth and eighteenth centuries writers in England, who developed the form into something close to the idea of character in fiction. The essay has an equally venerable history, and, like the sketch, had an impact on the development of the modern short story.

Euphony: Language that creates a harmonious and pleasing effect; the opposite of cacophony, which is a combination of harsh and discordant sounds.

Existentialism: A philosophy and attitude of mind that gained wide currency in religious and artistic thought after the end of World War II. Typical concerns of existential writers are human beings' estrangement from society, their awareness that the world is meaningless, and their recognition that one must turn from external props to the self. The novels of Albert Camus and Franz Kafka provide examples of existentialist beliefs.

Exposition: The part or parts of a work of fiction that provide necessary background information. Exposition not only provides the time and place of the action but also introduces readers to the fictive world of the story, acquainting them with the ground rules of the work. In the short story, exposition is usually elliptical.

Expressionism: Beginning in German theater at the start of the twentieth century, expressionism became the dominant movement in the decade following World War I. It abandoned realism and relied on a conscious distortion of external reality in order to portray the world as it is "viewed emotionally." The movement spread to fiction and poetry. Expressionism influenced the plays of Eugene O'Neill, Tennessee Williams, and Thornton Wilder and can be found in the novels of Franz Kafka and James Joyce.

Fable: One of the oldest narrative forms. Usually takes the form of an analogy in which animals or inanimate objects speak to illustrate a moral lesson. The most famous examples are the fables of Aesop, who used the form orally in 600 B.C.

Fabliau: a short narrative poem, popular in medieval French literature and during the English Middle Ages. Fabliaux were usually realistic in subject matter, bawdy, and made a point of satirizing the weaknesses and foibles of human beings. Perhaps the most famous are Geoffrey Chaucer's "The Miller's Tale" and "The Reeve's Tale."

Fabulation: A term coined by Robert Scholes and used in contemporary literary criticism to describe novels that are radically experimental in subject matter, style, and form. Like the magic realists, fabulators mix realism with fantasy. The works of Thomas Pynchon, John Barth, Donald Barthelme, and William Gass provide examples.

Fairy tale: A form of folktale in which supernatural events or characters are prominent. Fairy tales usually depict a realm of reality beyond that of the natural world and in which the laws of the natural world are suspended.

Figurative language: Any use of language that departs from the usual or ordinary meaning to gain a poetic or otherwise special effect. Figurative language embodies various figures of speech, such as irony, metaphor, simile, and many others.

Fin de siècle ("end of the century"): refers to the last decade of the nineteenth century, a transitional period in which artists and writers were aware that they were living at the close of a great age and deliberately cultivated a kind of languor, world weariness, and satiety. Associated with the period of aestheticism and the Decadent movement exemplified in Oscar Wilde.

Flashback: A scene that depicts an earlier event; it can be presented as a reminiscence by a character in a story, or it can simply be inserted into the narrative.

Folktale: A short prose narrative, usually handed down orally, found in all cultures of the world. The term is often used interchangeably with myth, fable, and fairy tale.

Form: The organizing principle in a work of literature, the manner in which its elements are put together in relation to its total effect. The term is sometimes used interchangeably with structure and is often contrasted with content: if form is the building, content is what is in the building and what the building is specifically designed to express.

Frame story: A story that provides a framework for another story (or stories) told within it. The form is ancient and is used by Geoffrey Chaucer in *The Canterbury Tales* (1387-1400). In modern literature, the technique has been used by Henry James in *The Turn of the Screw* (1898), Joseph Conrad in *Heart of Darkness* (1902), and John Barth, in *Lost in the Funhouse* (1968).

Framework: When used in connection with a frame story, the framework is the narrative setting, within which other stories are told. The framework may also have a plot of its own. More generally, the framework is similar to structure, referring to the general outline of a work.

Genre study: The concept of studying literature by classification and definition of types or kinds, such as tragedy, comedy, epic, lyrical, and pastoral. First introduced by Aristotle in *The Poetics* (fourth century B.C.), the genre principle has been an essential concomitant of the basic proposition that literature can be studied scientifically.

Gothic genre: A form of fiction developed in the late eighteenth century that focuses on horror and the supernatural. Examples include Matthew Gregory Lewis' *The Monk* (1797), Mary Wollstonecraft Shelley's *Frankenstein* (1818), and the short fiction of Edgar Allan Poe. In modern literature, the gothic genre can be found in the fiction of Truman Capote.

Grotesque: Characterized by a breakup of the everyday world by mysterious forces, the form differs from fantasy in that the reader is not sure whether to react with humor or horror. Examples include the stories of E. T. A. Hoffmann and Franz Kafka.

Hasidic tale: Hasidism was a Jewish mystical sect formed in the eighteenth century. The term Hasidic tale is used to describe some American short fiction, much of it written in the 1960's, which reflected the spirit of Hasidism, particularly the belief in the immanence of God in all things. Saul Bellow, Philip Roth, and Norman Mailer have been attracted to the genre, as has the Israeli writer Shmuel Yosef Agnon, who won the Nobel Prize in Literature in 1966.

Historical criticism: In contrast to formalist criticism, which treats literary works as self-contained artifacts, historical criticism emphasizes the social and historical context of literature and allows itself to take into consideration the relevant facts and circumstances of the author's life. The method emphasizes the meaning that the work had in its own time rather than interpreting it for the present.

Hyperbole: The term is Greek for "overshooting" and refers to the use of gross exaggeration for rhetorical effect, based on the assumption that the reader will not be persuaded of the literal truth of the overstatement. Can be used for serious or comic effect.

Imagery: Often defined as the verbal stimulation of sensory perception. Although the word betrays a visual bias, imagery, in fact, calls on all five senses. In its simplest form, imagery re-creates a physical sensation in a clear, literal manner; it becomes more complex when a poet employs metaphor and other figures of speech to re-create experience.

In medias res: Latin phrase used by Horace, meaning literally "into the midst of things." It refers to a literary technique of beginning the narrative when the action has already begun. The term is used particularly in connection with the epic, which traditionally begins *in medias res.*

Initiation story: A story in which protagonists, usually children or young persons, go through an experience, sometimes painful or disconcerting, that carries them from innocence to some new form of knowledge and maturity. William Faulkner's "The Bear," Nathaniel Hawthorne's "Young Goodman Brown," Alice Walker's "To Hell with Dying," and Robert Penn Warren's "Blackberry Winter" are examples of the form.

Interior monologue: Defined by Édouard Dujardin as the speech of a character designed to introduce the reader directly to the character's internal life, the form differs from other monologues in that it attempts to reproduce thought before any logical organization is imposed upon it. An example is Molly Bloom's long interior monologue at the conclusion of James Joyce's *Ulysses* (1922).

Interpretation: An analysis of the meaning of a literary work. Interpretation will attempt to explicate the theme, structure, and other components of the work, often focusing on obscure or ambiguous passages.

Irrealism: A term often used to refer to modern or postmodern fiction that is presented self-consciously as a fiction or fabulation rather than a mimesis of external reality. The best-known practitioners of irrealism are John Barth, Robert Coover, and Donald Barthelme.

Lai/Lay: A song or short narrative poem. The term was first applied to twelfth and thirteenth centuries French poems and to English poems in the fourteenth century that were based on them, including Geoffrey Chaucer's "The Franklin's Tale." In the nineteenth century, the term was applied to historical ballads such as Sir Walter Scott's *The Lay of the Last Minstrel* (1805).

Legend: A narrative that is handed down from generation to generation, usually associated with a particular place and a specific event. A legend may often have more historical truth than a myth, and the protagonist is usually a person rather than a supernatural being.

Leitmotif: From the German, meaning "leading motif." Any repetition—of a word, phrase, situation, or idea—that occurs within a single work or group of related works.

Literary short story: A term that was current in American criticism in the 1940's to distinguish the short fiction of Ernest Hemingway, Eudora Welty, Sherwood Anderson, and others from the popular pulp and slick fiction of the day.

Local color: Usually refers to a movement in literature, especially in the United States, in the latter part of the nineteenth century. The focus was on the environment, atmosphere, and milieu of a particular region. For example, Mark Twain wrote about the Mississippi region; Sarah Orne Jewett wrote about New England. The term can also be used to refer to any work that represents the characteristics of a particular region.

Lyric short story: A form in which the emphasis is on internal changes, moods, and feelings. The lyric story is usually open-ended and depends on the figurative language usually associated with poetry. Examples of lyric stories are the works of Ivan Turgenev, Anton Chekhov, Katherine Mansfield, Sherwood Anderson, Conrad Aiken, and John Updike.

Lyrical ballad: The term is preeminently associated with William Wordsworth and Samuel Taylor Coleridge, whose *Lyrical Ballads* (1798), which drew on the ballad tradition, was one of the seminal books of the Romantic age. *Lyrical Ballads* was a revolt against eighteenth century poetic diction; it was an attempt to create a new kind of poetry by using simple language and taking as subject the everyday lives of common folk and the strong emotions they experience.

Malaprop/Malapropism: A malapropism occurs when one word is confused with another because of a similarity in sound between them. The term is derived from the character Mrs. Malaprop in Richard Brinsley Sheridan's *The Rivals* (1775), who, for example, uses the word "illiterate" when she really means "obliterate" and mistakes "progeny" for "prodigy."

Märchen: German fairy tales, as collected in the works of Wilhelm and Jacob Grimm or in the works of nineteenth century writers such as Novalis and E. T. A. Hoffmann.

Medieval romance: Medieval romances, which originated in twelfth century France, were tales of adventure in which a knight would embark on a perilous quest to win the hand of a lady, perform a service for his king, or seek the Holy Grail. He had to overcome many obstacles, including dragons and other monsters; magic spells and enchantments were prominent, and the romance embodied the chivalric ideals of courage, honor, refined manners, and courtly love. English romances include the anonymous *Sir Gawain and the Green Knight* and Sir Thomas Malory's *Le Morte D'Arthur* (1485).

Memoir: Usually written by a person prominent in public life, a memoir is the authors' recollections of famous people they have known and great events they have witnessed. Memoir differs from autobiography, in that the emphasis in the latter is on the life of the authors.

Metafiction: Refers to fiction that manifests a reflexive tendency, such as Vladimir Nabokov's *Pale Fire* (1962), and John Fowles's *The French Lieutenant's Woman* (1969).

The emphasis is on the loosening of the work's illusion of reality to expose the reality of its illusion. Such terms as "irrealism," "postmodernist fiction," and "anti-fiction" are also used to refer to this type of fiction.

Metaphor: A figure of speech in which two dissimilar objects are imaginatively identified (rather than merely compared) on the assumption that they share one or more qualities: "She is the rose, the glory of the day" (Edmund Spenser). The term is often used in modern criticism in a wider sense to identify analogies of all kinds in literature, painting, and film.

Metonymy: A figure of speech in which an object that is closely related to a word comes to stand for the word itself, such as when one says "the White House" when meaning the "president."

Minimalist movement: A school of fiction writing that developed in the late 1970's and early 1980's and that John Barthes has characterized as the "less is more school." Minimalism attempts to convey much by saying little, to render contemporary reality in precise, pared-down prose that suggests more than it directly states. Leading minimalist writers are Raymond Carver and Ann Beattie. A character in Beattie's short story "Snow" (in *Where You'll Find Me*, 1986) seems to sum up minimalism: "Any life will seem dramatic if you omit mention of most of it."

Modern short story: The modern short story dates from the nineteenth century and is associated with the names of Edgar Allan Poe (who is often credited with inventing the form) and Nathaniel Hawthorne in the United States, Honoré de Balzac in France, and E. T. A. Hoffmann in Germany. In his influential critical writings, Poe defined the short story as being limited to "a certain unique or single effect," to which every detail in the story should contribute.

Monologue: Any speech or narrative presented by one person. It can sometimes be used to refer to any lengthy speech, in which one person monopolizes the conversation.

Moral tract: A propaganda pamphlet on a political or religious topic, usually distributed free. The term is often associated with the Oxford Movement in nineteenth century England, which was a movement to reform the Church of England.

Motif: An incident, situation, or device that occurs frequently in literature. Motif can also refer to particular words, images, and phrases that are repeated frequently in a single work. In this sense, motif is the same as leitmotif. Motif is similar to theme, although the latter is usually more abstract.

Myth: An anonymous traditional story, often involving supernatural beings or the interaction between gods and human beings, and dealing with the basic questions of how the world and human society came to be as they are. Myth is an important term in contemporary literary criticism. Northrop Frye, for example, has said that "the typical forms of myth become the conventions and genres of literature." By this, he means that the genres of comedy, romance, tragedy, and irony (satire) correspond to seasonal myths of spring, summer, autumn, and winter.

Narrative: An account in prose or verse of an event or series of events, whether real or imagined.

Narrative persona: Persona means literally "mask": it is the self created by the author and through whom the narrative is told. The persona is not to be identified with the author, even when the two may seem to resemble each other. The narrative persona in George Gordon, Lord Byron's *Don Juan* (1819-1824), for example, may express many sentiments of which Byron would have approved, but he is nevertheless a fictional creation who is distinct from the author.

Narrator: The character who recounts the narrative. There are many different types of narrators: the first-person narrator is a character in the story and can be recognized by his or her use of "I"; third-person narrators may be limited or omniscient. In the former, the narrator is confined to knowledge of the minds and emotions of one or, at most, a few characters. In the latter, the narrator knows everything, seeing into the minds of all the characters. Rarely, second-person narration may be used. (An example can be found in Edna O'Brien's *A Pagan Place*, 1973.)

Novel: A fictional prose form, longer than a short story or novelette. The term embraces a wide range of types, but the novel usually includes a more complicated plot and a wider cast of characters than the short story. The focus is often on the development of individual characterization and the presentation of a social world and a detailed environment.

Novella, novelette, Novelle, nouvelle: These terms all refer to the form of fiction that is longer than a short story and shorter than a novel. *Novella*, the Italian term, is the term usually used to refer to American works in this genre, such as Joseph Conrad's *Heart of Darkness* (1902) and Henry James's *The Turn of the Screw* (1898). *Novelle* is the German term; *nouvelle* the French; "novelette" the British. The term novel derived from these terms.

Objective correlative: A key concept in modern formalist criticism, coined by T. S. Eliot in *The Sacred Wood* (1920). An objective correlative is a situation, an event, or an object that, when presented or described in a literary work, expresses a particular emotion and serves as a precise formula by which the same emotion can be evoked in the reader.

Oral tale: A wide-ranging term that can include everything from gossip to myths, legends, folktales, and jokes. Among the terms used by Stith Thompson to classify oral tales (*The Folktale*, 1951) are märchen, fairy tale, household tale, *conte populaire*, novella, hero tale, local tradition, migratory legend, explanatory tale, humorous anecdote, merry tale.

Oral tradition: Material that is transmitted by word of mouth, often through chants or songs, from generation to generation. Homer's epics, for example, were originally passed down orally and employ formulas to make memorization easier. Often, ballads, folklore, and proverbs are also passed down in this way.

Oriental tale: An eighteenth century form made popular by the translations of *The Arabian Nights' Entertainments* (*The Thousand and One Nights*) collected during the period. Oriental tales were usually solemn in tone, contained little characterization, and focused on improbable events and supernatural places.

Oxymoron: Closely related to paradox, an oxymoron occurs when two words of opposite meaning are placed in juxtaposition, such as "wise fool," "devilish angel," or "loving hate."

Parable: A short, simple, and usually allegorical story that teaches a moral lesson. In the West, the most famous parables are those told in the Gospels by Christ.

Paradox: A statement that initially seems to be illogical or self-contradictory yet eventually proves to embody a complex truth. In New Criticism, the term was used to embrace any complexity of language that sustained multiple meanings and deviated from the norms of ordinary language use.

Parataxis: The placing of clauses or phrases in a series without the use of coordinating or subordinating terms.

Parody: A literary work that imitates or burlesques another work or author for the purpose of ridicule. Twentieth century parodists include E. B. White and James Thurber.

Periodical essay/sketch: Informal in tone and style and applied to a wide range of topics, the periodical essay originated in the early eighteenth century. It is associated in particular with Joseph Addison and Richard Steele and their informal periodical, *The Spectator.*

Personification: A figure of speech that ascribes human qualities to abstractions or inanimate objects, as in these lines by W. H. Auden: "There's Wrath who has learnt every trick of guerrilla warfare,/ The shamming dead, the night-raid, the feinted retreat." Richard Crashaw's "Hope, thou bold taster of delight" is another example.

Plot: Plot refers to how authors arrange their material not only to create the sequence of events in a play or story but also to suggest how those events are connected in a cause and effect relationship. There are a great variety of plot patterns, each of which is designed to create a particular effect.

Point of view: The perspective from which a story is presented to the reader. In simplest terms, it refers to whether narration is first person (directly addressed to the reader as if told by one involved in the narrative) or third person (usually a more objective, distanced perspective.)

Portmanteau words: The term was coined by Lewis Carroll to describe the creation of a new word by telescoping two existing words. In this way, "furious" and "fuming" can be combined to create "frumious." The works of James Joyce, as well as Carroll's *Through the Looking Glass and What Alice Found There* (1871), provide many examples of portmanteau words.

Prosody: The study of the principles of verse structure. Includes meter, rhyme, and other patterns of sound such as alliteration, assonance, euphony and onomatopoeia, and stanzaic patterns.

Protagonist: Originally, in the Greek drama, the "first actor," who played the leading role. The term has come to signify the most important character in a drama or story. It is not unusual for a work to contain more than one protagonist.

Pun: A pun occurs when words that have similar pronunciations have entirely different meanings. The result may be a surprise recognition of an unusual or striking connection, or, more often, a humorously accidental connection.

Realism: A literary technique in which the primary convention is to render an illusion of fidelity to external reality. Realism is often identified as the primary method of the novel form; the realist movement in the late nineteenth century coincided with the full development of the novel form.

Reminiscence: An account, written or spoken, of remembered events.

Rhetorical device: Rhetoric is the art of using words clearly and effectively, in speech or writing, in order to influence or persuade. A rhetorical device is a figure of speech, or way of using language, employed to this end. It can include such elements as choice of words, rhythms, repetition, apostrophe, invocation, chiasmus, zeugma, antithesis, and the rhetorical question (a question to which no answer is expected).

Rogue literature: From Odysseus to Shakespeare's Autolocus to Huckleberry Finn, the rogue is a common literary type. He is usually a robust and energetic comic or satirical figure whose roguery can be seen as a necessary undermining of the rigid complacency of conventional society. The picaresque novel (*picaro* is Spanish for "rogue"), in which the picaro lives by his wits, is perhaps the most common form of rogue literature.

Romance: Originally, any work written in Old French. In the Middle Ages, romances were about knights and their adventures. In modern times, the term has also been used to describe a type of prose fiction in which, unlike the novel, realism plays little part. Prose romances often give expression to the quest for transcendent truths. Examples of the form include Nathaniel Hawthorne's *The Scarlet Letter* (1850) and Herman Melville's *Moby Dick* (1851).

Romanticism: A movement of the late eighteenth century and the nineteenth century that exalted individualism over collectivism, revolution over conservatism, innovation over tradition, imagination over reason, and spontaneity over restraint. Romanticism regarded art as self-expression; it strove to heal the cleavage between object and subject and expressed a longing for the infinite in all things. It stressed the innate goodness of human beings and the evils of the institutions that would stultify human creativity.

Saga: Originally applied to medieval Icelandic and other Scandinavian stories of heroic exploits and handed down by oral tradition. The term has come to signify any tale of heroic achievement or great adventure.

Satire: A form of literature that employs the comedic devices of wit, irony, and exaggeration to expose, ridicule, and condemn human folly, vice, and stupidity. Justifying satire, Alexander Pope wrote that "nothing moves strongly but satire, and those who are ashamed of nothing else are so of being ridiculous."

Setting: The circumstances and environment, both temporal and spatial, of a narrative. The term also applies to the physical elements of a theatrical production, such as scenery and properties. Setting is an important element in the creation of atmosphere.

Shishōsetsu: Literally translated as "I novel," *shishōsetsu* is a Japanese genre, a form of autobiographical or confessional writing used in novels and short stories. The protagonist and writer are closely identified. The genre originated in the early part of the twentieth century; a good example is *An'ya Koro* (1921-1928; *A Dark Night's Passing*, 1958), by Shiga Naoya.

Short story: A concise work of fiction, shorter than a novella, that is usually more concerned with mood, effect, or a single event than with plot or extensive characterization.

Simile: A type of metaphor in which two things are compared. It can usually be recognized by the use of the words "like," "as," "appears," or "seems": "Float like a butterfly, sting like a bee" (Muhammad Ali); "The holy time is quiet as a nun" (William Wordsworth).

Skaz: A term used in Russian criticism to describe a narrative technique that presents an oral narrative of a lowbrow speaker.

Sketch: A brief narrative form originating in the eighteenth century, derived from the artist's sketch. The focus of a sketch is on a single person, place, or incident; it lacks a developed plot, theme, or characterization.

Story line: The story line of a work of fiction differs from the plot. Story line is merely the events that happen; plot is how those events are arranged by the author to suggest a cause and effect relationship.

Stream of consciousness: A narrative technique used in modern fiction by which an author tries to embody the total range of consciousness of a character, without any authorial comment or explanation. Sensations, thoughts, memories, and associations pour out in an uninterrupted, prerational and prelogical flow. Examples are James Joyce's *Ulysses* (1922), Virginia Woolf's *To the Lighthouse* (1927), and William Faulkner's *The Sound and the Fury* (1929).

Structuralism: Structuralism is based on the idea of intrinsic, self-sufficient structures that do not require reference to external elements. A structure is a system of transformations that involves the interplay of laws inherent in the system itself. The structuralist literary critic attempts, by using models derived from modern linguistic theory, to define the structural principles that operate intertextually throughout the whole of literature as well as principles that operate in genres and in individual works.

Style: Style is the manner of expression, or how the writer tells the story. The most appropriate style is that which is perfectly suited to conveying whatever idea, emotion, or other effect that the author wishes to convey. Elements of style include diction, sentence structure, imagery, rhythm, and coherence.

Subjective/Objective: Terms used in critical theory. Subjective refers to works that express the ideas and emotions, the values and judgments of the authors, such as William Wordsworth's *The Prelude* (1850). Objective works are those that appear to be free of the personal sentiments of authors, who take a detached view of the events they record.

Symbolism: A literary movement encompassing the work of a group of French writers in the latter half of the nineteenth century, a group that included Charles Baudelaire, Stéphane Mallarmé, and Paul Verlaine. According to Symbolism, a mystical correspondence exists between the natural and spiritual worlds.

Synesthesia: Synesthesia occurs when one kind of sense experience is described in terms of another. Sounds may be described in terms of colors, and so on. For example, these lines from Keats's poem "Isabella," "O turn thee to the very tale,/ And taste the music of that vision pale," combine the senses of taste, hearing, and sight. Synesthesia was used especially by the nineteenth century French Symbolists.

Tale: A general term for a simple prose or verse narrative. In the context of the short story, a tale is a story in which the emphasis is on the course of the action rather than on the minds of the characters.

Tall-tale: A humorous tale popular in the American West; the story usually makes use of realistic detail and common speech, but it tells a tale of impossible events that most often focus on a single legendary, superhuman figure, such as Paul Bunyan or David Crockett.

Technique: Refers both to the method of procedure in creating an artistic work and to the degree of expertise shown in following the procedure.

Thematics: According to Northrop Frye, when a work of fiction is written or interpreted thematically, it becomes an illustrative fable. Murray Krieger defines thematics in *The Tragic Vision* (1960) as "the study of the experiential tensions which, dramatically entangled in the literary work, become an existential reflection of that work's aesthetic complexity."

Theme: Loosely defined as what a literary work means, theme is the underlying idea, the abstract concept, that the author is trying to convey: "the search for love," "the growth of wisdom," or some such formulation. The theme of William Butler Yeats's poem "Sailing to Byzantium," for example, might be interpreted as the failure of man's attempt to isolate himself within the world of art.

Tone: Strictly defined, tone is the authors' attitude toward their subject, their persona, themselves, their audience, or their society. The tone of a work may be serious, playful, formal, informal, morose, loving, ironic, and so on; it can be thought of as the dominant mood of a work, and it plays a large part in the total effect.

Trope: Literally "turn" or "conversion"; a figure of speech in which a word or phrase is used in a way that deviates from the normal or literal sense.

Vehicle: Used with the term "tenor" to understand the two elements of a metaphor. The tenor is the subject of the metaphor, and the vehicle is the image by which the subject is presented. The terms were coined by I. A. Richards. As an example, in T. S. Eliot's line, "The whole earth is our hospital," the tenor is "whole earth" and the vehicle is the "hospital."

Verisimilitude: When used in literary criticism, verisimilitude refers to the degree to which a literary work gives the appearance of being true or real, even though the events depicted may in fact be far removed from the actual.

Vignette: A sketch, essay, or brief narrative characterized by precision, economy, and grace. The term can also be applied to brief short stories, less than five hundred words long.

Yarn: An oral tale or a written transcription of what purports to be an oral tale. The yarn is usually a broadly comic tale, the classic example of which is Mark Twain's "Baker's Bluejay Yarn." The yarn achieves its comic effect by juxtaposing realistic detail and incredible events; tellers of the tale protest that they are telling the truth; listeners know differently.

Bryan Aubrey

INDEX

INDEX

Predicament," 385-386; "A Sick Call," 387-388; "A Wedding Dress," 385.

Calvino, Italo, 391-397; "Adam, One Afternoon," 393-394; "The Adventure of a Bather," 394-395; "The Aquatic Uncle," 395; "The Crow Comes Last," 394; "Games Without End," 395.

"Camberwell Beauty, The" (Pritchett), 1936.

"Camionista, I." *See* "Lorry Driver, The."

"Camp Cataract" (Bowles, J.), 271-272.

Campaspe (Lyly), 1529-1530.

Camus, Albert, 398-403, 2671, 2743-2744; "The Adulterous Woman," 399-400; "The Artist at Work," 402; *Exile and the Kingdom,* 399; "The Growing Stone," 401-402; "The Guest," 400-401, 2743-2744; "The Renegade," 402; "The Silent Man," 402.

Canby, H. S., 2676.

Cancerqueen (Landolfi), 1396-1397.

Cancroregina. See *Cancerqueen.*

Candide (Voltaire), 2359, 2645.

"Candy-Man Beechum" (Caldwell), 372.

Cane (Toomer), 2297-2302.

canon, **2803.**

"Canon Alberic's Scrapbook" (James, M.), 1269.

Canterbury Tales, The (Chaucer), 488-496.

Cantilena of St. Eulalia, 2605.

"Cantleman's Spring-Mate" (Lewis), 1486.

"Cap for Steve, A" (Callaghan), 389.

Capote, Truman, 404-409; "Master Misery," 407-408; "A Tree of Night," 405-407.

Card, Orson Scott, 410-415; "Kingsmeat," 411-413; "The Porcelain Salamander," 413-414.

caricature, **2803.**

Carleton, William, 416-422; "The Lough Derg Pilgrim," 419; "Ned M'Keown," 417-418; "Phelim O'Toole's Courtship," 419-420; "The Three Tasks or The Little House Under the Hill," 418-419; "Tubber Derg," 420-421.

Carmen (Mérimée), 1657.

"Carmilla" (Le Fanu), 1445-1446.

Carpentier, Alejo, 423-427; "Like the Night," 424-426.

Carr, John Dickson, 428-433; "All in a Maze," 430-431; "The Door to Doom,"

430; "The Incautious Burglar," 431; "The Shadow of the Goat," 430.

Carver, Raymond, 434-443, 2755-2756; "Boxes," 441-442; "The Bridle," 440-441; "Fat," 436; "Neighbors," 437; *What We Talk About When We Talk About Love,* 437-439; "Where I'm Calling From," 439-440; "Why Don't You Dance?," 438-439; *Will You Please Be Quiet, Please?,* 436-437.

"Cask of Amontillado, The" (Poe), 2687.

Cassill, R. V., 444-449; "The Biggest Band," 445-446; "The Crime of Mary Lynn Yager," 447-448; "In the Central Blue," 446-447; "The Sunday Painter," 447.

Cassirer, Ernst, 2679-2680.

"Catastrophe" (Buzzati), 351-352.

"Catch, The" (Ōe), 1776-1777.

Cathedral Folk, The (Leskov), 1467.

Cather, Willa, 450-456; *My Ántonia,* 454; "Neighbor Rosicky," 454; "Paul's Case," 452-453, 2714; "The Sculptor's Funeral," 451-452; "Uncle Valentine," 453.

"Cat's Meow, The" (Morris), 1680-1681.

"Cavalleria rusticana." See "Rustic Chivalry."

"Cave, The" (Zamyatin), 2536.

"Ceci n'est pas un conte." *See* "This Is Not a Story."

"Ceil" (Brodkey), 332-333.

"Celebrated Jumping Frog of Calaveras County, The" (Twain), 2327-2328, 2704.

"Celestial Omnibus, The" (Forster), 888.

Celtic Twilight, The (Yeats), 2525.

Cena Trimalchionis (Petronius), 1879, 1882-1883.

"Census Taker, The" (Oates), 1738.

Cervantes, Miguel de, 457-466; "Colloquy of The Dogs," 460-463; *Don Quixote de la Mancha,* 460; *The Exemplary Novels,* 457, 460; "The Glass Scholar," 463-464; "Rinconete and Cortadillo," 464-465.

Chabon, Michael, 467-473; "The Little Knife," 471-472; "A Model World," 469-471; *A Model World and Other Stories,* 467-472; "S ANGEL," 468-469.

"Chac Mool" (Fuentes), 926.

Chaereas and Callirhoe (Chariton), 2573.

"Chain of Love, A" (Price), 1923-1924.

"Jilting of Granny Weatherall, The" (Porter), 1909.
Jin xin gu zhi lian (Wang Anyi), 2398.
"Jockey, The" (McCullers), 1540.
"Joe Eliot" (Farrell), 843-844.
"John Gardner" (Gardner), 960.
"John Redding Goes to Sea" (Hurston), 1241-1242.
"John Sherman" (Yeats), 2526-2527.
"Johnny Pye and the Fool-Killer" (Benét), 213-214.
Johnson, Samuel, 1283-1289; *The Adventurer,* 1285; *Rasselas,* 1285-1288; *The Idler,* 1285; *The Rambler,* 1284-1285, 2642-2643.
"Jolly Corner, The" (James, H.), 1265-1266.
"Jongleur de Notre-Dame, Le." *See* "Juggler of Our Lady, The."
"Jordan's End" (Glasgow), 1003-1004.
"Joshua" (Grau), 1058-1059.
"Journey to Petrópolis" (Lispector), 1492.
"Journey to the Seven Streams, A" (Kiely), 1332.
Joyce, James, 1290-1299, 2672; "Araby," 1297; "The Dead," 1294-1295, 1298, 2727-2728; *Dubliners,* 1292-1298; "An Encounter," 1297; "Eveline," 1297; "Grace," 1295; "Ivy Day in the Committee Room," 1296, 1297-1298; "A Little Cloud," 1294, 1297; "A Painful Case," 1295, 1297; "The Sisters," 1293; *Stephen Hero,* 2727.
"Joycelin Shrager Story, The" (Disch), 746.
"Juan Darién" (Quiroga), 1989.
"Judas Tree, The" (Welch), 2425-2426.
"Judgement Day" (O'Connor, Flannery), 1764.
"Judgment, The" (Kafka), 1302-1304.
"Juggler of Our Lady, The" (France), 901.
Jules Verne Steam Balloon, The (Davenport), 687.
"Julia and the Bazooka" (Kavan), 1314-1315.
"Julia Cahill's Curse" (Moore, George), 2726-2727.
Jungle Book, The (Kipling), 1363.
"Junior" (Lewis), 1485.
"Junius Maltby" (Steinbeck), 2208.
"Jūrokusai no Nikki." *See* "Diary of a Sixteen-Year-Old."

"Just Like a Tree" (Gaines), 935-936.
Just So Stories (Kipling), 1363-1364.

"Kabnis" (Toomer), 2300-2302.
Kafka, Franz, 1300-1309; "Before the Law," 1305; "The Bucket Rider," 1305-1306; "A Country Doctor," 1306-1308; "Give It Up!," 1304-1305; "The Judgment," 1302-1304; "The Metamorphosis," 2718.
"Kafkas" (Wiggins), 2469.
"Kagebōshi." *See* "Shadow Figure, The."
Kagi. See Key, The.
Kalendergeschichten. See Tales from the Calendar.
"Kamennoe serdtse." *See* "Heart of Stone, A."
"Kamienny świat." *See* "World of Stone."
Kappa (Akutagawa), 36.
"Karusel." *See* "Merry-Go-Round, The."
"Kataude." *See* "One Arm" (Kawabata).
"Katherine Comes to Yellow Sky" (Helprin), 1161.
"Katrina, Katrin" (Helprin), 1161.
Kavan, Anna, 1310-1316; "Asylum Piece," 1312-1313; *Asylum Piece and Other Stories,* 1312-1313; "The Birthmark," 1312; "Going Up in the World," 1312; *The House of Sleep,* 1313-1314; "I Am Lazarus," 1313; "Julia and the Bazooka," 1314-1315; *My Soul in China,* 1315; "The Old Address," 1314; "The Palace of Sleep," 1313; "There Is No End," 1313; "The World of Heroes," 1314.
Kawabata, Yasunari, 1317-1323; "Diary of a Sixteen-Year-Old," 1319; *The House of the Sleeping Beauties,* 1321; "The Izu Dancer," 1319-1320; "The Man Who Did Not Smile," 1320; "The Mole," 1320; "The Moon on the Water," 1320-1321; "Of Birds and Beasts," 1320; "One Arm," 1321-1322.
"Keela, the Outcast Indian Maiden" (Welty), 2433.
Keillor, Garrison, 1324-1330; *Happy to Be Here,* 1328; *Lake Wobegon Days,* 1328; *Leaving Home: A Collection of Lake Wobegon Stories,* 1326-1329; "95 Theses 95," 1326-1327; *A Prairie Home Companion,* 1324, 1325-1326;

INDEX

XXXIII

INDEX

"Unlucky for Pringle" (Lewis), 1484.
"Unzen" (Endō), 835.
Updike, John, 2332-2343, 2754; "A &
P," 2335-2336; "The City," 2342; "A
Dogwood Tree," 2754; "Flight," 2335;
"The Hermit," 2337; "The Music
School," 2754; "Separating," 2339;
"Slippage," 2341; "Sublimating," 2338;
"Transaction," 2339-2341; "Trust Me,"
2341; "Wife-wooing," 2336.
"Upstairs in a Wineshop" (Lu Hsün),
1523-1524.
"Uroki francuzskogo." *See* "French
Lessons."
"Urteil, Das." *See* "Judgment, The."

"V podvale." *See* "In the Basement."
"V stepi." *See* "In the Steppe."
"Valaida" (Wideman), 2465.
"Vale of Tears" (Leskov), 1469.
"Valiant Woman, The" (Powers), 1918-1919.
"Valley Between, The" (Marshall), 1614.
"Vanity and Some Sables" (Henry), 1179.
Vapnfjord Men, The, 2592.
"Various Temptations" (Sansom), 2054.
"Vasily and Vasilisa" (Rasputin), 1993-1994.
vehicle, **2819.**
"Veldt, The" (Bradbury), 305.
"Venduta e comprata." *See* "Bought and
Sold."
"Vengeful Creditor" (Achebe), 2-3.
"Veni, Vidi . . . Wendt" (Stern),
2213-2214.
Venus of Ille, The (Mérimée), 1657-1658.
Verga, Giovanni, 2344-2349; "Gramigna's
Mistress," 2347; "The Last Day," 2348;
"Property," 2347-2348; "Rosso Malpelo,"
2347; "Rustic Chivalry," 2346-2347;
"The She-Wolf," 2347.
Vergil, 2350-2355, 2570, 2572; *Aeneid,*
2351-2354, 2570; *Eclogues,* 2350;
Georgics, 2350, 2351.
verisimilitude, **2819.**
"Vermont Tale, A" (Helprin), 1164.
"Vertical Ladder, The" (Sansom),
2051-2052.
"Verwandlung, Die." *See* "Metamorphosis,
The."
"Very Old Man with Enormous Wings, A"
(García Márquez), 953.
"Vesna v Fialte." *See* "Spring in Fialta."

Via crucis do corpo, A (Lispector), 1493.
Viagem a Petrópolis. *See* "Journey to
Petrópolis."
"Viaggio, La." *See* "Adrianna Takes a
Trip."
"Viaggio di nozze." *See* "Wedding Trip."
Victory Over Japan (Gilchrist), 987-988.
"Vieja moralidad." *See* "Old Morality,
The."
"Views of My Father Weeping"
(Barthelme), 166.
vignette, **2819.**
"Village of the Dead" (Hoch), 1206-1207.
"Villager, The" (Jackson), 1252.
"Vintage Thunderbird, A" (Beattie),
180-181.
"Violet." *See* "Epilogue II."
"Virgin Violeta" (Porter), 1908.
"Virtue" (Maugham), 1628.
"Vision of Mizrah, The" (Addison), 16.
"Visit, The" (Jackson), 1253-1254.
"Visit to Grandpa's, A" (Thomas),
2265-2266.
"Visitation, The" (Woiwode), 2494.
"Visitor, The" (Thomas), 2270.
Vita nuova (Dante), 663.
"Viy" (Gogol), 1017-1018.
"Vodianaia feeriia." *See* "Water Ballet, A."
"Voice from the Woods, A" (Humphrey),
1235.
"Voices of Adamo, The" (Laurence), 1408.
"Voitel'nitsa." *See* "Amazon, The."
Volksmärchen (Tieck, Ludwig), 2647.
*Völsunga Saga. See Saga of the Volsungs,
The.*
Voltaire, 2356-2363, 2645; *Babouc,*
2359-2360; *Candide,* 2359, 2645; *Jeannot
and Colin,* 2360; *Memnon,* 2359-2360;
Zadig, 2358-2359.
Vonnegut, Kurt, Jr., 2364-2371;
"Go Back to Your Precious Wife
and Son," 2368-2370; *God Bless You,
Mr. Rosewater,* 2365-2366; "Harrison
Bergeron," 2367-2368; *2BRO2B,* 2366;
"Welcome to the Monkey House,"
2366-2367; *Welcome to the Monkey
House,* 2365.
"Vor dem Gesetz." *See* "Before the Law."
Voss, Arthur, 2669.
Voyage of St. Brendan, 2603.
"Vystrel." *See* "Shot, The."

Wahre Muftoni, Der (Meckel), 1645.
Wain, John, 2372-2376; "The Life Guard," 2374; "Master Richard," 2373; "The Message from the Pig-Man," 2373-2374; "While the Sun Shines," 2374.
"Wakefield" (Hawthorne), 1146.
"Wald, Der" (Walser), 2389, 2391.
Waldo, Edward Hamilton. *See* Sturgeon, Theodore.
Walk and Other Stories, The (Walser), 2391.
Walker, Alice, 2377-2386; "The Child Who Favored Daughter," 2380; "Fame," 2383; *In Love and Trouble,* 2378-2381; "Nineteen Fifty-five," 2382-2383; "The Revenge of Hannah Kemhuff," 2380; "Roselily," 2379-2380; "Source," 2384; "To Hell with Dying," 2381; *You Can't Keep a Good Woman Down,* 2382-2384.
"Wall, The" (Sansom), 2050.
"Wall, The" (Sartre), 2065-2067.
Wall, The (Sartre), 2065-2069, 2743.
"Walls of Avila, The" (Connell), 600.
"Wally" (Auchincloss), 113-114.
Walpole, Horace, 2674-2675.
Walser, Robert, 2387-2393; *Cinderella,* 2389-2390; *Fritz Kochers Aufsätze,* 2389; "Oskar," 2390; "Response to a Request," 2390; *A Slap in the Face et cetera,* 2391-2392; *Snowwhite,* 2389-2390; "A Strange City," 2390; "Der Wald," 2389, 2391; *The Walk and Other Stories,* 2391.
"Walter Kömpff" (Hesse), 1185-1186.
Waltharius, 2602-2603.
"Waltz, The" (Parker), 1848.
"Wanderer, dommst du nach Spa .." *See* "Stranger, Bear Word to the Spartans, We .."
Wandering (Lu Hsün), 1522-1524.
"Wandering Willie's Tale" (Scott), 2087-2088.
Wang Anyi, 2394-2400; "And the Rain Patters On," 2395; *Baotown,* 2397; "The Base of the Wall," 2396; "Destination," 2396; *Jin xin gu zhi lian,* 2398; *Lapse of Time,* 2396-2397; *Love in a Small Town,* 2398; *Love on a Barren Mountain,* 2397-2398.
"Wants" (Paley), 1838.
"War Baby, The" (Lewis), 1485-1486.
"War Generation, The" (Endō), 838.

"Warawanu Otoko." *See* "Man Who Did Not Smile, The."
Ward, Alfred C., 2676-2677.
"Warden, The" (Gardner), 959.
Warner, Sylvia Townsend, 2401-2409; "But at the Stroke of Midnight," 2406; *"Hee-Haw!,"* 2403; *The Innocent and the Guilty,* 2406-2407; "A Love Match," 2404-2405; "Oxenhope," 2407; *Scenes of Childhood,* 2407-2408; "Swans on an Autumn River," 2405-2406; "Winter in the Air," 2403-2404.
Warren, Robert Penn, 2410-2416; "Blackberry Winter," 2411; "The Circus in the Attic," 2413; "Prime Leaf," 2412-2413; "When the Light Gets Green," 2411-2412.
Waste of Timelessness and Other Early Stories (Nin), 1722.
"Watakushi." *See* "Thief, The."
"Watashi no mono." *See* "My Belongings."
"Water Ballet, A" (Zoshchenko), 2560.
"Water Message" (Barth), 154.
"Water Them Geraniums" (Lawson), 1432-1433.
Watercress Girl and Other Stories, The (Bates), 176.
"Way Back, The" (Grau), 1060.
We, in Some Strange Power's Employ (Delany), 704.
"—We Also Walk Dogs" (Heinlein), 1154-1155.
We Are Still Married: Stories and Letters (Keillor), 1329.
"Wedding Day" (Boyle, K.), 283-286.
"Wedding Dress, A" (Callaghan), 385.
"Wedding Trip" (Pavese), 1861-1862.
Weidman, Jerome, 2417-2421; "The Horse That Could Whistle Dixie," 2419-2420; "I Knew What I Was Doing," 2419; "My Father Sits in the Dark," 2418; "Three-Two Pitch," 2419.
Welch, Denton, 2422-2429; "At Sea," 2423-2424; "Brave and Cruel," 2426-2427; "The Coffin on the Hill," 2423; "The Diamond Badge," 2428; "The Fire in the Wood," 2427; "The Hateful Word," 2427-2428; "The Judas Tree," 2425-2426; "The Trout Stream," 2426; "When I Was Thirteen," 2424-2425.